Creating Connections

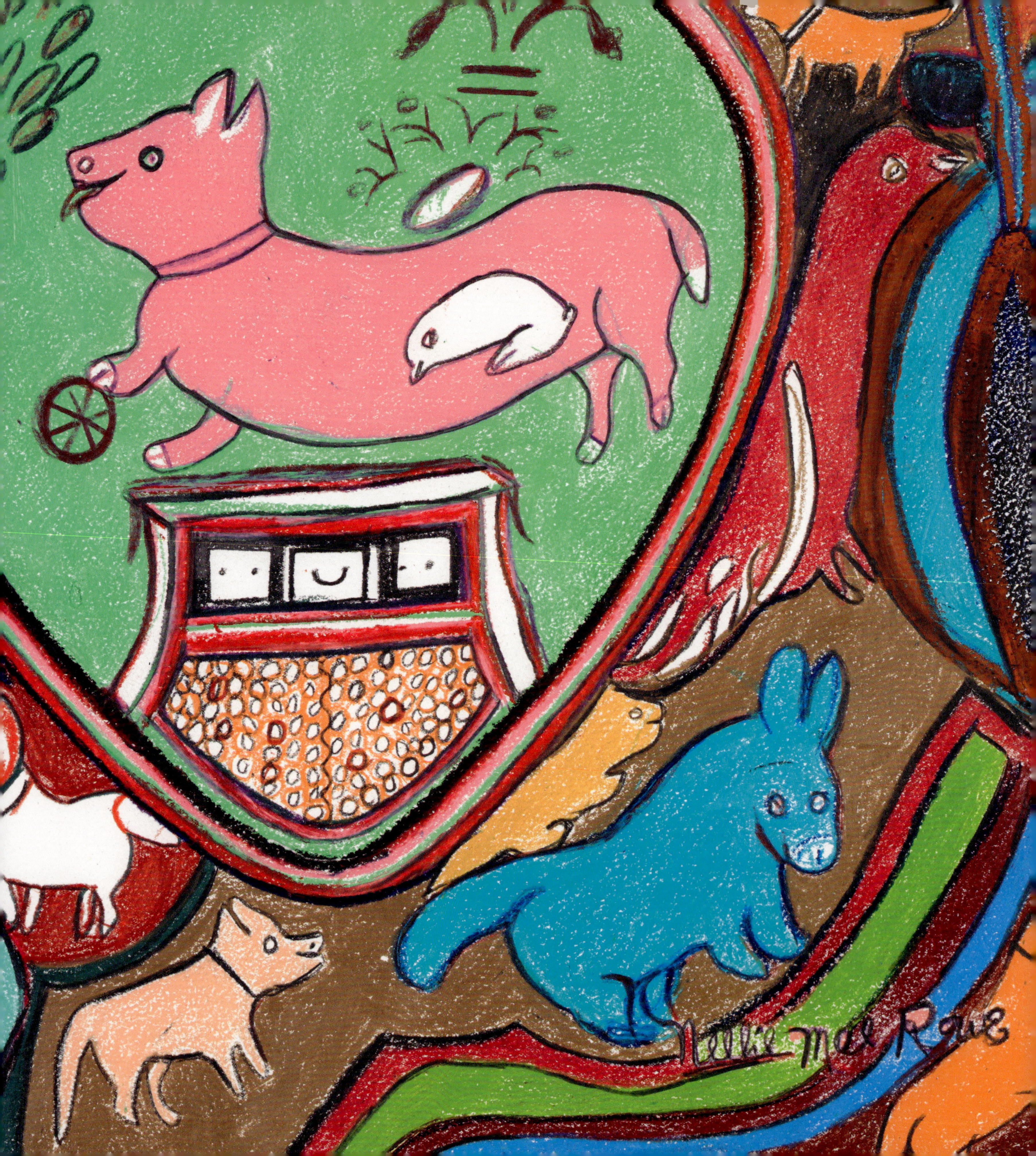
Nellie Mae Rowe

Creating Connections

Self-Taught Artists in the Rosenthal Collection

Edited by Julie Aronson

Interview with Richard Rosenthal by Julie Aronson
Contributions by Olivia Sagan and Charles Russell

Cincinnati Art Museum
in association with D Giles Limited

cincinnati art museum

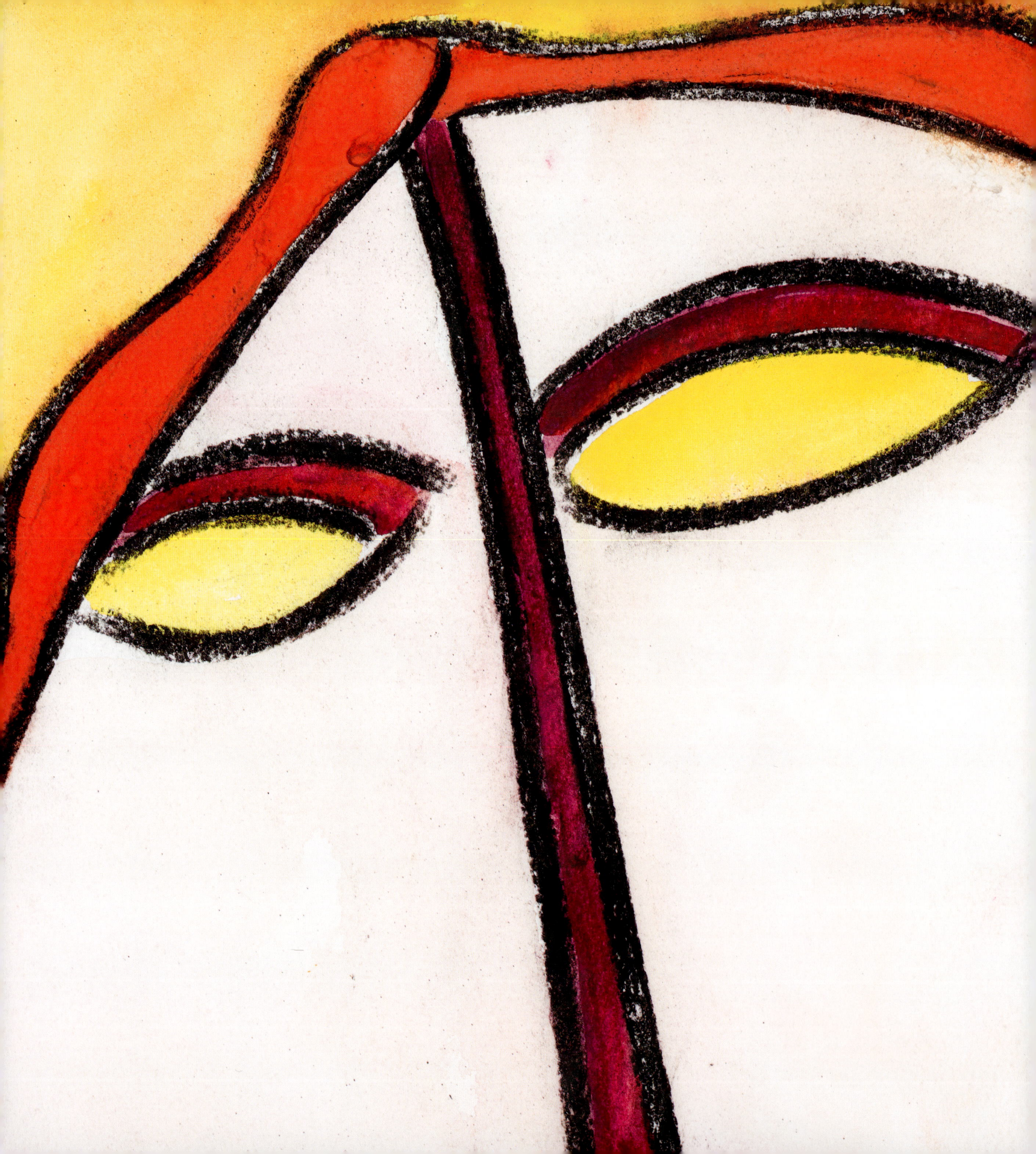

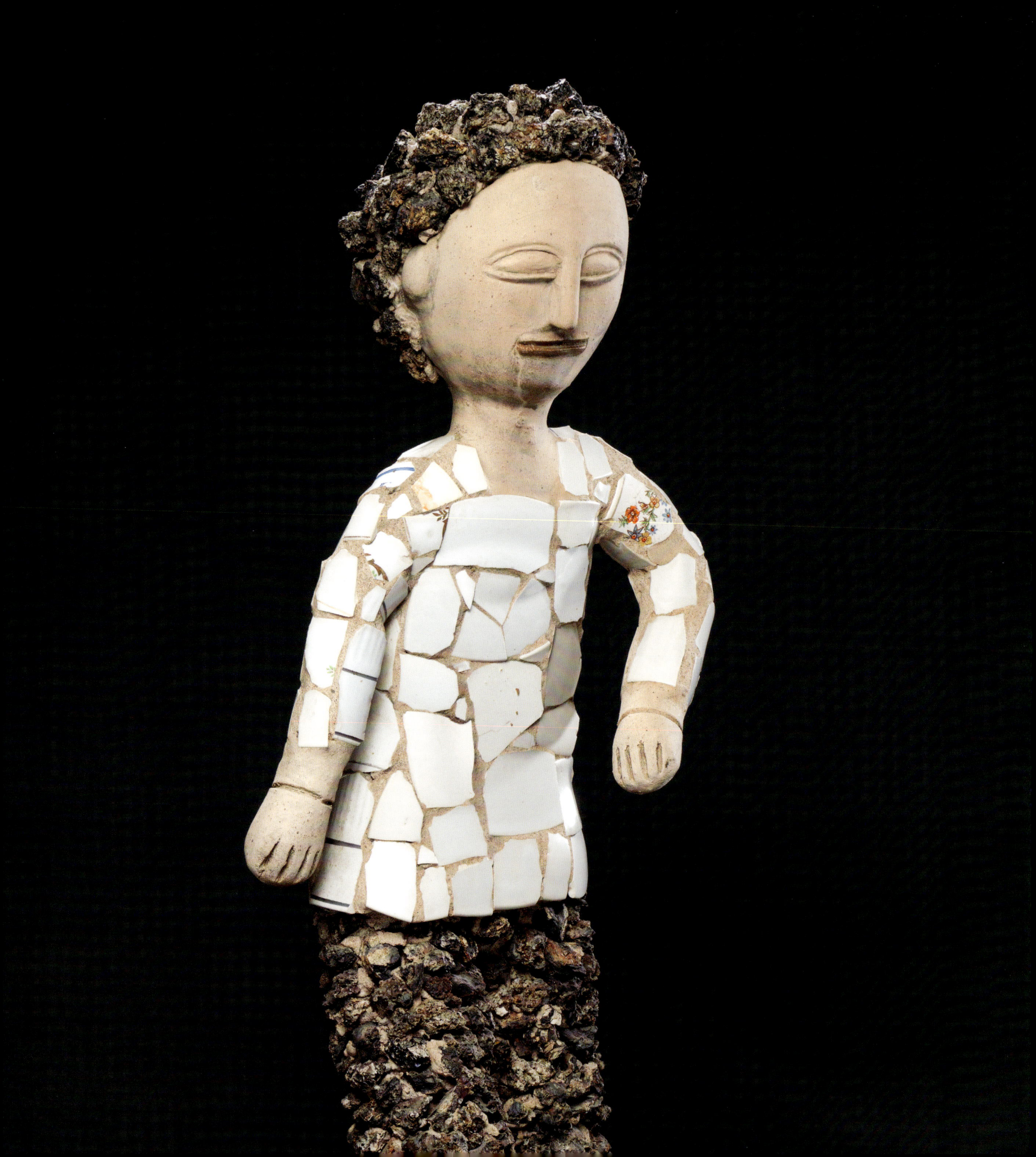

Director's Foreword

Over the years I have had the good fortune to know numerous self-taught and visionary artists alongside individuals who find inspiration in their artmaking. Each interaction has made an indelible mark and memory in my own experience. Several have changed my outlook; each has altered how I think about a public museum, where people, art, artists, humanism, and spirituality interweave.

In conversation with the community of collectors who share experiences with the artists in these pages, I am reminded that they often think differently about art. Every narrative begins with *who* before what, why, or when. Deep interpersonal touches are filled with joy and emotion in each recitation. Oftentimes, discussion centers on stories of meeting the artists and reciprocating their welcome and embracing their differing realities.

Richard Rosenthal, whose expansive collection includes a wonderful promised bequest of works to the Cincinnati Art Museum, is a visionary in his own right. He has built arts institutions, invested in our city, lifted up our aspirations, and found authentic connection to so many in his wide circle. He is a true believer in the virtuosity of people. I am grateful for his friendship.

The artists within the gift encompass two dozen individualistic talents who expand our knowledge of the diversity of art history, including Thornton Dial, William Hawkins, Bessie Harvey, Ronald Lockett, Nellie Mae Rowe, Bill Traylor, and Martín Ramírez. Jean Dubuffet is represented in two magnificent works. Nek Chand, Adolf Wölfli, and Edmund Monsiel enlarge the worldview, while Mary K. Borkowski is of our own region. All but two are new to the museum's holdings.

My admiration is extended to Dr. Julie Aronson and the Cincinnati Art Museum team of professionals who have cared for this project from its inception. The passion and affection for the artists and for the Rosenthals is evident throughout. I am thankful to Olivia Sagan and Charles Russell for their thoughtful essays and to all of our museum supporters, including ArtsWave, anchoring arts investment in Greater Cincinnati.

As I consider the artists within this catalogue and in the galleries of the Cincinnati Art Museum in intersection with the ebullient journey of the Rosenthal family, I come to a realization. Preceding the story of a collection and collectors, herein is a story of *connectors* and human *connections*. I invite you to share in the joyful encounters with artists throughout.

Cameron Kitchin
Louis and Louise Dieterle Nippert Director
Cincinnati Art Museum

Cat. 31 (detail)
Nek Chand, *Standing Man*

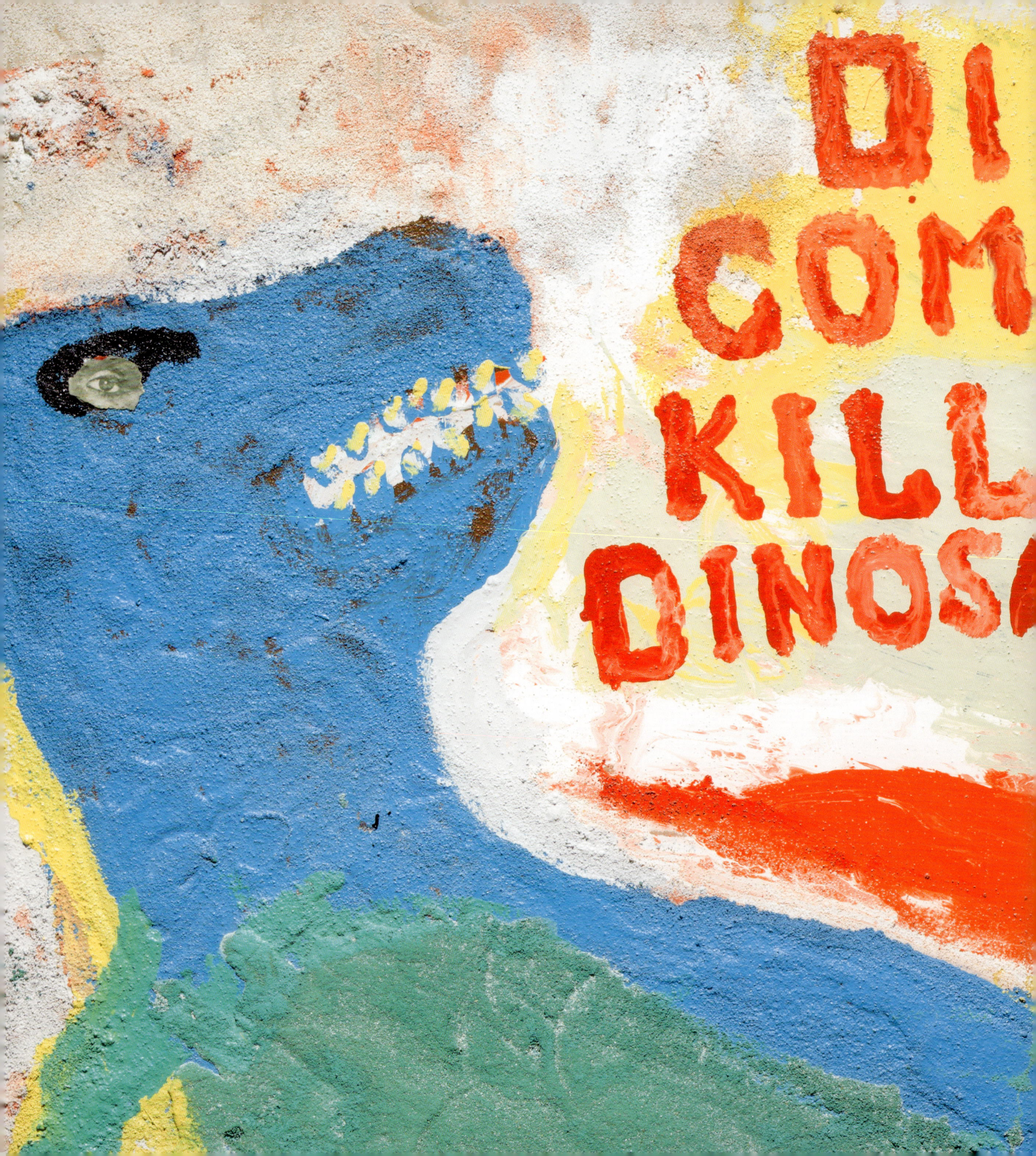
DI
COM
KILL
DINOS

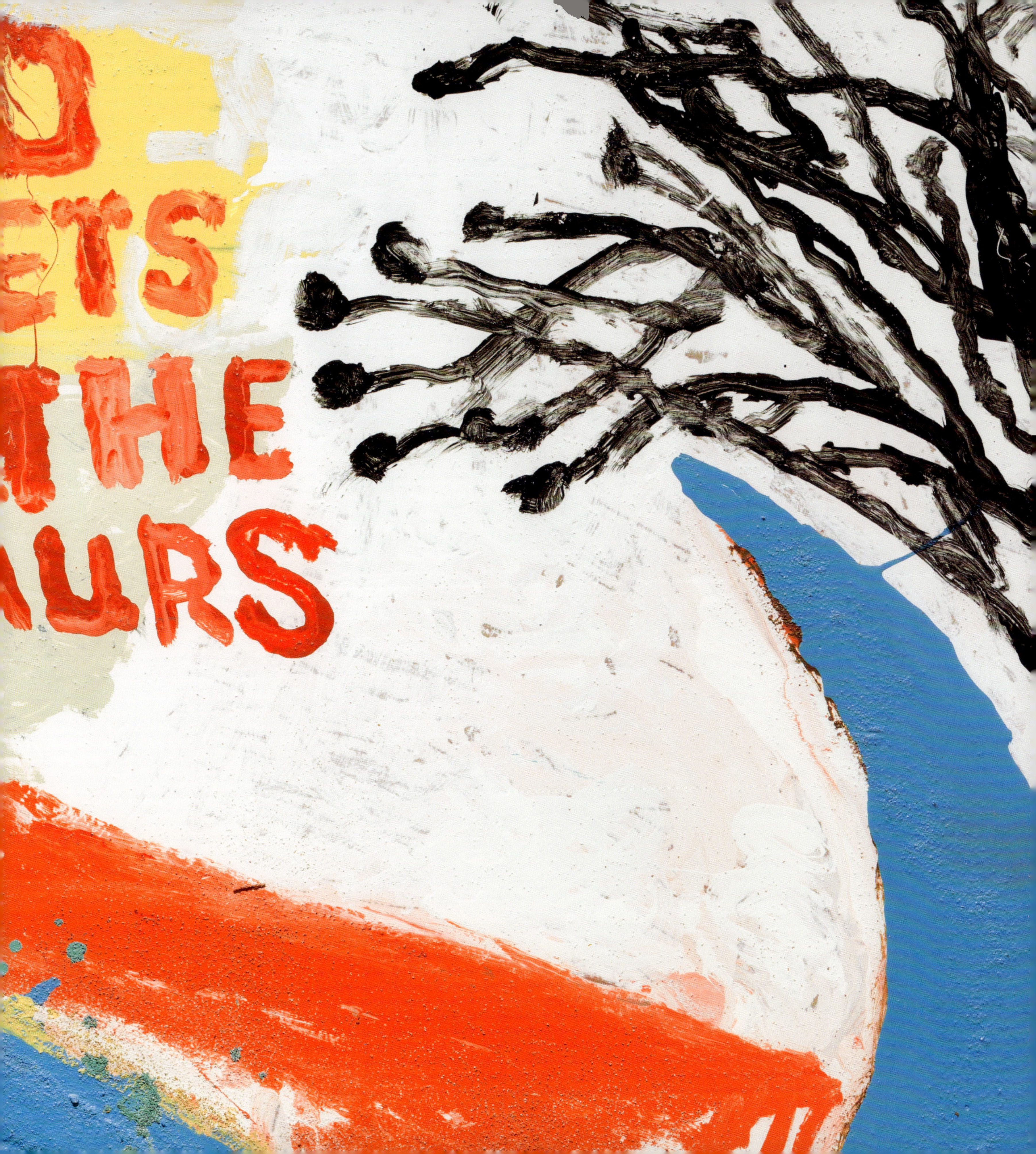
ETS
THE
URS

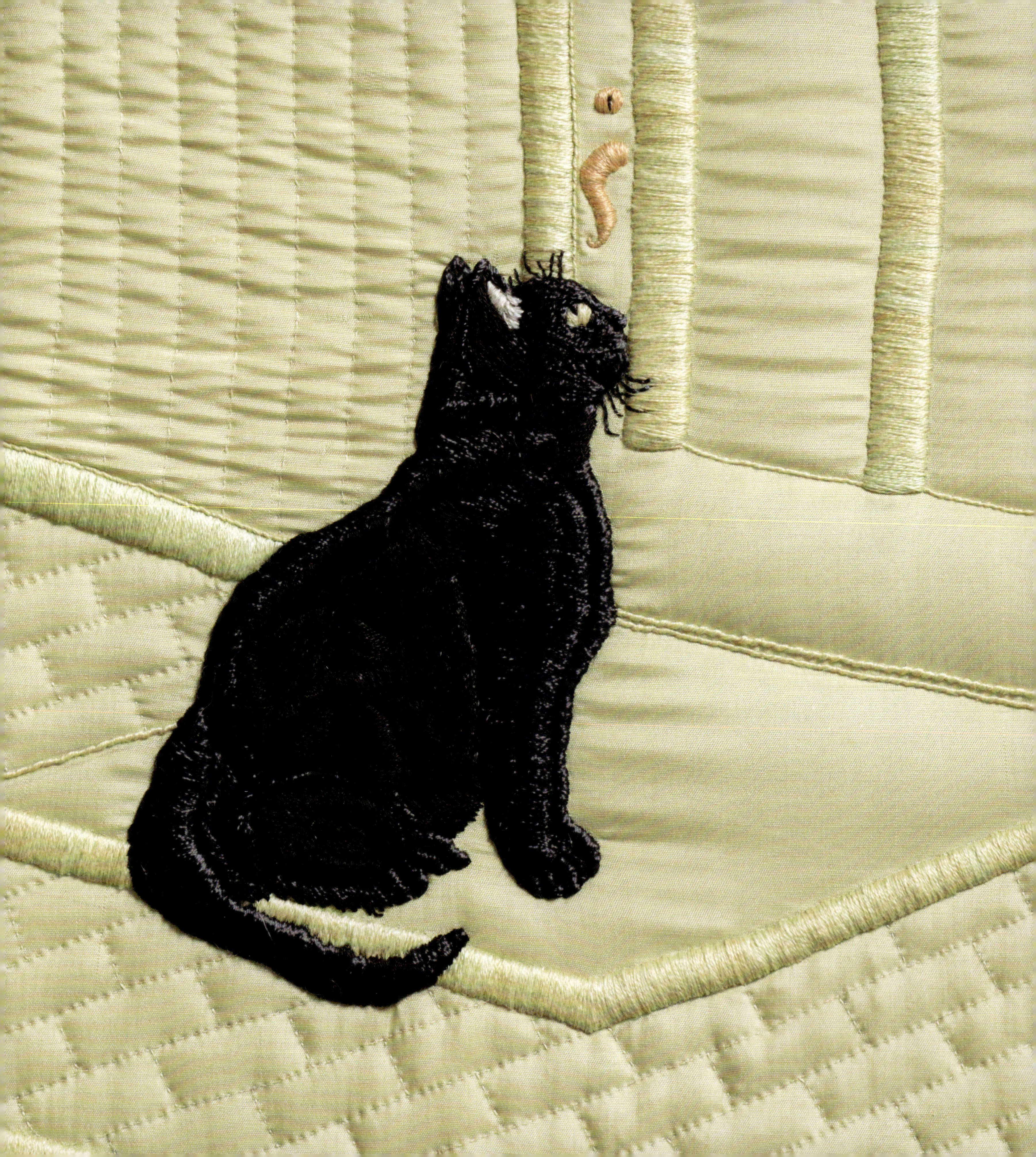

Acknowledgments

Working with Richard Rosenthal has been a tremendous pleasure. His generosity in sharing this extraordinary collection, its stories, and his knowledge are inspiring. Katherine Rosenthal also deserves our heartfelt thanks for her enthusiastic participation in this endeavor. Special recognition is due as well to Anne Buening, Curatorial Assistant for American and European Paintings, Sculpture, and Drawings and my ever-cheerful right hand on this project. Anne's enthusiasm for this material, sleuthing skills, managerial acumen, and dedication to detail have been indispensable.

This handsome and engaging catalogue is a tribute to the expertise of all those who contributed to its content and production. Foremost, we warmly thank our distinguished authors, Dr. Olivia Sagan and Dr. Charles Russell, for embracing the challenge; their essays—astute, scholarly, and often poignantly moving—offer stimulating and compassionate approaches to the way we engage with the work of self-taught artists (or any artists, in fact). The exquisite photography of the works of art is a credit to Rob Deslongchamps, and we are grateful to Tony Walsh for the stunning interior photographs of the Rosenthals' beautiful mid-century modern home. I am also indebted to the museum's new copyeditor, Franck Mercurio, who delved into this manuscript on his second day on the job, and to our colleagues at D Giles Limited, especially Dan Giles, Liz Japes, Allison McCormick, Louise Ramsay, Jodi Simpson, and Alfonso Iacurci.

Exhibitions involve every member of the superb museum team—so please take a bow! With apologies to those whose names do not appear, I offer thanks here to the following individuals. First, I express my gratitude to Director Cameron Kitchin, Chief Curator Cynthia Amnéus, and Director of Collections and Exhibitions Susan Hudson. Exhibitions Registrar Jenifer Linnenberg proficiently coordinated movement of the artwork to and from the museum—not once but twice, so objects could be photographed in studio lighting. Conservator Cecile Mear unframed and examined each work on paper, and conservators Serena Urry, C. Obie Linn, and Kelly Rectenwald lent their expertise to a project notable for unconventional materials. Galina Lewandowicz and Jennifer Hardin of the Mary R. Schiff Library provided research support. Additional employees deserving recognition are designers Lauren Walker, Victoria Karoleff, and their staffs; Emily Holtrop and the Learning and Interpretation team; Kim Flora and the expert crew of installers, preparators, and carpenters; Kirby Neumann and the Philanthropy Division; Darcy Schwass and the Marketing and Communications team; Carol Edmondson and the Finance and Operations Division; and Terrie Simons with Special Events. I also acknowledge Haley Babcock, Sara Birkofer, Amy Burke, Summer Cook, e.m.i., Erica Farler, Caitlin Tracey-Miller, and Fiona Vieh.

Beyond the museum, several others kindly extended valuable advice, information, and insights. Importantly, Richard Rosenthal has shared with us the research of scholar Michael Bonesteel, whom he engaged to catalogue, gather literature, and provide insight on selected artists and their works. We also appreciate the kindness of Matthew Bauman, Transylvania University, Lexington, Kentucky; Henry Boxer, of the Henry Boxer Gallery, Richmond, England; Katherine Jentleson, High Museum of Art, Atlanta; Leslie Umberger, Smithsonian American Art Museum, Washington, DC; Barb Vogel, an artist based in Columbus, Ohio, for her knowledge of Mary Borkowski; and Elaine Y. Yau, Berkeley Art Museum and Pacific Film Archive, University of California, Berkeley. Our deepest gratitude goes to the artists herein represented for sharing work that is amazing, startling, thought-provoking, challenging, ravishing. It is to these creative individuals we dedicate this book.

Julie Aronson
Curator of American Paintings, Sculpture, and Drawings

Cat. 35 (detail)
Mary K. Borkowski, *House Huntin'*

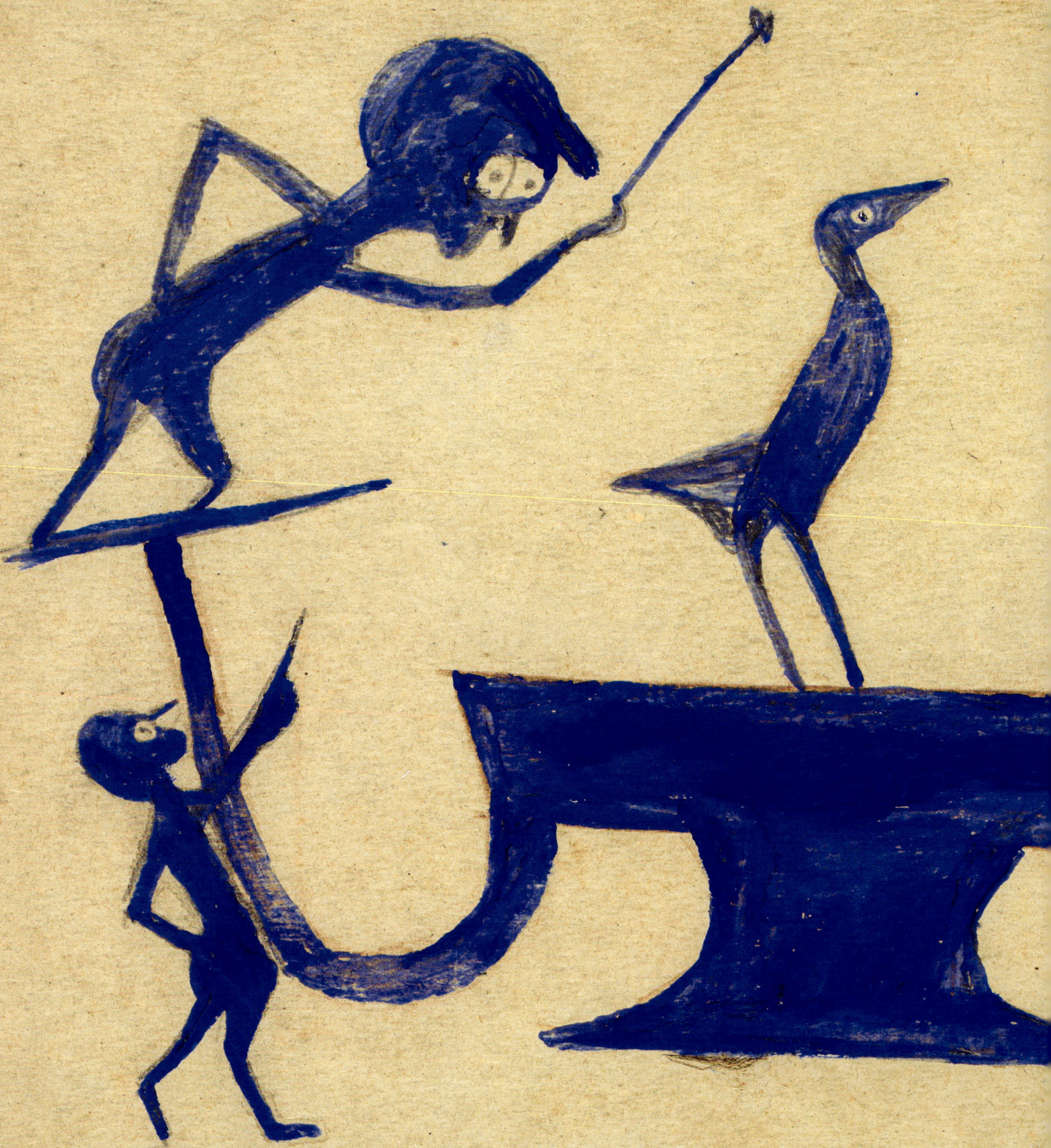

Graceful Mysteries

Olivia Sagan

In Elizabeth Strout's quietly surprising novel *Olive, Again*, the enigmatic protagonist proposes that our job in life is simply "to bear the burden of the mystery with as much grace as we can."[1] Art, its making, and our encounters with it are amongst the handful of things known to make the burden of that mystery lighter. And while lightening the burden, art also deepens the mystery—but what mystery, after all, does not benefit from a deepening?

In this essay to celebrate the experience of this remarkable exhibition, *Creating Connections: Self-Taught Artists in the Rosenthal Collection*, I offer a few things. In the tradition of narrative, it will tell a story of how one might think up an image, think of an image, think through as well as by and in an image—prepositions, small and unassuming things, being so very important. It will also lightly explore the attention by which an image is apprehended, and by whom.

As a story, it offers a framework on which to hang your own thoughts and plot your own encounter with an image, or your own creating of one. That framework acts as a scaffold with transoms joining genres and disciplines and diagonal braces securing narrative strands from my research. This research, with artists with long histories of mental ill health, for whom art, in the words of the painter Dorothea Tanning, "has always been the raft onto which we climb to save our sanity,"[2] mines auto/biography and re-membering and summons us into a better understanding of the self-taught artist. The scaffold will ask you for a while to join in the deep mystery of the art encounter and to examine the texture of the transformative potential of aesthetic experience. It asks that you join me in questions that have exercised not only art historians, philosophers, anthropologists, and psychologists, but, crucially, the layperson, too, who stops to stare and wonder and feel and in so doing has the burden of the mystery of life altered. With the mystery lightened and deepened, it, and we too, are increased, enhanced, entranced. And we go on our way.

An exhibition such as this poses messy, playful, and rich questions. Questions about what a pedagogy of art can be, and how learning is "uncannily organized by repetitions of past investments and conflicts."[3] Questions about exactly what *is* that drive to make an image, to externalize something from one's mind's eye, to lose sleep in the doing of it, to despair, but then to exult at the one tiny stroke or fleeting moment that feels right, like a private coming home. How does art making act so poignantly as balm, as provocation, as distraction, as galvanizer of other journeys, "simply" through what the scholar Ellen Dissanayake referred to as the "making special" through art?[4] Such an exhibition

Cat. 7 (detail)
Bill Traylor, *Exciting Event in Blue: Four Wild Men, Barking Dog, Perched Bird, and Construction*

asks us, too, to explore what happens to *us* in the viewing and remaking of the image in our encounter with it, who are we that comes thus to the image, and are shaken or bored by it, mocked or celebrated in it, slandered or validated by it. I hope this short piece will challenge, inform, and perhaps add a layer of thought and celebration to your viewing of this marvelous collection.

Attention

> Bare attention has a sort of purity about it. It's not a cluttered concept. – Nina Coltart[5]

When I watch people deeply gazing at, or feeling, art there is a *look* on their face. That look, in which ripples of awe, confusion, wonderment, disgust, or even revulsion free-play minutely, speaks of the ineffability of art and its enduring power. How we choose the tools with which to chip away at the ineffable—indeed, whether we regard something as ineffable at all—are questions which lie within our subterranean researcher, and, as with Heraclitus's river, no work of art can be entered the same way twice. So that chipping away is a fluid, dynamic thing, needing a light, open but steady attention.

The attention behind the look is worth thinking about, and worth attending to. Because this is not the attention that can easily be captured or commodified by the attention economy, corporate platforms cannot bid for, buy, and sell it. It is an attention of depth and subtlety, a *free floating* attention,[6] a "negative capability," comfortable existing with "uncertainties, mysteries, doubts, without any irritable reaching after fact and reason."[7] As Jenny Odell writes in her thoughtful and playful polemic about the attention economy, it is a close attention, one that can "help us see into nuanced ecologies of being and identity."[8]

This kind of attention needs practice, and when practiced becomes not perfect but heightened, increasing us. It is the very opposite of the splintered attention that twitches at clickbait, or the frenzied attention we give to our social media platforms, or the hungry, animalistic attention we apply to shopping in the multiple virtual windows of our phones, appearing through the clever but unidimensional, hard-edged, and limited alchemy of algorithms. It is a slow, mindful, soulful attention. One that the philosopher Martin Buber would suggest is a meeting of I-Thou—an encounter untainted, wherein one experiences the other in (thine) irreducibility, with no interpretation, objectification, or agenda.[9] Thinkers from Buddha through to Odell remind us this attention is a radical act, a form of resistance in itself.

Something happens, then, in the space between the object and the viewer (and the term *viewer* here includes those who sense and feel the art as well as those who "see" it). That space, one the psychoanalyst Donald Winnicott

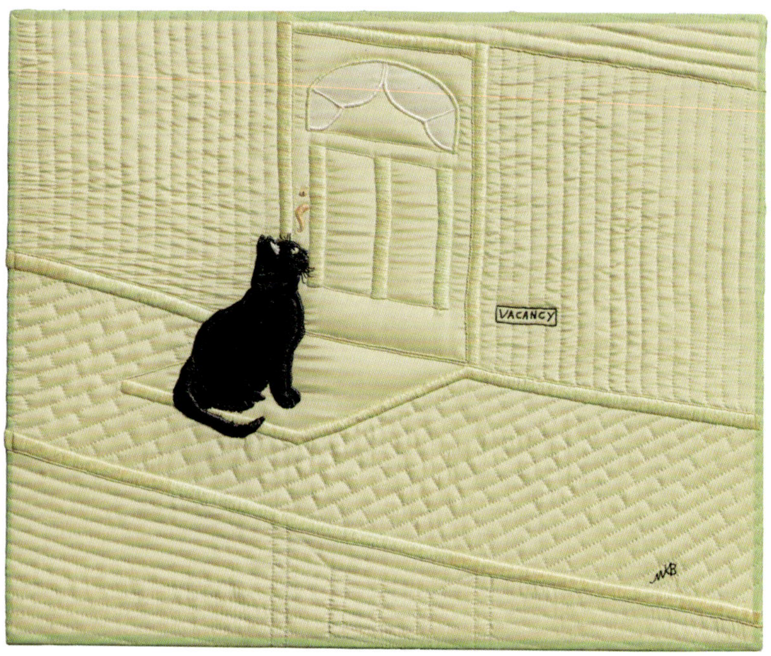

Cat. 35
Mary K. Borkowski (American, 1916–2008), *House Huntin'*, 1967

termed *potential space*, is one of play;[10] an "area of the transitional object and phenomena, the analytic space, the area of cultural experience, and the area of creativity."[11] It is a space of wonder where small eruptions of awe and questioning, unsettlement and homecoming, yearning and satiating occur. We play there, rest there, and grow there, in that simple moment of attentively apprehending art in its myriad forms. The verb *attend* is from the Latin *attendere*, meaning to "stretch toward," as in to stretch your mind towards something. So let's stretch fully towards this exhibition and be increased by the art to which we attend.

Story

> Life must be understood backwards. But it must be lived forwards. – Søren Kierkegaard[12]

When we allow ourselves to see with a bare attention, we are rewarded. This reward for me can be likened to the crystalline shock of stepping out into a clear, cold Scottish day. In that moment, colors burst their bounded palette, texture exudes abundance, and line exceeds boundary, edge, contour in being *just fine*. And that attention beckons us into a story, narrative species that we are, about ourselves, about the space we are bodily inhabiting, about the object itself and its creator. This veritable traffic of stories becomes a new one in the transitional space of bare attention.

I want us here to consider the story of the creator, who, particularly in the case of this exhibition, brings multiple story strands—of race, ethnicity, gender, poverty, solitude, suffering, disability, distress, striving, as well as strands of joy, resilience, courage, and power. These intersect to form a rich fabric of narrative. Such a fabric, like a fine silk, shakes down and alters its sheen and glow over time. The "truths" of the narrative lie not "in their faithful representation of a past world, but in the shifting connections they forge between past, present, and future."[13] The narrative of the life lived forward and understood backward is scripted and rescripted, art offering a precious chance to address, to re-dress. For psychoanalysts such as Kenneth Wright, artistic activity may be one way of making up for "deficiencies of response" of, for example, the early environment: a way of "making good the original deficit."[14] From this perspective, drawing on the work of Daniel Stern, in which the need of infants for reciprocal, validating facial responses from a primary caregiver was shown to be vital to development, the rescripting that artistic endeavor allows is "a way of realizing and restoring the self."[15] Ellen Dissanayake, who has spent decades on the anthropological, philosophical, and, most recently, interpersonal neurobiological exploration of art and culture, goes further, proposing that ritualized mother-infant interaction *gave rise* to the arts.[16]

Such realizing and restoring is also much called for in lives peppered with testimonial injustice,[17] where there

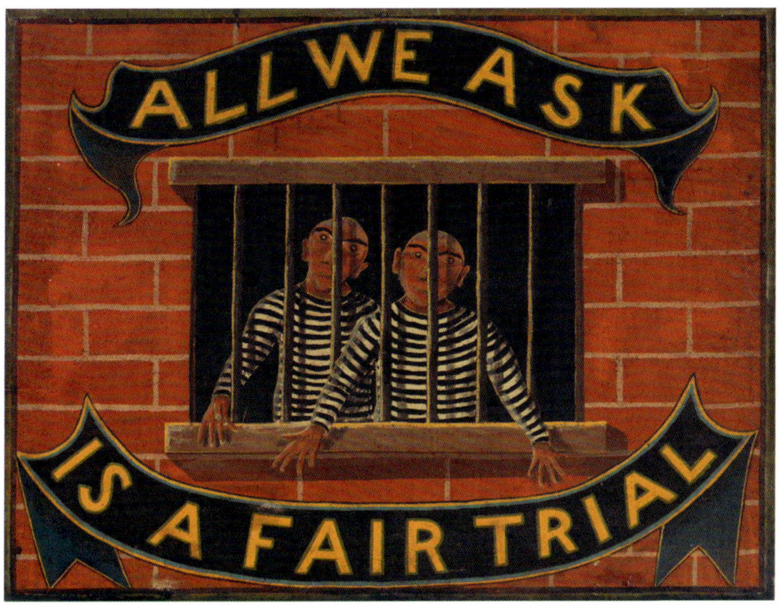

Cat. 6
Unidentified Artist (American),
All We Ask Is a Fair Trial,
late 19th–early 20th century

have been persistent microacts of marginalizing, silencing, overlooking, and invalidating. Art making can, for some makers, be one way to see yourself, to show yourself, and finally be *seen*. Strong medicine. And perhaps in this rescripting, through which art offers its balm to the creator, we, the viewers, may also share to some degree, and re-make ourselves too. As psychologists Sean Akerman and Suzanne Ouellette put it, "artists serve as models for us all as they draw upon the past and transcend it both to lose and to reconstruct the self and identity."[18]

Art performs its mystery in other ways, too. Psychoanalysis has long provided its rich lexicon to probe how art works, with its language for hurt and trauma, for silences, betrayal, and the work of psychic repair. It is, in the words of Michael Eigen, "a language of wounds."[19] To this I would add that it is also a language of discovery, connection, and profound empowerment. Artists speak of making art as a journey, a difficult one, into an interior, one on which they experience joy, release, excavation, redemption, connection, and reparation.[20] Kleinian theory and its later elaborations[21] offer explorations of art and its relation to the inner world and mental wellbeing that are sophisticated, at times opaque, yet which also have a welcome common-sense appeal. It resolutely positions the human psyche as social by nature, object-seeking and resilient, not only able to repair damage but *compelled* to repair damage. And it is not a linear journey. Kayleigh, one of the artists in my research with a long history of abuse and self-harm, described how she worked at one piece "over and over . . . it kind of . . . took hold of me. It wasn't pretty, the image, nor the feeling, but it kept recurring and I kept dealing with it and it kept defeating me . . . and I'd bin it. Only to come back to it. Eventually some sort of . . . er . . . penny dropped . . . about what I was trying to get 'right' . . . it was about the body, my body."

Artists spoke to me of cycles of creative production within one piece of art and also cycles or spirals spanning weeks, years even—iterative, sometimes compulsive excavations of persistence and bravery. In the classic *The Hidden Order of Art*, Anton Ehrenzweig conceptualized three phases of art production,[22] and this temporal nature of our rescripting through art watermarked the stories of artists in my research. They used phrases such as "evacuation phase," "resolution episode," "rebirth period." There was also description of phases of single-minded creative pursuit, suspended time of almost oceanic texture and autotelic experience,[23] the sense that the activity is intrinsically rewarding or worthwhile in its own right, corresponding to the "flow states" of optimal engagement of psychologist Mihaly Csikszentmihalyi.[24] But there were also other states, dreaded times, spoken of in sometimes dull, dreadful monotone, when illness took over and nothing was made, with the fear that it would never again be made, that *one* would never be remade.

For some, again, art making functions perhaps more simply as a distraction—from dark places and the thoughts that arise in their cavernous reaches. For others still, it is a release valve, whereby, as the writer Lionel Shriver put it, "Anger generates narrative drive."[25] Anger, its pent-up, malign, and insidious growth, charges into story in words, in picture, in form. There it is. Feel my anger.

In my research I have interviewed artists who have had years, sometimes decades of tussles, all-out battles, and some wins too, with mental illness. Many of them will testify that we make a mistake to think the psychic repair processes of excavation, analysis, acceptance, and healing are confined to the clinic and couch. As art therapists attest, many people struggle with verbal language, working better in symbol,

Cat. 57 (detail)
Charles Benefiel, *Random Numeric Repeater #5*

color, metaphor, texture. Indeed, the sociologist Kathy Charmaz reminds us that "the raw experience of suffering may fit neither narrative logic nor the comprehensible content of a story."[26]

And we make a similar misjudgment if we hold that an expert in the room to guide us in this difficult process is a crucial component of the journey. Many artists I spoke to eschewed the clinical model for its asymmetry of power relations, and critical psychology is alive to such limitations.[27] The profession of art therapy itself has, in recent years, urged therapists to take greater responsibility for social justice by acknowledging the importance of power, race, privilege, and oppression within its framework.[28]

So steeped are we, however, in our post-enlightenment, post-developed worldview of mental "illness"[29]—as something to be talked about with an expert who wields their analytic skills like a scalpel, ready to lance the problematic abscess through disclosure—that we fail to explore alternative ways of confronting distress, trauma, atypicality. Such ways are now being given the time and study they deserve, and one is through making art, which, in the words of one of my interviewees, "has been instrumental in helping me to stay sane."

Tara, a forty-seven-year-old reclusive artist whose description of forty years of psychiatric interventions makes for hard listening, says simply that she makes art because while the story of things that happen to us is "deep, too deep for language," it is "not too deep for the eye."

So, as we view each of the works in this exhibition with a clear and uncluttered attention, let's delight in being the next part of the narrative, share in the experience of it being made, and be mindful of the story and the *life* that made it.

Space

In *A Room of One's Own*, Virginia Woolf famously wrote that in order for a woman to write fiction she must have two things: a room of her own and enough money to support herself.[30] There is much more, of course, in that suggestion that creativity is best nurtured in certain conditions. There is the politics of privilege and ease; the unjust ways in which the quietening of hunger is or is not achieved; the recognition that some groups of people (in this case, women) not only have less hope than others of the luxury of privacy, abundance, and time, but less chance of even being seen as entitled to such. The tale, therefore, of many Outsider and self-taught artists is even more compelling, as in many cases their art is honed in lack, forged in poverty, cultivated in the very absence of a room or studio or even home of one's own.

These tales are those of artists in this collection: Minnie Evans, an African American who, born into poverty, pursued her art despite the restrictions and hardships placed on her (cat. 9). Ralph Fasanella, Bronx-born to immigrant parents, was a tireless advocate for laborers' rights (cat. 17). Bill Traylor, another African American, was born into slavery and

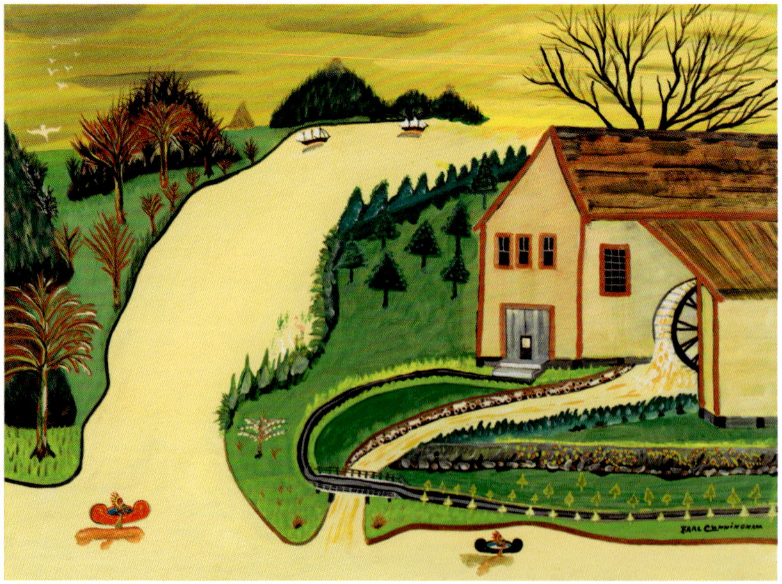

Cat. 37
Earl Cunningham (American, 1893–1977), *Mill*, 1949–77

spent most of his life after emancipation as a sharecropper (cat. 7). Nan Phelps (whose mother Lula Mae Hinkle is represented in cat. 30), one of eleven children born to an impoverished Kentucky family, began drawing with crayons at her desk in school before her family's economic situation forced her to leave formal education to care for her siblings. Ken Grimes, self-taught and diagnosed with paranoid schizophrenia in his early twenties, now creates playfully intense monochrome works featuring open vistas of outer-space imagery, aliens, and interstellar signals (cat. 69).

So while space, time, privilege, and a full belly help one learn to create, what is remarkable about self-taught artists is that they do what they do despite the odds: as one artist I interviewed put it, "I cannot *not* do this," and Mary K. Borkowski (cats. 35, 36, 38), another artist in this collection, said, "The world is on fire, and I have something to say about it." American sociologist Gary Fine describes the works created by such artists as "authentic because of the biographical contours of their creators—life stories of *difference* that infuse the content of the work."[31]

I have spoken to artists in psychiatric wards, in hospitals, in refuges, and hostels for the homeless. They have made their art at kitchen tables; on the street; in borrowed hallways while they sofa-surfed; in the grim shared room of a cheap hotel; in a refugee shelter of corrugated iron and plastic sheeting; in the dank front rooms of tenements and council flats where the noise of traffic, breaking glass, fighting, and shrieking children comes into the room through cardboard-thin walls. They have used whatever material they have, whatever they can get: wallpaper, cardboard boxes, children's crayons, spray paint. They have worked, like Thornton Dial in this collection (cats. 11–13), with found objects, lost objects, any objects, any*thing*, to find ways to say what, sometimes, has been impossible to put into words. Henri, an artist I interviewed with dissociative identity disorder, described the difficulty inherent in using spoken language to communicate nonverbal or preverbal experience. She spoke haltingly of her wariness of the dangers of the "colonization" of her words,[32] echoing the Russian philosopher Mikhail Bakhtin who pithily stated that words are always "populated with the intentions of others."[33]

So, what makes some artists outsiders is that for the most part they don't get to come in: into the warmth, the privacy, or the cushioned. Into the studio, the gallery, the recognition, and the luster. And into everything that comes with all that: art fluency, cultural capital, confidence, trust, financial reward, and being seen, in more ways than one. French sociologist Pierre Bourdieu gave us useful tools with which to analyze how the working class is excluded from art by their lack of familiarity with the requisite aesthetic codes.[34] He spoke of how "habitus," our "feel for the game"—the result of a long process of inculcation that begins in childhood—endows some with an entry point into culture while denying others, and how such cultural capital, this internalized code or cognitive acquisition, equips some with an almost "innate" competence for deciphering cultural relations and artifacts. His analysis lays bare the power relations in social life and partly explains the *outside* in *Outsider Art*. Such analysis and critique of the political and economic realities of the contemporary art world illuminate the stark divisions of the domains that flowed in and out of the narratives of artists with whom I spoke, who described how making art with no hope of ever showing it was a fraught experience, rife with tension. Caught in the confluence of the competing discourses of high art, community and Outsider Art, user empowerment, self-help, and an enduring language of artist as individual, these artists were making difficult choices about their identity, their art, and their health—and battling the constraints on mobility from one domain to another.

Yet precisely on such troubled boundaries do some artists find a space conducive to working productively and creatively, imagining and reimagining themselves, working with rhizomatic networks of people similarly "unhomed" but not homeless. Gilles Deleuze and Félix Guattari in their philosophical work *A Thousand Plateaus* speak of "striated spaces" as hierarchical, rule-intensive, strictly bounded, and confining, and "smooth spaces" that are open, dynamic, and allow for transformations and reimaginings to occur.[35] In this way, "all becoming occurs in smooth space," echoing artists with whom I spoke; they were adept at moving between deterritorialization, freeing themselves from the restrictions and boundaries of controlled, striated spaces, and reterritorialization,[36] repositioning themselves within new forms of striated spaces. In such a space, competing allegiances can play, and both agency and dissent find expression. Many I spoke to rejected categories such as "self-taught" or "Outsider" or "naïve"—not wanting to be categorized or consigned to any one label, or be driven to self-determine. One artist said that "to become an artist allowed me to live on the peripheries of myself—to reinvent perpetually," any form of pigeonholing being anathema to that for which he was striving.

Yet still indisputable were the lack, stigma, and hardship amongst the people I spoke with, who told me about the dearth of opportunity, of access, of materials, of space, of connections. One artist, shrugging her shoulders at the memory of going to see the owner of a small exhibition space, said, "I just didn't have the words, like, to sell myself, to talk about what I did, it was like there was a whole language I didnae know. That's when I actually did feel on the outside."

Margins

> The essence of creativity is going against the crowd.
> – Arthur Cropley[37]

As a species we are cognitive misers. We seek patterns, categories, classifications—and this serves our overstimulated and crowded, noisy brains well. It is also useful for capitalist economies and their instruments, not least the aforementioned algorithms of surveillance capitalism, which "know" us through our patterns, all the better to sell us stuff. The art in this collection will therefore fall inescapably into categories of Outsider Art, *Art Brut*, folk art, vernacular, naïve, primitive, self-taught art. And

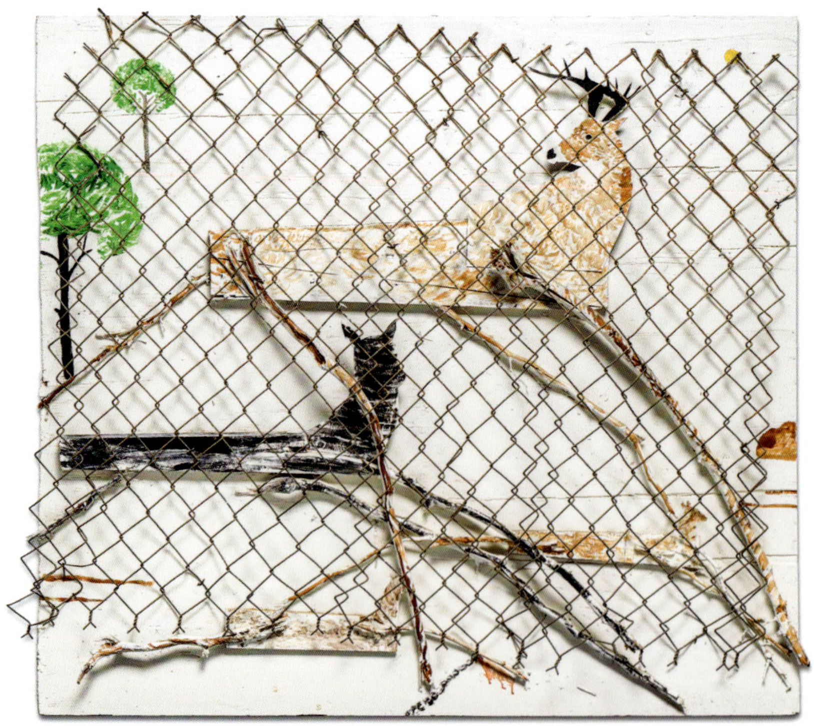

Cat. 14
Ronald Lockett (American, 1965–1998), *Traps*, circa 1989

Cat. 14 (detail)

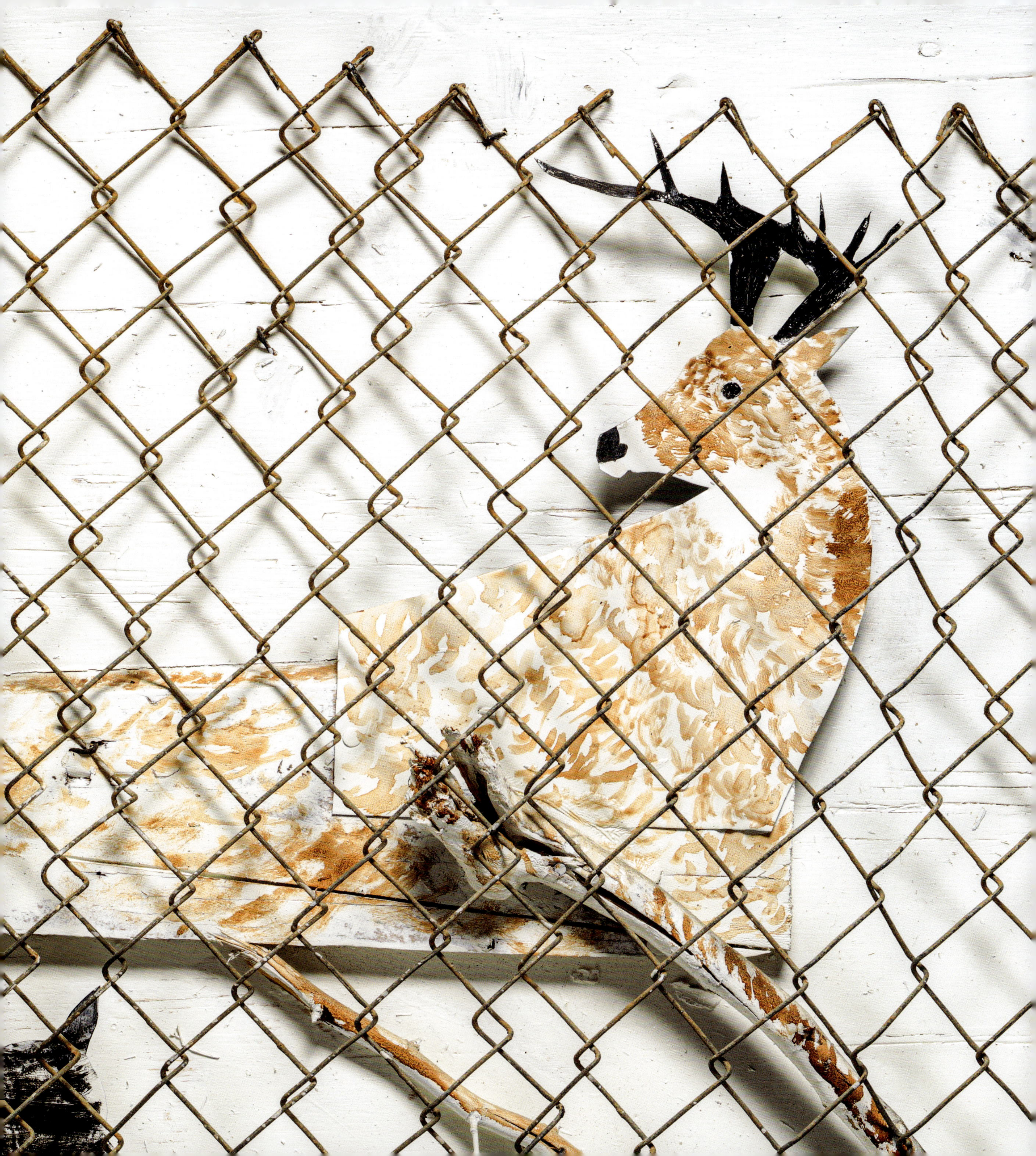

whilst categories and nomenclature will dissipate the more your attention becomes honed, tribute does need to be paid to the difficult road traveled by Outsider Art as a broad category before it became an insider interest—as this fascinating history adds further layers to this collection of art from many margins.[38]

After the witch hunts across Europe and other horrors of the Middle Ages, with their formulations of madness based on a frenzied Christian theological mix of the divine, the diabolical, and the depraved, the Age of Reason placed great weight on rationality. By dint of this, by the end of the seventeenth century, madness was increasingly seen as an organic, *physical* phenomenon, no longer involving the soul or moral responsibility. So began the shift towards a medicalized discourse that would recast madness as "mental illness," a term now contested in the twenty-first century for its "dubious scientific validity."[39]

The new cult of reason gave rise to asylums for the insane and the assertion that madness, far from being a path to higher states, was in fact an *in*ability to participate meaningfully in the society of the day. The mad, by this logic, required incarceration. The proliferation of workhouses and poorhouses—in short, the institution—was one response to the new social relations that left families, the fodder of the developing industrialized economy, less able to look after relatives in need. Workhouses and poorhouses, some of which contained a ward exclusively for "lunatics," acted as a means by which paupers, prostitutes, orphans, invalids, the old, beggars, the criminal, and the mad could be corralled and subdued. Historian and philosopher Michel Foucault has famously argued that such institutional confinement was based on a condemnation of idleness and an articulation of the imperative of labor, expressing an emerging normative order of modern society and a switch from punishment of the body to punishment of the mind.[40] Thus we arrive at a focus on the "productive citizen" and the proposed relationship between being busy in the labor force, being included in society, and being sane—a focus that was to endure. As we approach the first quarter of the twenty-first century, the notion of the productive, networked citizen as the lifeblood of neoliberal societies is reaching a new zenith, with new nadirs for those not deemed productive, networked, solvent, sane, or able.[41]

Asylums in the eighteenth century ushered in new thinking about treatment and mechanisms of restraint and control. They made liberal use of straightjackets, chains, handcuffs, and iron collars, with treatments that included medieval favorites such as bloodletting and purging. But by the end of the 1700s a new movement emerged, the Moral Treatment Movement, which somewhat radically advocated kindness towards the mentally ill, along with purposeful activity. The French physician and philosopher Philippe Pinel along with the English Quaker William Tuke recommended that treatment should include the use of literature, music, physical exercise, and work. Suggestions such as these gradually led to postwar industrial therapy in psychiatric hospitals and to modern-day occupational therapy practice. The beginnings of the idea of art as therapy would soon take root.

With the change in activity and treatments prescribed for the incarcerated came a growing interest in lives that had previously elicited little actual concern. Observations of the art making of the "mad" began, and Pinel has been credited with being the first to write about the art of the mentally ill in his 1801 *Medico-Philosophical Treatise on Mental Alienation or Mania*. In 1810 John Haslam, an English apothecary and physician from the Bethlem Hospital,[42] became probably the first clinician to reproduce patient work in his *Illustrations of Madness*. Another proponent of Moral Treatment was the doctor William Browne, who advocated activities for patients such as writing and drama, and pioneered early forms of art therapy, initiating one of the earliest collections of artistic work by patients in a psychiatric hospital.

The art of the mentally ill became an established area of clinical and academic interest. It also caught the attention of the literati, with madness representing for the Romantics an alluring, privileged, and exalted state that opened vistas onto hidden realms.[43] The physician Cesare Lombroso, another amongst the first to form a collection of the art of the insane, pioneered study in another vein: the long-expounded links between creativity, madness, and genius, a line of study that persists to this day. Lombroso, accredited with being the father of criminology, concluded in his 1881 work *The Man of Genius* that both the madman and the genius were types of "degenerate." He drew on the work of French physician Bénédict Morel who, in 1857, proposed a theory of "hereditary degeneracy." Degeneration theory was to have some staying power as a tool of social control, with certain of its tenets enduring in the work of eugenicists and social Darwinists. Lombroso's student Max Nordau expanded on Morel and Lombroso's ideas in his own 1892 volume *Degeneration*, which was to later inform the Nazis' wholesale condemnation of "degenerate art"—just one example of the "use" to which theories that conflate madness, creativity, and a regression to humankind's unbridled passions have been put.

The nineteenth century would offer up other seminal works ensuing from the continued interest into the art of those deemed mad. In 1907, a French psychiatrist, Marcel Réja, published *The Art of the Insane*, claiming that this art provides us with a way into understanding creativity more generally. Psychiatrist and art historian Hans Prinzhorn elevated the debate by assembling a small collection of creative works from psychiatric hospitals at the University of Heidelberg, and enthusiasm grew through his 1922 illustrated book *Artistry of the Mentally Ill*, in which he used psychoanalytic theories to present the cases of individual artist-patients. Prinzhorn also, for the first time, linked the art of the mentally ill with that of children and folk artists, an idea that was to gather momentum in the hands of French painter Jean Dubuffet.

Dubuffet was impressed by the art of schizophrenic patients he encountered on his 1945 journey to the asylum of Waldau in Switzerland. He felt he was observing expressions of an extreme individualism, free from all social and cultural constraints. It was raw—hence his coining of the now well-known term *Art Brut*. Translated by Roger Cardinal in the early 1970s as "Outsider Art," the term, including its controversies and, indeed, the market for its artifacts, survives—in fact, thrives—well into the present day. An umbrella term "for everything that is ostensibly raw, untutored, and irrational in art,"[44] Outsider Art continues to offer both an identity and a genre for the work of the mentally ill, but also, arguably, to delineate and stereotype.

The association of the raw and the primitive with madness, and the relationship with folk, primitive, and children's art, was one exploited by both the Surrealists and the Expressionists. In his 1912 diary entry, the artist Paul Klee logged a visit to an exhibition of Wassily Kandinsky's group Der Blaue Reiter (The Blue Rider) and reflected on the primordial and the art of both children and the

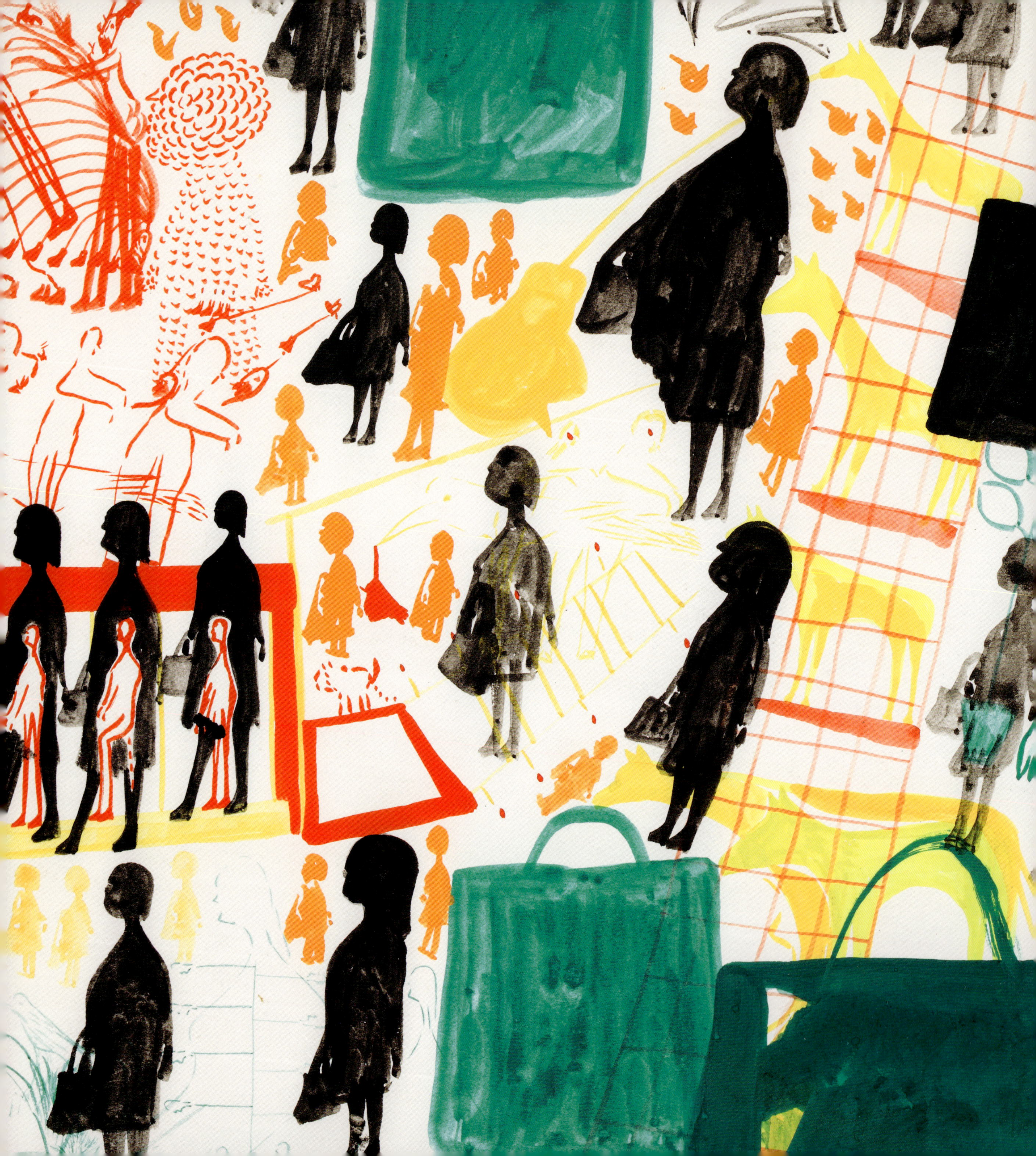

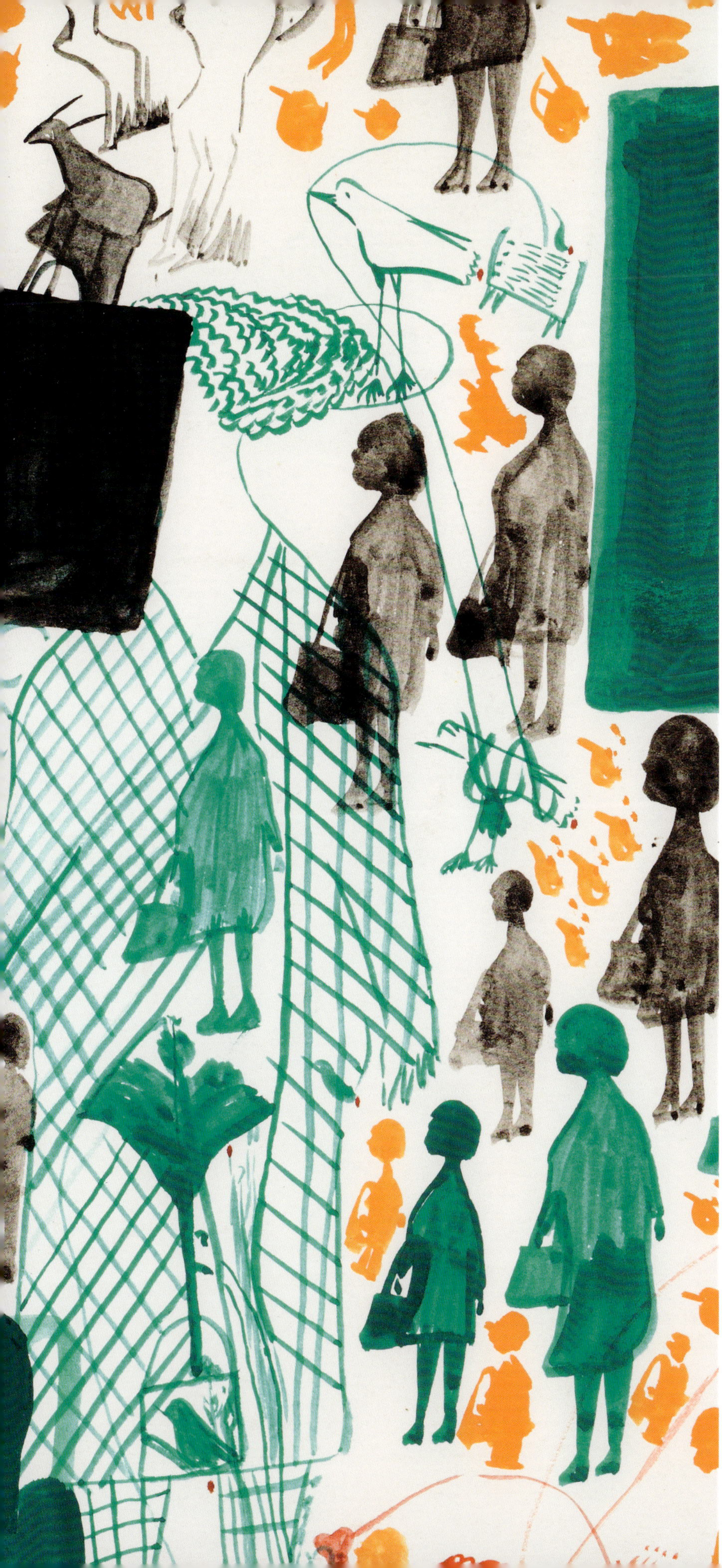

mentally ill. References to the spontaneity of such art and the conflation of art with raw passion further fortify stereotypes of madness as belonging to the untamed, wild, and dangerous—stereotypes that persist, with fear, stigma, and discrimination subsequently enduring in tandem.

The episteme of madness continued its movement from theology, through philosophy and into the then-emerging science of psychology. In the early twentieth century Sigmund Freud was developing psychobiography, using this to investigate art and its makers. He and his former pupil, colleague, and later archrival Carl Jung were to diverge dramatically in their thinking about the purpose and value of art and its relationship to the mind of the maker and beholder, and residues of this schism remain as a watermark in theories today of symbolism and creative expression.

In 1942 the artist and therapist Adrian Hill coined the term *art therapy*, having discovered the benefits of painting and drawing while recovering from tuberculosis. Meanwhile, in the United States, the psychologist Margaret Naumburg did much to establish the discipline through her *Dynamically Oriented Art Therapy* (1966). By the late 1960s in both Europe and the United States, the debate about how art works to alleviate psychological distress was well underway, and making art began to be encouraged in hospitals, psychiatric and rehabilitation centers, prisons, and community centers, with community art projects proliferating as part of humanitarian work with the displaced, orphaned, traumatized, and vulnerable.

A new receptivity to the "uncooked" art of individuals without formal training grew, and exhibitions of "Outsider Art" proliferated. This has continued, but not without critics, who question, for example, the consumption of "lowbrow" cultural artifacts by the "highbrow" elite.

Cat. 50 (detail)
Carlo Zinelli, *Untitled*

Professor of Sociology Vera L. Zolberg points out that, after all, "The existence of outsider art implies an insider art,"[45] and such lively debate underscores the continued contentious nature of the genre and its lasting ability to unsettle and provoke.

By the 2000s, Outsider Art had become a tour de force inside the art world. The insider/outsider binary has become at best smudged and debated, and at worst problematic and exploitative, with the art world cashing in on art often created in poverty and isolation by artists oftentimes unrecognized during their lifetime and not fully, if at all, benefitting from financial reward. It remains an example for some of the appropriation by powerful agents of the creative expression of the socially excluded.

Some of the artists I interviewed tussled with nomenclature, the tyranny of labels, and the conundrum of being interesting as an artist because of your biography. Leonne, one artist in my research, commented:

> I'm not a "mental health artist" [makes scare quotes with fingers]. I'm not an outsider artist. Just because I'm bipolar doesn't mean I have to stay in community arts or work with others who have a mental health condition, but it's like . . . [pause] I'm not interesting unless I'm a "Bipolar Artist" so I can't escape that . . . that label, again.

Much has been written about the value of labels and identity politics to the art world. Mónica Kjellman-Chapin argues that the centrality of biography to Outsider Art is not simply an integral part of its categorization and valuation but is chosen intentionally as a marketing device,[46] feeding what Professor of Art History Miwon Kwon calls a "lust for authentic histories and identities."[47] Curator and critic Lyle Rexer cautions that while the term *Outsider Art* has the potential to add positive value to the artist's work, it can, by the same token, imprison.[48] Professor of Philosophy Jesse Prinz, meanwhile, notes that "Outsider Art" and "Outsider Artist" are not neutral concepts, and like any concepts, they "both reflect and impose power relations."[49]

Attention, story, space, and margins have formed the scaffold of this preamble. It has scattered around a few thoughts about how our psychologies, creativity, and auto/biography[50] are complexly hewn through the interstices of power, heredity, and the socioeconomic ideologies in which we find ourselves enmeshed. I hope they have added to the experience of looking at this collection and peeling back its many layers. Let's begin by just applying an open, bare attention and step lightly into this mystery.

Cat. 60 (detail)
Janet Sobel, *Untitled* (*JS-070*)

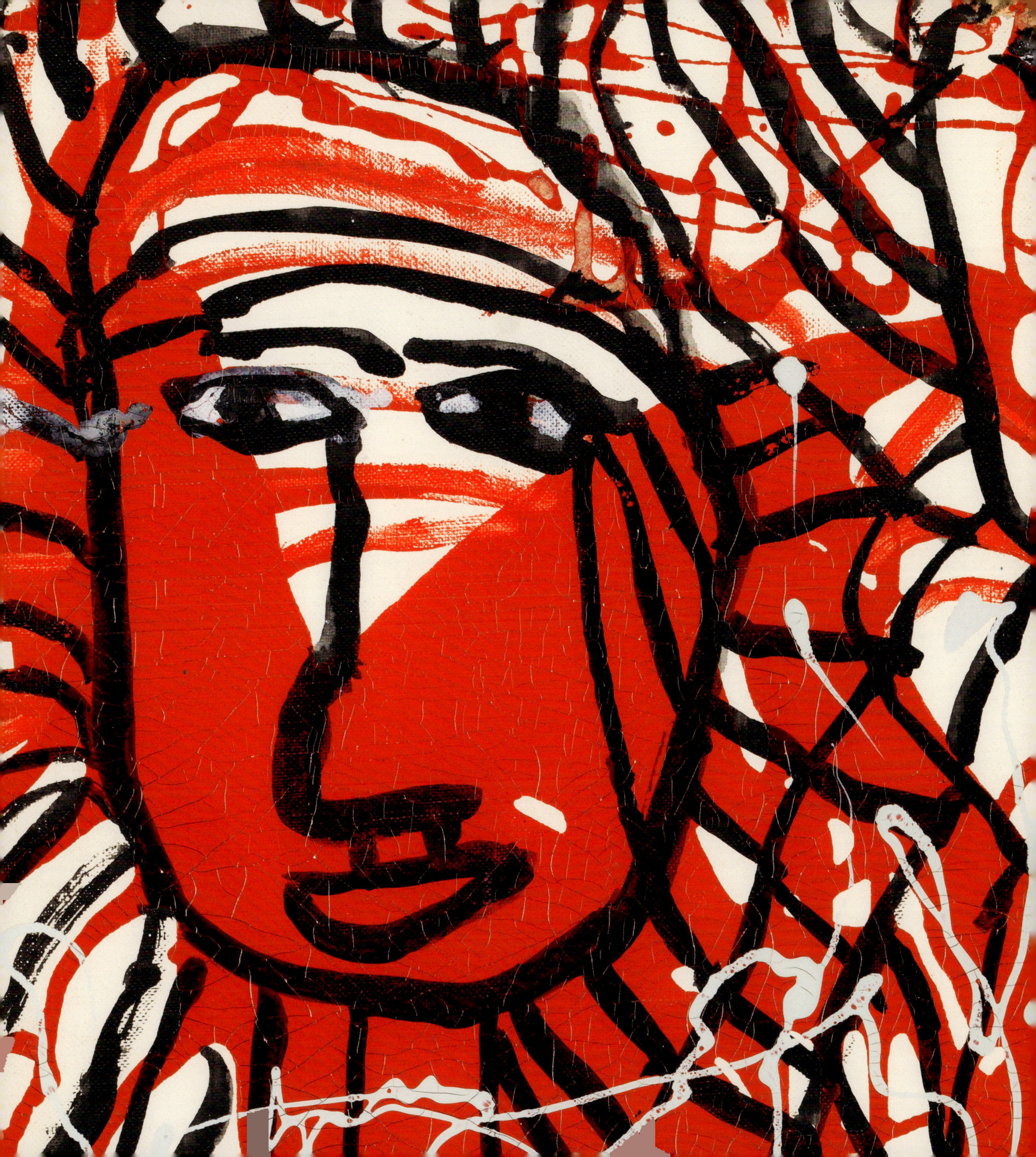

1. Elizabeth Strout, *Olive, Again* (London: Penguin Books, 2020), 116.
2. Dorothea Tanning quoted in John Glassie, “Oldest Living Surrealist Tells All,” *Salon*, February 11, 2002, https://www.salon.com/2002/02/11/tanning/.
3. Alice Pitt and Deborah Britzman, “Speculations on Qualities of Difficult Knowledge in Teaching and Learning: An Experiment in Psychoanalytic Research,” *International Journal of Qualitative Studies in Education* 16, no. 6 (November 2003): 761, https://doi.org/10.1080/09518390310001632135.
4. Ellen Dissanayake, *Homo Aestheticus: Where Art Comes From and Why* (Seattle: University of Washington Press, 1995), 58.
5. Nina Coltart quoted in Anthony Molino, ed., *Freely Associated: Encounters in Psychoanalysis with Christopher Bollas, Joyce McDougall, Michael Eigen, Adam Phillips, Nina Coltart* (New York: Free Association Books, 1997), 205.
6. Wilfred Ruprecht Bion, *Attention and Interpretation* (London: Karnac Books, 1970).
7. John Keats quoted in Bion, *Attention and Interpretation*, 125.
8. Jenny Odell, *How to Do Nothing: Resisting the Attention Economy* (New York: Melville House, 2019), 155.
9. Martin Buber, *I and Thou* (New York: Howard Books, 2008).
10. Donald Woods Winnicott, *Playing and Reality* (New York: Pelican Books, 1985), 153.
11. Thomas Ogden, *The Matrix of the Mind: Object Relations and the Psychoanalytic Dialogue* (London: Karnac Books, 1992), 203.
12. “It is quite true what philosophy says: that life must be understood backwards. But they forget the other clause—that it must be lived forwards.” Søren Kierkegaard, *Papers and Journals: A Selection*, trans. Alastair Hannay (London: Penguin, 1996; ebook 2015), 43 IV A 164, https://www.google.com/books/edition/Papers_and_Journals/kSNqCAAAQBAJ.
13. Catherine Riessman Kohler, “Analysis of Personal Narratives,” in *Handbook of Interview Research: Context and Method*, ed. Jaber F. Gubrium and James A. Holstein (London: Sage Publications, 2000), 705.
14. Kenneth Wright, *Mirroring and Attunement: Self-Realization in Psychoanalysis and Art* (London: Routledge, 2009), 49.
15. Daniel Stern, *The Interpersonal World of the Infant* (New York: Basic Books, 1985).
16. Ellen Dissanayake, “Ethology, Interpersonal Neurobiology, and Play: Insights into the Evolutionary Origin of the Arts,” *American Journal of Play* 9, no. 2 (Winter 2017): 143–68, https://files.eric.ed.gov/fulltext/EJ1141577.pdf.
17. Miranda Fricker, *Epistemic Injustice: Power and the Ethics of Knowing* (Oxford: Oxford University Press, 2009).
18. Sean Akerman and Suzanne C. Ouellette, “What Ricoeur’s Hermeneutics Reveal about Self and Identity and Aesthetic Experience,” *Theory & Psychology* 22, no. 4 (August 2012): 385, https://doi.org/10.1177/0959354311401483.
19. Michael Eigen, *Emotional Storm* (Middletown, CT: Wesleyan University Press, 2005), 51.
20. Olivia Sagan, *Narratives of Art Practice and Mental Wellbeing: Reparation and Connection* (London: Routledge, 2014).
21. For example, see Sandra Gosso, ed., *Psychoanalysis and Art: Kleinian Perspectives* (London: Karnac Books, 2004); and Nicky Glover, *Psychoanalytic Aesthetics: An Introduction to the British School* (London: Harris Meltzer Trust, 2009).
22. Anton Ehrenzweig, *The Hidden Order of Art* (Los Angeles: University of California Press, 1971).
23. Jeanne Nakamura and Mihaly Csikszentmihalyi, “The Concept of Flow,” in *The Handbook of Positive Psychology*, ed. Shane J. Lopez and Charles R. Snyder (New York: Oxford University Press, 2002).
24. Mihaly Csikszentmihalyi, *Creativity: Flow and the Psychology of Discovery and Invention* (New York: HarperCollins, 1996).
25. Lionel Shriver, *So Much for That* (London: HarperCollins, 2010), 543.
26. Kathy Charmaz, “Stories and Silences: Disclosures and Self in Chronic Illness,” *Qualitative Inquiry* 8, no. 3 (June 2002): 303, https://doi.org/10.1177/107780040200800307.
27. Thomas Teo, “Critical Psychology: A Geography of Intellectual Engagement and Resistance,” *American Psychologist* 70, no. 3 (January 2015): 254, https://doi.org/10.1037/a0038727.
28. Erin Kuri, “Toward an Ethical Application of Intersectionality in Art Therapy,” *Art Therapy* 34, no. 3 (September 2017): 118–22, https://doi.org/10.1080/07421656.2017.1358023.
29. For a critique of the pathologization of individuals in contemporary neoliberal society, see Heidi Rimke, “Introduction—Mental and Emotional Distress as a Social Justice Issue: Beyond Psychocentrism,” *Studies in Social Justice* 10, no. 1 (August 2016): 4–17, https://doi.org/10.26522/ssj.v10i1.1407.
30. Virginia Woolf, *A Room of One’s Own* (London: Hogarth Press, 1929).
31. Gary Alan Fine, *Everyday Genius: Self-Taught Art and the Culture of Authenticity* (Chicago: University of Chicago Press, 2004), 6.
32. Olivia Sagan, “Art-Making and Its Interface with Dissociative Identity Disorder: No Words That Didn’t Fit,” *Journal of Creativity in Mental Health* 14, no. 1 (August 2018): 23–36, https://psycnet.apa.org/doi/10.1080/15401383.2018.1499062.
33. Mikhail Bakhtin, *The Dialogic Imagination*, ed. Michael Holquist, trans. Caryl Emerson and Michael Holquist (Austin: University of Texas Press, 1981), 294.
34. Pierre Bourdieu, *The Logic of Practice*, trans. Richard Nice (Cambridge: Polity Press, 1990), 66.
35. Gilles Deleuze and Félix Guattari, *A Thousand Plateaus* (London: Bloomsbury Academic, 2013), 486.

36. Maria Tamboukou, "Machinic Assemblages: Women, Art Education and Space," *Discourse: Studies in the Cultural Politics of Education* 29, no. 3 (September 2008): 359–75, https://doi.org/10.1080/01596300802259129.
37. Arthur J. Cropley, "The Dark Side of Creativity: What Is It?" in *The Dark Side of Creativity*, ed. David H. Cropley, Arthur J. Cropley, James C. Kaufman, and Mark A. Runco (Cambridge: Cambridge University Press, 2010), 8.
38. For example, see Roger Cardinal, *Outsider Art* (New York: Praeger Publishers, 1972); and David Maclagan, *Outsider Art: From the Margins to the Marketplace* (London: Reaktion Books, 2010).
39. Rimke, "Introduction—Mental and Emotional Distress," 5.
40. Michel Foucault, *Discipline & Punish: The Birth of the Prison*, 2nd ed., trans. Alan Sheridan (London: Vintage Books, 1995).
41. James Davies, *Sedated: How Modern Capitalism Created our Mental Health Crisis* (London: Atlantic Books, 2021).
42. Readers may be interested to explore the continued tradition of Bethlem at the Bethlem Gallery, https://bethlemgallery.com/.
43. The bidirectional relationship of Romanticism and Outsider Art continues to be explored and critiqued. See, for example, Joanne Cubbs, "Rebels, Mystics, and Outcasts: The Romantic Artist Outsider," in *The Artist Outsider*, ed. Michael D. Hall and Eugene W. Metcalf Jr. (Washington, DC: Smithsonian Institution Press, 1994), 77–83.
44. Lyle Rexer, *How to Look at Outsider Art* (New York: Harry N. Abrams, 2005), 6.
45. Oliver Hahl, Ezra W. Zuckerman, and Minjae Kim, "Why Elites Love Authentic Lowbrow Culture: Overcoming High-Status Denigration with Outsider Art," *American Sociological Review* 82, no. 4 (August 2017): 828–56, https://doi.org/10.1177/0003122417710642.
46. Mónica Kjellman-Chapin, "Fake Identity, Real Work: Authenticity, Autofiction, and Outsider Art," *SPECS Journal of Art and Culture* 2, no. 1 (2009): 148–59, https://scholarship.rollins.edu/specs/vol2/iss1/51.
47. Miwon Kwon, *One Place after Another: Site Specific Art and Locational Identity* (Cambridge, MA: MIT Press, 2002), 139.
48. Rexer, *How to Look at Outsider Art*.
49. Jesse Prinz, "Against Outsider Art," *Journal of Social Philosophy* 48, no. 3 (September 2017): 265, https://dx.doi.org/10.1111/josp.12190.
50. The use of the slash in *auto/biography* was introduced by Liz Stanley (1992) and denotes autobiography as co-constructed by both the subject and their interaction with other(s) and their environment and experiences. Liz Stanley, *The Auto/Biographical I: Theory and Practice of Feminist Auto/Biography* (Manchester: Manchester University Press, 1992).

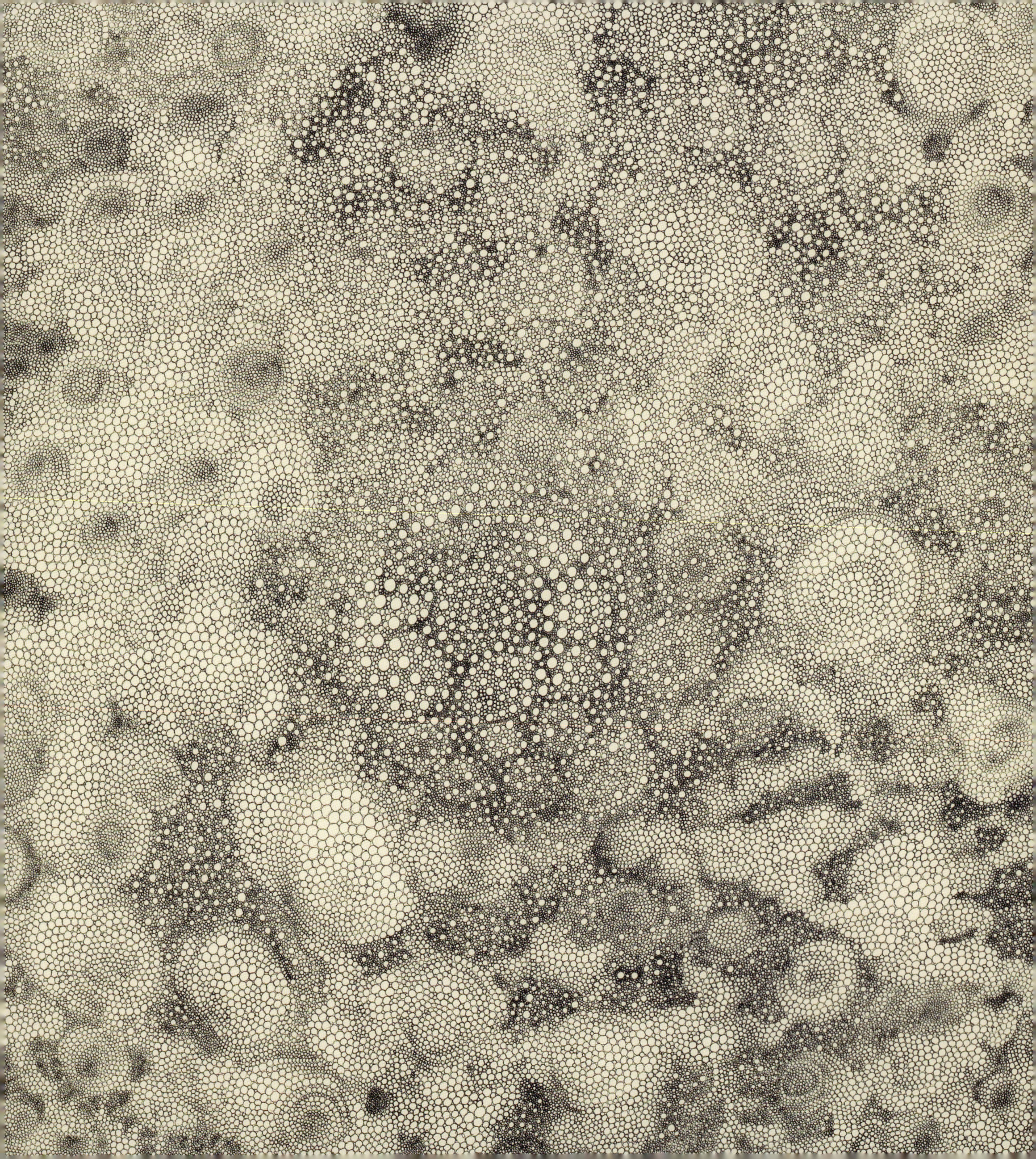

A Shepherd of the Art

Collector Richard Rosenthal in Conversation, March 24, 2022

Julie Aronson

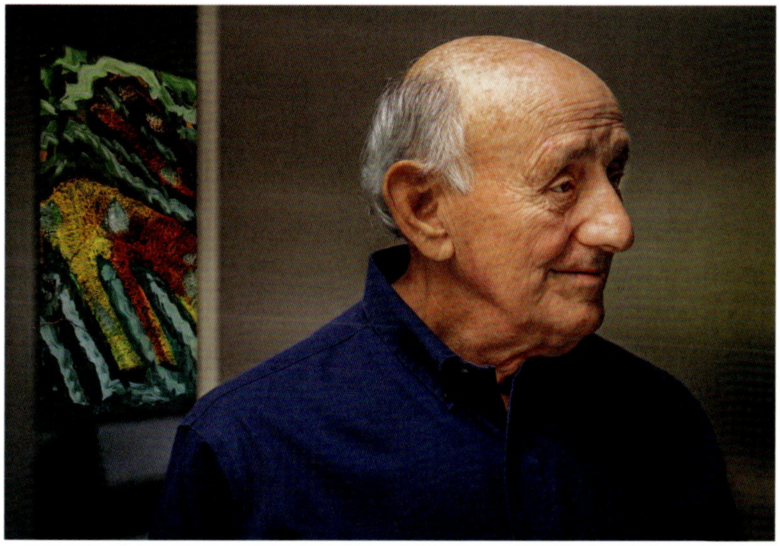

Richard Rosenthal, 2022

Julie Aronson — How did you become interested in art?
Richard Rosenthal — Well, art as well as arts, plural—entirely my mother. My five siblings and I had little choice about whether or not we were going to like art. We were surrounded by it; we participated in it. I played the violin. My mother was a wonderful pianist. We were taken to plays, concerts of all sorts, and my younger brothers and I were in a Saturday-morning studio program at the Cincinnati Art Museum when we were very young kids. We weren't very good at it but appreciating art versus making it has always been something that I have loved.

When and how did you start collecting?
My late wife Lois and I started collecting shortly after we were married. So, this could go back to the mid- to late '60s. And the first thing we collected was painted American furniture. That morphed into Shaker furniture. We became friendly with the Shaker community in Sabbathday Lake, Maine, and became very interested in their lifestyle, attending some of their meetings on Sundays, and so on. So, we had a number of wonderful pieces of Shaker furniture and baskets. That then somehow morphed into folk art of the Grandma Moses type, which then moved right on over about fifteen years ago to Outsider folk art or *Art Brut*, among many other names for this particular genre.

I know that you *do* like nineteenth-century things.
Yes, especially furniture. But the focus of the collection is contemporary. It is contemporary in time made rather than appearance.

Cat. 58 (detail)
Hiroyuki Doi, *Untitled*

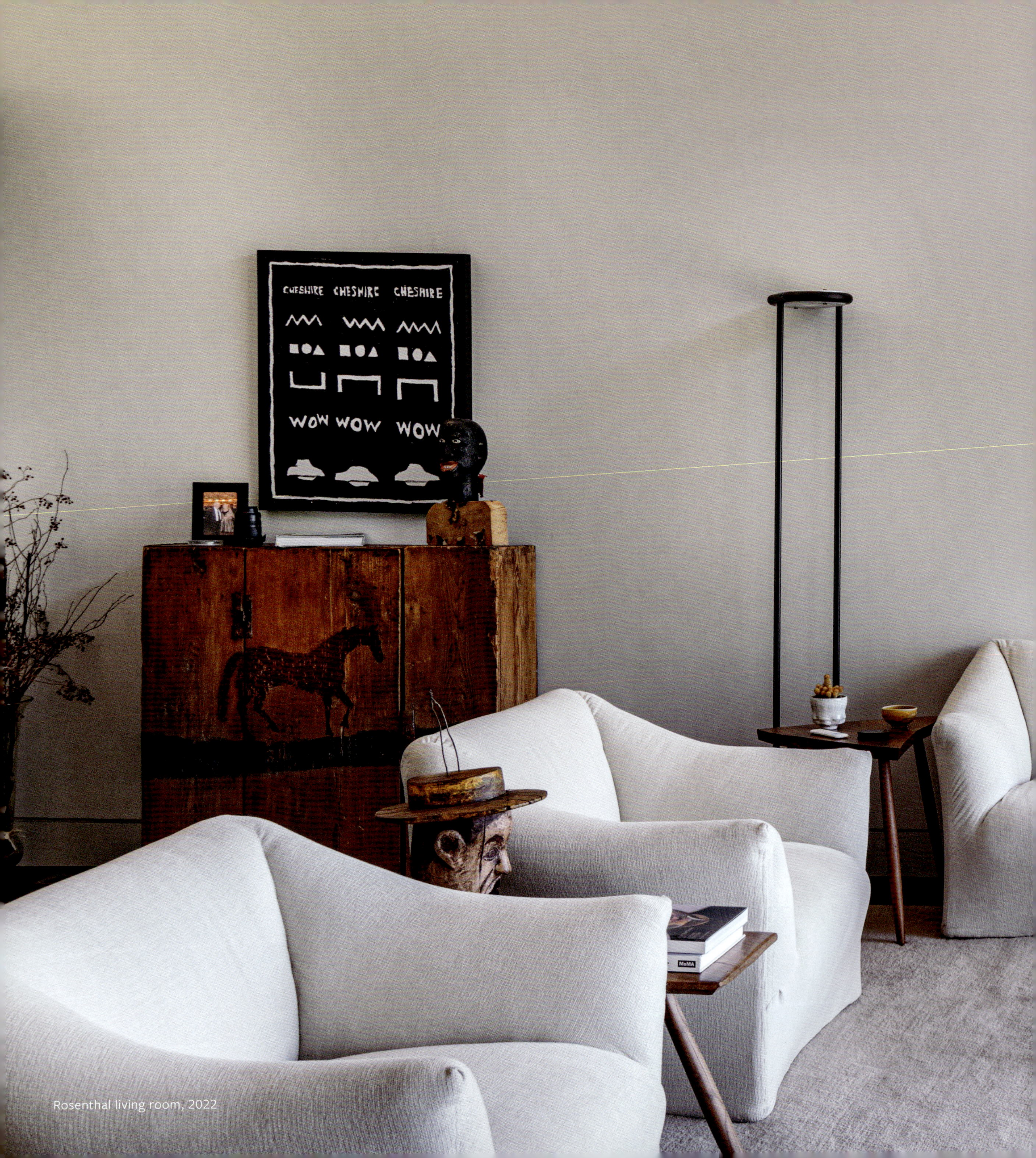

Rosenthal living room, 2022

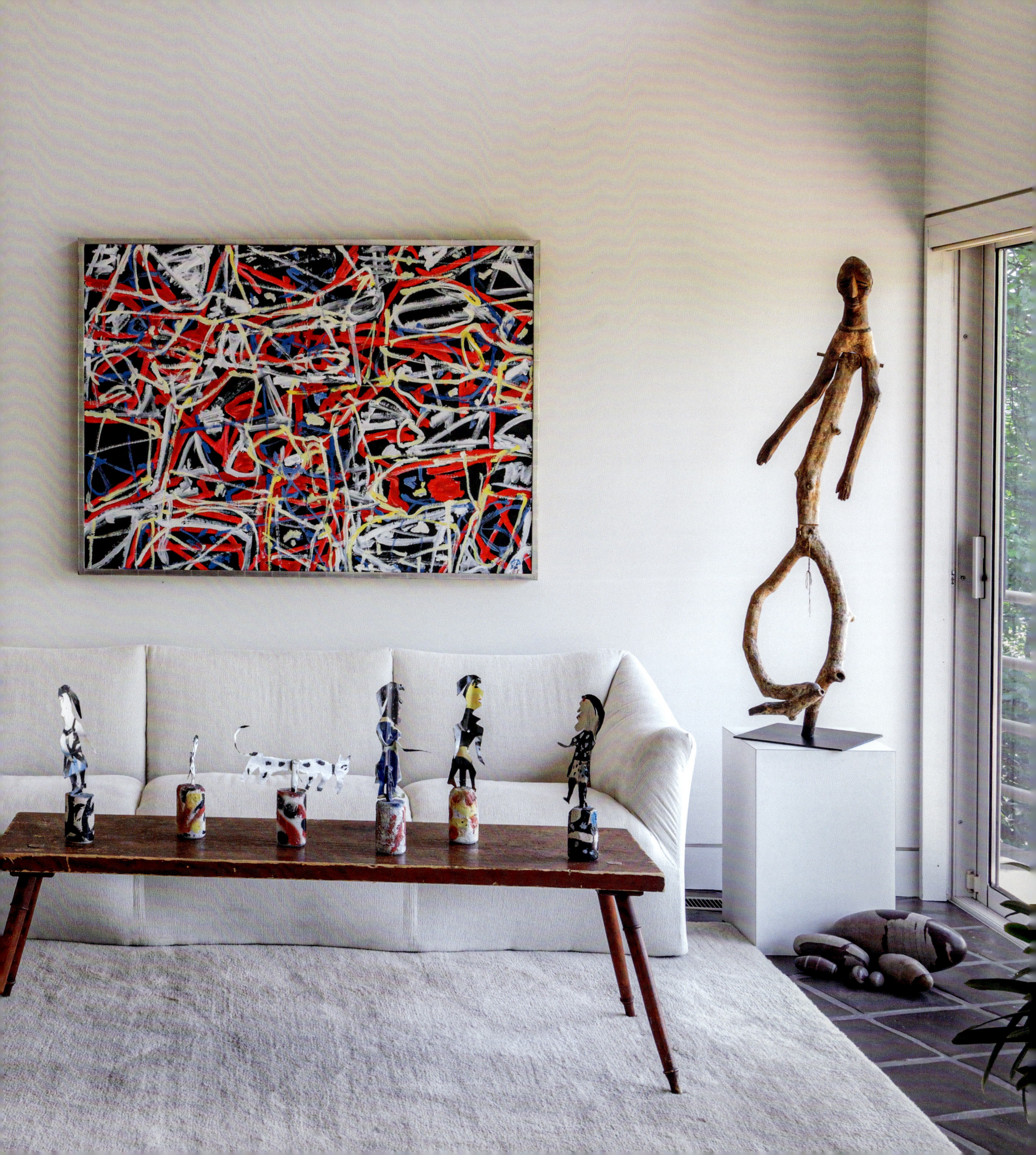

How do you define your collection? Do you put parameters on it?

I really don't. We collected things to which we had an almost immediate response, and our rule for collecting or buying was that, if Lois and I both just loved whatever it was we were looking at, and it wasn't totally outside what we could afford to buy, we'd buy it. If one of us loved it and the other of us was not really sure, we would likely buy it, but it would be located somewhere near the person who loved it—usually, in my case, my office, or, with Lois, if there was something she loved that I thought was just okay, then it would be located in an area of the house where she spent most of her time.

Beyond that, there are some pieces by Dubuffet (cats. 43, 44, 59) which, although he is not a self-taught or folk artist, I love because I want to honor that he legitimized the field. There was an exhibition of folk art in Paris. He saw it, fell in love with it, and said, "Wait a minute, this is great art. It's communicating a message in a very unique and representative way." And boom! Because of his reputation, his opinion was heard and accepted. His work is a connector for me personally—to have him on the walls of my home and to have a variety of his work—because his art was immensely eclectic.

Have there been advisors or mentors who have helped you along the way, informing the collection?

Early on, I bought a number of pieces of folk art from Jay Johnson's America's Folk Heritage Gallery in Manhattan. Jay helped at that time to fashion the collection. He would say things like "This is an artist whose work you don't have, and this is one of his better pieces, and you need to have him in your collection." One other influencer is a man by the name of Laurent Danchin. Until he died a few years ago, he was the European editor for *Raw Vision* magazine and lived in France. We took a number of trips with him to artists' studios in and around Paris, and he opened up new worlds of work by artists from that part of the world.

Have you met any of the artists whose work you have in the collection?

I have, which has been one of the most interesting and enjoyable parts of collecting this genre of art, because there are wonderful stories behind every single piece. Those stories say so much about the art. For me, it helps deepen the meaning, the message, and the pure enjoyment of each work.

For example, we have a large painting, about ten feet wide by four and a half feet high, by Ralph Fasanella, who I met probably forty years ago (cat. 17 and fig. 1). And while I liked his art, Lois really did not. We did not buy a piece of his art at that time, nor when I ran into him about twenty years ago. He was a short, first-generation Italian man, cigar-smoking and a little bit aloof. But a man of strong priorities. Of importance for him were the Brooklyn Dodgers, number one; God, number two; family, number three. I remarked that I was a Dodgers fan, but he didn't believe it. I said, "Well, Ralph, if you'd like to name a late 1940s Dodgers team, I will give you the player of each position." Well, he did, and I did. And, all of a sudden, we became buddies because I passed his most important test. So, at any rate, about five years ago in New York, I found a work [by Fasanella] I really liked very much and bought it. As he was a union organizer, this was a theme that was prominent in much of his work. The painting depicts a strike that ended in a very bloody way in Lawrence, Massachusetts, in 1912—the wool workers' strike. The experience of meeting the artist and [hearing]

Cat. 43 (detail)
Jean Dubuffet, *Annal XII* (*Annale XII*)

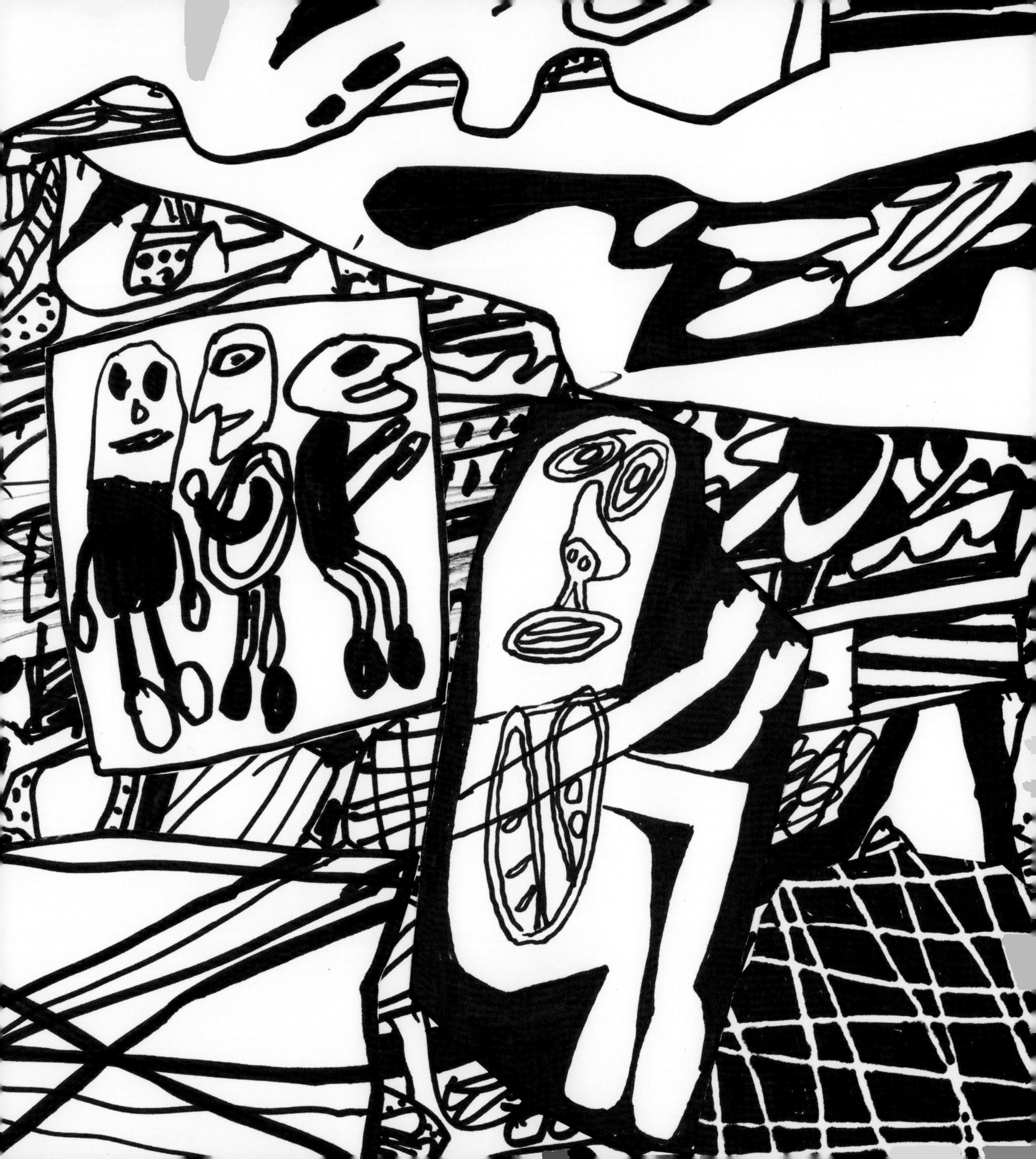

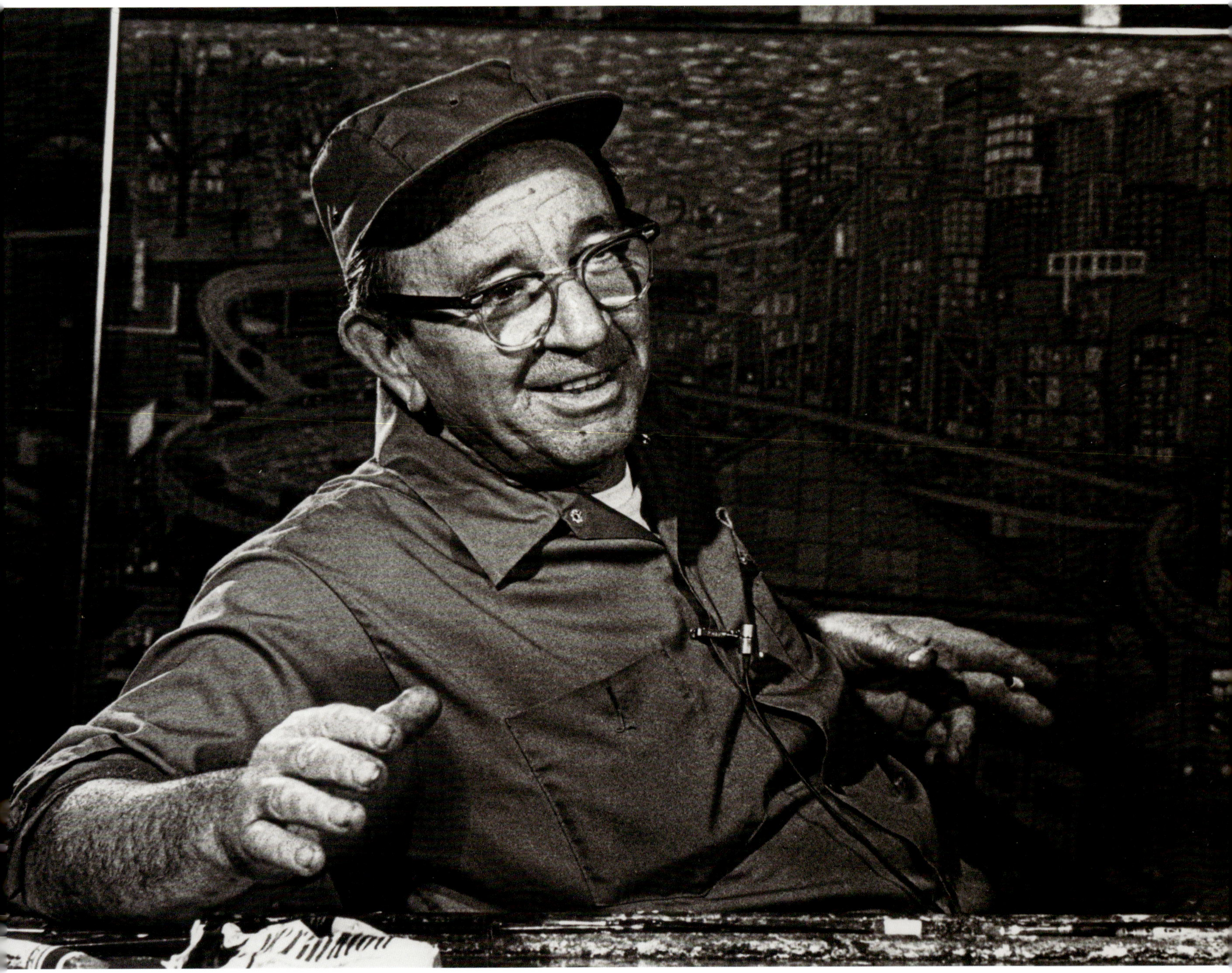

Fig. 1
Charmian Reading (American, 1931–2014), *Ralph Fasanella*, 1972, black and white print, American Folk Art Museum Archives, gift of the estate of Ralph Fasanella, 2009

all of these stories bundled together make for the unique enjoyment I get every time I walk past that piece of art. All those memories come pouring right out of the canvas.

Your collection is very diverse. Are there things you see linking the works together?

There is not a common thread. As I mentioned earlier, a lot of the art that Lois and I purchased, and that I've purchased since her death, has had something that immediately attracted us. We both liked color and, frequently, the bolder the better. It might have been the subject, or the medium, or the message. I don't think there's a theme here, but there's certainly an influence. And the more fascinating the story about the painting and the painter or the sculptor, which gives a deeper meaning, the better. It just makes that piece of art perpetually exciting. I never get tired of looking at any of the pieces that are in the collection.

Having said that, I find that there are some pieces that . . . it's not that I don't like them anymore, it's just that I like something else better. I have only so many walls. And so, while I do rotate art from time to time, I find that I wind up selling some of the art—somewhat painfully, because they're all my children, and I love them all. But the artist wanted them shared with other people and sitting in art storage in my home doesn't allow that.

Are you still out there looking?

Sure. I love to look, and if something special about a piece strikes me, I will certainly want to learn more about the artist and possibly buy it. Now, my wife Kitty and I, together, have bought a number of pieces. So, yes, I'm an active collector.

What are you looking for or thinking about when you go to the Outsider Art Fair or into a gallery?

I look at all art with what I call "the innocent eye." I am totally neutral when I walk into a gallery or a show. And if the art says something to me—drawing me to it almost like a magnet—then I buy it. By the same token, I will quickly walk away if there isn't some emotional response to the piece.

I am somewhat influenced by other collectors, curators, and dealers who say, "This is a new face in the field, and you have to have his or her piece of art." And so, I will look at that because I want to learn from people who are more expert than I. I have works I would call iconic pieces of art. I do like them very much, but would I have bought them if they weren't iconic? I'm not sure. But I certainly was influenced, and still am influenced, by the reputation of the artist. For me, however, it is purely secondary or tertiary in terms of the importance of owning it. I am frequently not sold. I am more likely to buy a piece of art because of my own personal experience with it. There are some artists who are very important to other collectors—but not [to] me. [Joseph] Yoakum for example. I'm just not a fan. Nevertheless, I'm glad other people like his work because that's good for the artist.

I'm drawn to things that are . . . I think *clever* is not quite the right word, but maybe even more phantasmagorical, if you would. I really get a kick out of that. I am, however, very much aware that a cartoon is only funny once. A piece of art can be funny, but it has to be funny forever. And that, for any artist or any art collector, I should think, would be very, very difficult to find. So, I would not say that I have any comedic art. Maybe some of it's a little bit amusing, but I have very little of that, frankly.

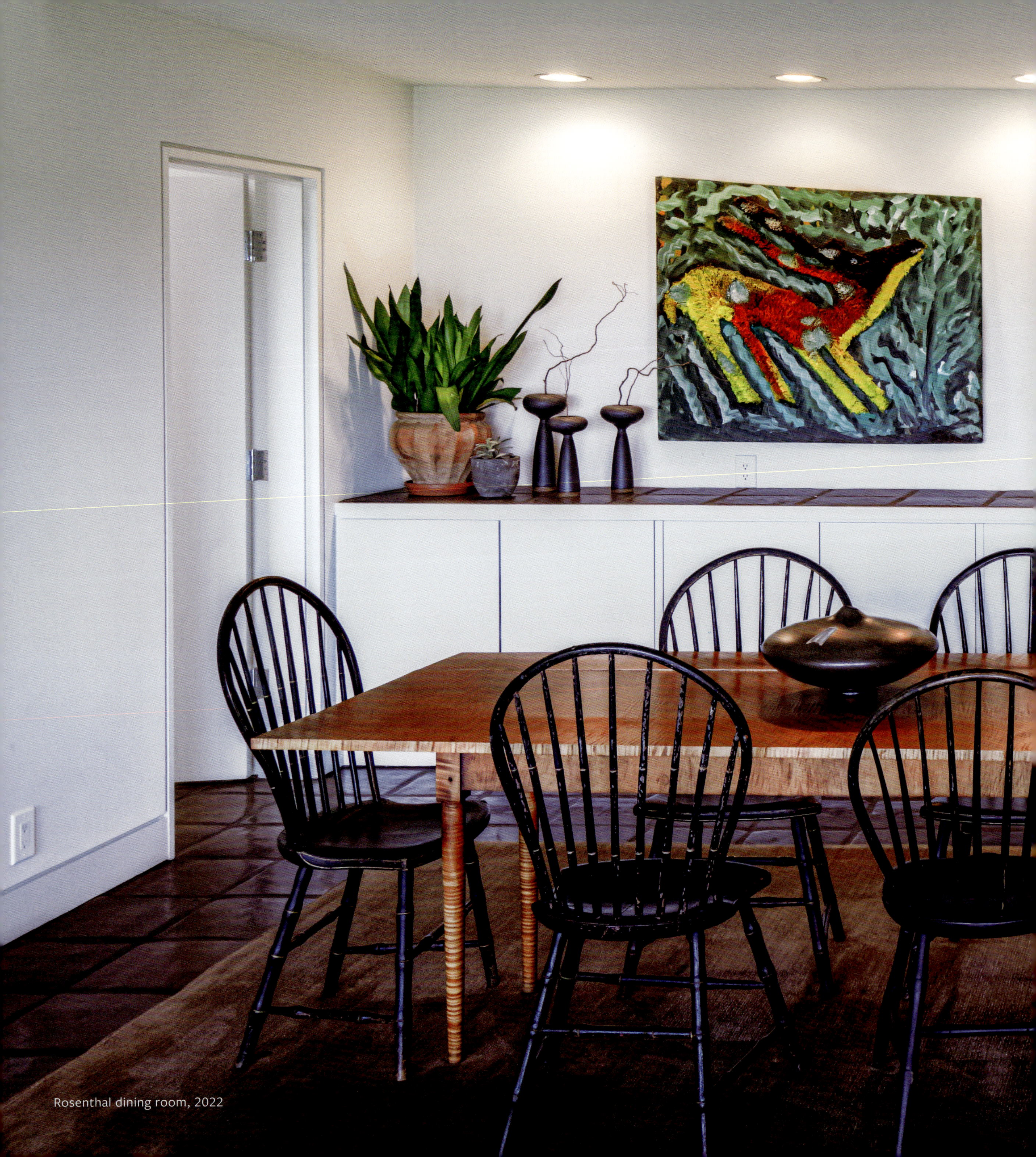

Rosenthal dining room, 2022

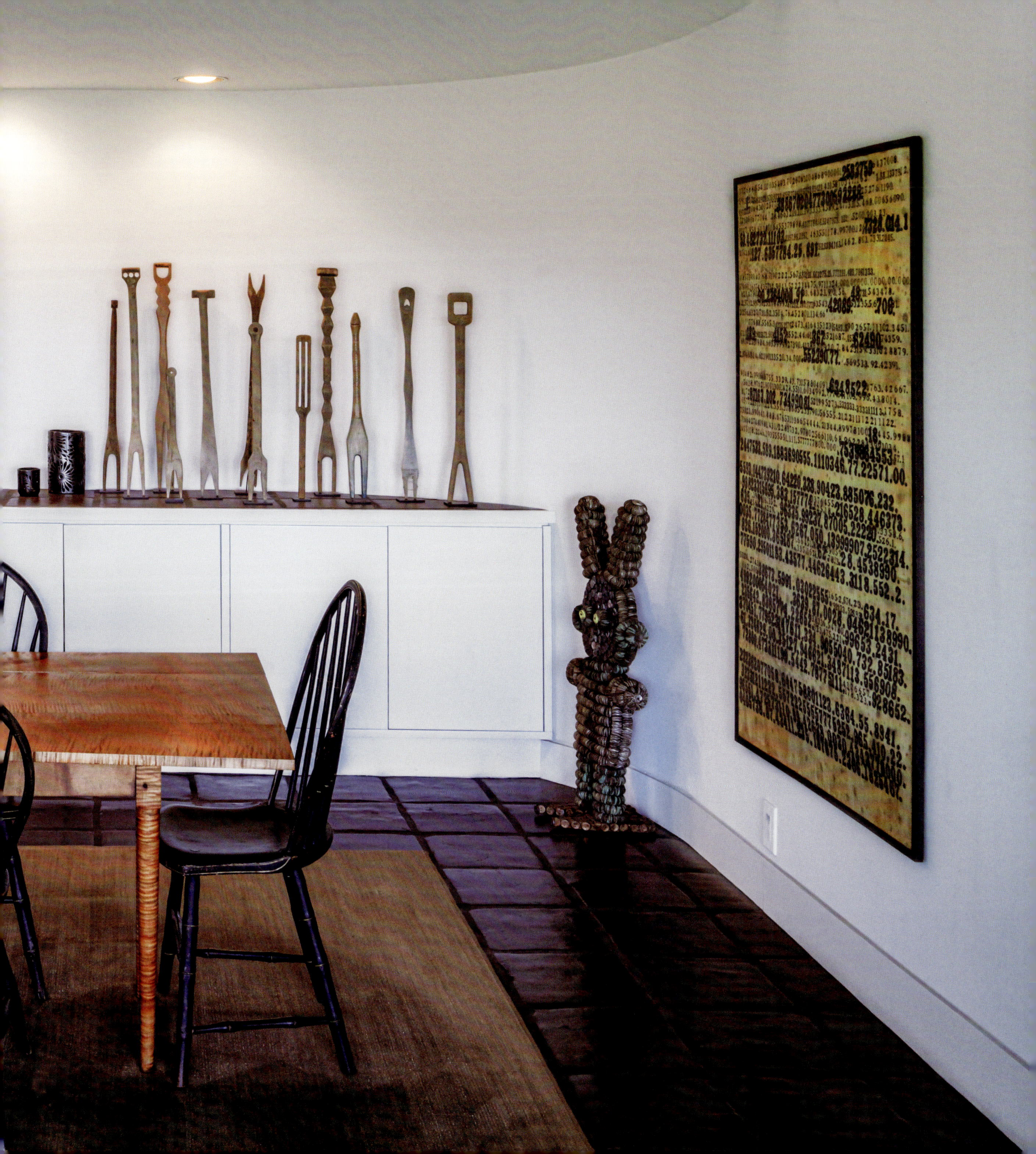

Do you have favorite pieces?

The Fasanella would certainly be one of those and a small collage by Dubuffet (cat. 43). There is a "thread painting" of a farm scene by Mary Borkowski (cat. 38) that I just love so much. She was a wonderful woman, very kind, very giving. I tried to help with her desire to make her work more widely popular, but I failed. I introduced her to a couple of dealers who did not agree with me that she was somebody they could market.

I like a lot of the work of Ned Cartledge (cats. 20–23). I think he's one who does have a very sarcastic sense of humor, which I happen to spark to. Some of it is politically engendered. I'm thrilled to have a couple of his darker pieces because of the amazing story behind his work. Just a brilliant, creative individual.

The Hiroyuki Doi (cat. 58) is one that I love to sit on that couch and just—I won't say stare at it—but just focus on it. And it moves. The pieces in it move. Too often we use the expression *organic*, but it does become organic for me.

Were you on the ground during the founding of *Raw Vision*, and what's been your involvement with the magazine?

No. I was not there for the launch, but I've been involved with it as a director [for] at least fifteen years. As a former

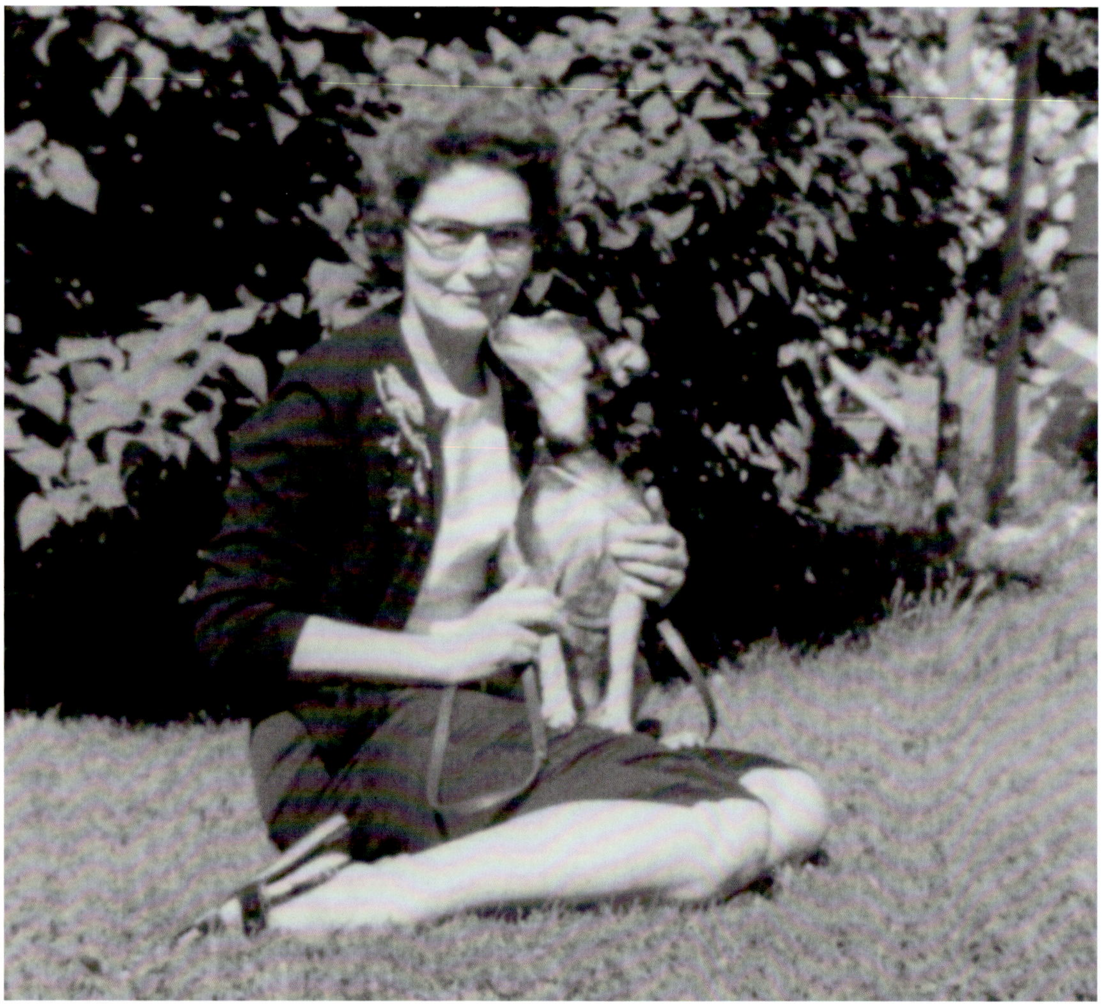

Fig. 2
Mary K. Borkowski with her dog Midgie, 1960s, from *The Pets in My Life* (Columbus, OH: Barb Vogel, 2002), 14

Cat. 38 (detail)
Mary K. Borkowski, *Toil, Strength, and Devotion*

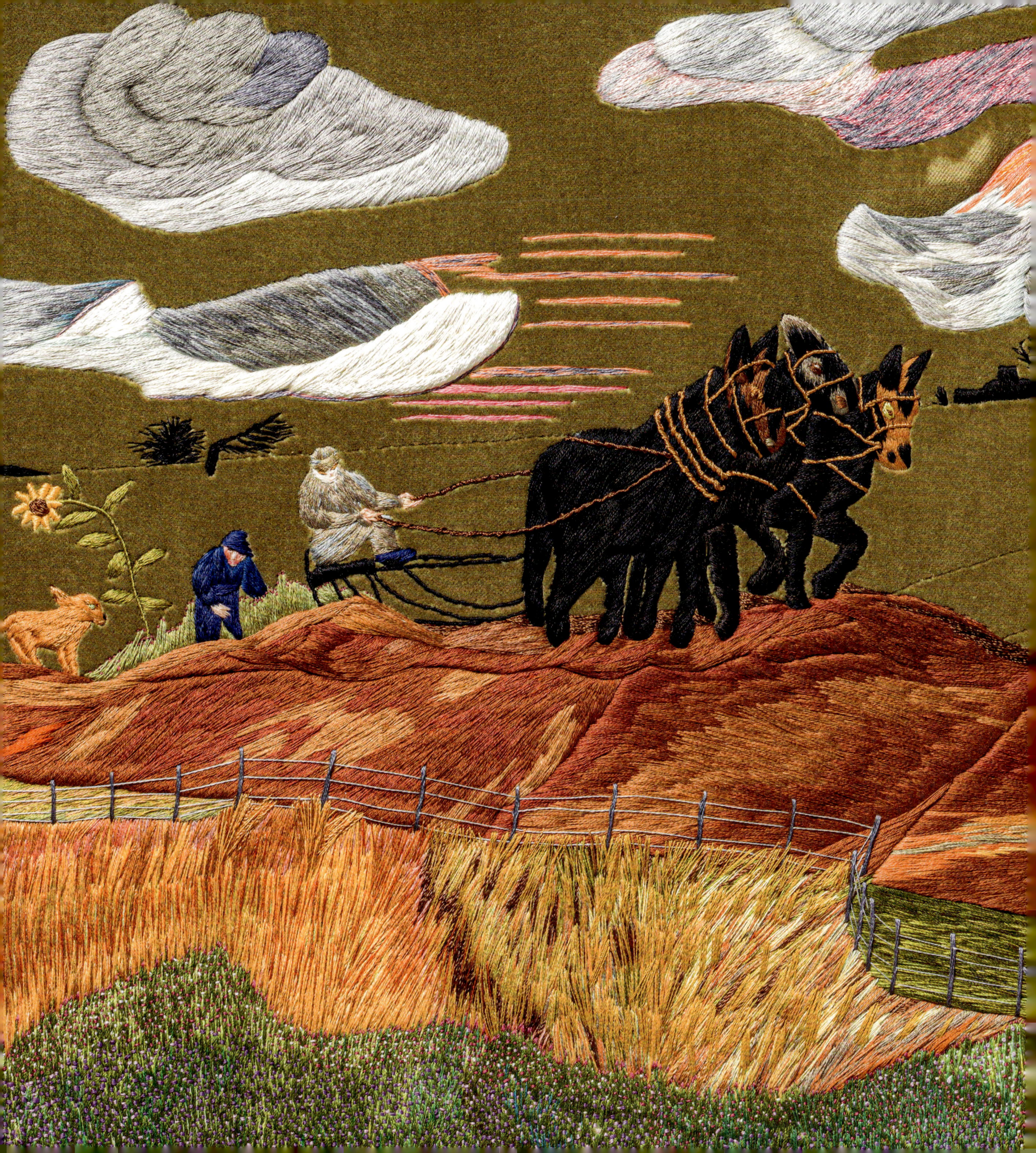

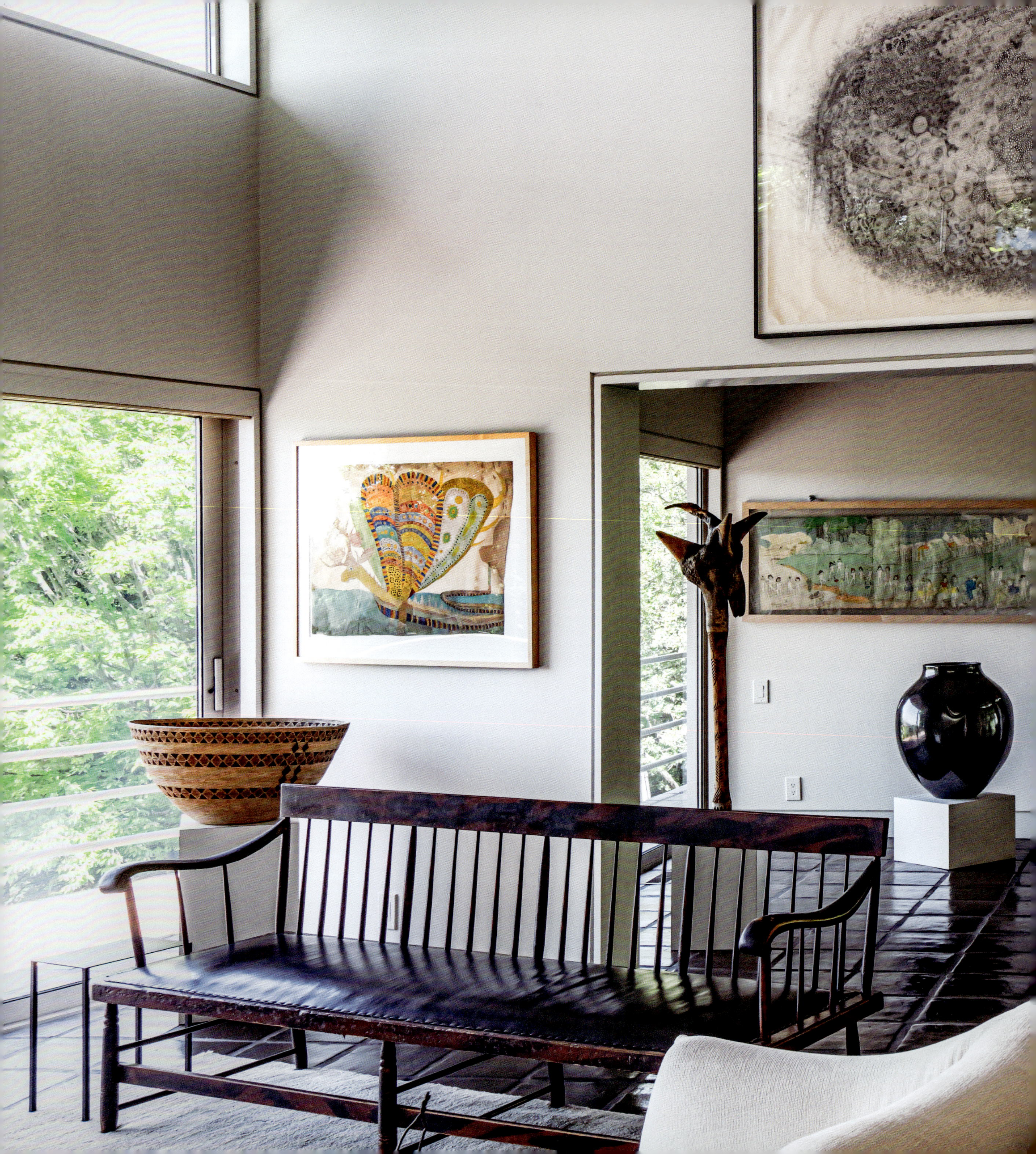

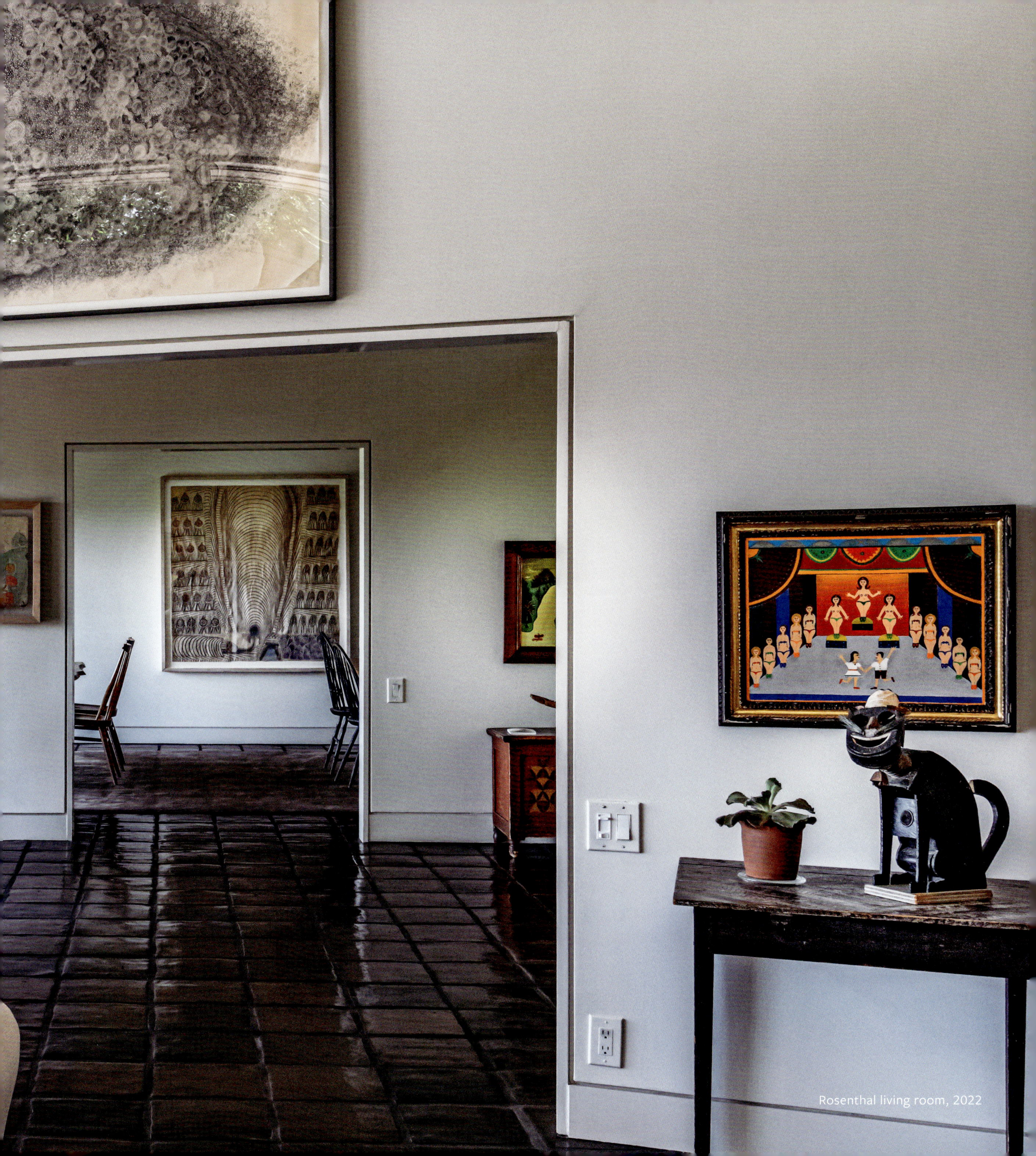

Rosenthal living room, 2022

magazine publisher, I was extremely interested in the magazine—for content, obviously—and worked pretty closely with its publisher, John Maizels, with everything from the design, [to] the type, to how the articles read, to how to better build circulation for it. I even found a number of people who sold advertising for him. So, I was really an unpaid assistant publisher, if you will. Of course, having been in that business, but having been out of it for at least five years at that time, I had very itchy fingers to get back into it on some level. I critiqued maybe half a dozen issues and saw John make changes based on what I said, but it was more than I could do on any ongoing basis.

So, today, I devour each issue, and occasionally let John know this or that about the issue. I enjoy spending time with him when I'm in London. Like Laurent did in Paris, John does for me in London, where we visit artists with him. That's great fun for me and also introduces me to artists I would not otherwise know. So, the connection with the magazine has been very positive and good fun for me.

There is a lot of discussion around the terminology to use for this type of artwork, attempts to devise a term that is both appropriate for the art and empowering to the artist—or not disempowering to the artist, I would say. *Self-taught*, that's the one most museums and scholars are using now. But a lot of different genres of artists are self-taught. Do you have any thoughts about that?

I don't have a well-defined thought, unfortunately. And you heard me vacillate, myself, from *Art Brut* to *Outsider*. *Untrained* is another one I think is a little demeaning. I hope it's not off-putting to anyone, but I think that *Art Brut*—raw art—is my favorite, but I'm not married to it. A big problem with *Art Brut* is that if you don't know what it means, it means nothing. And it sounds a little snobbish, or as my mother would say, "highfalutin."

Do you see intersections between your collection and your commitment to social justice? Does your activity as a collector dovetail with your other philanthropic activities in the community?

I think, certainly, the pieces by Ned Cartledge (cats. 20–23) intersect with my feelings about everything from social justice to religion and the hypocrisy of some religions. There are some other connections politically. The painting *All We Ask Is a Fair Trial* (cat. 6) is certainly about social justice. I've never thought about this, but obviously it has been a strong influence in the collection.

I'm thinking about the people who made these things, too. There are many artists who've had all kinds of trauma and challenges from being institutionalized or experiencing racism. But somehow their work is a triumph.

Well, you just opened up a whole area: a strong part of my upbringing [was] my mother being a musical therapist, my sister an art therapist. My mother practiced at what was then called Longview State Mental Hospital. Many of the Outsider folk artists are people who have mental health issues, and it drives the art that they do. And certainly, that voice is one that I've picked up without really articulating that connection. I have very good examples of work by people who were institutionalized, and art [was] used as a therapy for them. But I should say that in that therapy, they are sending messages. It's a very clear communication, frequently.

Cat. 6 (detail)
Unidentified Artist, *All We Ask Is a Fair Trial*

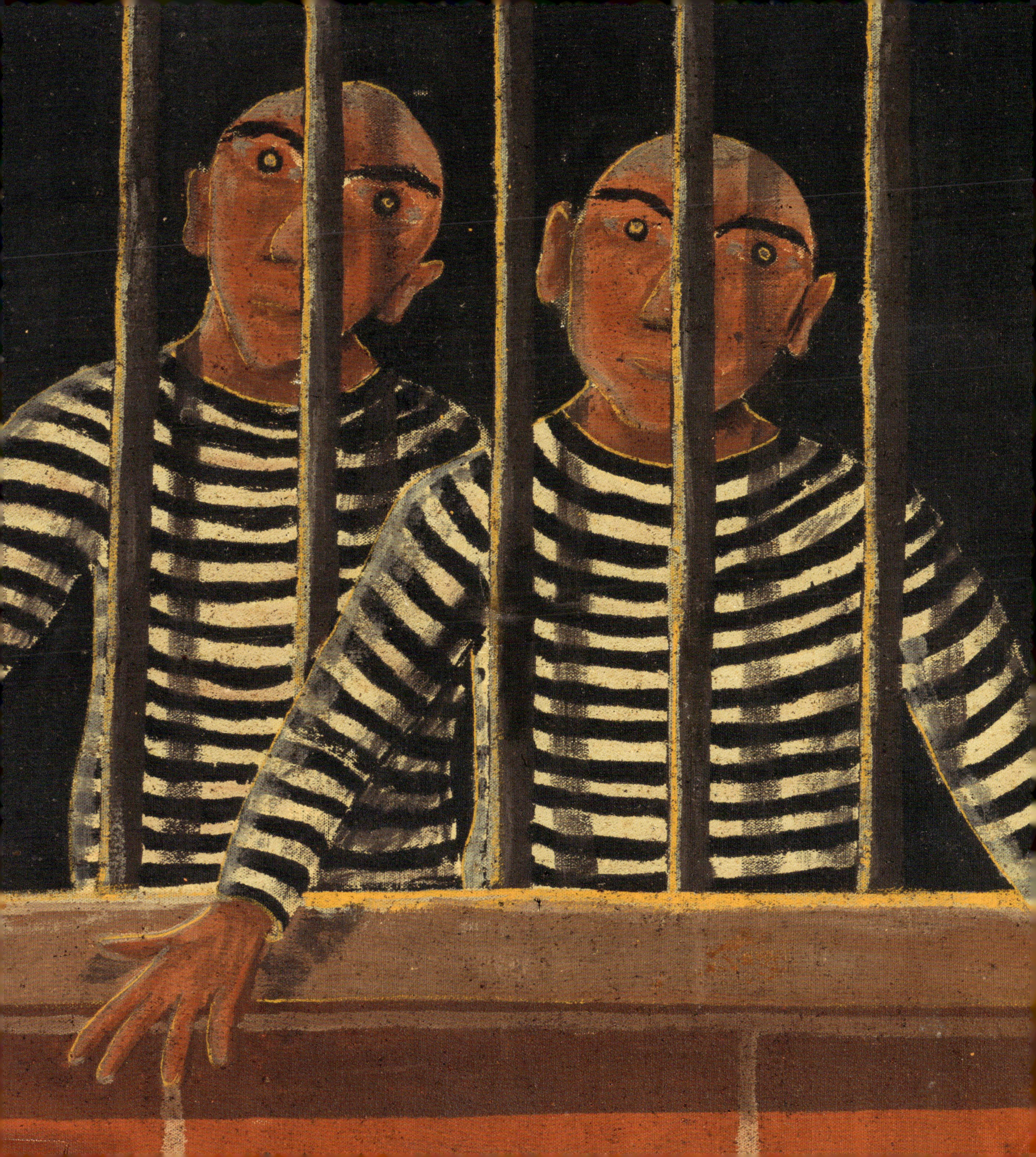

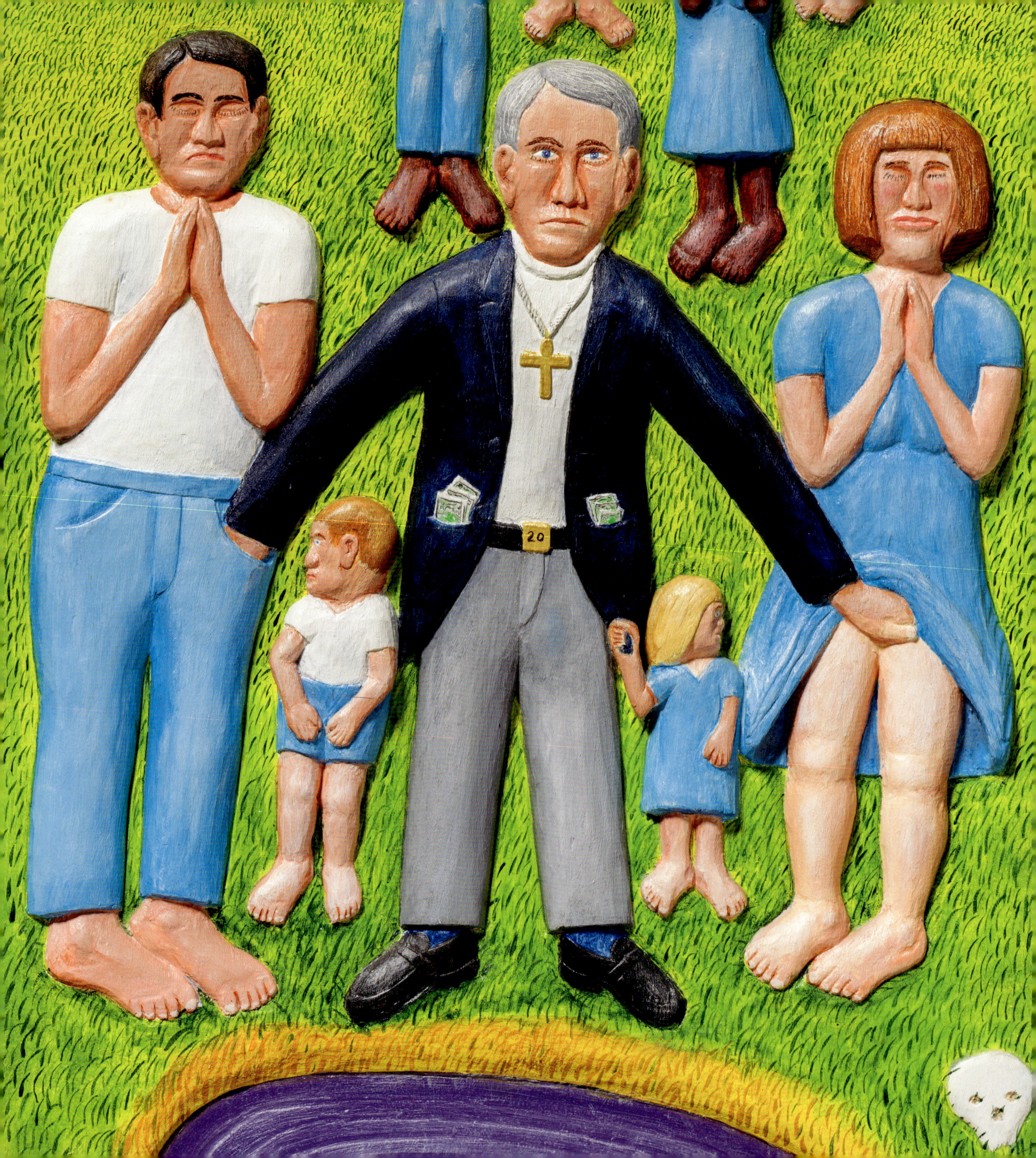
20

Have you seen changes in the field and in the market over the time you have been acquiring this material?

I think both a good and a bad thing is that big money from collectors has come into the field. Kitty and I were at the apartment of a collector who had thirty-some [Bill] Traylors. To me, it is limiting the exposure of that artist's work. Exposure is something that means a lot to me and more to the artist. And yes, this particular collector has a whale of a lot of money. And yes, he can do whatever he wants to do with it, and he's not doing anything illegal. So, yes, I have seen money come into it, and that's disturbing to me. It's almost like hoarding. It lessens the joy of the art, of seeing the art, experiencing the art, sharing the art.

You are bequeathing an important selection of work from your collection to the Cincinnati Art Museum. What do you hope to accomplish in doing that? And what are your hopes for the future and the work of artists like these?

Well, I hope my collection will raise the importance and quality of that genre at the museum, and entice other collectors, especially in the Cincinnati area, but also around the country, to do the same thing that I've done. It is art that is accessible. And there are people who have deep wealth but not deep appreciation for this particular genre who might see it and feel "Well, that's something that I like and would like to help support."

I feel that I'm a shepherd of the art. I don't really *own* it. It's owned by the maker and whomever else is going to be looking at it. That's why it's going to the museum, where it will be seen in perpetuity. And I think it's especially true of both folk art and Outsider folk art that the maker made it to be seen. They usually have a message, and they want to share that message or preach that message, as the case may be, to as wide an audience as possible. So, I'm simply the middleman for the artist at this time in my life.

Cat. 22 (detail)
Ned Cartledge, *Beware of False Prophets*
(or *Beware of Imposters*)

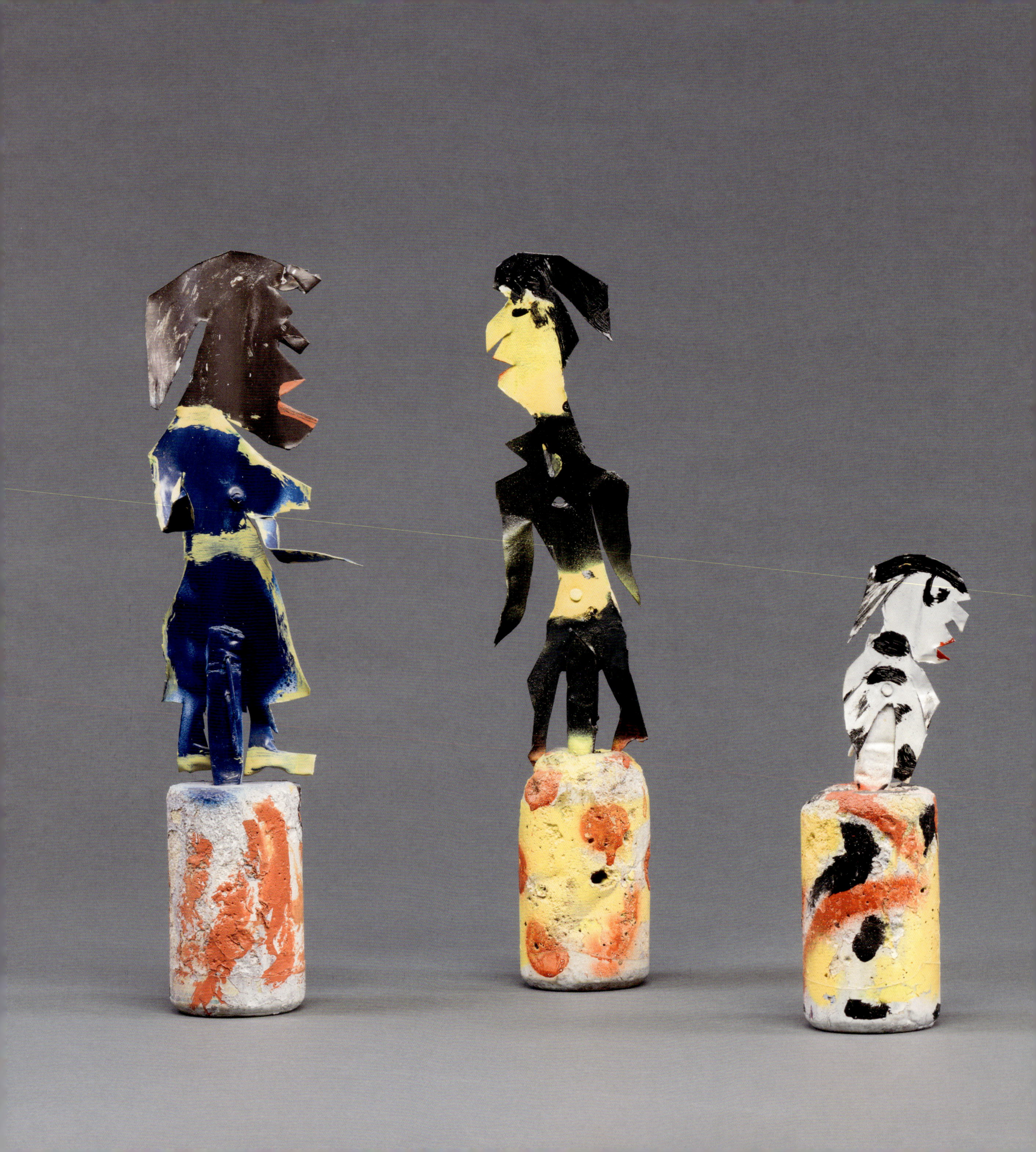

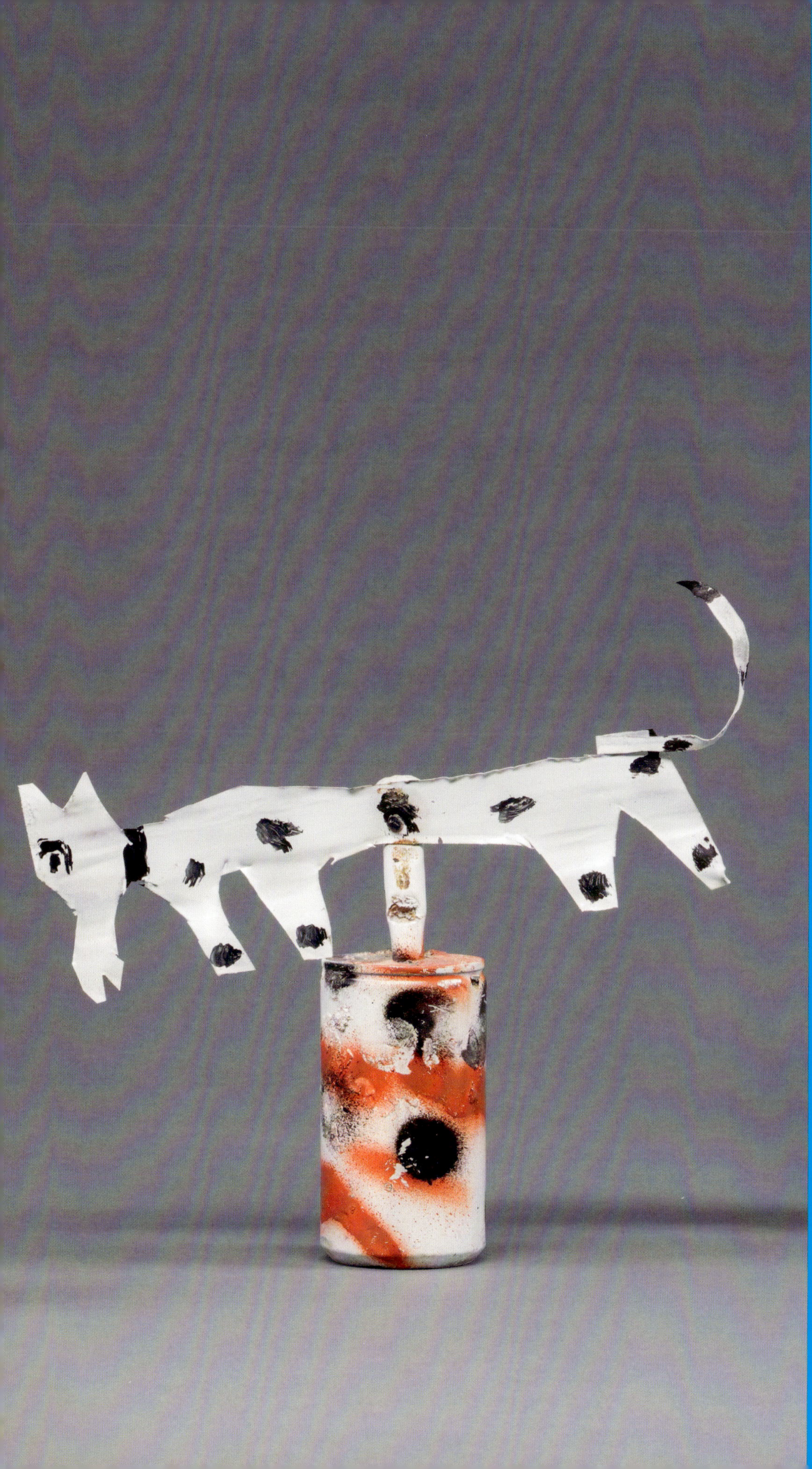

Part 1

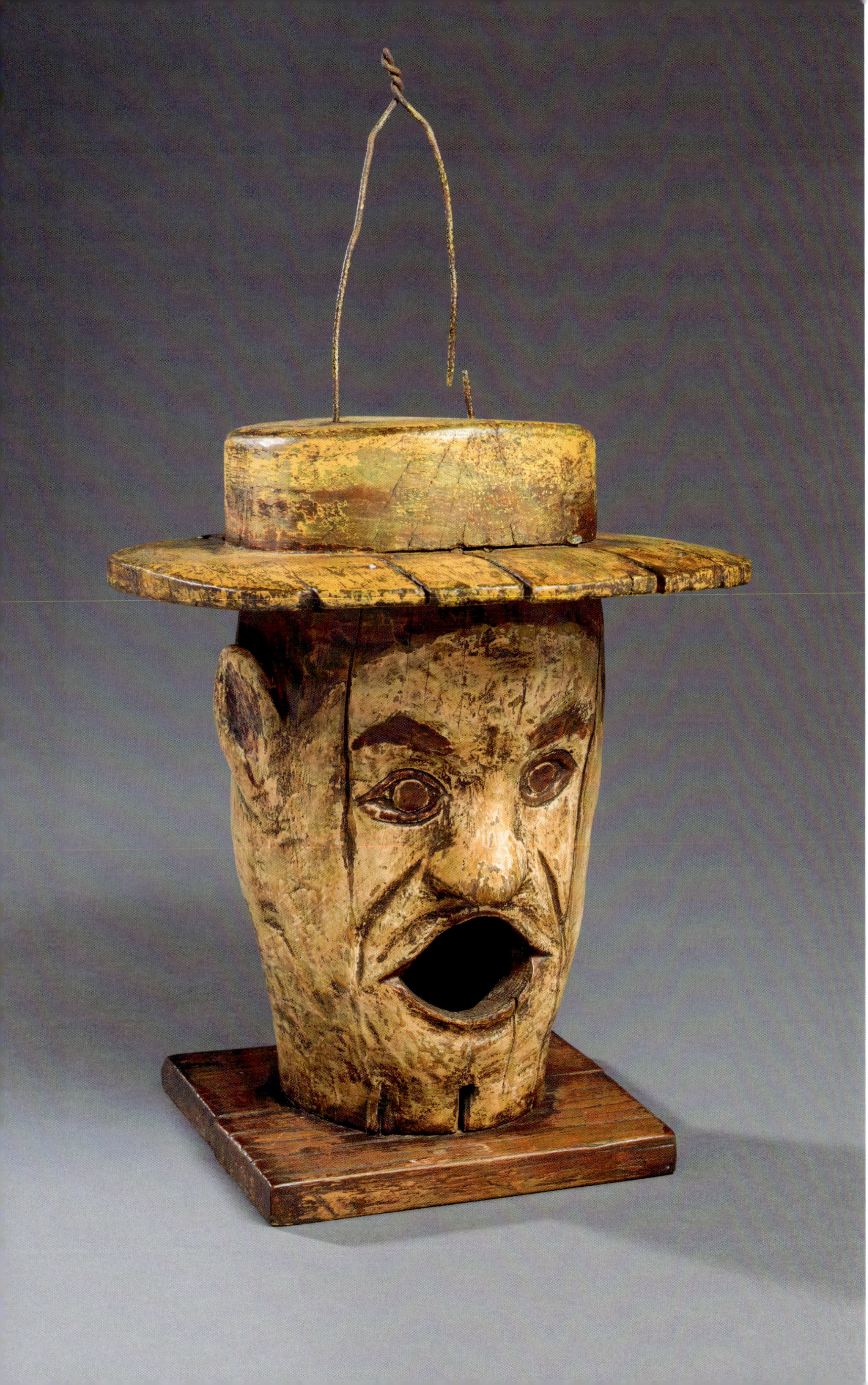

Cat. 1
Unidentified Artist (American)

Bird House
circa 1920–30
carved and painted wood and wire
18½ × 10 × 11½ in.
(47 × 25.4 × 29.2 cm)

"As a boy my husband delivered newspapers in the 1930s and was fascinated by this birdhouse as it sat on a fence post. We only live three doors away from the homestead now. The original owner (in the 1930s) was Ed Lewis. There was only one other that came out of a garage sale in Punxsutawney (7 miles) not as nice. . . . I was always sorry I sold it but I've watched it change hands at least 5 times. I think you are very safe in saying it is Western Pennsylvania, and probably definite on the date give or take a few."

Jacqueline Homan, June 4, 1990, quoted in Richard Rosenthal files.

Cat. 2
Adélard Turgeon
Born 1883 Saint-Anselme, Quebec, Canada
Died 1968 Saint-Anselme, Quebec, Canada

Hunter's Delight
circa 1950
carved and painted wood
20¼ × 25 × 14 in.
(51.4 × 63.5 × 35.6 cm)

In this whimsical, crisply detailed sculpture, a hunter in a bright red coat perches on a branch surrounded by a variety of wildlife. The critters include an oversized rabbit and a beaver, species that in nature do not climb trees. Like other farmers who turned to carving, Adélard Turgeon whittled as a pastime and made sculptures to entertain children.

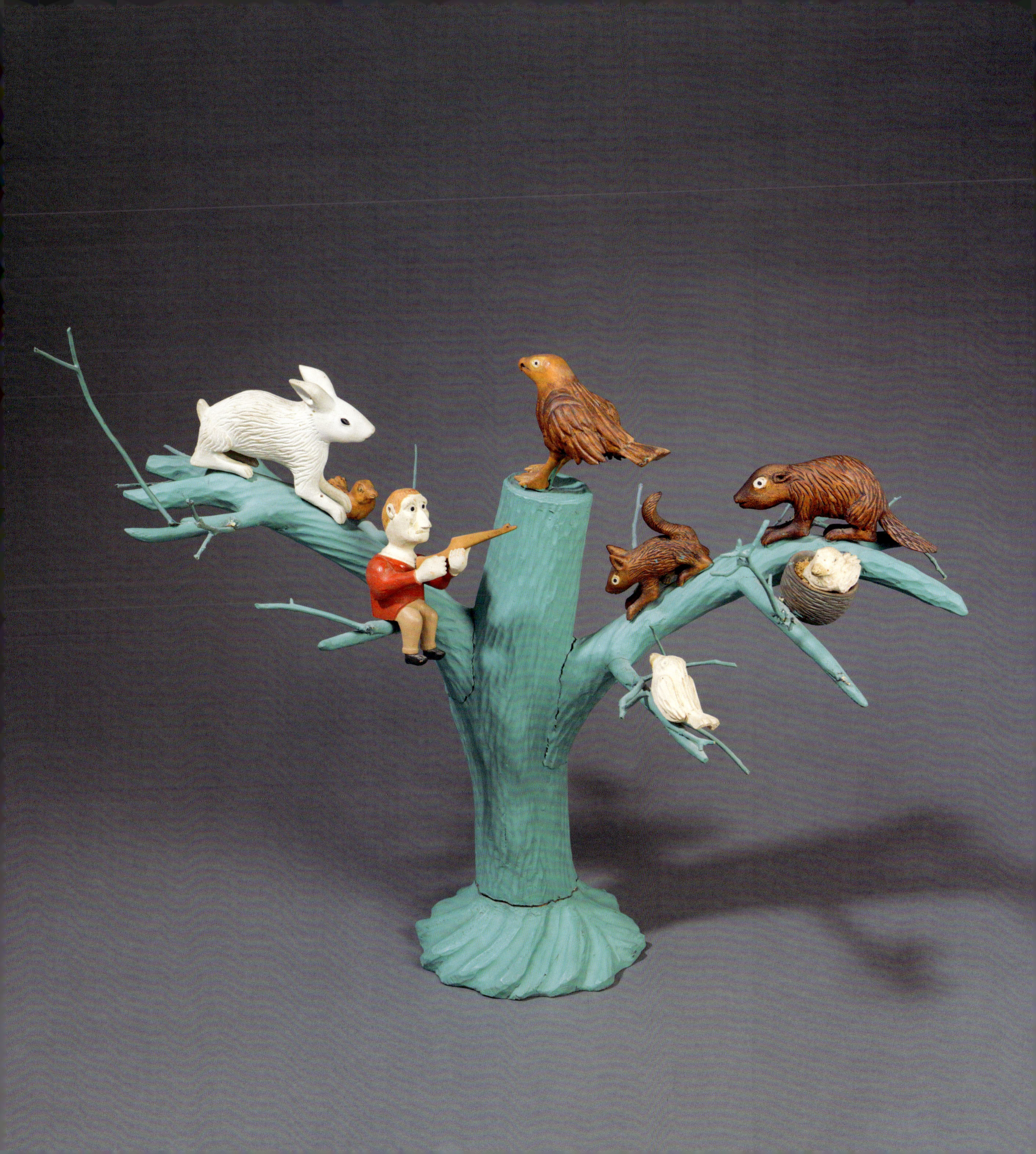

Cat. 3
Unidentified Artist (American)

Cat Post
20th century
painted wood and found objects
63½ × 14 × 14 in.
(161.3 × 35.6 × 35.6 cm)

The unknown artist who made this piece used meager materials in a creative way. Two sticks, a few other repurposed items, and a judicious application of black and white paint turned a mundane post into a delightful cat.

Cat. 4
Unidentified Artist (American)

Spotted Hen
circa 1890
painted pine, sheet copper, and metal
with mount 13⅞ × 8½ × 14½ in.
(35.2 × 21.6 × 36.8 cm)

Posing engaging views from every direction, this hen stretching her legs and spreading her wings has an elegant form decoratively embellished with paint.

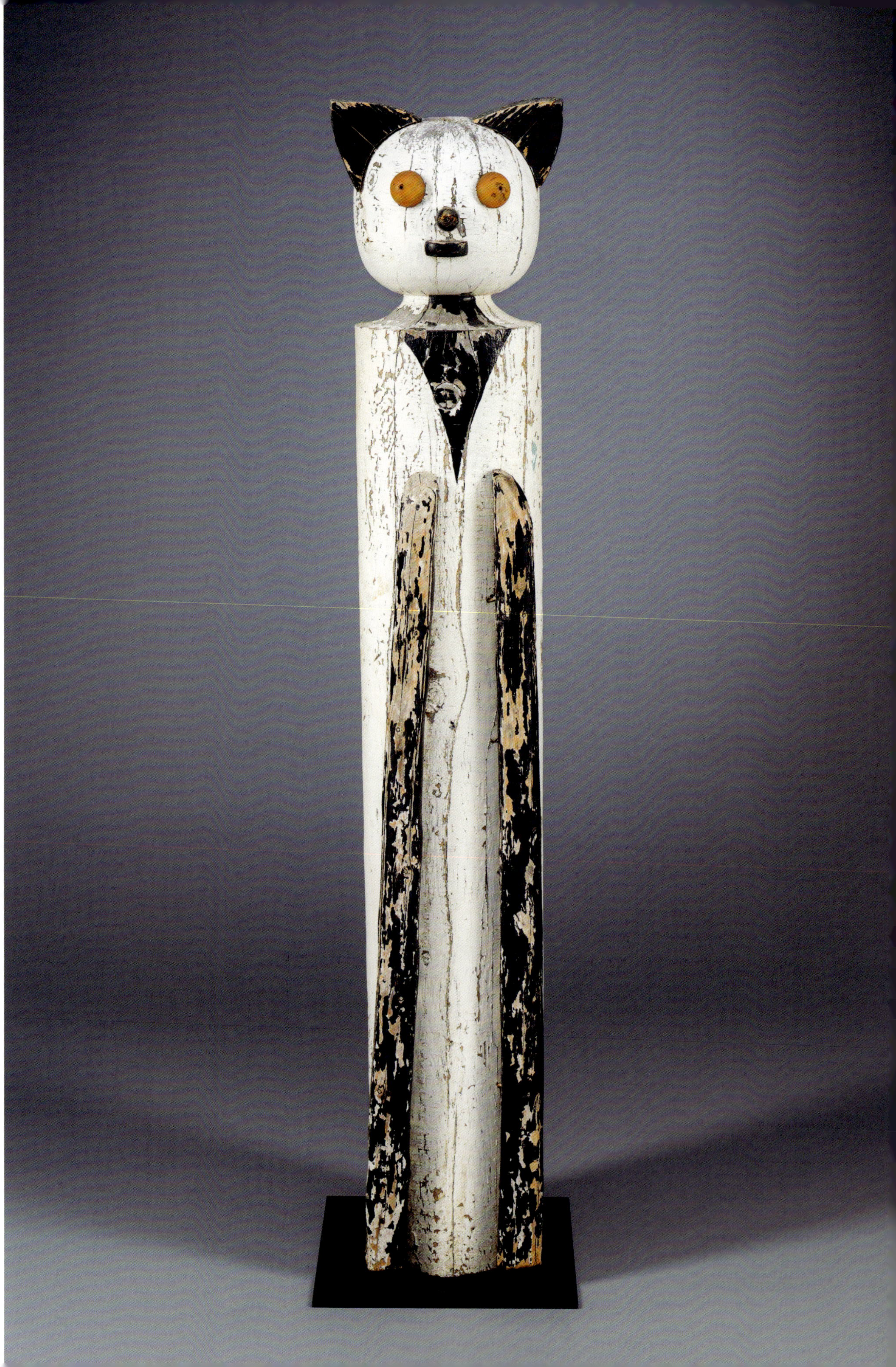

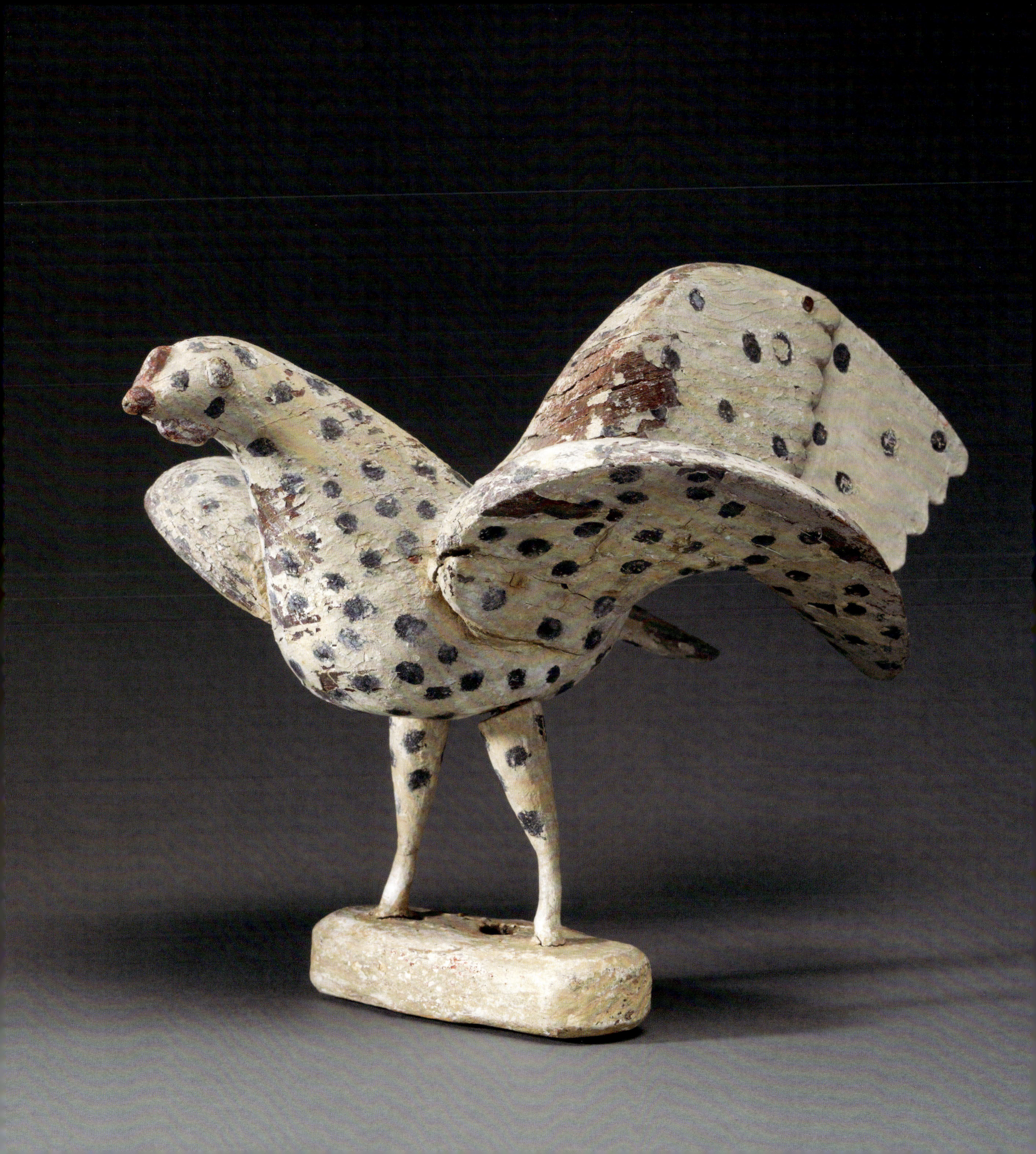

Cat. 5

Unidentified Artist (American)

Hairpiece or Hat Mannequin
late 19th or early 20th century
carved wood with paint
with mount 17 × 10 × 10 in.
(43.2 × 25.4 × 25.4 cm)

This hairpiece mannequin or hatmaker's stand is a compelling work of sculpture, transcending its utilitarian objective. The individuality, visual power, and abstracted form of objects such as this attracted those artists seeking to break free of established conventions of "fine art."

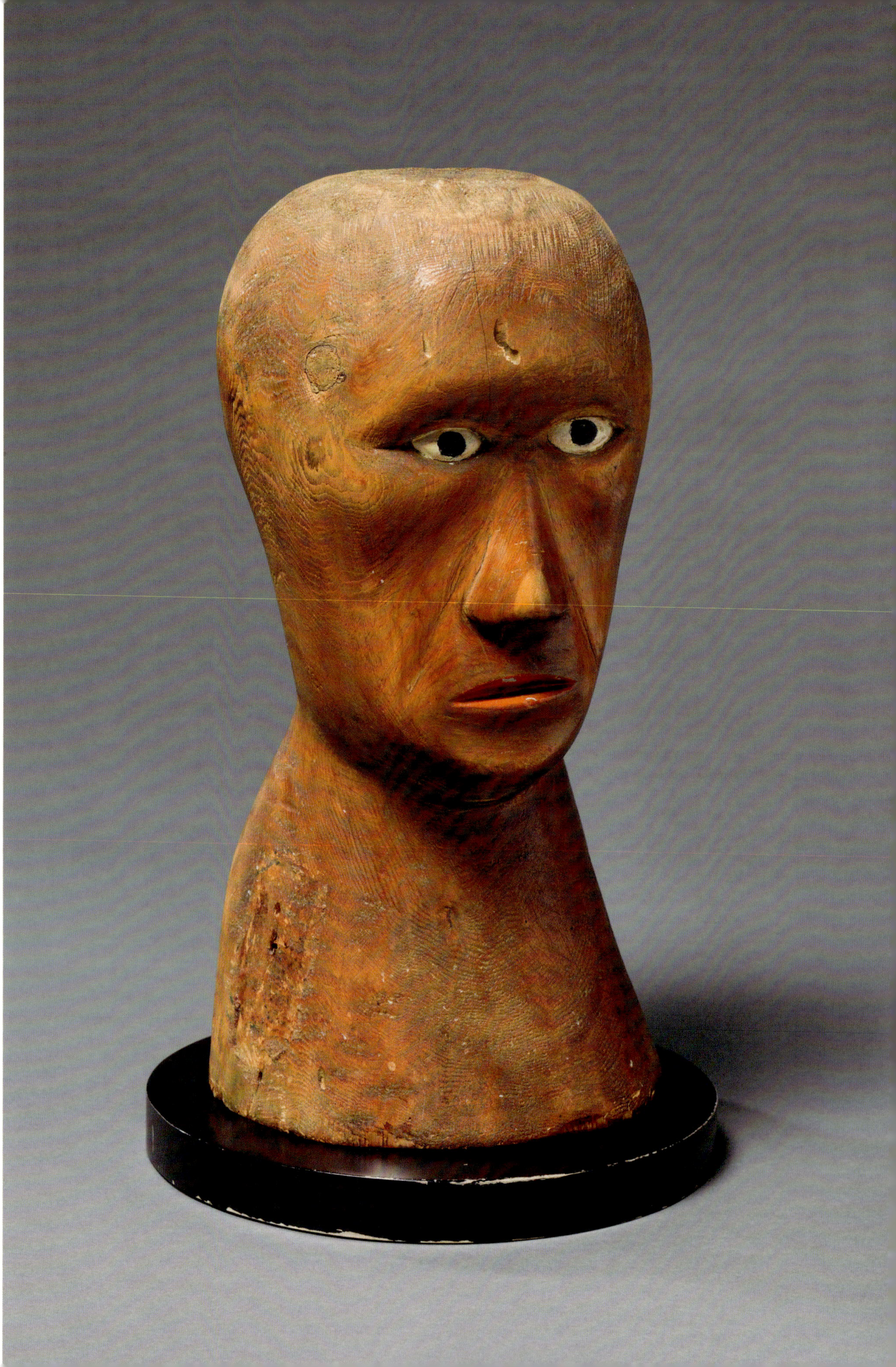

Cat. 6
Unidentified Artist (American)

All We Ask Is a Fair Trial
late 19th–early 20th century
oil on canvas mounted
on wood panel
36 × 46 in. (91.4 × 116.8 cm)

As the banners and bold graphic qualities resemble shop signs of the late nineteenth century, this painting may be the work of a commercial artist. It brings to mind the famous Sacco and Vanzetti trial of the 1920s, but the style of the painting suggests an earlier date. More than a century later, this plea for justice still resonates with viewers.

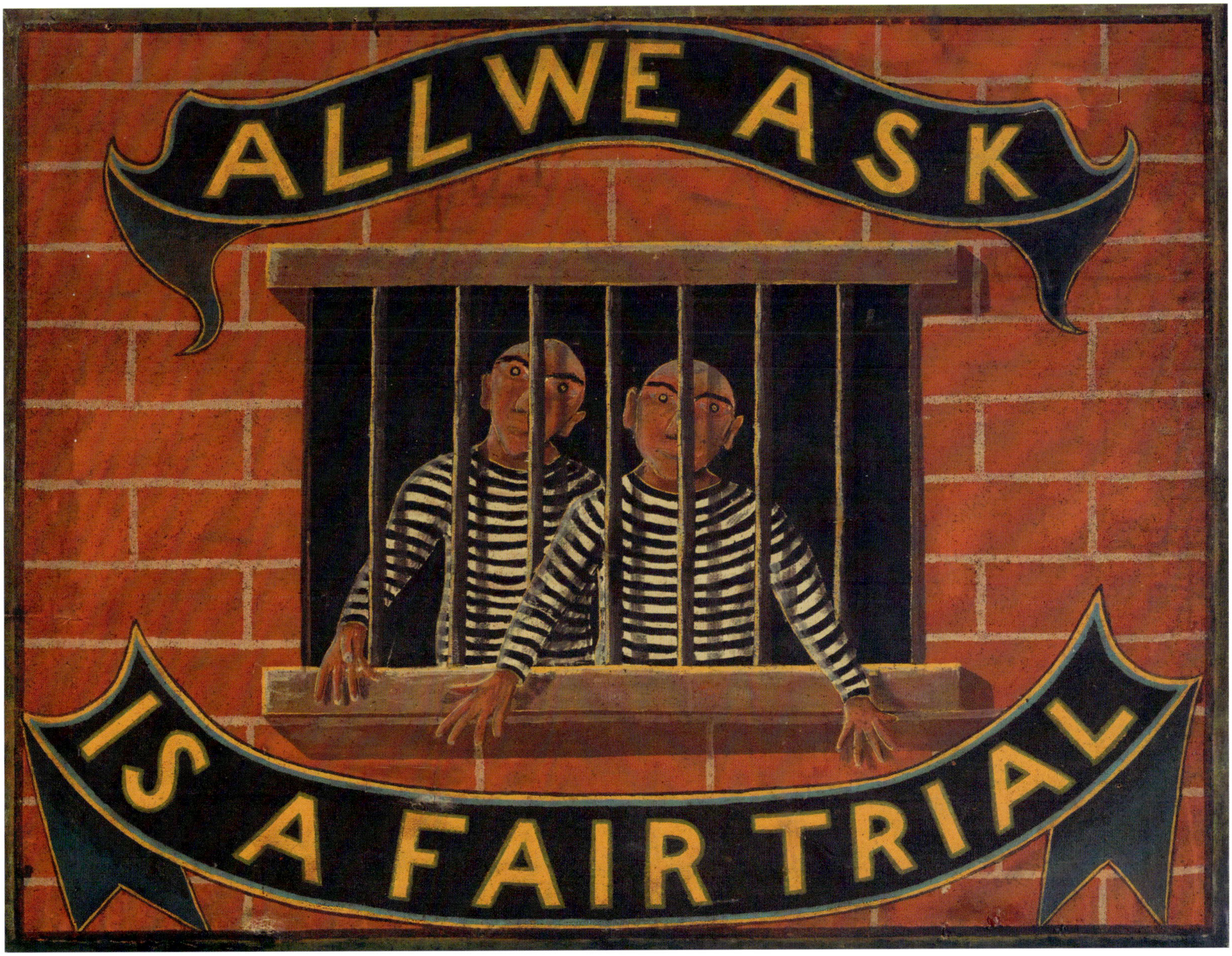

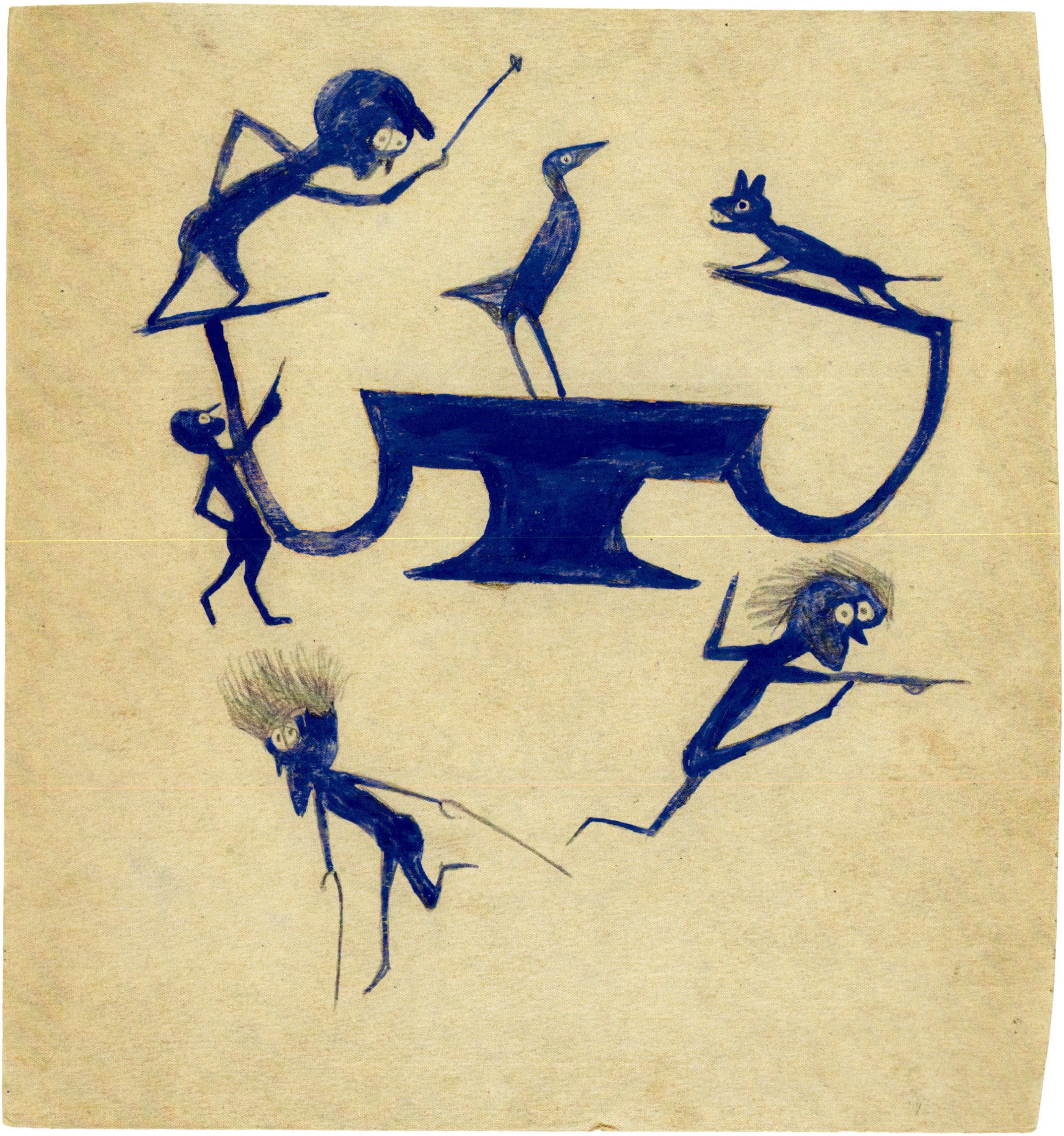

Cat. 7
Bill Traylor
Born circa 1853 Dallas County (near Pleasant Hill), Alabama
Died 1949 Montgomery, Alabama

Exciting Event in Blue: Four Wild Men, Barking Dog, Perched Bird, and Construction
circa 1939–42
tempera, graphite pencil, and ink (or watercolor) on thin cardboard
14⅞ × 13⅞ in. (37.8 × 35.2 cm)

This complex composition has a jangling energy. Surrounding what may be a fountain is a circular arrangement of gesturing figures moving in various directions. Formerly enslaved on an Alabama plantation, where he continued to labor for decades after emancipation, Bill Traylor began making art in Montgomery at the age of eighty-six. His personal symbolism and narratives are rooted in his experiences of plantation life and the urban South.

Cat. 8
Bessie Harvey
Born 1929 as Bessie Ruth White, Dallas, Georgia
Died 1994 Alcoa, Tennessee

Peace
1987
found wood, beads, and paint
41 × 32 × 30 in.
(104.1 × 81.3 × 76.2 cm)

"I talk to the trees. . . . There's souls in the branches and roots. I frees them," said Bessie Harvey of her transformation of natural materials into powerful, spiritual sculptures. A housekeeper's aid at a Tennessee hospital, Harvey began making her "dolls" around 1974, seeing faces and figures in the organic shapes and adding paint, putty, brightly colored beads, turkey bones, and other objects.

Bessie Harvey quoted in Chuck and Jan Rosenak, *Museum of American Folk Art Encyclopedia of Twentieth-Century American Folk Art and Artists* (New York: Abbeville Press, 1990), 152.

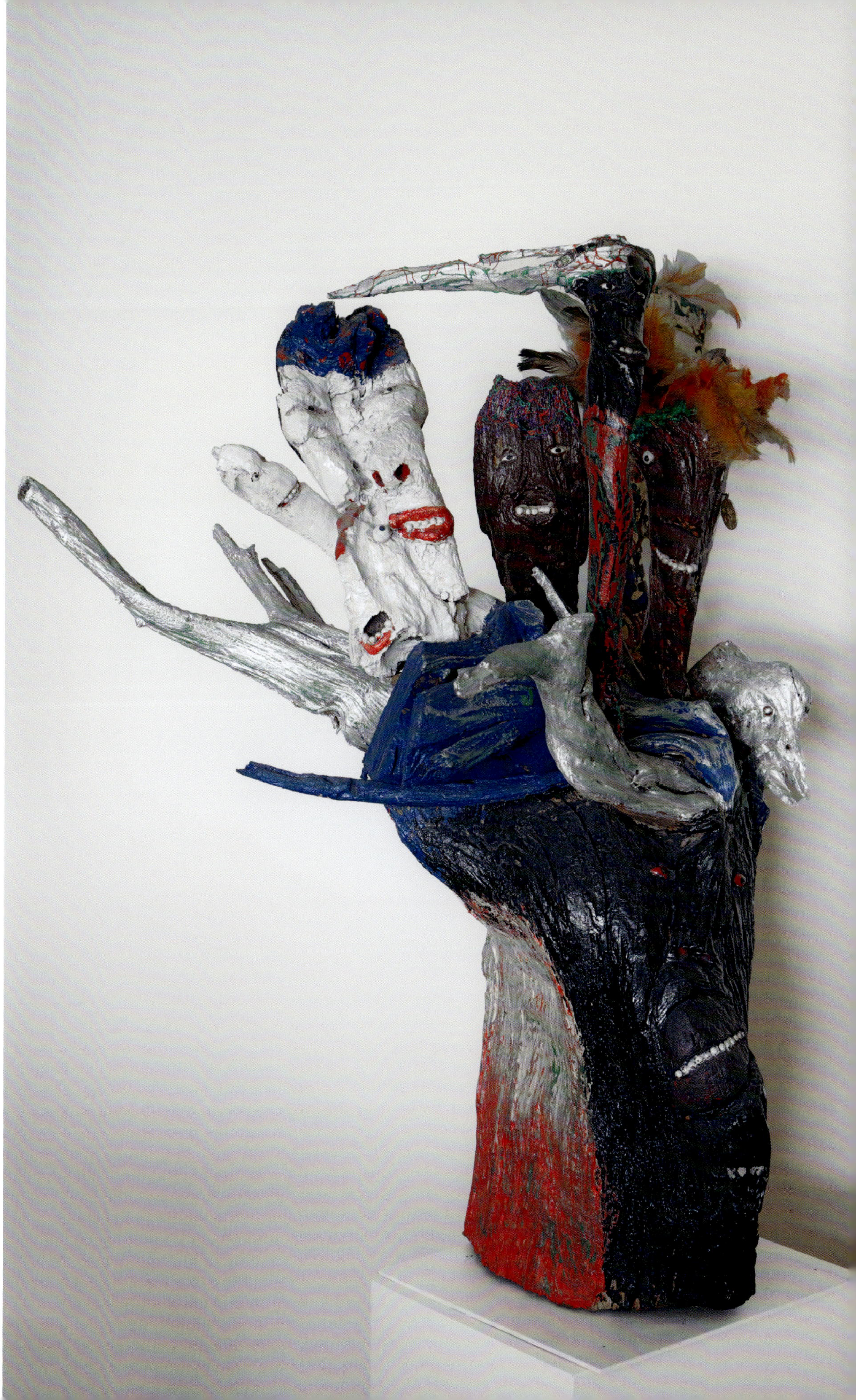

Cat. 9
Minnie Evans
Born 1892 as Minnie Jones, Long Creek, North Carolina
Died 1987 Wilmington, North Carolina

No. 79
1946
crayon, pen and ink (several colors), and graphite pencil on paper mounted on a second sheet of paper
8¾ × 11⅝ in. (22.2 × 29.6 cm)

Minnie Evans, long the gatekeeper at Airlie Gardens in Wilmington, North Carolina, claimed her lyrical, imaginative drawings appeared spontaneously without forethought. "God has sent me teachers. . . . The angel that stands by me, answers me . . . and directs me what to do."

Minnie Evans quoted in Mary E. Lyons, *Painting Dreams: Minnie Evans, Visionary Artist* (Boston: Hougthon Mifflin Company, 1996), 24.

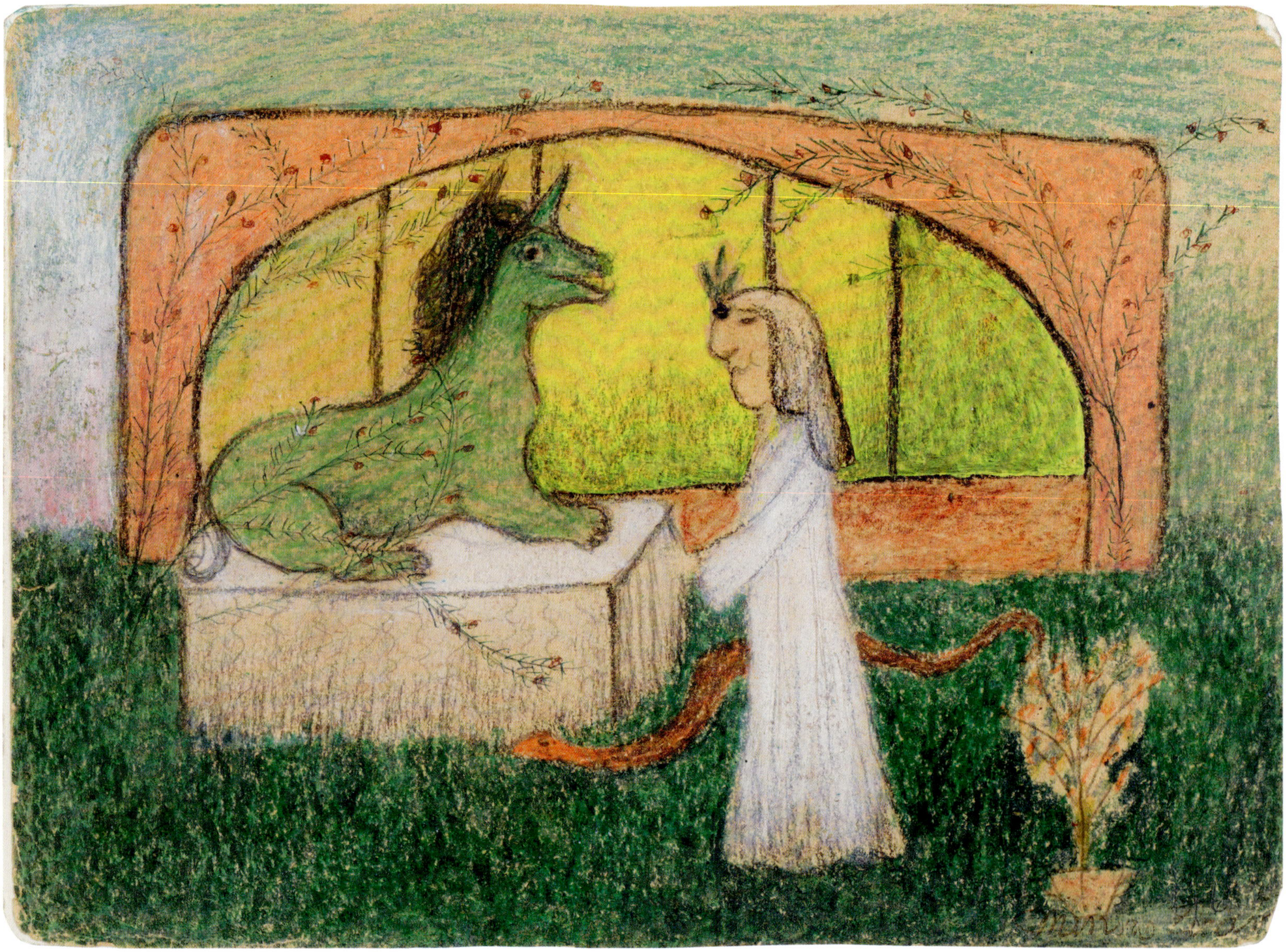

Cat. 10

Sister Gertrude Morgan

Born 1900 as Gertrude Williams,
Lafayette, Alabama
Died 1980 New Orleans, Louisiana

Mothers Day

circa 1960–74
crayon, tempera or gouache,
and pen and ink (blue, black,
and silver) on cardboard
7 13/16 × 12 3/16 in. (19.9 × 30.9 cm)

Sister Gertrude Morgan was a Pentecostal Christian who had moved to New Orleans by 1939. Her vivid, freely composed works proclaim her joyful intimacy with the Lord. The "PRECIOUS BRIDE" dressed in white represents Morgan herself, declaring her marriage to God. "DADA" in Morgan's text refers to Christ, who deserves gratitude for a mother's love.

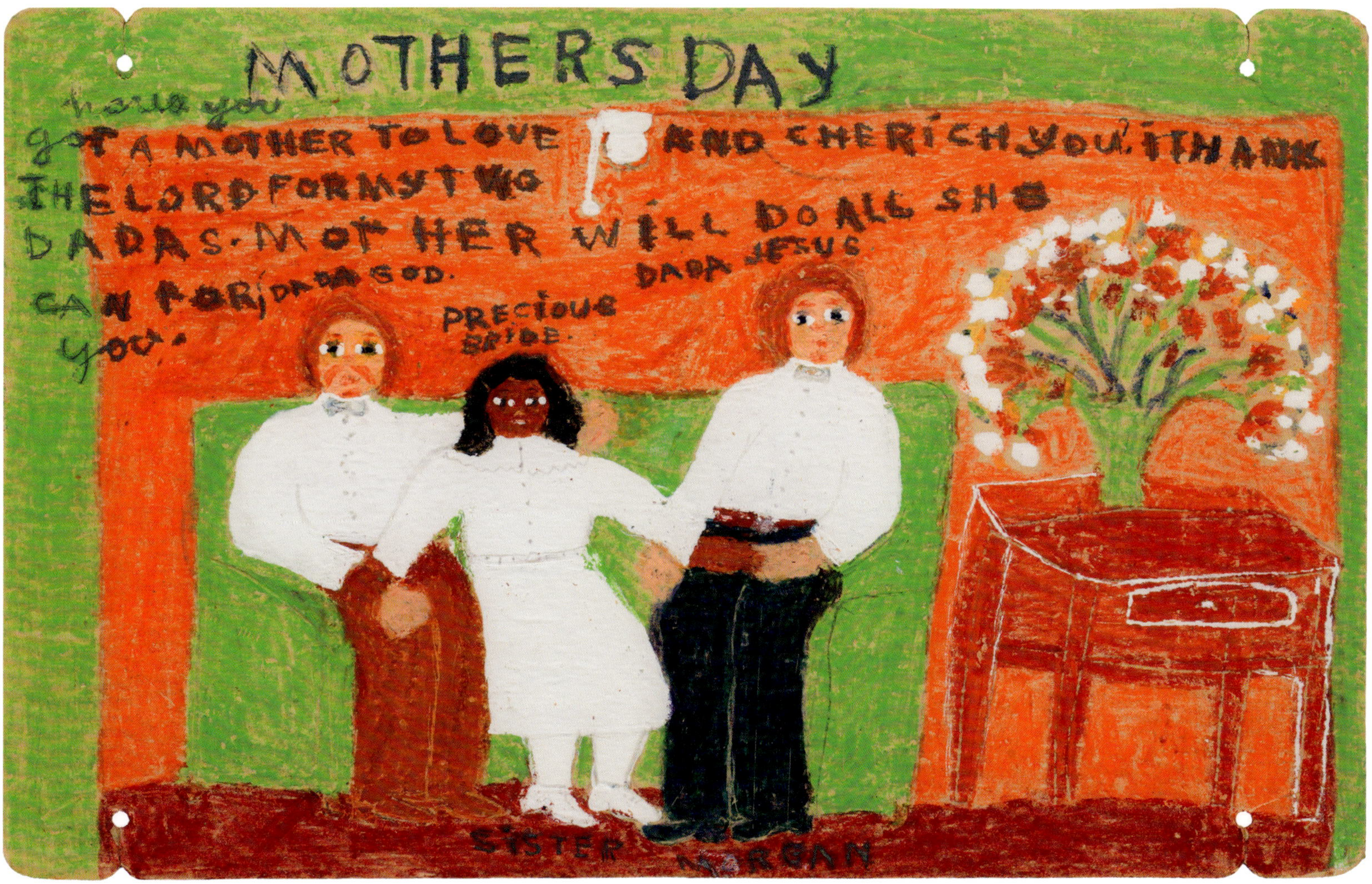

Cat. 11

Thornton Dial

Born 1928 Emelle, Alabama
Died 2016 McCalla, Alabama

Street People

1988
painted cut sheet metal and concrete
from left to right
a: 15 × 4½ × 3¼ in. (38.1 × 11.4 × 8.3 cm)
b: 15 × 3¼ × 2½ in. (38.1 × 8.3 × 6.4 cm)
c: 9⅛ × 3 × 2½ in. (23.2 × 7.6 × 6.4 cm)
d: 10¾ × 11½ × 3 in. (27.3 × 29.2 × 7.6 cm)
e: 14⅜ × 3¼ × 3 in. (36.5 × 8.3 × 7.6 cm)
f: 14¼ × 4¼ × 2¾ in. (36.2 × 10.8 × 7 cm)

Thornton Dial's *Street People* may relate to a community project he conceived for employing the disadvantaged: casting construction bricks in concrete in discarded tin cans. In these spirited tabletop sculptures, the concrete bricks become bases for individualized figures Dial cut from can lids and perhaps other discarded metal then painted.

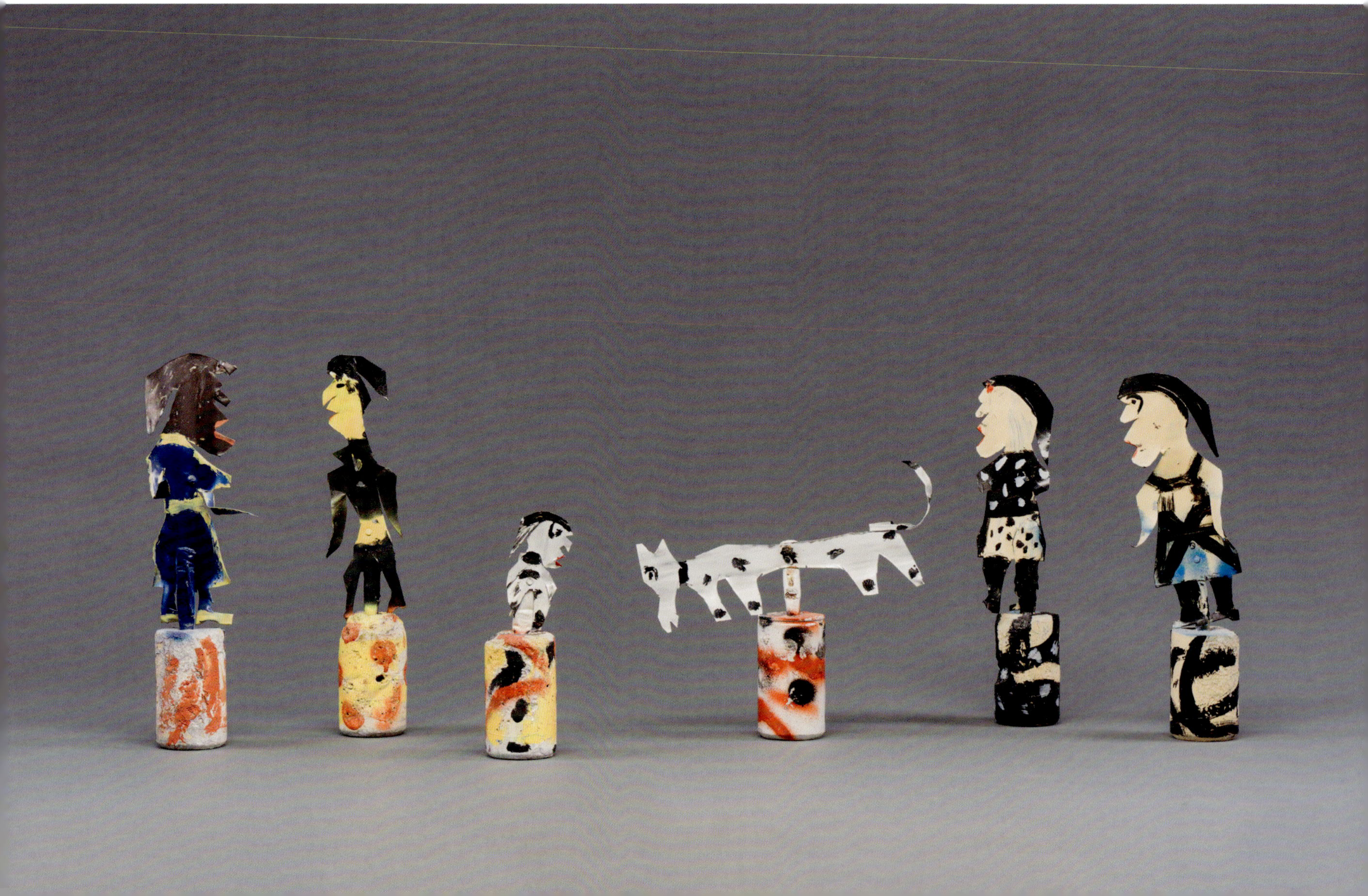

Cat. 12a
Thornton Dial

Can Man (Red)
1989
painted concrete-filled metal can with collage elements and painted cut sheet metal
17 × 13¼ × 4¾ in.
(43.2 × 33.7 × 12.1 cm)

Dial, who worked for thirty years in Alabama's railway car manufacturing industry, stated that out of necessity Black people in America have had to be resourceful. "I only want materials that have been used by people . . . that have did people some good but once they got the service out of them they throwed them away. So I pick it up and make something new out of it."

Thornton Dial, interviews by William Arnett, 1995 and 1996, quoted in "Thornton Dial," Souls Grown Deep, https://www.soulsgrowndeep.org/artist/thornton-dial, accessed June 23, 2022.

Cat. 12b
Thornton Dial

Can Man (Blue)
1989
painted concrete-filled metal can with collage elements and painted cut sheet metal
17 × 19 × 12 in.
(43.2 × 48.3 × 30.5 cm)

"Cutting out tin and carpet and stuff come natural like drawing. The mind do the imagining. I got where I could bend and twist the old materials as beautiful as I could draw it out with a pencil."

Thornton Dial, interviews by William Arnett, 1995 and 1996, quoted in "Thornton Dial," Souls Grown Deep, https://www.soulsgrowndeep.org/artist/thornton-dial, accessed June 23, 2022.

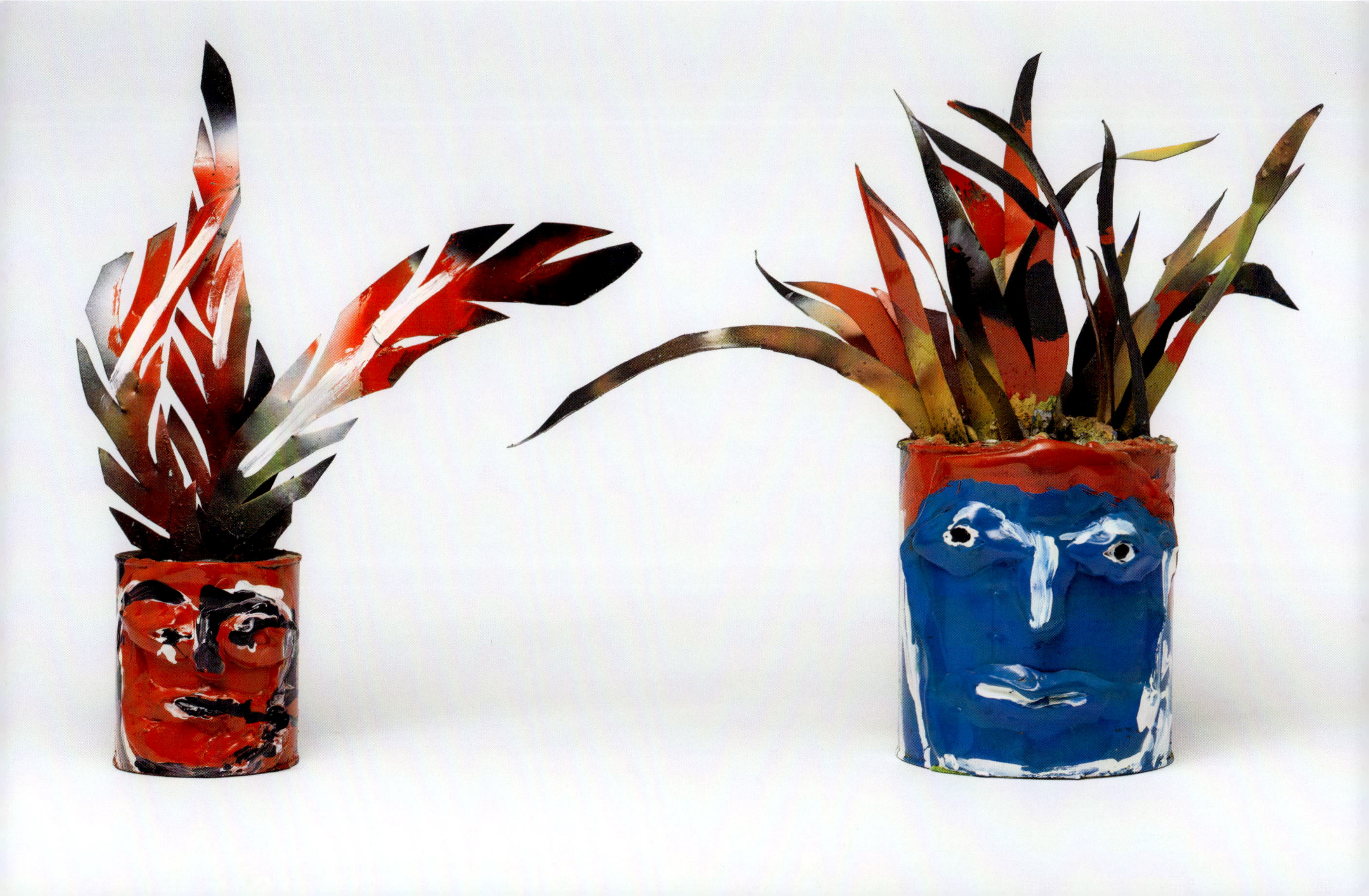

Cat. 13
Thornton Dial

A Moose That Has a Back Can Do Anything in the Woods
1989
paint and cut and painted high-pile carpet on canvas mounted on board
in frame 36 ½ × 48 ¼ in.
(92.7 × 122.6 cm)

Animals in the personal symbolism of Alabama artist Thornton Dial are sometimes stand-ins for Black men or the artist himself. Racism and the power dynamics in American society are among the foremost thematic concerns of this art museum star, praised for his fierceness and expressive deployment of found materials.

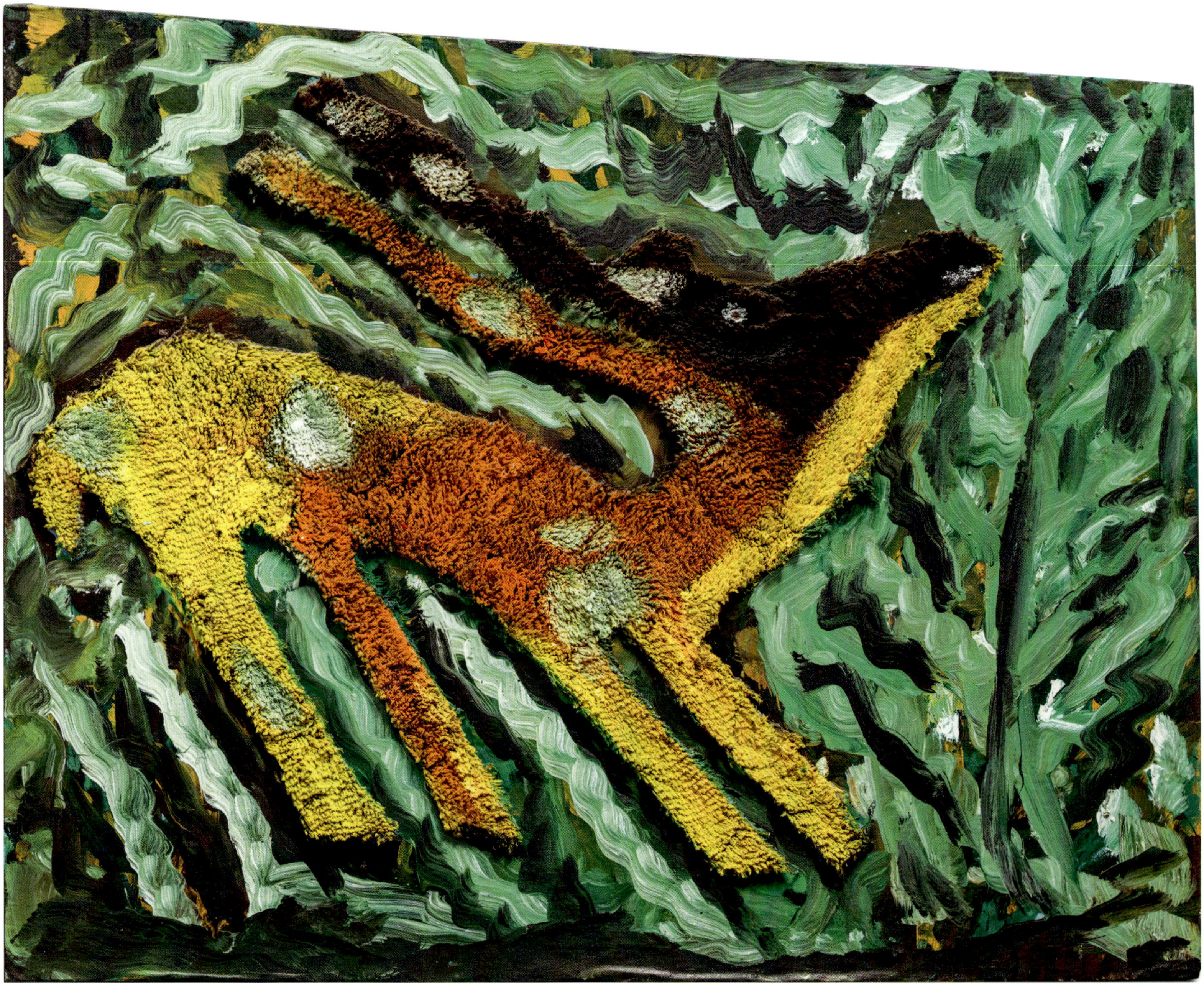

Cat. 14

Ronald Lockett

Born 1965 Bessemer, Alabama

Died 1998 Bessemer, Alabama

Traps

circa 1989

wire, painted wood, chain-link fencing, found sticks, cut sheet metal, and nails

49 × 54 × 4 in.

(124.5 × 137.2 × 10.2 cm)

In Bessemer, Alabama, Ronald Lockett found role models for making compelling art out of scrap materials. He felt the influence and encouragement of his older cousin Thornton Dial and regional creators of artistic environments. Lockett's emotionally resonant work, notably his *Traps* series, eloquently explores the human condition, the environment, and racial discrimination.

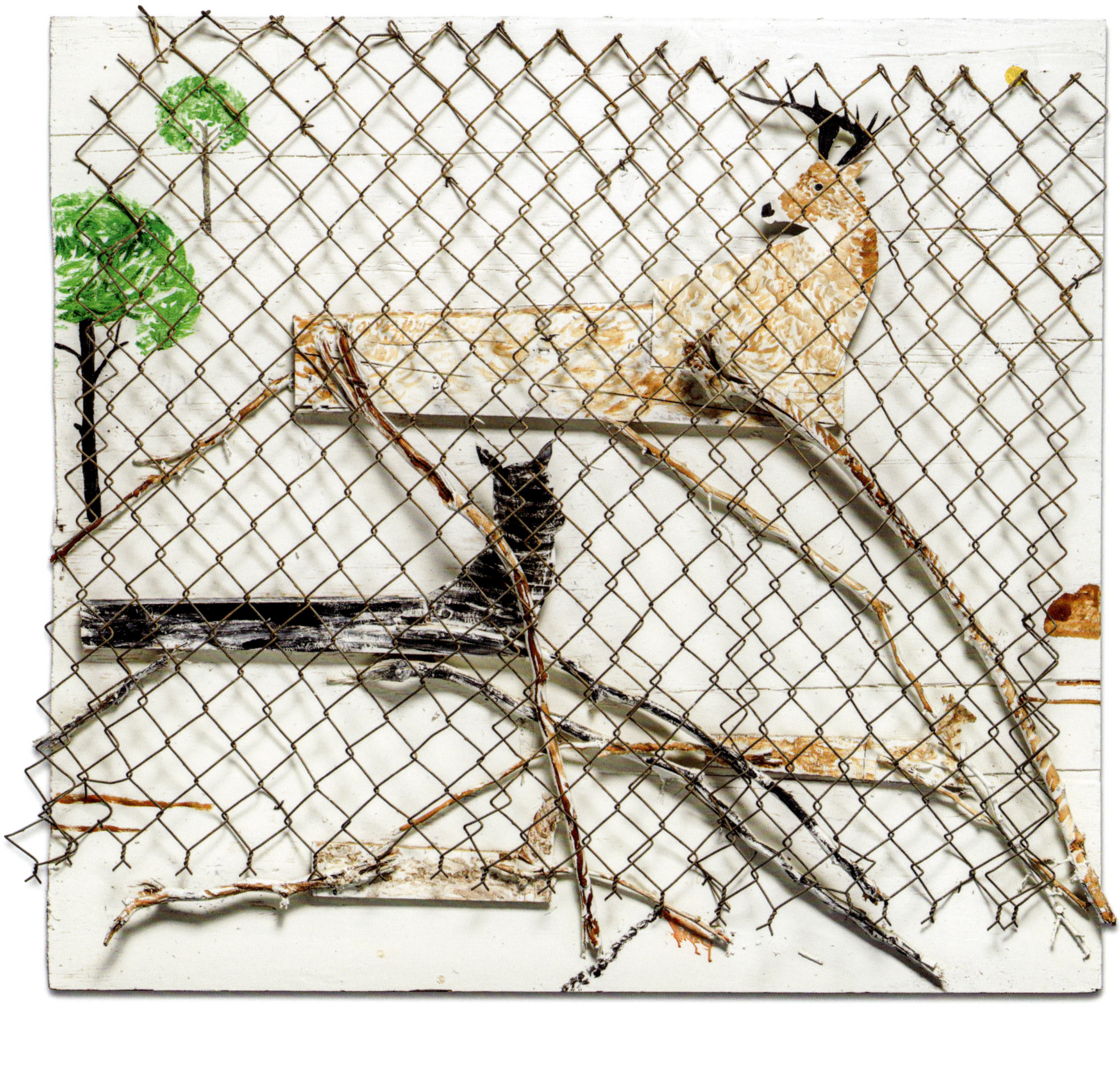

Cat. 15
Tony Fitzpatrick
Born 1958 Chicago, Illinois

Roberto Clemente
1987
colored pencil and oil
pastel on slate
slate $11\frac{15}{16} \times 8\frac{1}{16}$ in. (30.3 × 20.4 cm);
with decorated frame $13\frac{7}{16} \times 9\frac{5}{8}$ in.
(34.2 × 24.4 cm)

For Tony Fitzpatrick, baseball has a spiritual dimension and he treats the players with reverence. Hence, Roberto Clemente, the beloved Pittsburgh Pirates right fielder, sprouts angel wings and assumes a prayerful attitude (while poised to catch a fly ball).

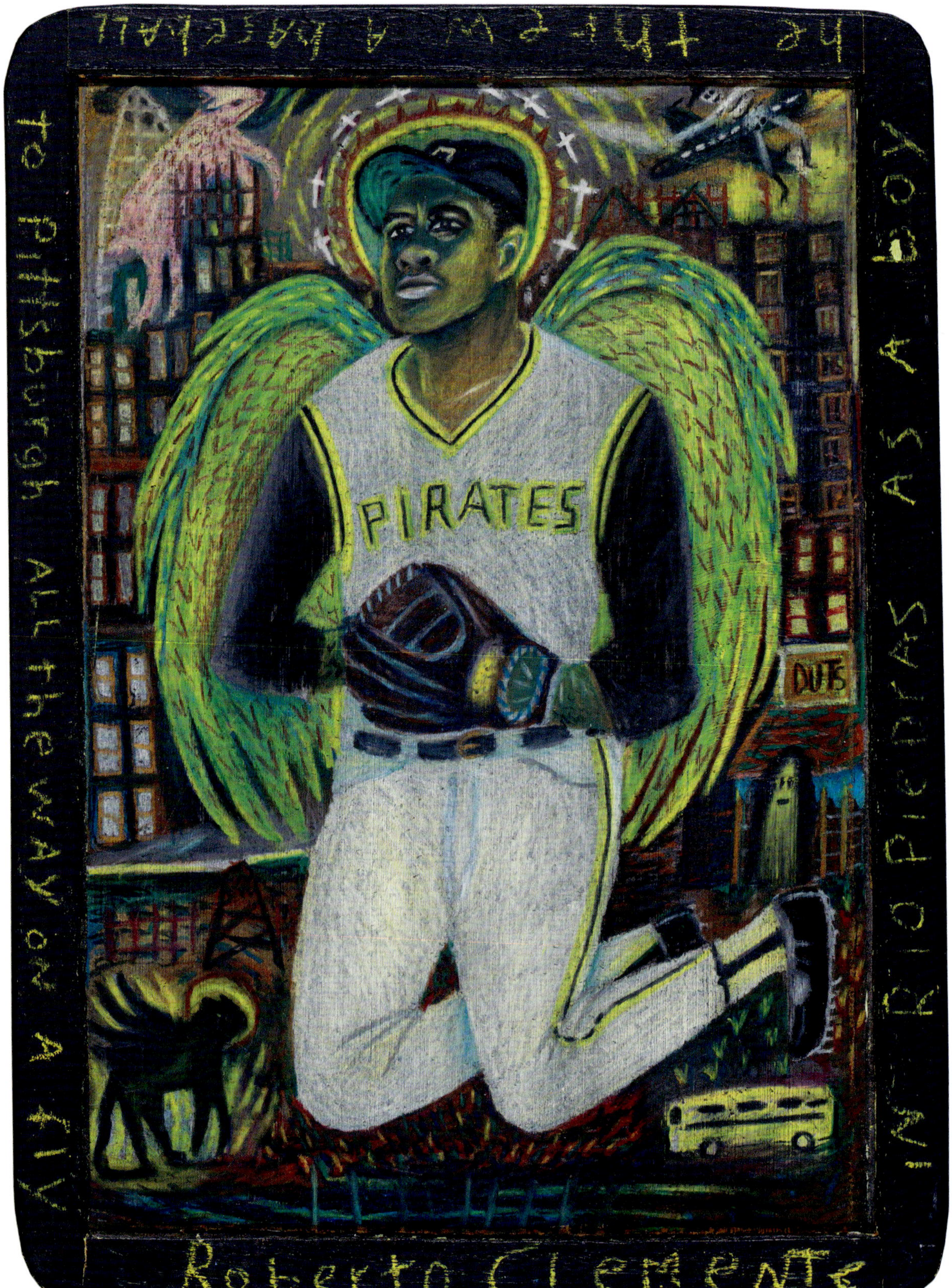

Cat. 16
Tony Fitzpatrick

Willie Mays
1987
colored pencil and oil pastel on slate
slate $11\frac{15}{16} \times 8\frac{1}{16}$ in. (30.3 × 20.4 cm); with decorated frame $13\frac{7}{16} \times 9\frac{1}{2}$ in. (34.2 × 24.2 cm)

Visits to the Art Institute of Chicago and other museums, says Tony Fitzpatrick, provided the best art education he could have wished for. Religious art (as well as comic books) had a strong appeal. He puts old, discarded objects, like the children's chalk boards he used for this series, to the service of storytelling. The hooded Ku Klux Klan–like figure seen here alludes to the threats of racial violence Black players like Willie Mays confronted.

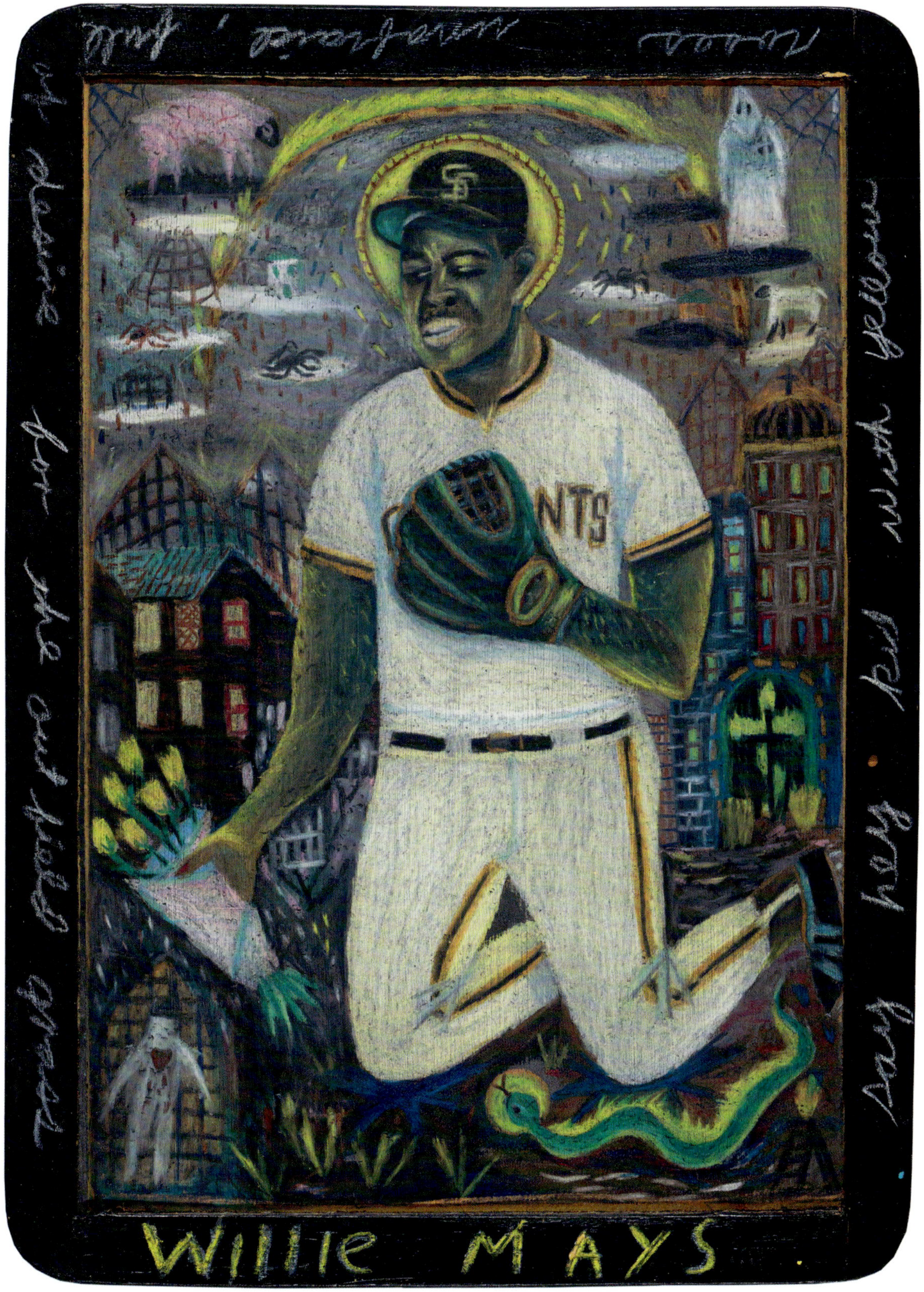

Cat. 17
Ralph Fasanella
Born 1914 New York City
Died 1997 Yonkers, New York

Meeting at the Commons—Lawrence 1912
1977
oil on canvas
50 × 120 in. (127 × 304.8 cm)

Experiences in an Italian immigrant family and as a union activist gave rise to Ralph Fasanella's deep sympathy for working people and impassioned commitment to social justice. For a series of large, cinematic paintings devoted to the "Bread and Roses" textile workers strike of 1912 in Lawrence, Massachusetts, he made studies of the site, conducted interviews, and pored over accounts of the historic events. The strike, with violent clashes and death, ultimately led to higher wages and safer working conditions for mill workers.

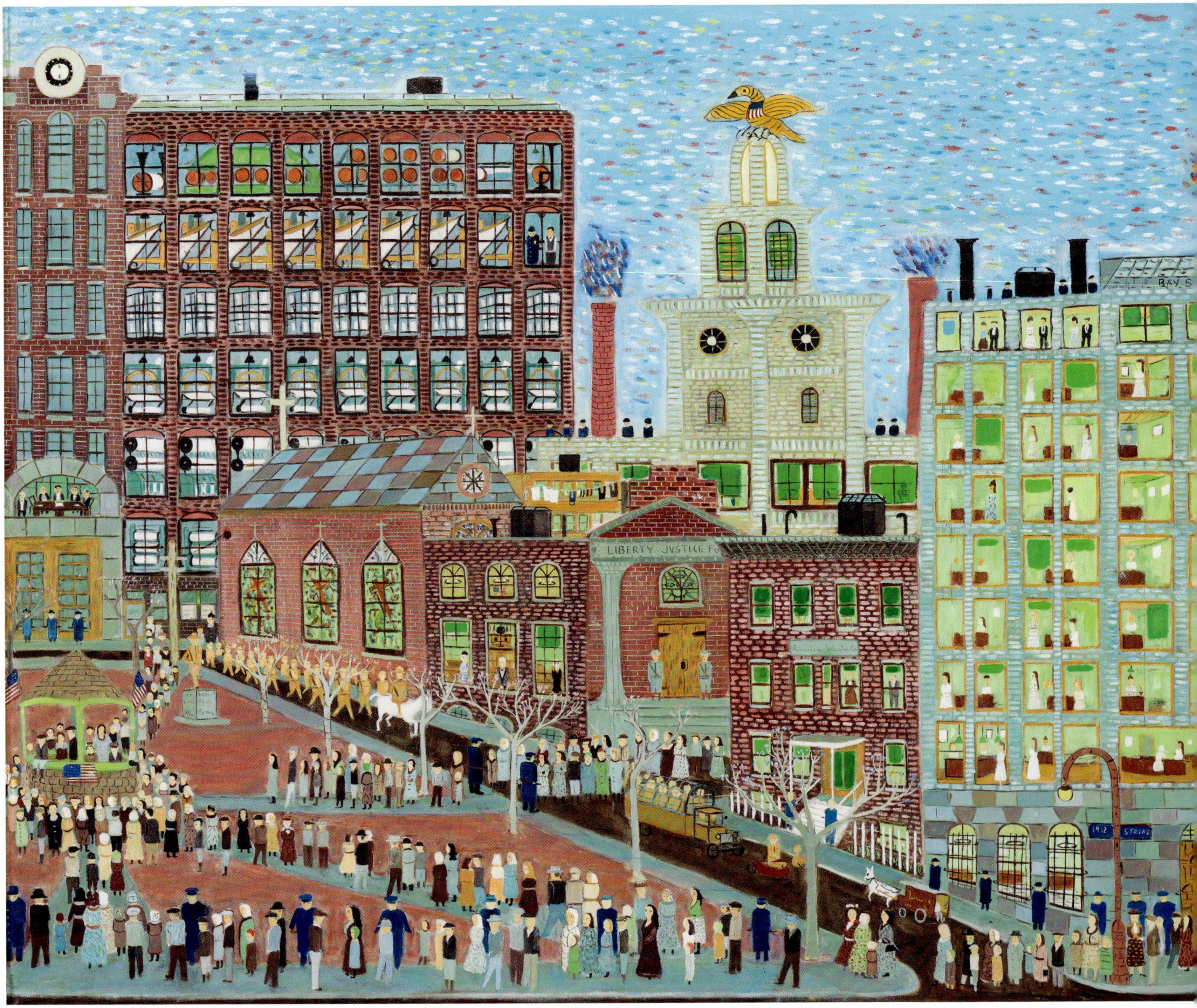

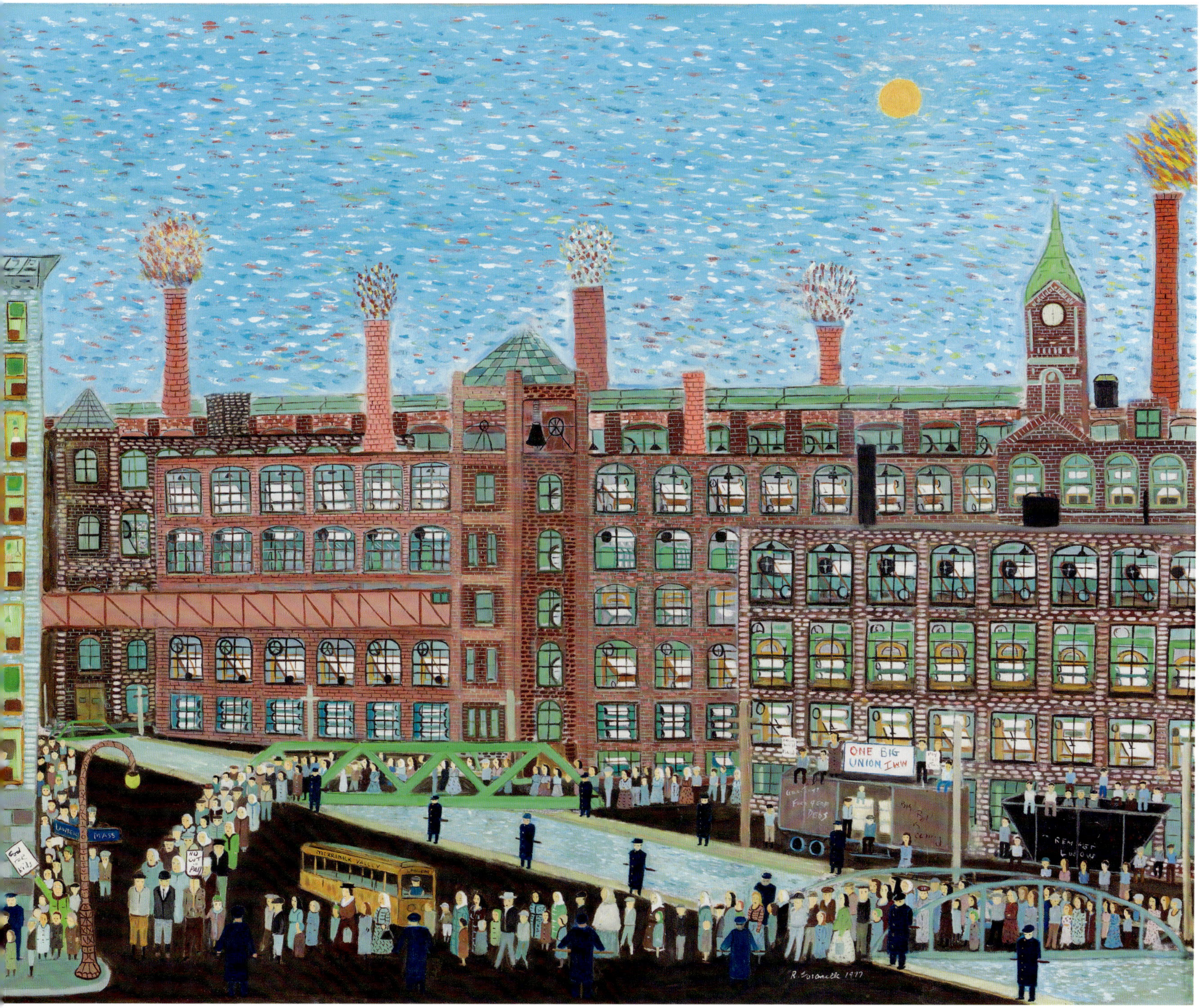
ONE BIG
UNION IWW
MASS

Cat. 18

Louis Monza

Born 1897 Turate, Italy
Died 1984 Redondo
Beach, California

An Apple and Its Counterpart

1944
oil on canvas
20 × 12 in. (50.8 × 30.5 cm)

Though brightly colored, some of Louis Monza's works grimly reflect on the brutality and price of war. Monza immigrated to the United States from his native Italy on the eve of World War I. He began to make art in the late 1930s after he fell from a scaffold while employed as a house painter.

Cat. 19

Louis Monza

Travesty (Book Burning)

1984
oil on canvas
$23\frac{5}{8} \times 19\frac{1}{4}$ in. (60 × 48.9 cm)

Lifetime recognition came to Louis Monza, whose imaginative works communicate on wide-ranging issues. Religion and politics are intertwined in this painting in which a soldier confronts a flaming tower of books. Encircling the pyre are the Crucifixion of Christ, the Statue of Liberty, the United States Capitol, and the Washington Monument inscribed "In God We Trust."

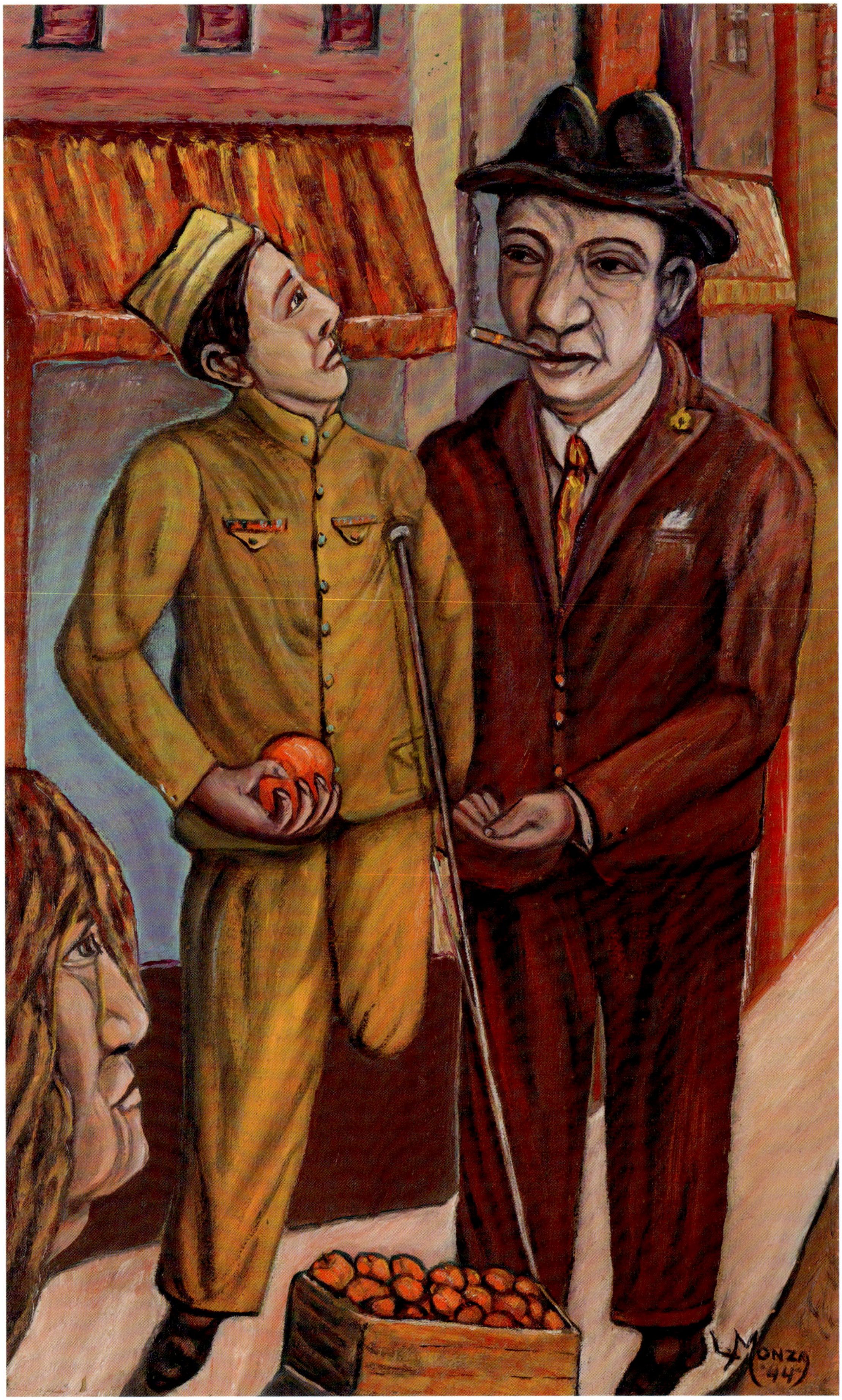

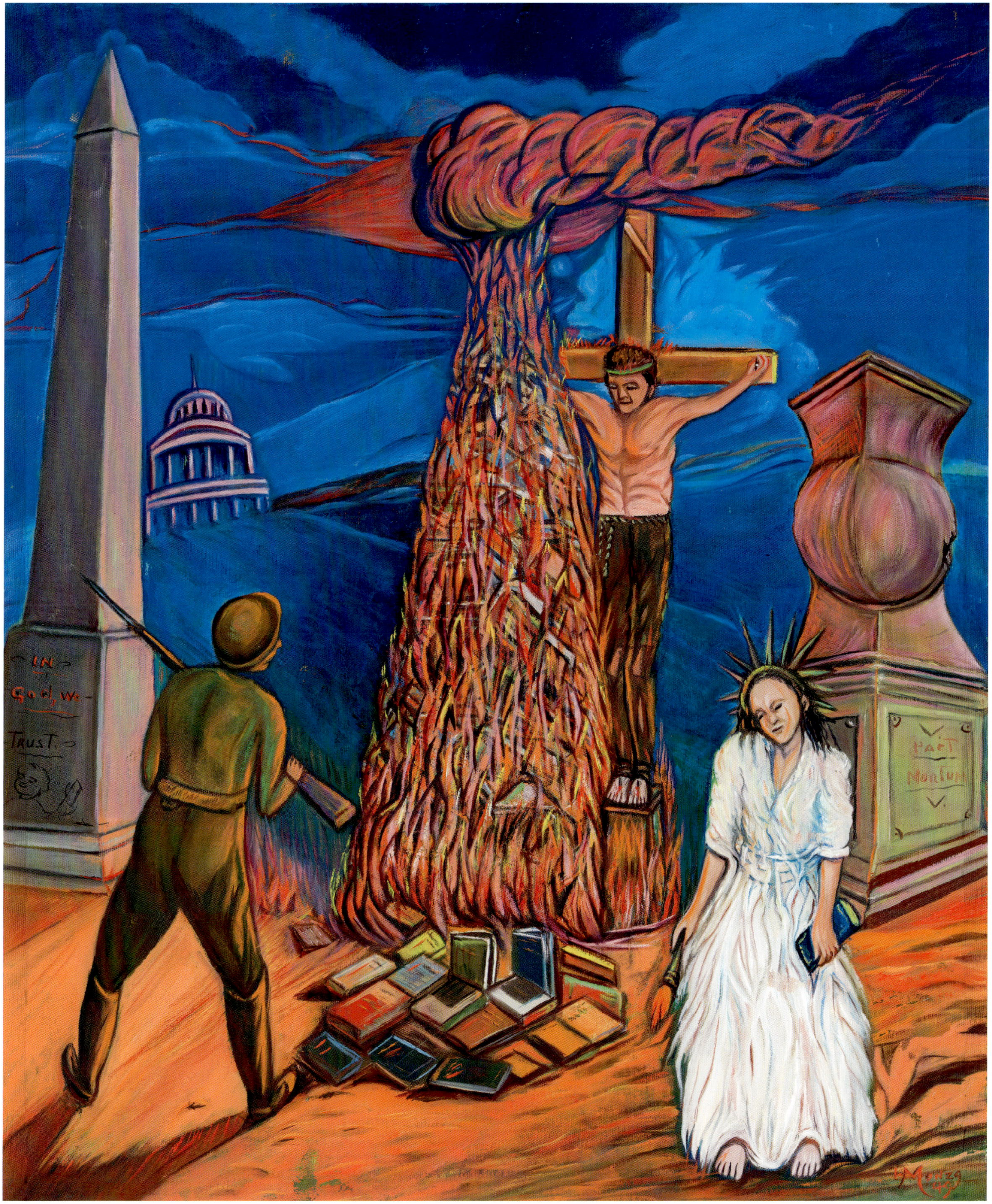
IN
God, We
Trust.
PacT
MorTum

Cat. 20

Ned Cartledge

Born 1916 Canon, Georgia
Died 2001 DeKalb, Georgia

Temperance

1970
carved and painted wood
32 × 36¼ in. (81.3 × 92.1 cm)

"I say what I want to say—
not cutesy things for folk art
collectors."

Ned Cartledge quoted in Chuck and Jan Rosenak, *Museum of American Folk Art Encyclopedia of Twentieth-Century American Folk Art and Artists* (New York: Abbeville Press, 1990), 68.

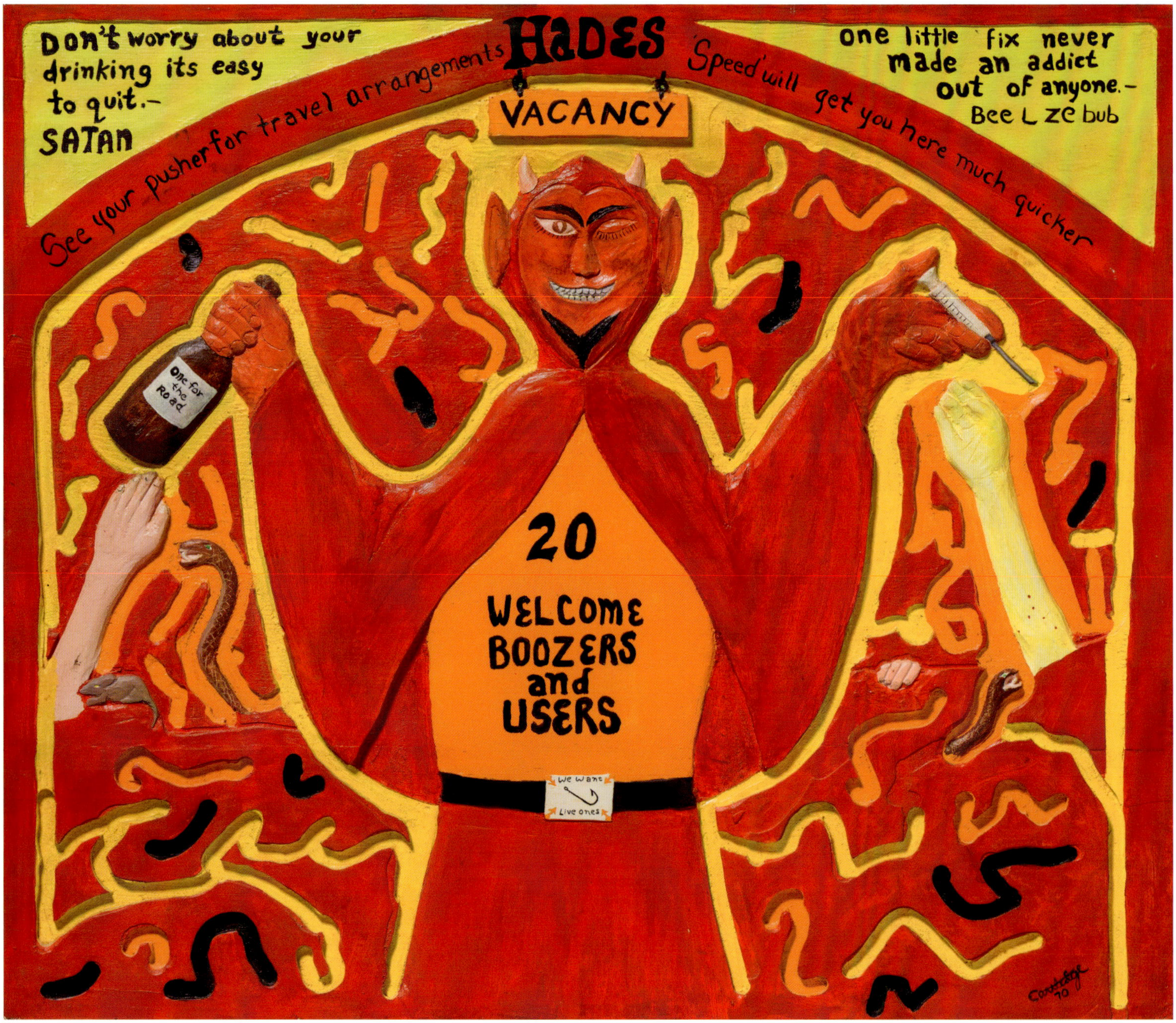

Cat. 21
Ned Cartledge

This Eagle Cannot Fly with Only the Right Wing
1981
carved and painted wood
20 × 25 in. (50.8 × 63.5 cm)

"Then along when the Vietnam War came along, I began to do what I call social and political comment. I was one of the old folks opposed to the . . . Vietnam War."

Ned Cartledge, interview by William Volkersz, March 12, 1984, Archives of American Art, Smithsonian Institution, https://www.aaa.si.edu/collections/items/detail/transcript-interview-ned-cartledge-22668.

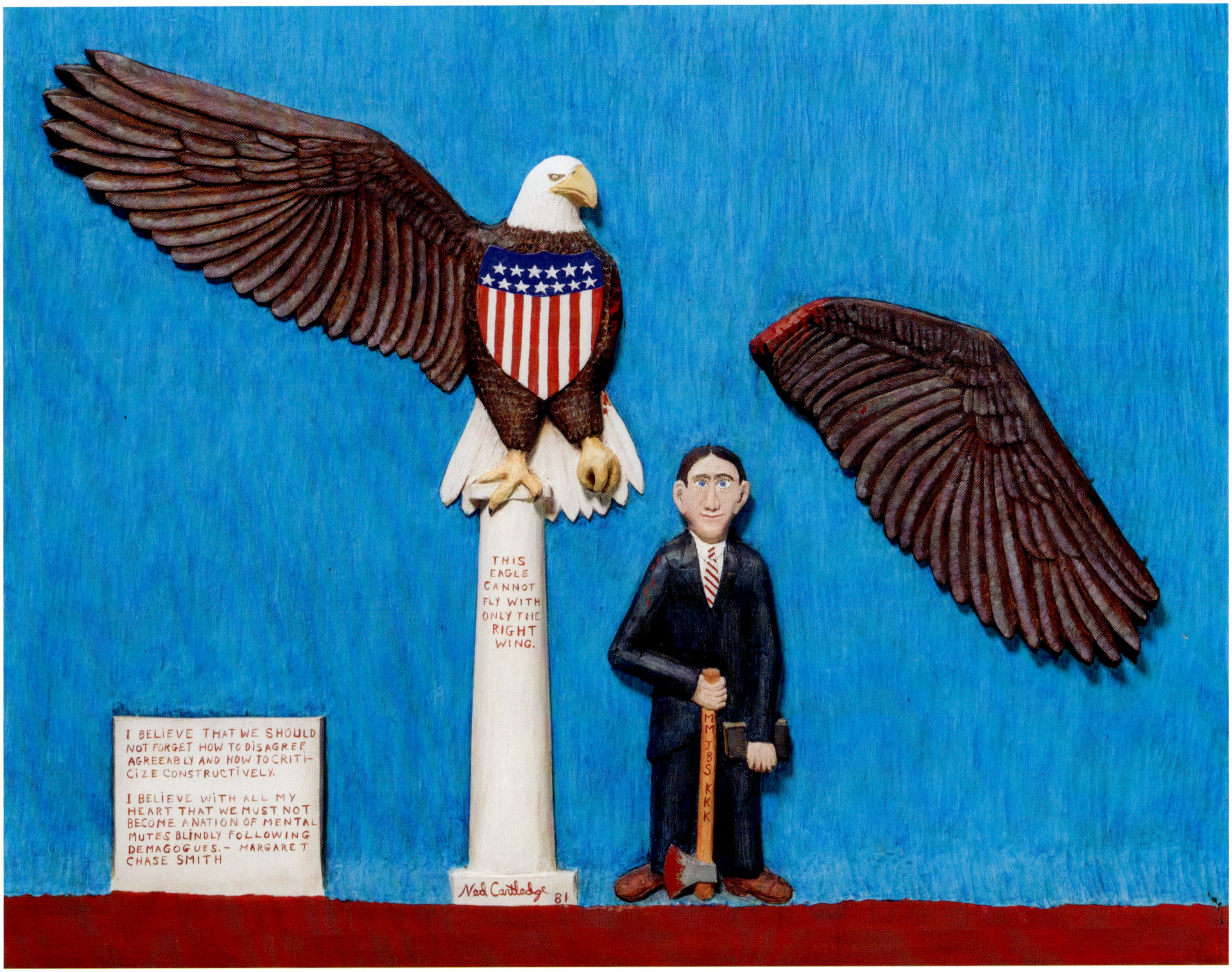

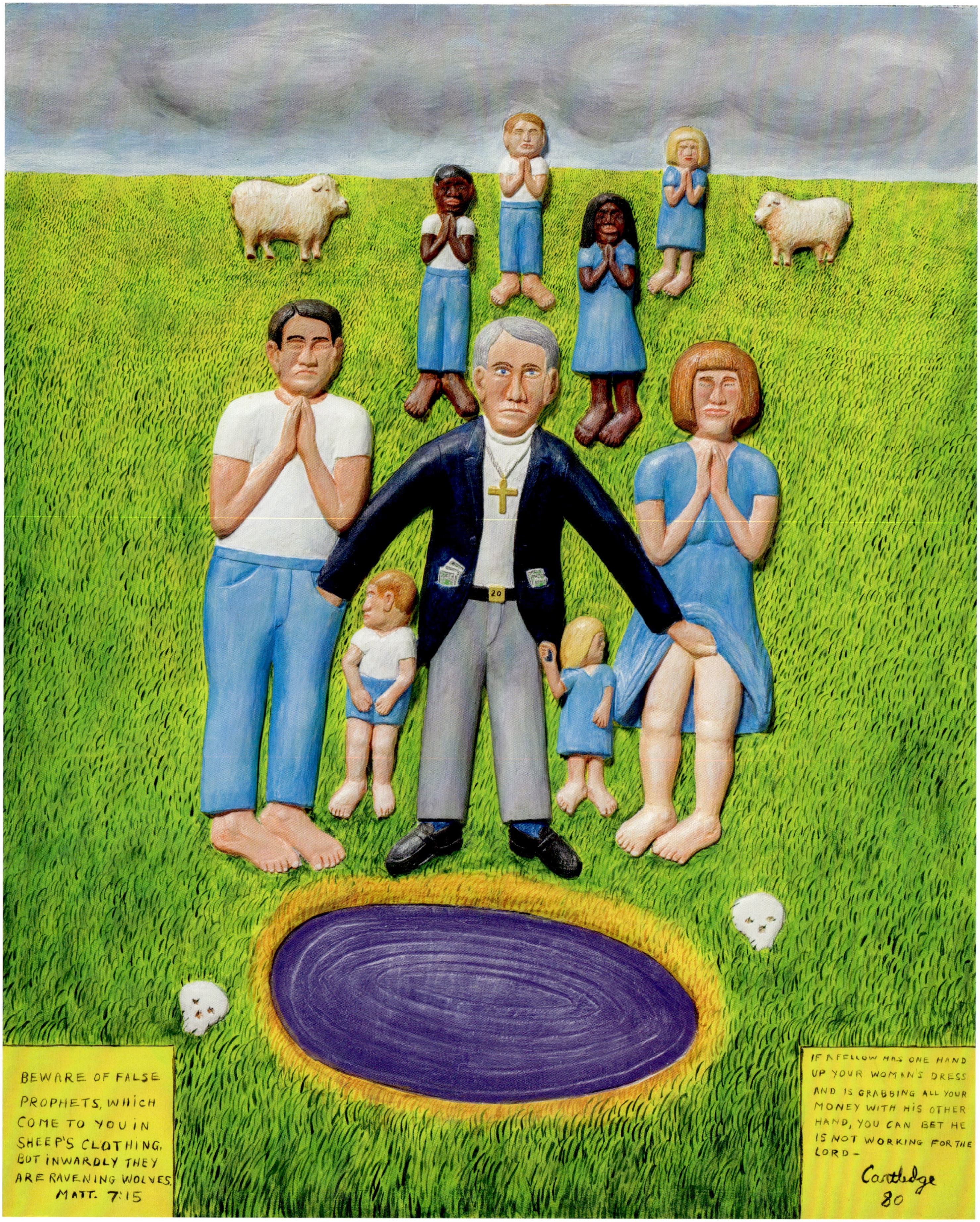
BEWARE OF FALSE PROPHETS, WHICH COME TO YOU IN SHEEP'S CLOTHING, BUT INWARDLY THEY ARE RAVENING WOLVES. MATT. 7:15
IF A FELLOW HAS ONE HAND UP YOUR WOMAN'S DRESS AND IS GRABBING ALL YOUR MONEY WITH HIS OTHER HAND, YOU CAN BET HE IS NOT WORKING FOR THE LORD –
Cartledge 80

Cat. 22

Ned Cartledge

Beware of False Prophets (or **Beware of Imposters**)
1980
carved and painted wood
23 × 18½ in. (58.4 × 47 cm)

"That's . . . on the Jim Jones type personality. He's got his big cross there fronting for him. . . . And his money's comin' out of his pockets, and all these people that are following him . . . they got their prayerful attitude, but they're blind. They go along, got their eyes closed, and of course there I got the sheep. . . . They're followers. . . . The only people in the picture that got their eyes open are the little children. . . . Of course, that's his purple Koolaid [with which Jones's followers committed mass suicide in Guyana]. . . . But he's leading them to destruction."

Ned Cartledge, interview by William Volkersz, March 12, 1984, Archives of American Art, Smithsonian Institution, https://www.aaa.si.edu/collections/items/detail/transcript-interview-ned-cartledge-22668.

Cat. 23

Ned Cartledge

Hell Ain't Half Full
1986
carved and painted wood
17¼ × 33½ in. (43.8 × 85.1 cm)

No subject was sacred for Atlanta artist Ned Cartledge, who as a child carved sculptures from pine grocery crates with his mother's paring knife. Working for decades in the cotton industry, then as a hardware salesman at a Sears, Roebuck store, Cartledge in his carvings often took aim at hypocrisy and greed.

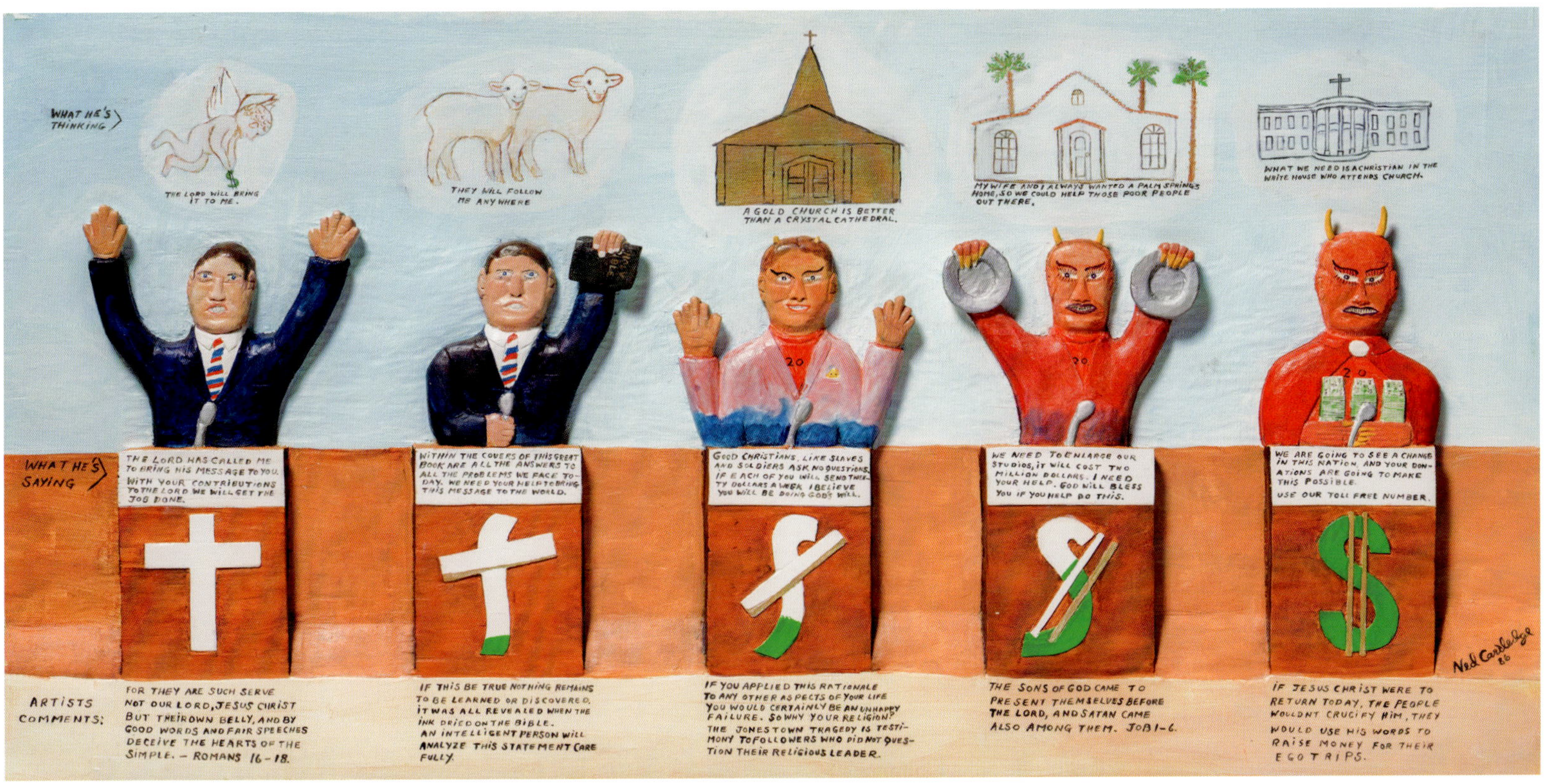

Cat. 24
William Hawkins
Born 1895 Union City, Kentucky
Died 1990 Columbus, Ohio

Did Comets Kill the Dinosaurs? #1
circa 1986
enamel house paint, cornmeal, and collage on Masonite
48 × 56½ in. (121.9 × 143.5 cm)

Dramatic scale, striking aesthetic choices, bold execution, and references to popular culture: these give the paintings of William Hawkins a formidable impact. His animals, including those no longer walking the earth, overflow with character, perhaps a tribute to the artist's rural Kentucky childhood.

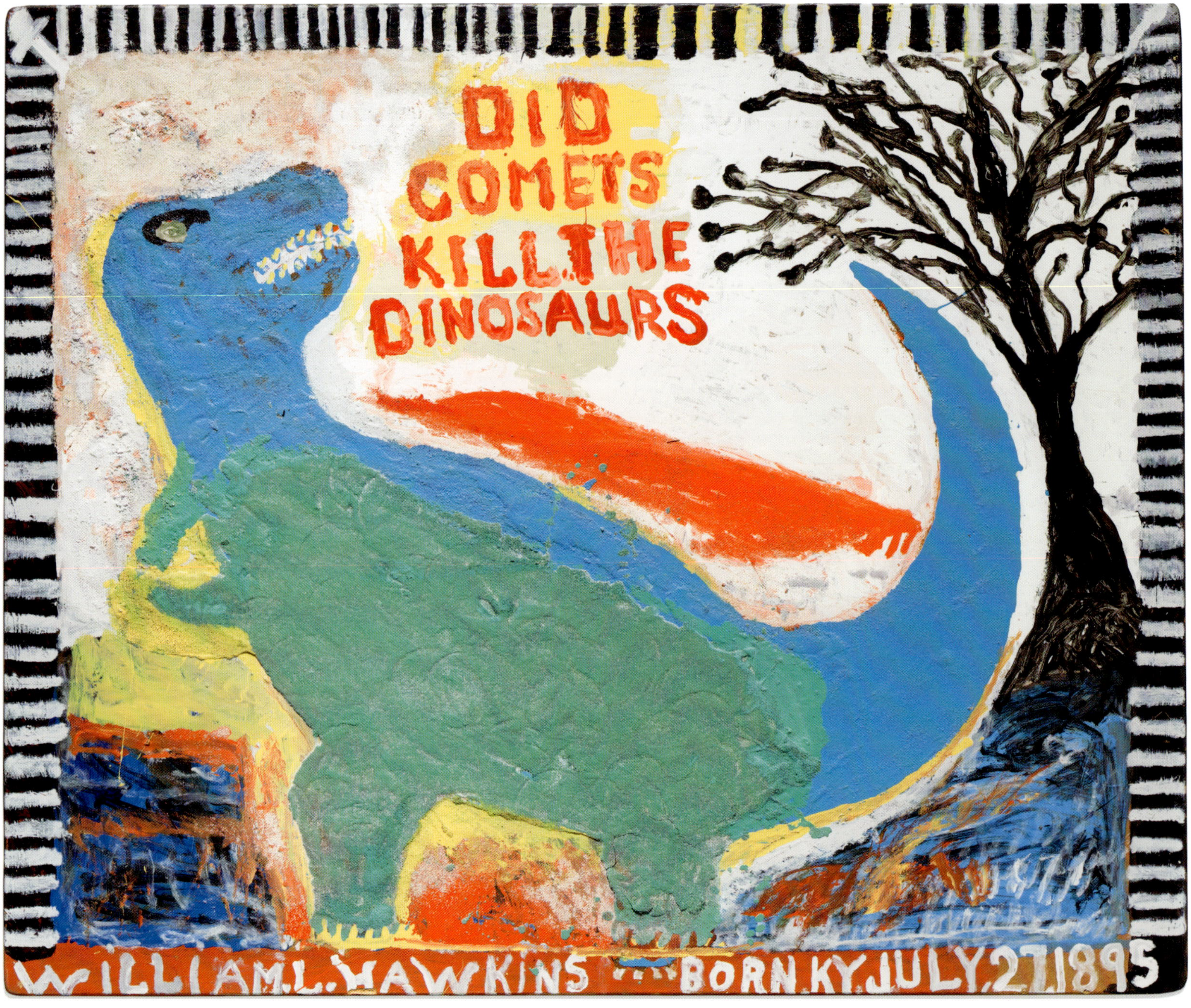

Cat. 25

Unidentified Artist (American)

White Bear

1920–30

carved and painted wood

14 × 29 × 11¾ in.

(35.6 × 73.7 × 29.8 cm)

This polar bear, possibly carved in Maine, would evoke terror in the most intrepid outdoorsman. The rugged carving, stocky build, jagged teeth, and bloody red mouth make this a fearsome creature.

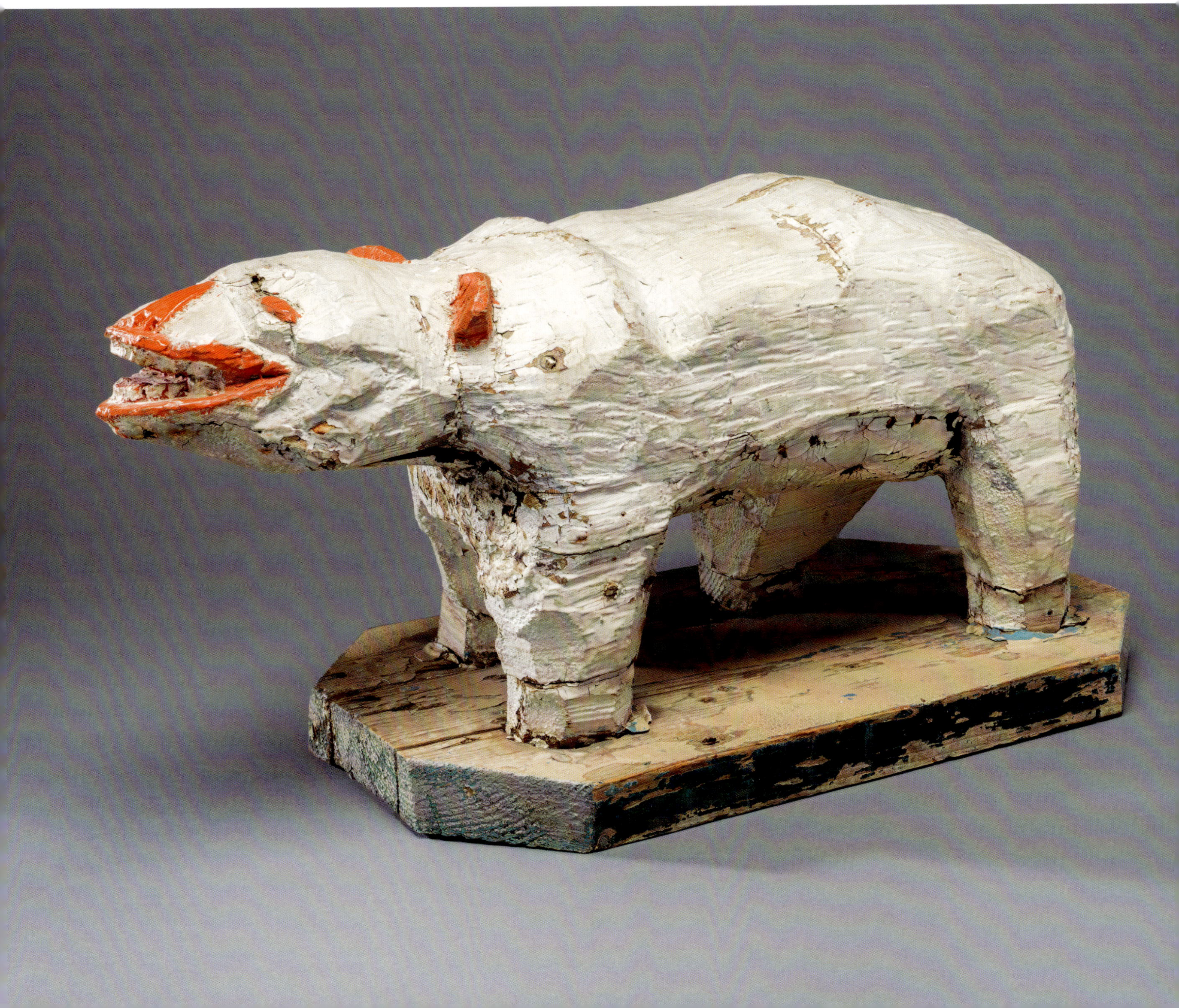

Cat. 26

Clarence Woolsey
Born 1909 Hugoton, Kansas
Died 1987 Waterloo, Iowa
and
Grace Woolsey
Born 1921 as Grace Evelyn Zingg, Thompson, Iowa
Died 1992 Waterloo, Iowa

Caparena Figure
1961–71
bottle caps, wire, wood, and nails
40 × 18½ × 13 in.
(101.6 × 47 × 33 cm)

"The World's Largest Pioneer Caparena" (or "Cap-Arena") was the name Clarence and Grace Woolsey gave a display of their work in Lincoln, Iowa, charging twenty-five cents admission. By this time in 1971, the farm couple had crafted more than 100 of these ingenious figures (which Clarence reportedly called "Bears") from pop bottle caps pierced and wired together over wood frames made from old fruit crates.

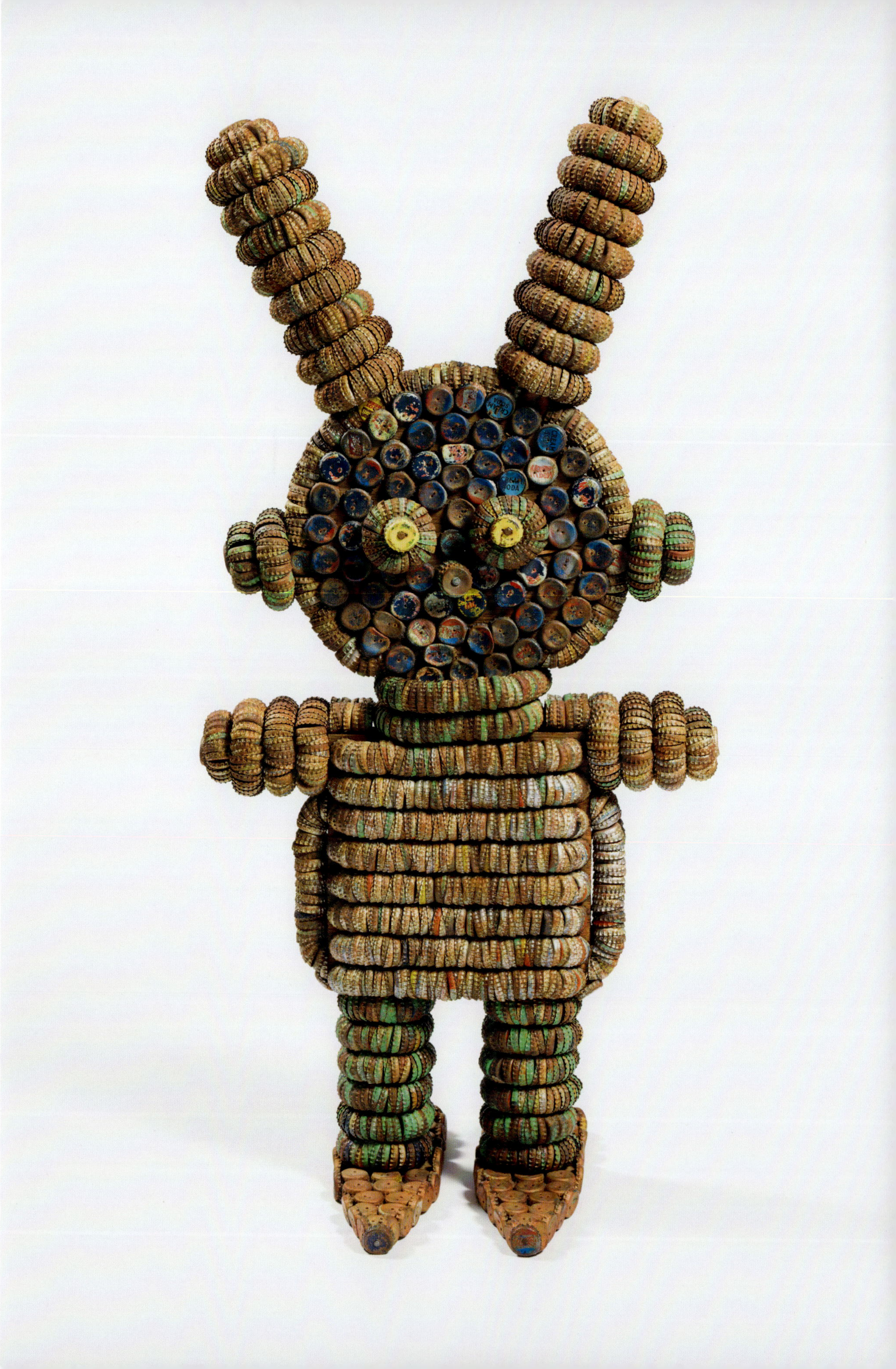

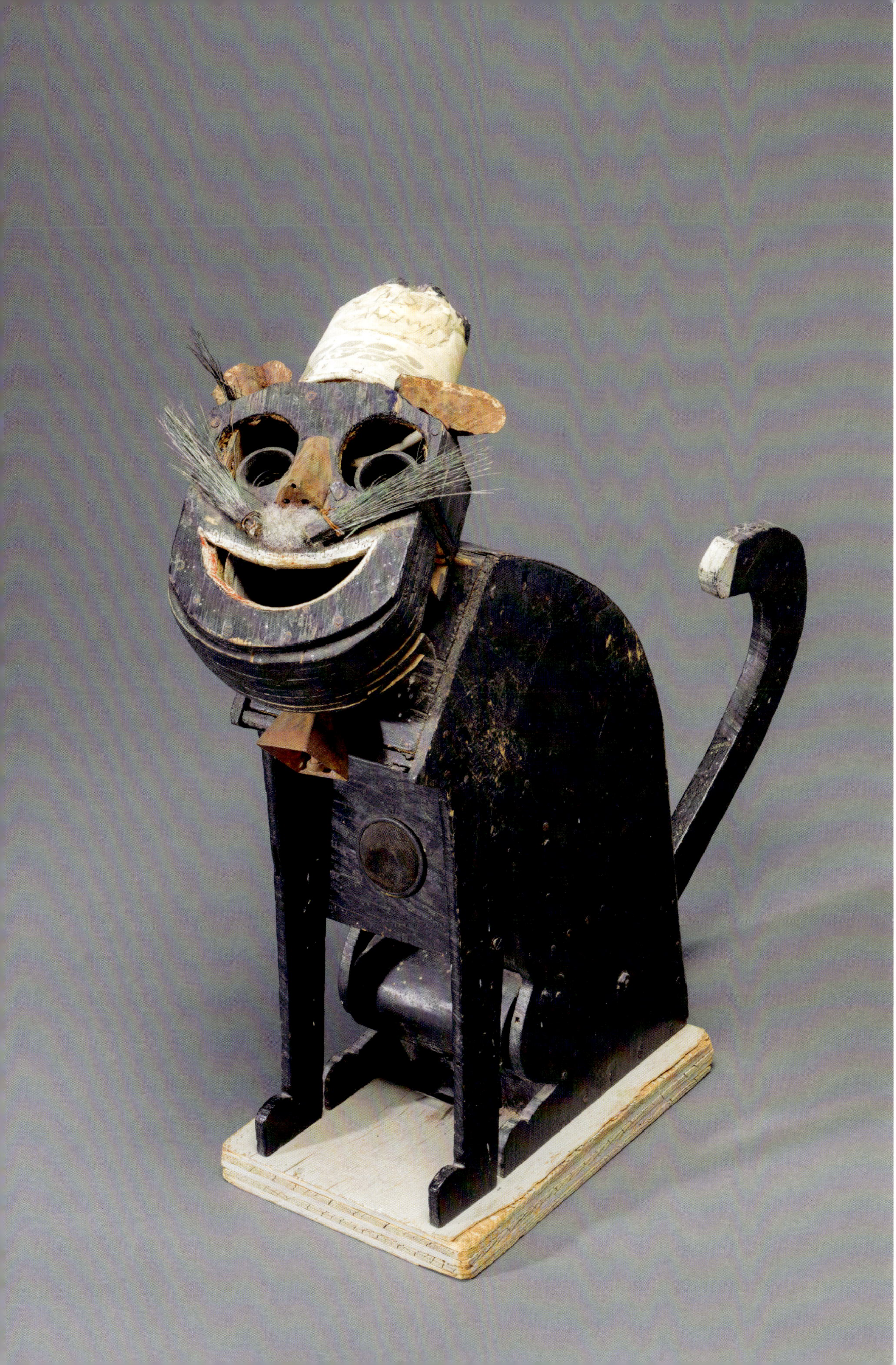

Cat. 27
Unidentified Artist (American or European)

Cat Bank
mid–late 20th century
wood, metal, paint, and found objects
16 ½ × 6 ¼ × 16 in.
(41.9 × 15.9 × 40.6 cm)

This bank in the form of a cat is cleverly assembled from an assortment of found objects selected for shape combined with elements probably cut for the purpose. The broad smile, bristly upturned whiskers, cup hat, bell, and white tail tip make this feline a spirited character.

Cat. 28

David Butler

Born 1898 Good Hope, Louisiana
Died 1997 Morgan City, Louisiana

Nativity Scene

circa 1980
painted cut sheet metal, plastic beads, and wire
28 × 42 ½ × 3 in.
(71.1 × 108 × 7.6 cm)

David Butler said divine inspiration guided him to beautify his environment with vivid works of art. This cut-and-painted tin religious scene was perhaps a window screen; we may well imagine the striking effects of light penetrating the cutouts in its intriguing design. Wires with found objects like beads set Butler's delightful conceptions in motion.

Cat. 29

David Butler

Fish

1980
painted cut sheet metal
9 ¾ × 16 ½ × 3 ¼ in.
(24.8 × 41.9 × 8.6 cm)

Those who visited the home of David Butler near Patterson, Louisiana, found themselves immersed in a fantasy world. After leaving employment due to an accident, Butler set about ornamenting his home; he cut roofing tin with a meat cleaver, a hammer, and an axe-head to create vibrant scenes and imaginative creatures, like this fierce-looking fish brightly decorated with house paints.

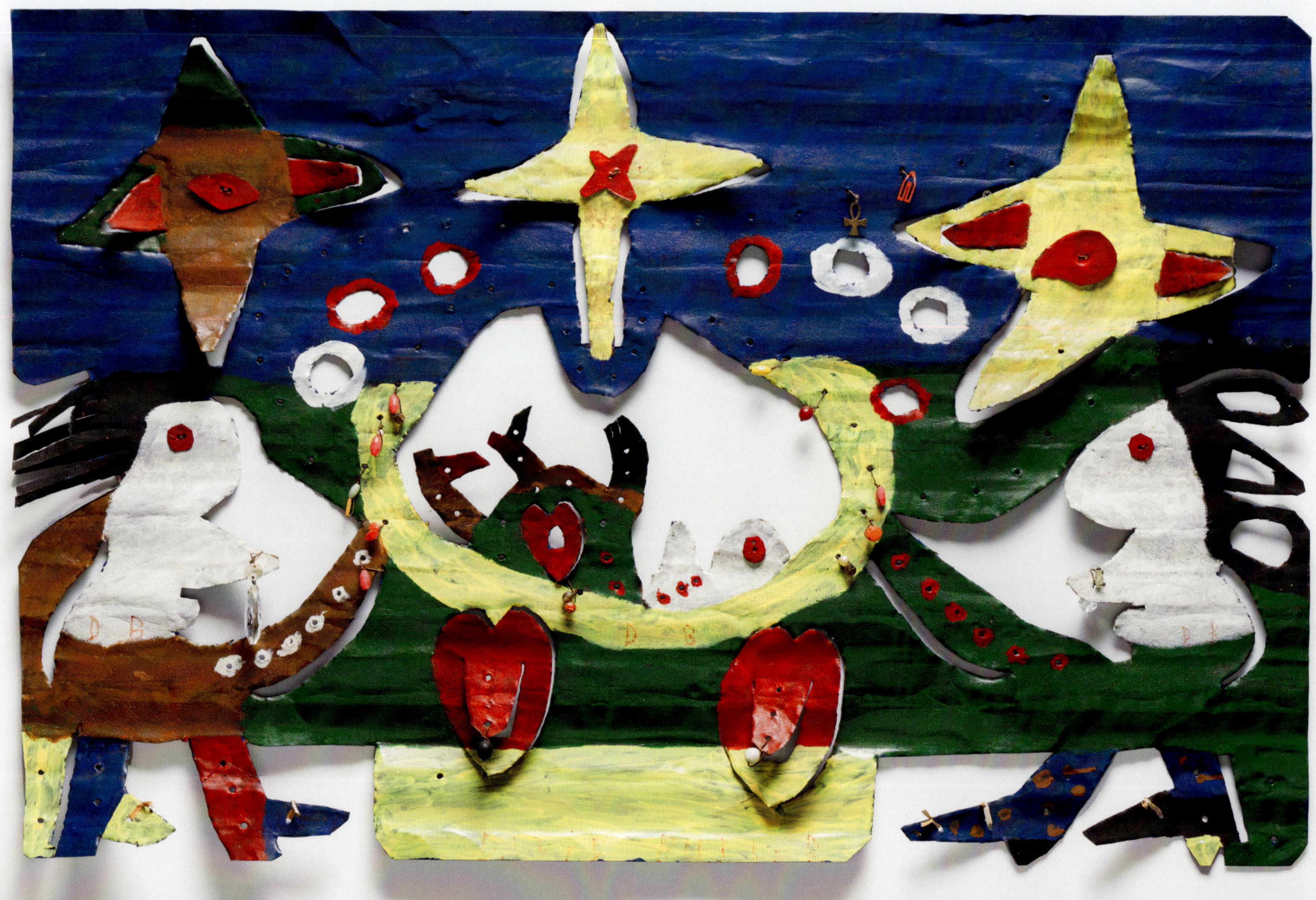

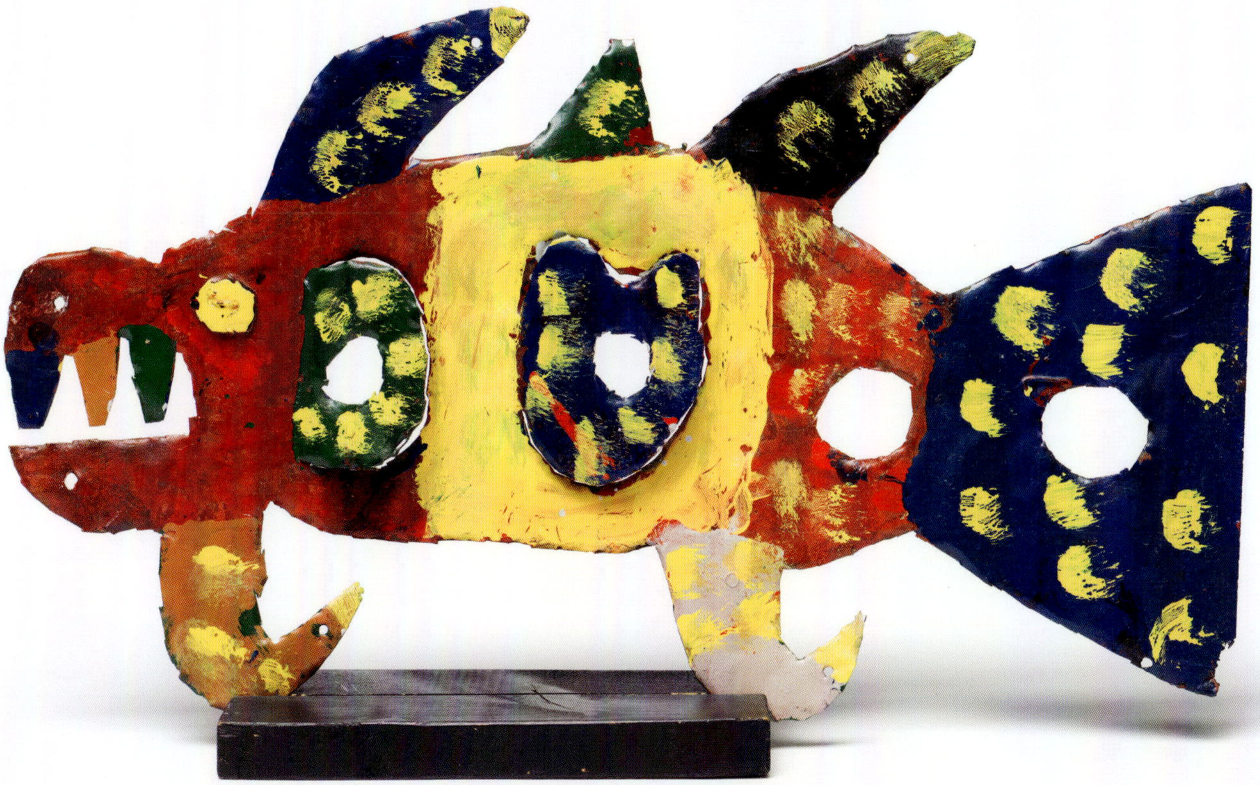

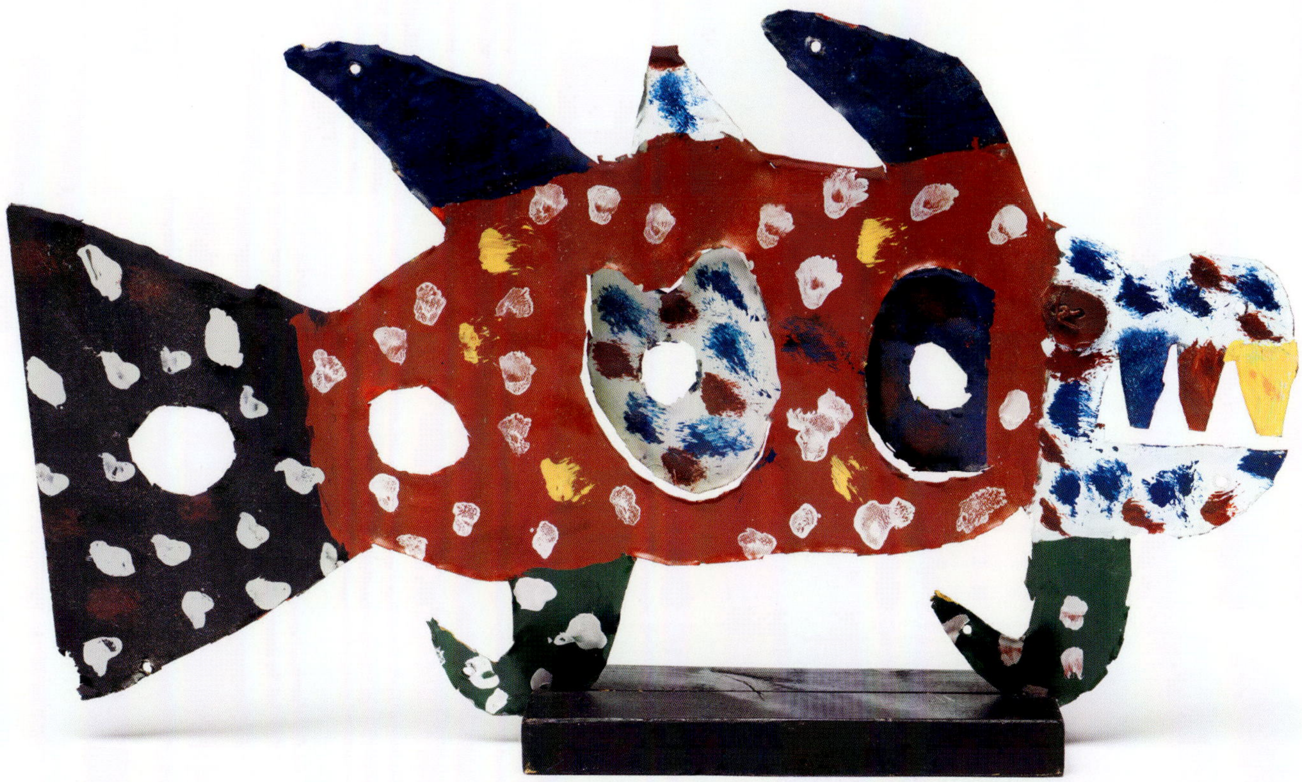

Cat. 30

Probably Lula Mae Hinkle

Born 1881 as Lula Mae Weaver, London, Kentucky

Died 1960 London, Kentucky

Garden Houses

circa 1920s–50s

concrete, glass, ceramic, and found objects

front row (left to right)

a: 29 × 13 × 10 in. (73.7 × 33 × 25.4 cm)

b: 22 × 12 × 13 in. (55.9 × 30.5 × 33 cm)

back row (left to right)

c: 34 × 10 × 15 in. (86.4 × 25.4 × 38.1 cm)

d: 35 × 10 × 10 in. (88.9 × 25.4 × 25.4 cm)

e: 31 × 11 × 11 in. (78.7 × 27.9 × 27.9 cm)

Richard and Lois Rosenthal acquired these fanciful garden sculptures from the self-taught painter Nan Phelps (1904–1990) of Hamilton, Ohio, who was so concerned for their preservation she insisted the collectors accept them as a gift. These diminutive fairy houses sparkling with colored glass were likely the creations of Nan's mother, Lula Mae Hinkle, whom her daughter painted making a quilt in 1957 (Cincinnati Art Museum).

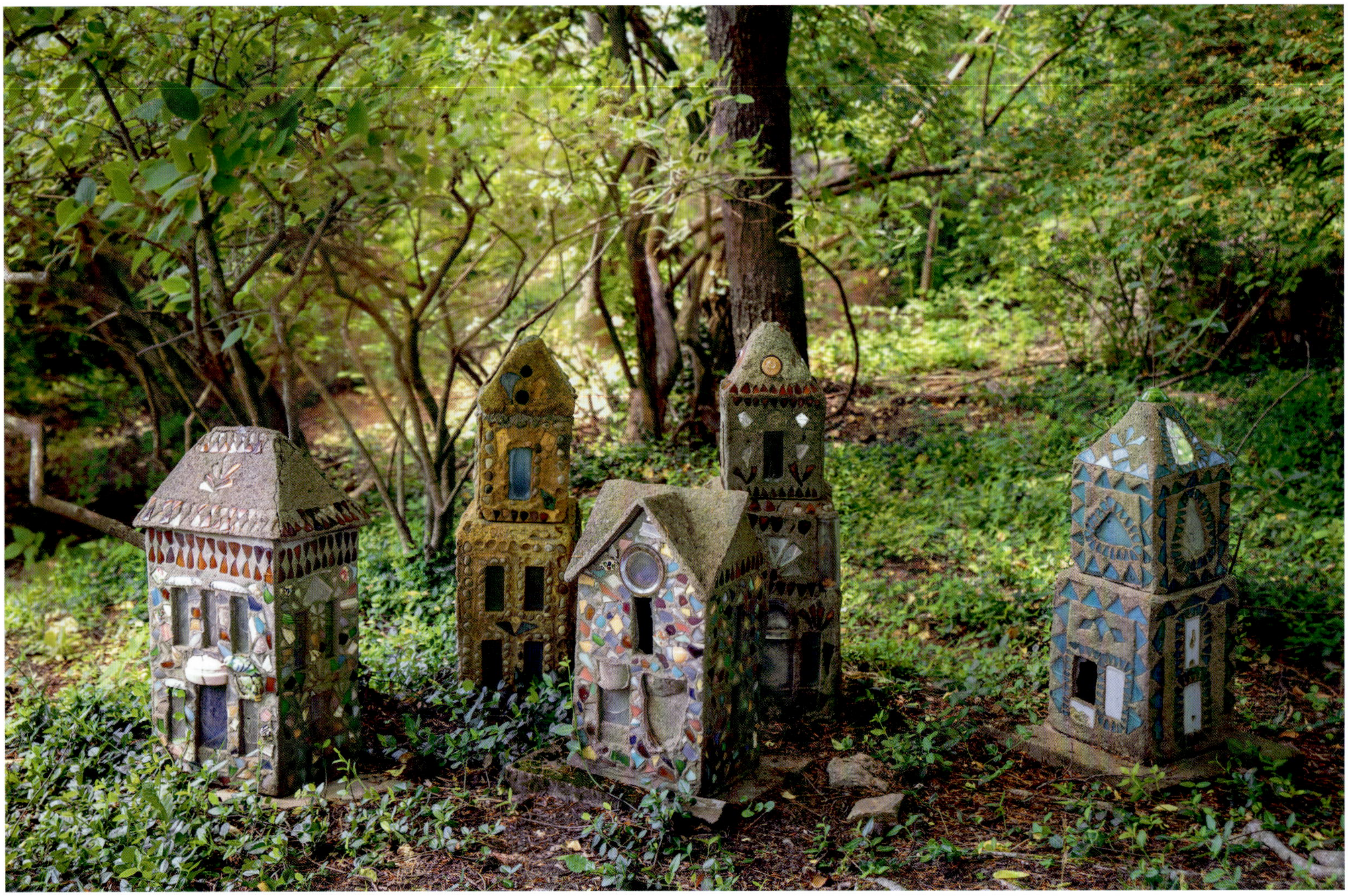

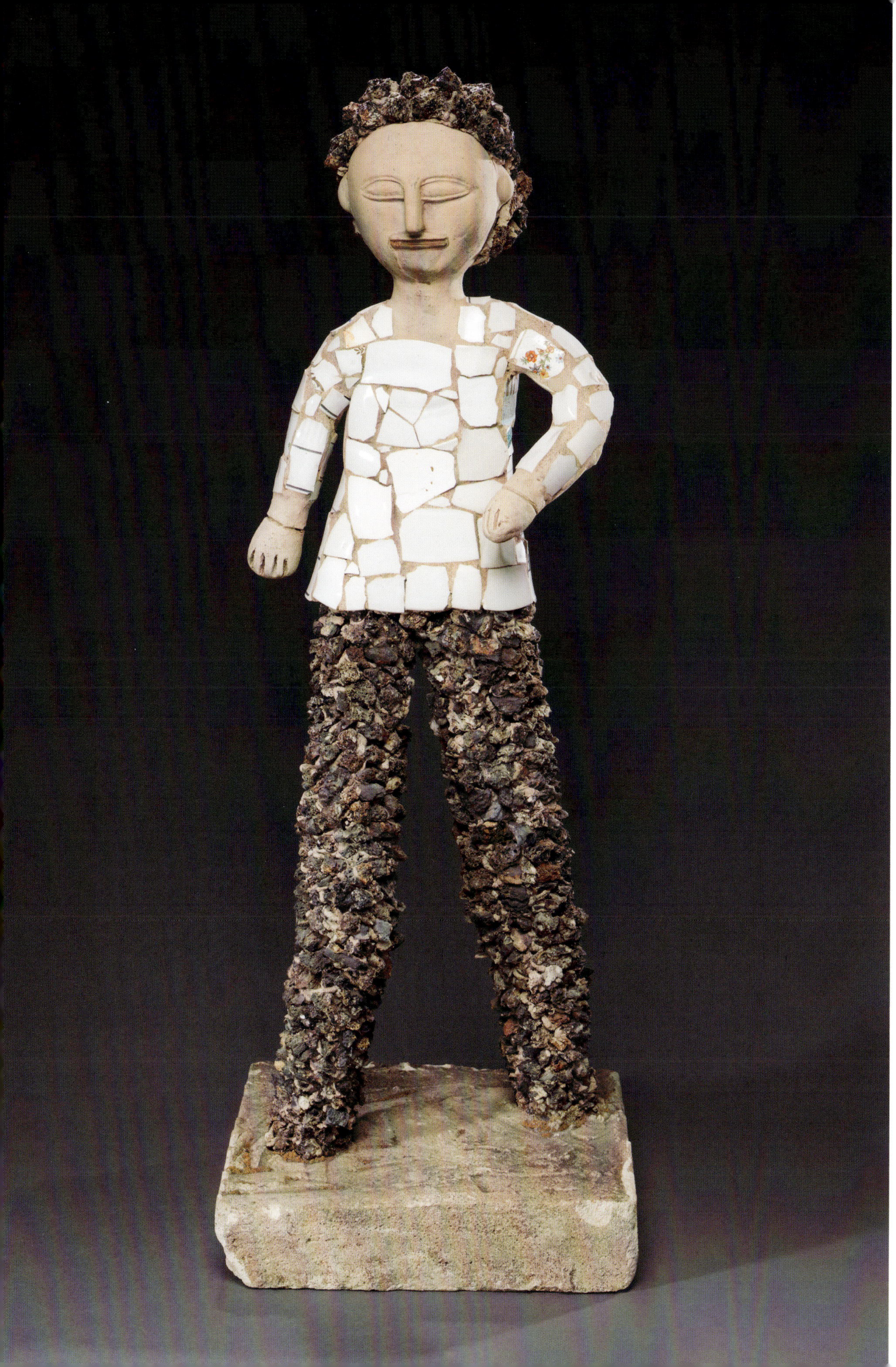

Cat. 31
Nek Chand
Born 1924 Barian Kalan
(now Pakistan)
Died 2015 Chandigarh, India

Standing Man
circa 1951–80
painted fired clay, broken china, rocks, and concrete
34½ × 12 × 12 in.
(87.6 × 30.5 × 30.5 cm)

A road inspector in Chandigarh, India, Nek Chand constructed figures, animals, and walls out of concrete and his collection of broken ceramics, rocks, bottles, pieces of cinder, and broken glass acquired at demolition sites. Working illegally on government property at the edge of the city, Chand created his Rock Garden, a mythical world he described as his poetry with rocks and a child's dream. Officially recognized in 1976 as a park, the Rock Garden is a 30-acre creative environment.

Charles Russell, *Groundwaters: A Century of Art by Self-Taught and Outsider Artists* (Munich and New York: Prestel Verlag, 2011), 157.

Cat. 32

Nellie Mae Rowe

Born 1900 Fayetteville, Georgia

Died 1982 Atlanta, Georgia

Pink Pig

mid-20th century

crayon on paper

16 1⁄16 × 20 1⁄16 in. (40.8 × 50.9 cm)

"I'm back to a child again. I'm seventy-five years old and I'm like a child. I get a kick out of drawin'. If I had the opportunity that children have now, I don't know what I would have done. I ain't had the opportunity. I had to go to the fields. . . . Now is the time for me to rest and play. I've worked my days, now I want to play these other days out. And God will let me do it, too. I'm goin' to play in my playhouse. I love it!"

Nellie Mae Rowe, interview by Charles Brown, Charleston Communication Center, 1975, quoted in Lee Kogan, *The Art of Nellie Mae Rowe: Ninety-Nine and a Half Won't Do* (Jackson: University Press of Mississippi, 1998), 31.

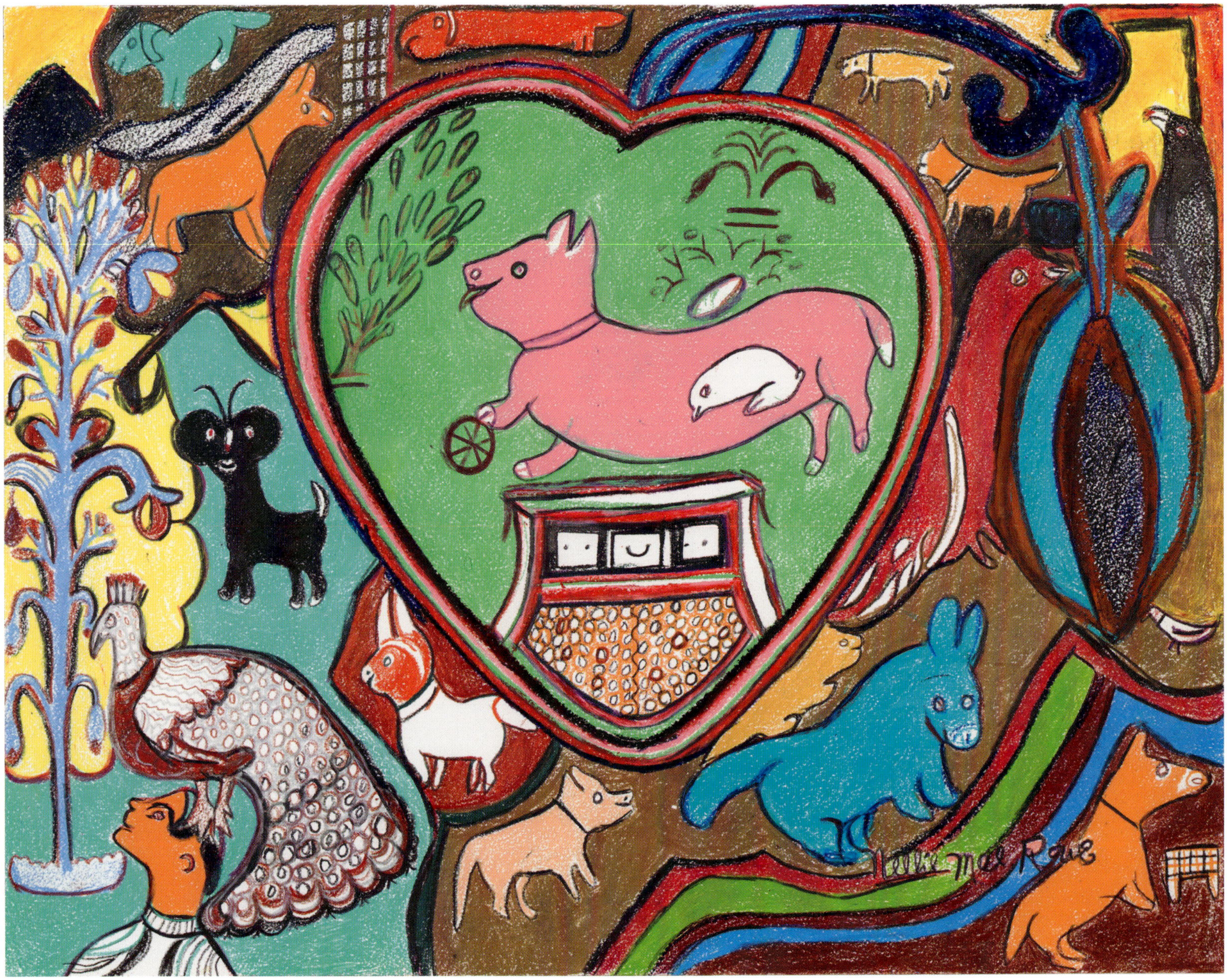

Cat. 33
Malcah Zeldis
Born 1931 as Malcah Brightman, New York City

Peaceable Kingdom
1977
enamel paint on Masonite
35 × 35 in. (88.9 × 88.9 cm)

Malcah Zeldis, who grew up in a Jewish neighborhood of Detroit, began to paint in earnest at the age of forty-three after graduating from Brooklyn College. Edward Hicks's *Peaceable Kingdom*, an icon of nineteenth-century American folk art, inspired this exuberant painting that celebrates living in harmony and may include Zeldis and her friends.

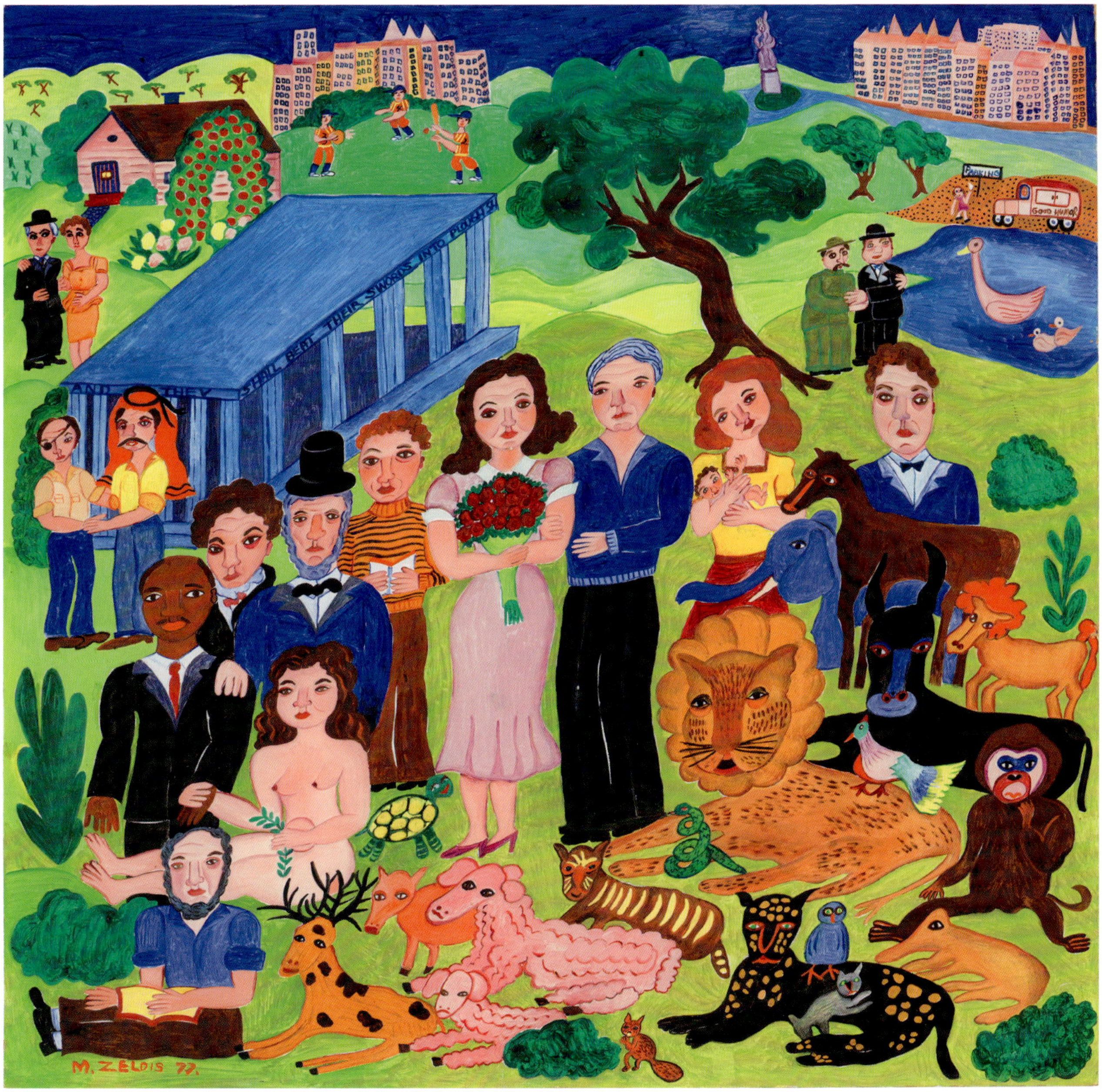

Cat. 34
Erich Grams
Born 1924 Altenfelde, East Prussia, Kingdom of Prussia
Died 1998 Germany

Playing Deer (Spielende Hirsche) (recto); **Untitled Fantasy** (verso)
1974
oil on wood panel
20 × 32 in. (50.8 × 81.3 cm); with decorated frame 21½ × 33¾ in. (54.6 × 85.7 cm)

After Erich Grams suffered two serious injuries while working in mining and in construction, he moved his family to Karlshausen in western Germany. One day in 1971, his young daughter asked her father to paint pictures on their house. Soon the entire home was covered inside and out. Grams also painted on boards, often working on the back and frame as well. Each painting is meant to depict an ideal, perfect world that has been lost.

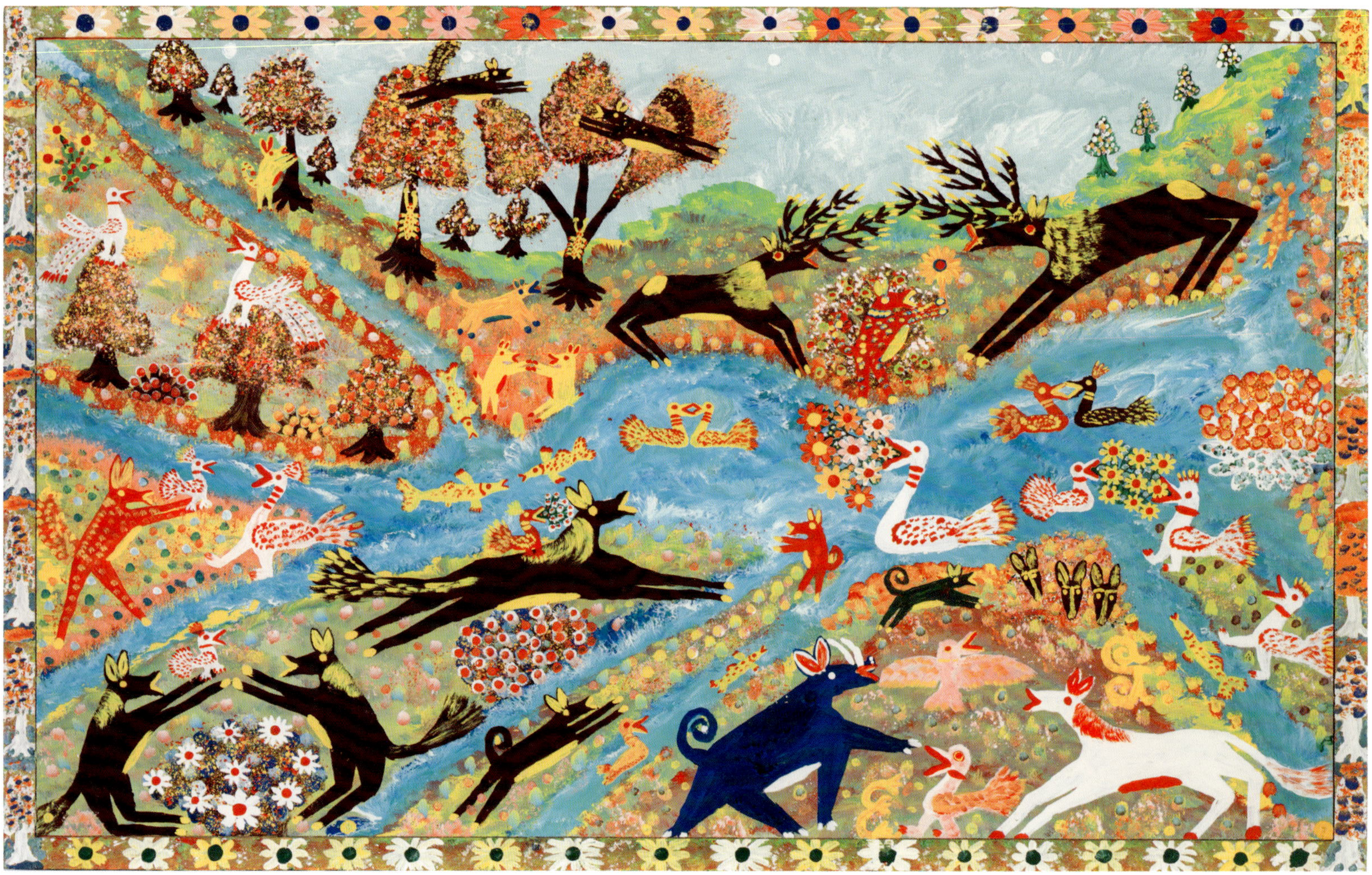

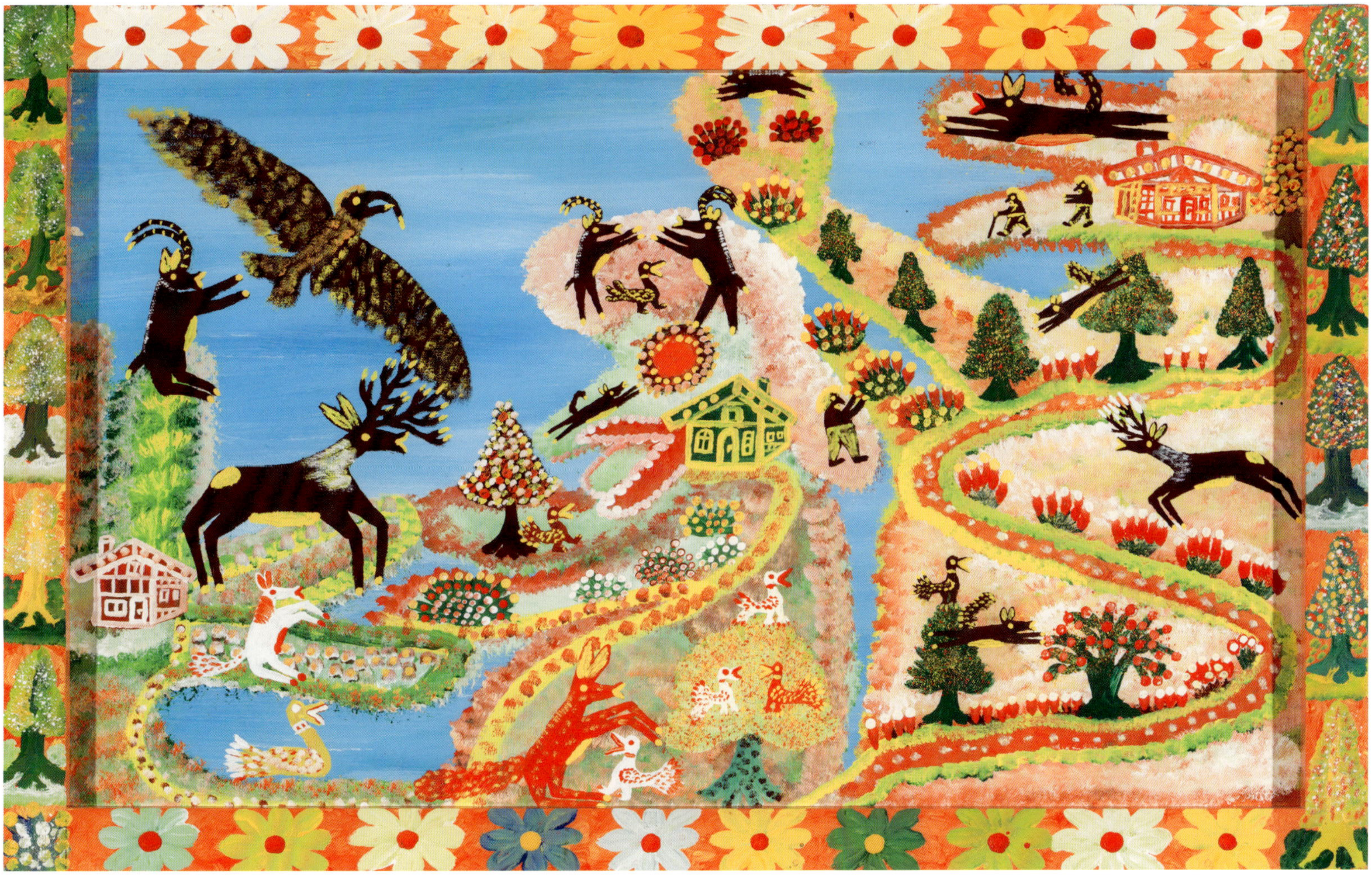

Cat. 35
Mary K. Borkowski
Born 1916 Sulphur Lick, Ohio
Died 2008 Dayton, Ohio

House Huntin'
1967
hand stitching, quilting, and appliqué on fabric
15¾ × 18¾ in. (40 × 47.6 cm)

"My cat, Sweetie Pie, came to me on Friday the thirteenth, in January 1967. My dog had died at the age of 18 the previous October, and I had a feeling that this little stray kitten knew there was a vacancy as she came straight to my door that dark cold night, bypassing all other houses."

Mary K. Borkowski, artist statement on reverse of *House Huntin'*.

Cat. 36
Mary K. Borkowski

Her Last Goodnight
1985
hand stitching and appliqué on fabric
26⅛ × 19⅛ in. (66.4 × 48.6 cm)

"Sweetie slept on the foot of my bed. Beginning one night, suddenly, and continuing every night for two weeks, she came up to me and licked first my left ear, then my right ear. One night she fell off the bed and couldn't get up, and died from a stroke on Friday, January 13. I realized her sudden licking of my ears was her way of telling me she loved me and was leaving now."

Mary K. Borkowski, "Sweetie," from *The Pets in My Life* (Columbus, OH: Barb Vogel, 2002), 17.

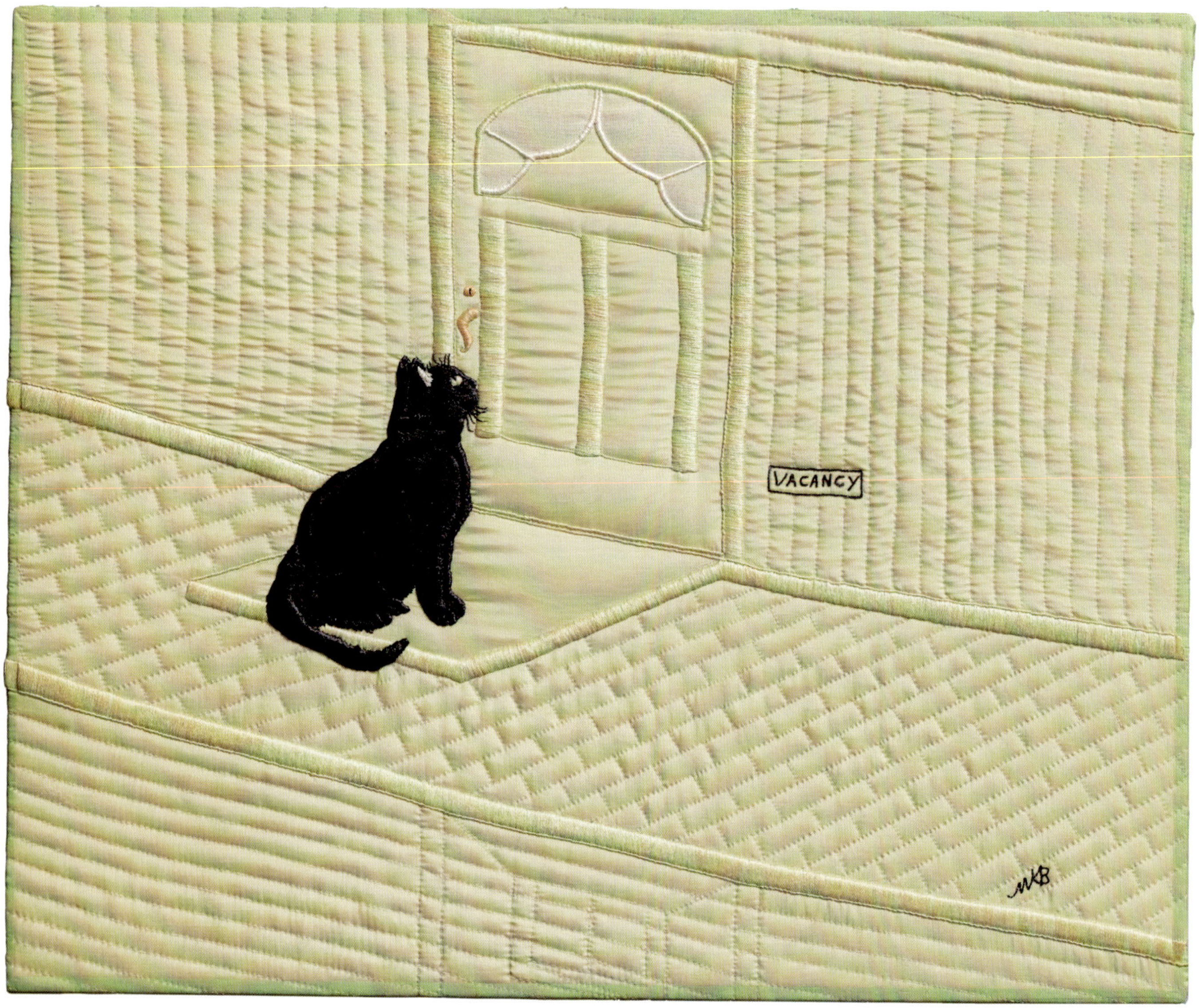

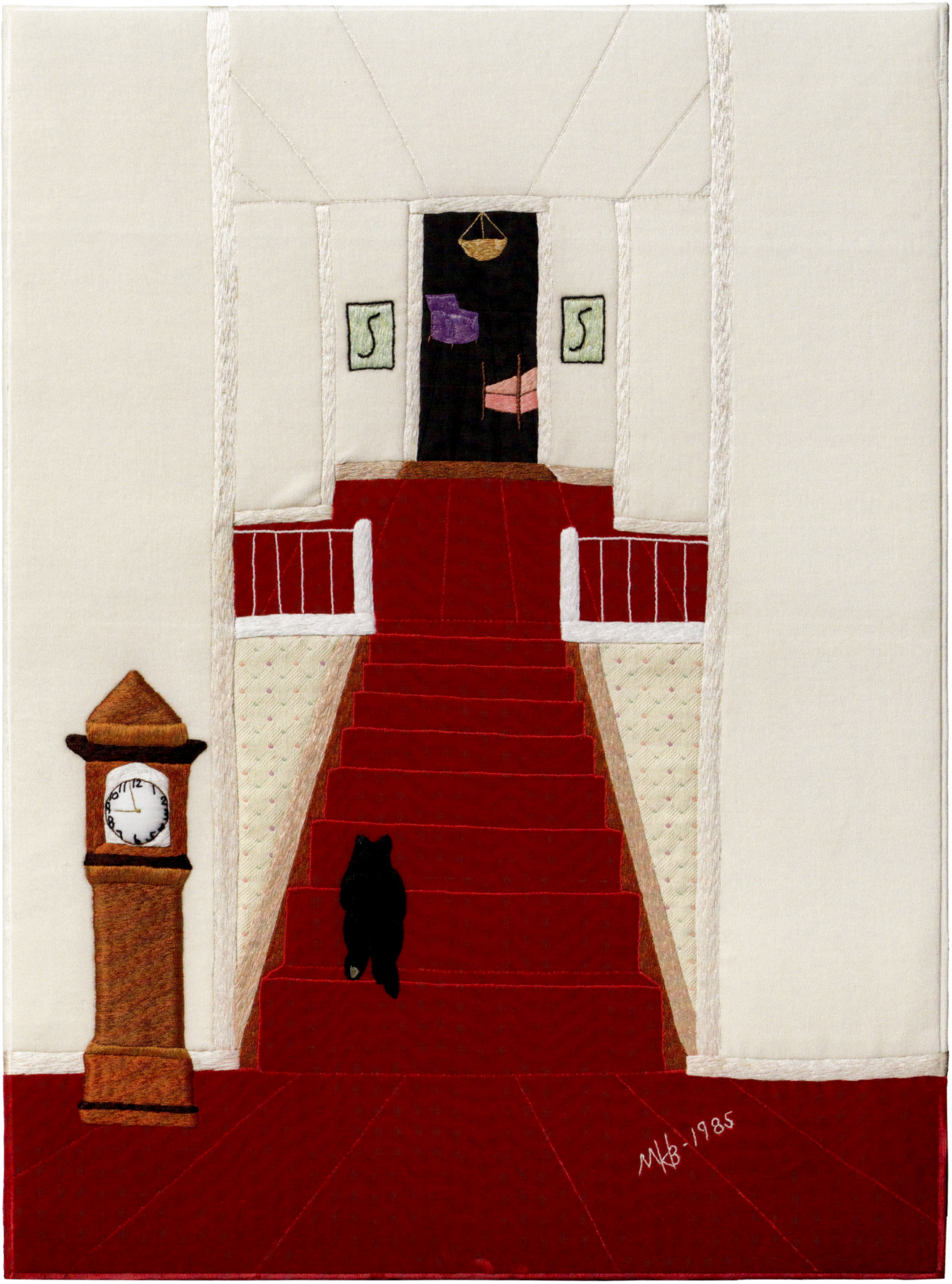
MKB-1985

Cat. 37
Earl Cunningham
Born 1893 Edgecomb, Maine
Died 1977 St. Augustine, Florida

Mill
1949–77
oil on fiberboard
18 × 24 in. (45.7 × 61 cm)

With pristine surfaces and bold designs, boatman and artist Earl Cunningham presents an idyllic, imagined nineteenth-century America. Perhaps hoping for the celebrity of Grandma Moses, Cunningham made business cards on which he touted himself a "primitive" artist.

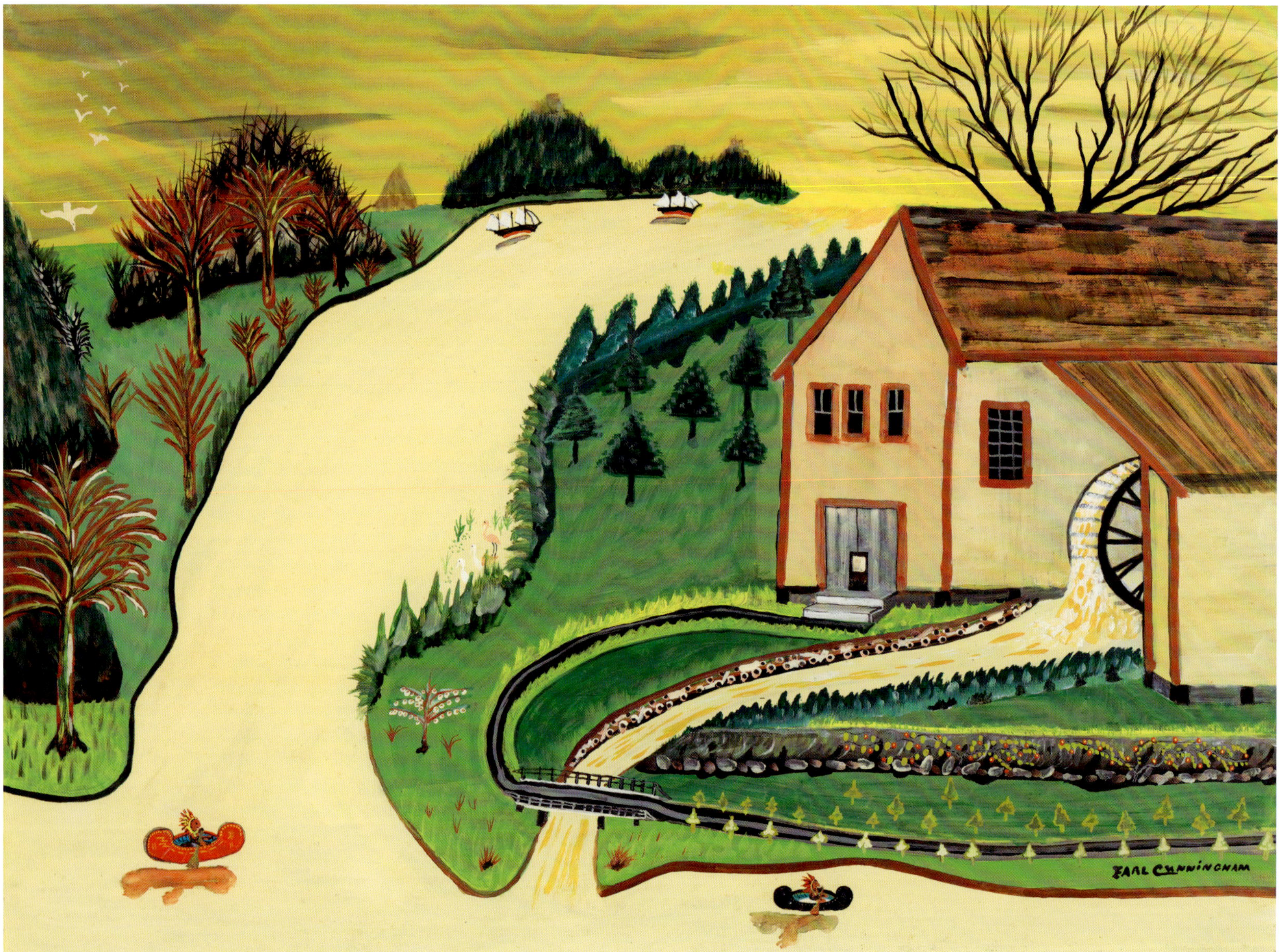

Cat. 38
Mary K. Borkowski
Born 1916 Sulphur Lick, Ohio
Died 2008 Dayton, Ohio

Toil, Strength, and Devotion
1973
hand stitching with silk thread on velvet
20⅛ × 29¼ in. (51.1 × 74.3 cm)

A collection of childhood memories on the family farm near Sulphur Lick, Ohio, inspired Mary K. Borkowski. Here, her father plants a field, diligently followed by the dog Tilly and Mary's beloved cat Sweetie Pie. Sheep turn toward her grandmother's home to escape the coming storm. "Tucked back in God's country, it was a big thing when we saw an airplane going over high in the sky. My favorite bird is the beautiful cardinal, so I had to include him and by his facing the horses in a test of bravery shows not by our size do we overcome."

Mary K. Borkowski, letter dated July 16, 1974, taped to reverse of *Toil, Strength, and Devotion*.

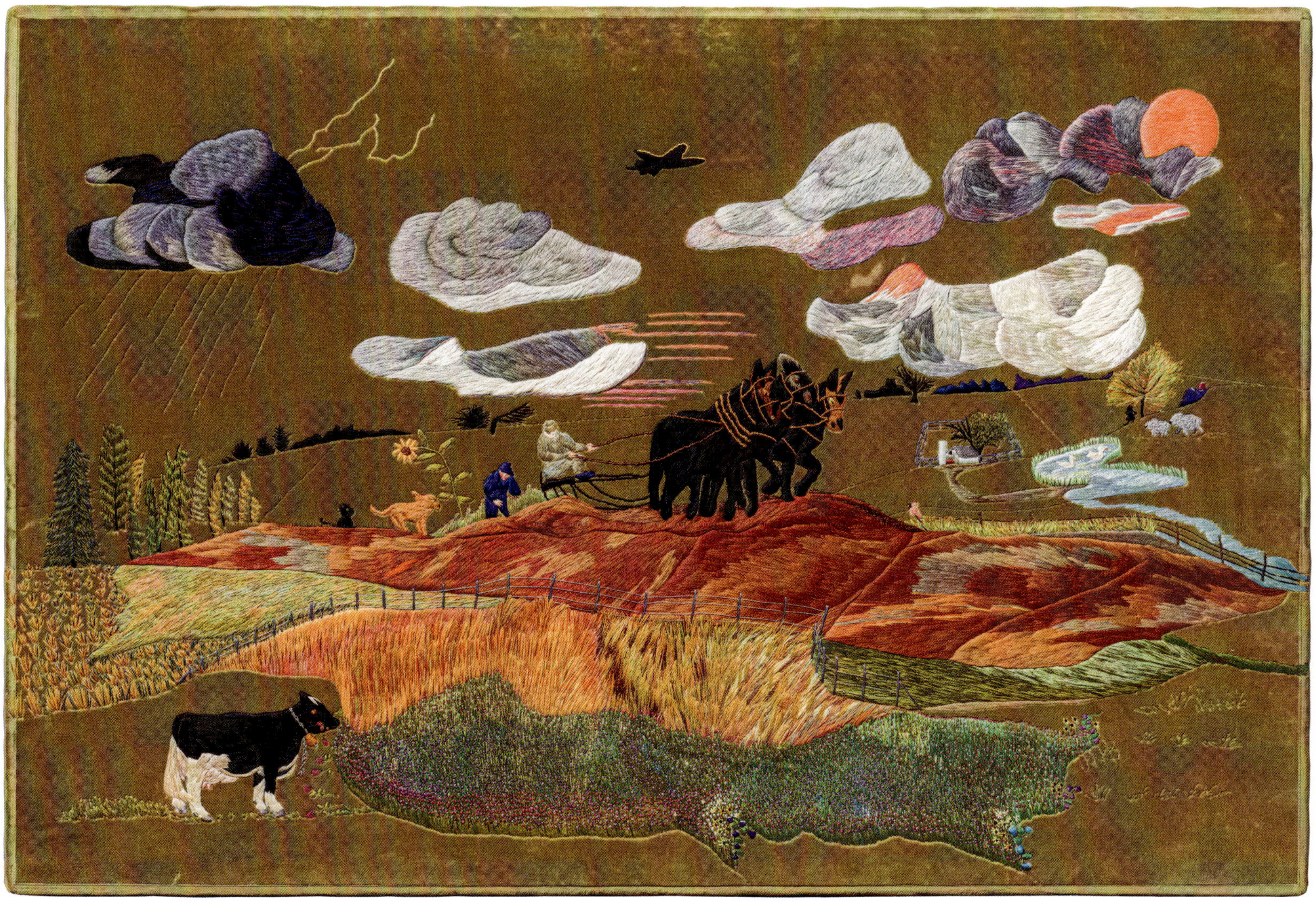

Cat. 39
Andy Kane
Born 1956 New York City

Welcome to N.Y.C.
1977
acrylic on canvas
30 × 40 in. (76.2 × 101.6 cm)

In *Welcome to N.Y.C.*, a subway train rattles in front of the city's skyline and cockroaches march along the bottom. This work was painted in New York City in the front room of the artist's aunt's apartment on 84th Street. It is one of his earliest attempts at acrylic painting, created when he was in his early twenties.

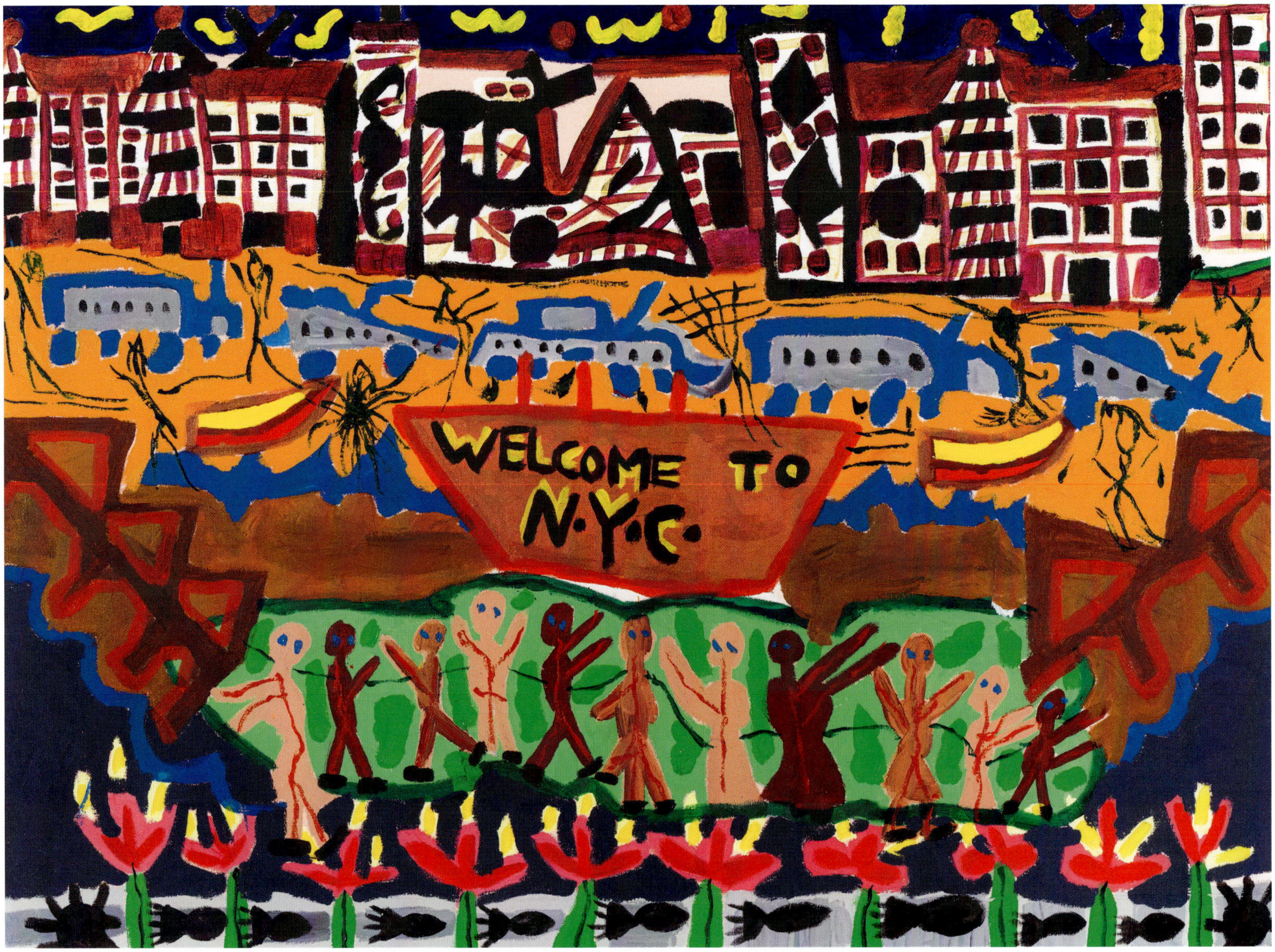

Cat. 40
Victor Joseph Gatto
Born 1893 New York City
Died 1965 Miami, Florida

The Train through the Mountains
1938–65
oil on canvas
25 × 30 in. (63.5 × 76.2 cm)

From New York City's Little Italy, Victor Joseph Gatto, who was frequently hard up for money, took up art at age forty-eight after seeing a $600 painting at an outdoor fair in Greenwich Village. His vivid, imaginative landscapes and other subjects gained him some renown.

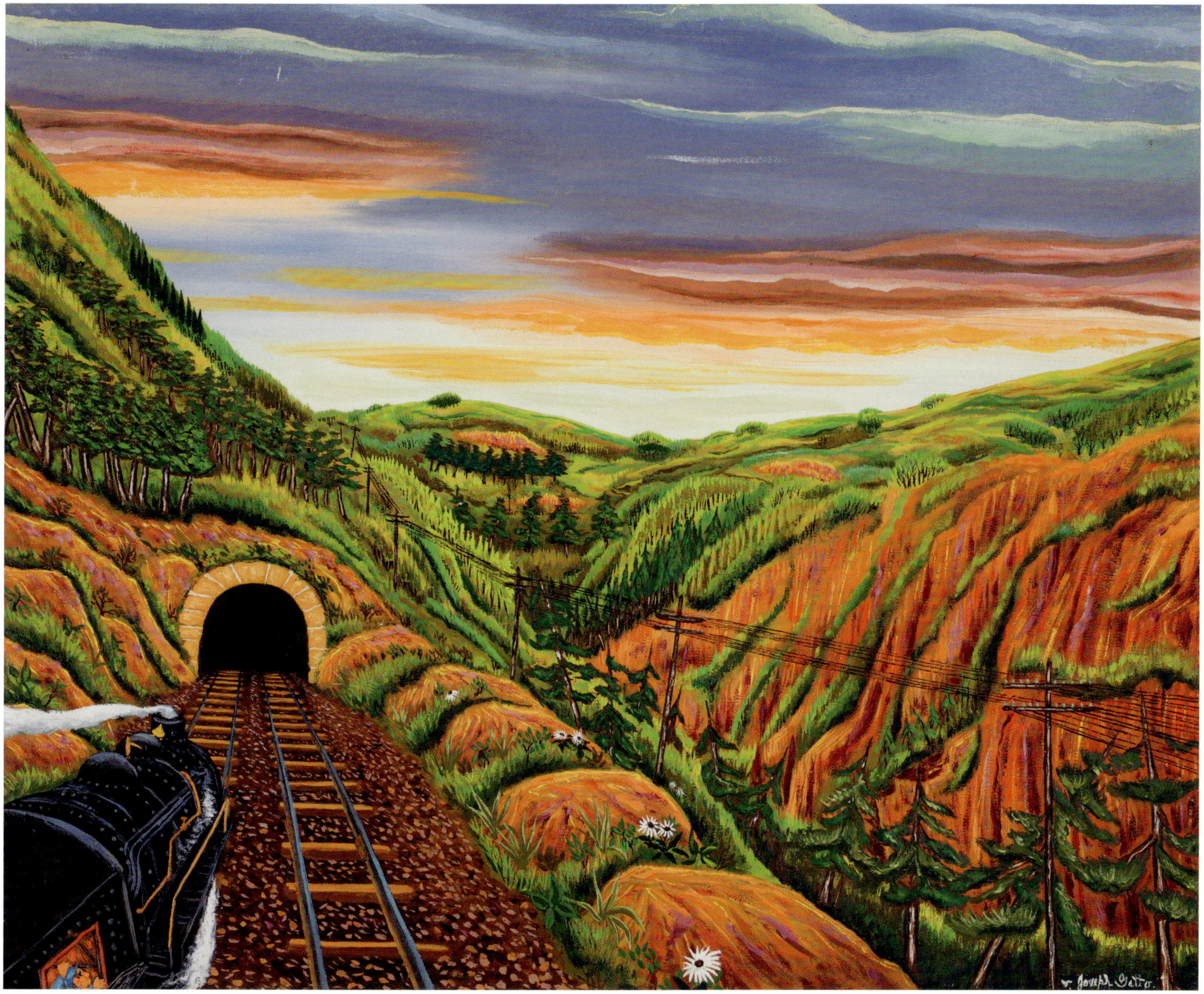

Cat. 41

David Zeldis

Born 1952 Israel, works in New York City

Untitled

1986

colored pencil on paper

8⅞ × 12 in. (22.6 × 30.5 cm)

Delicate, refined, surreal drawings are the hallmark of David Zeldis, the son of the self-taught artist Malcah Zeldis (see cat. 33). Complicating categorization, David Zeldis studied photography at the New York School of the Visual Arts. Museums have embraced his work, including those focused on the work of self-educated artists.

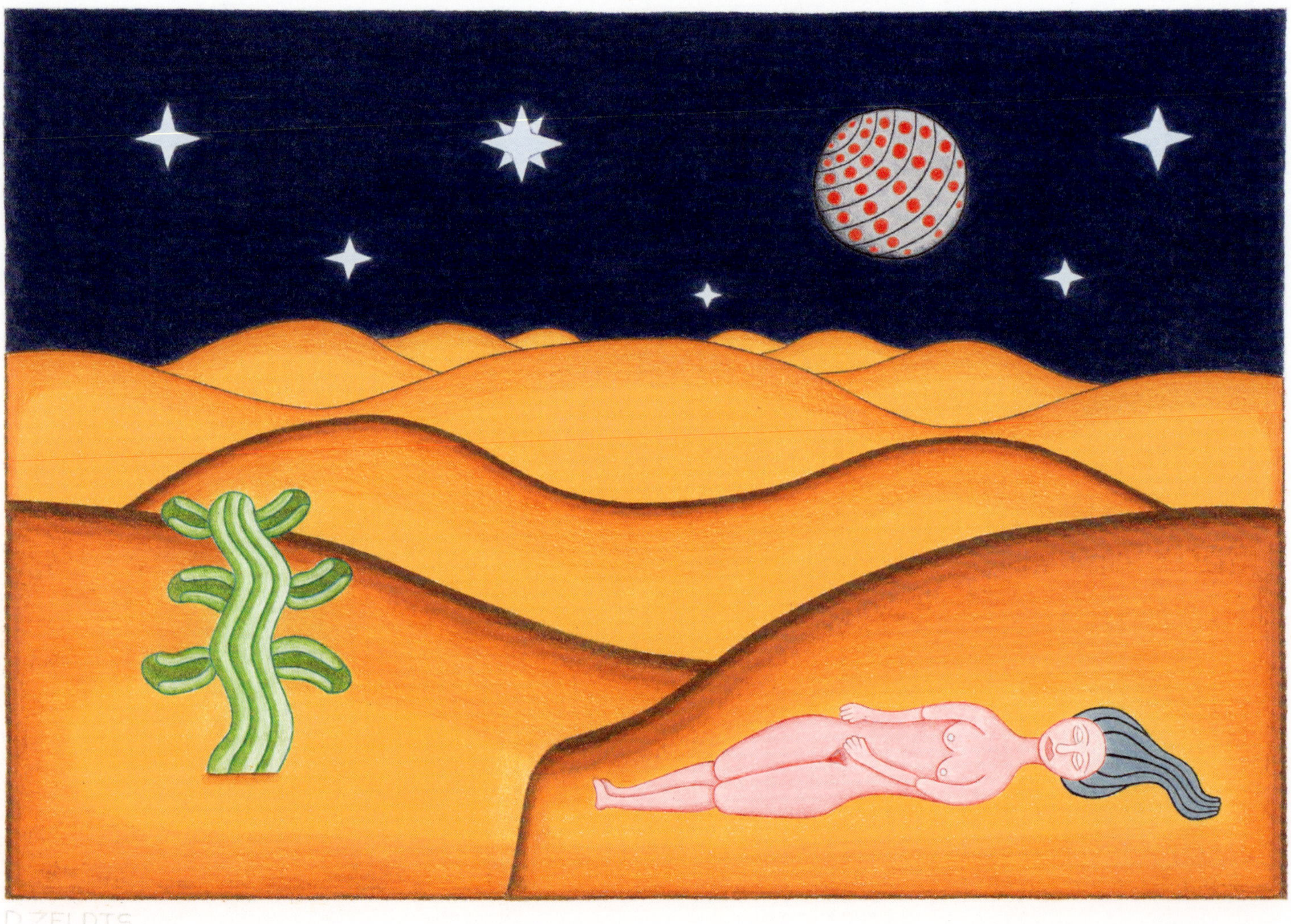

Cat. 42
Chan-Thien-My Company, Ltd.
Established 1996 Hanoi, Vietnam

Xuan
2016
embroidery on fabric
23½ × 32 in. (59.7 × 81.3 cm)

The Chan-Thien-My Company was founded in Hanoi in 1996 with the aim of providing people with disabilities with skills to allow them to become self-sustaining and offer support to their families and communities. Workshops in embroidery are among the offerings; a variety of landscape and still-life compositions in needlework are available to collectors via the organization's website.

Chan-Thien-My Company, http://hongngocvn.com, accessed June 30, 2022.

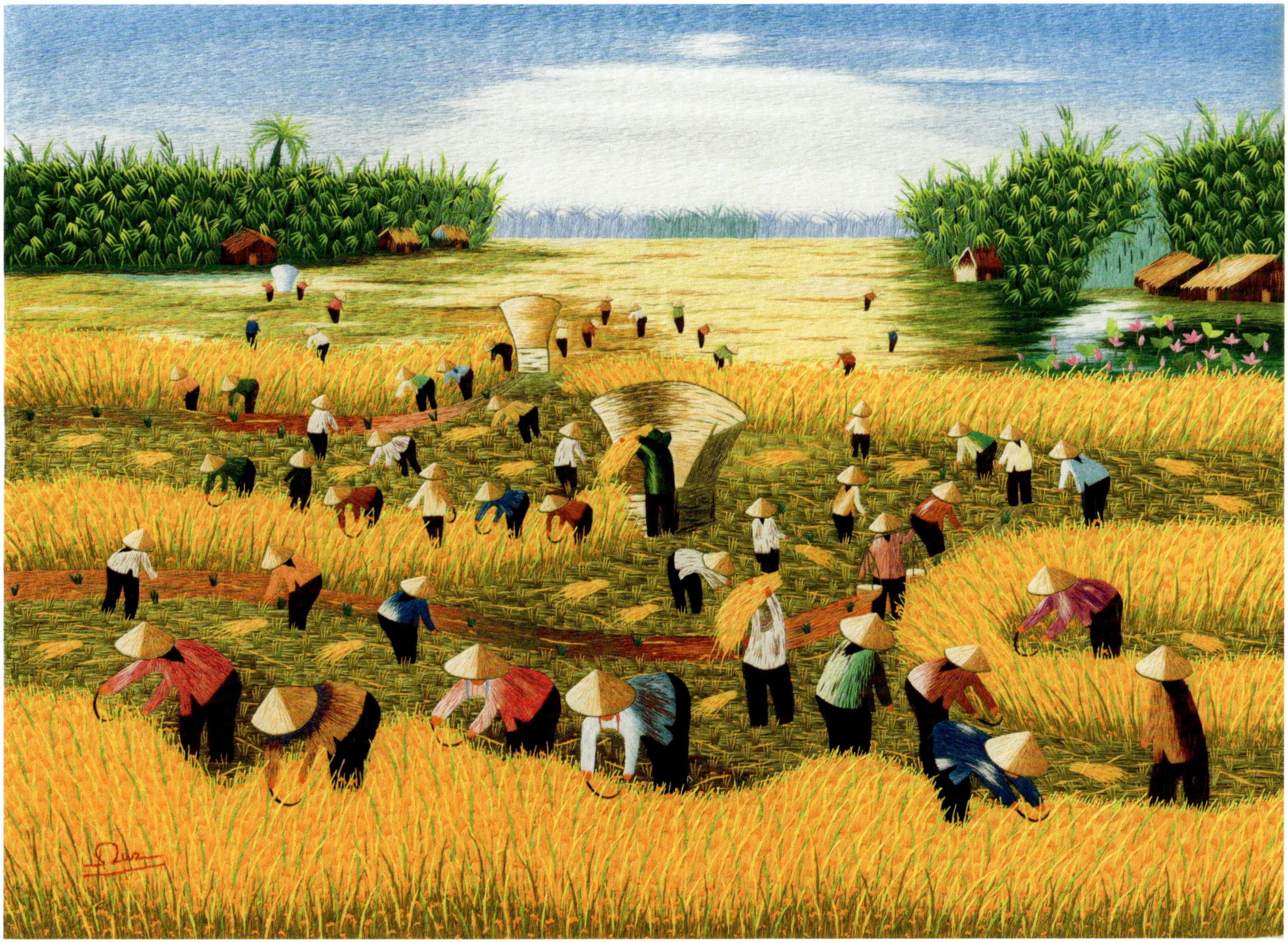

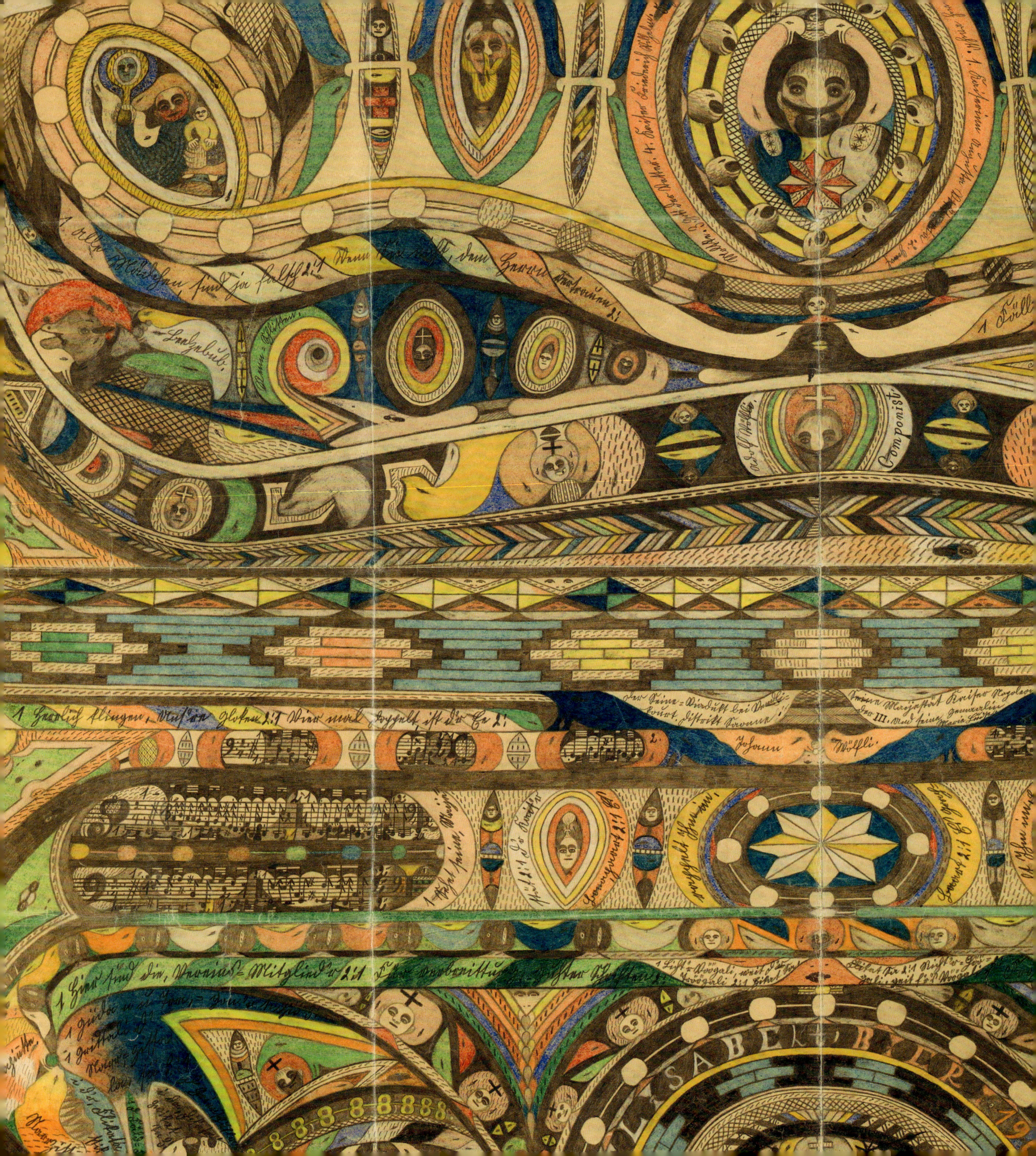
Componist
Johann
Wölfli.

Creating Connections

Reflections on the Rosenthal Collection

Charles Russell

The Rosenthal Collection presents a significant selection of works by a broad array of artists who have often been seen as representative of the fields of self-taught and "Outsider" art that emerged throughout the twentieth and early twenty-first centuries. These European, American, and international creations demonstrate a remarkable variety of aesthetic styles, media, and methods expressive of the personal intentions of artists creating largely independently of the dominant movements and primary concerns of modern art history. By entering the extensive holdings of the Cincinnati Art Museum, the Rosenthal Collection contributes to expanding our ways of understanding and appreciating the breadth and richness of art within our culture. It also encourages a larger and more nuanced historical overview of modern art.

This is an eclectic collection. What makes it so rich, yet at the same time so challenging to behold, is that while collectively the works exemplify many "types" of non-mainstream art, no single orientation dominates. Rather, there is a generous acceptance of multiple forms of individual and cultural visual creativity. Each individual artwork—and the collection as a whole—allows the museum viewer an opportunity (which the collector evidently enjoys) to encounter singular expressions of gifted, if untrained, artists and to appreciate how they illuminate and communicate both distinct and shared personal experiences across time and cultures.

Indeed, our viewing works in a collection such as this enables us to attend to the individuality of each creation in ways that may appear, at least initially, to be different from how we approach the artworks known to us from art history and previous museum exhibitions. Every piece seems to stand on its own before us, with little guiding art historical or biographical frames of reference. They each testify to a particular artist's need or desire to shape visual presentations of essential personal thoughts and feelings. Collectively, they demonstrate a fascinating range of creative self-expression and offer us as viewers the opportunity to recognize and respond as the distinct individuals that we are.

Although they are presented here as a collection, these works were created as manifestations of neither an art "movement" nor a school. Very few of their creators envisioned themselves participating in an "art world," or creating for the museum, and even more rarely did they see themselves as contributing to art history—although that is what they may increasingly do as we view them in this museum collection.

Cat. 45 (detail)
Adolf Wölfli, *Elisabeth Bieri*

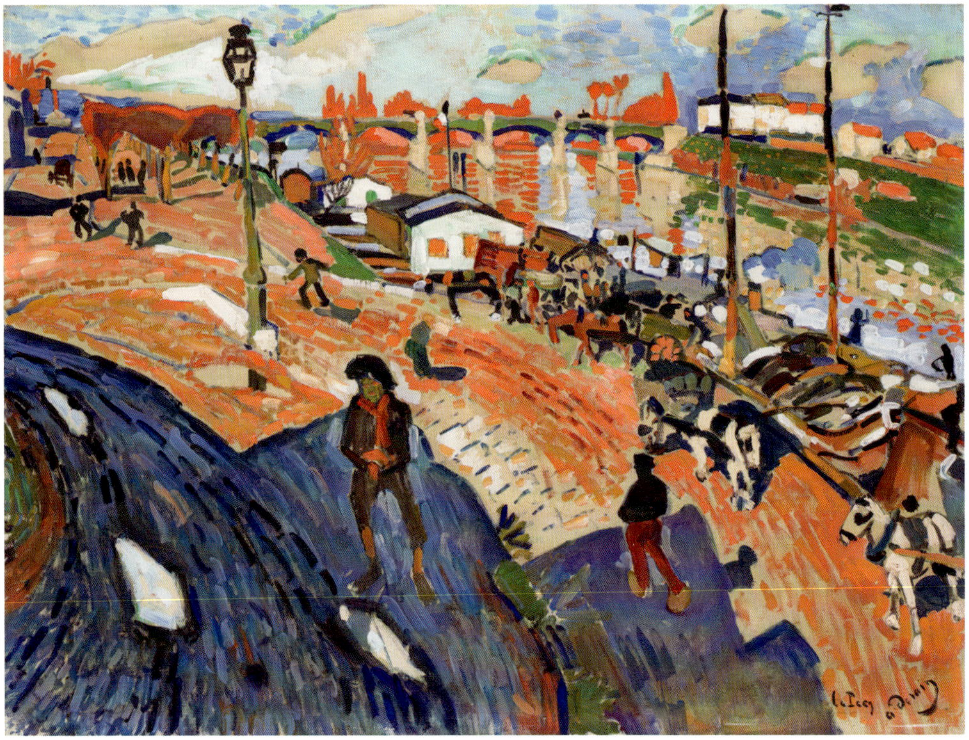

Fig. 3
André Derain (French, 1880–1954), *The Bridge at Le Pecq*, 1904–5, oil on canvas, 34¾ × 45½ in. (88.3 × 115.6 cm), Cincinnati Art Museum; Museum Purchase: Bequest of Mary E. Johnston, by exchange, and The Edwin and Virginia Irwin Memorial, 2005.16

While their creators may not have participated in any art movements, works like these in the Rosenthal Collection have frequently been grouped variously together under narrowly descriptive labels, each focusing on but a single, specific aspect of the ubiquitous creative activity in the lives of their makers and within the culture at large. Yet even those imperfect designations can suggest how these distinctive, if idiosyncratic, works attest to the great variety of artistic visual creativity unexpectedly to be found throughout society. Every term may tell us something about an artist's personal vision and the immediate cultural contexts from which artworks can emerge. Terms such as *primitive* and *naïve art* have referenced apparently unsophisticated stylistic elements that demonstrate a lack of artistic training. *Folk* and *vernacular art* have located artworks primarily within shared traditional and even contemporary regional, class, or ethnic visual styles and cultural behaviors. Alternatively, the terms *visionary* and *Art Brut* still invoke the presumably primal, even instinctual sources of creativity out of which arise passionate expressions of artistic freedom and uniquely personal vision. Furthermore, over the past several decades, works like those in the Rosenthal Collection have frequently been labeled either

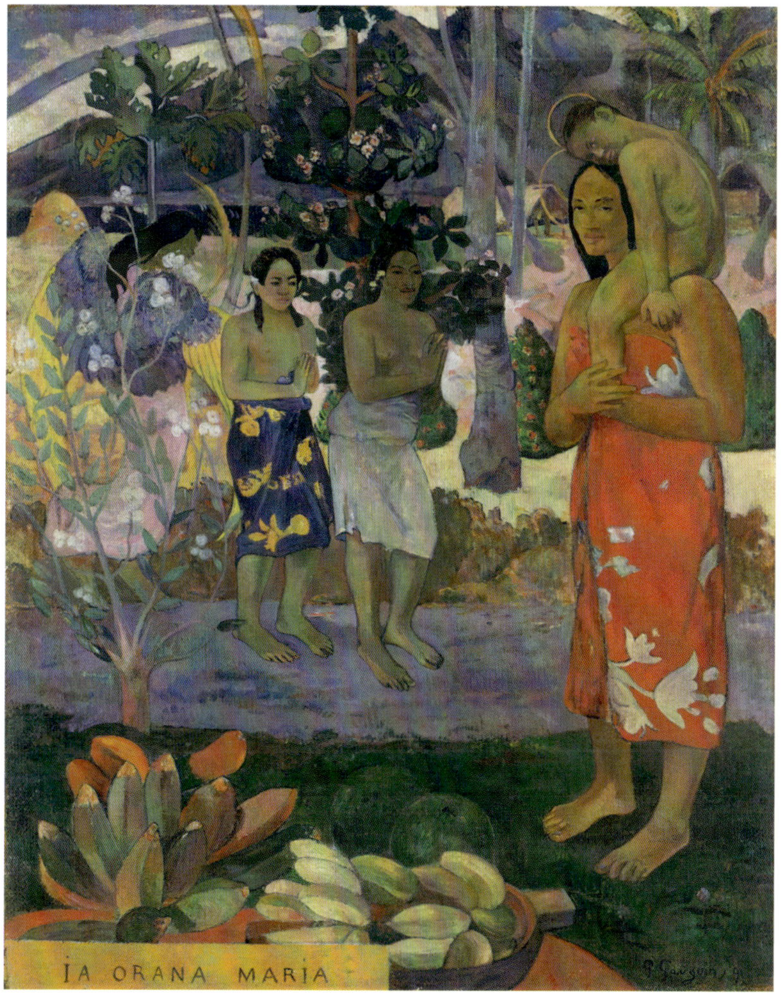

Fig. 4
Paul Gauguin (French, 1848–1903),
Ia Orana Maria (Hail Mary), 1891,
oil on canvas, 44¾ × 34½ in. (113.7 × 87.6 cm),
The Metropolitan Museum of Art, New York;
Bequest of Sam A. Lewisohn, 1951, 51.112.2

self-taught or *Outsider art*. *Self-taught* designates artists who have willfully developed their own distinctive aesthetic style, drawing freely from both individual experiences and observations of their local or mass culture visual environment. The category of the "Outsider" stresses an artist's cultural position, often on the margins of the social order, either because of intensely personal life choices or distressed mental condition, or merely that of creating "outside" the particular concerns of the dominant art world.

Yet, however illuminating these labels may be, concerning either individual works or their shared sensibilities and techniques, they act as reductive, qualifying terms limiting our awareness of the fullness of aesthetic behavior. The focus on particular elements serves to separate these artworks from the broader concept of "Art" in general. Each designated "type" of art is seen as lesser than what is usually considered as the art of art history, the art of the "art world." Of course, this institutional conception of the art world often bears similarly qualifying labels: *fine* art, *high* art, *mainstream* art, all terms that also signal the relativity and hierarchy of cultural values and should encourage us to question their contemporary relevance.

It is, however, art historically significant, and perhaps ironic, that the initial identification of "non-mainstream" art forms was itself a product of the modernist and vanguard art world. The self-taught and "Outsider" artists were largely "discovered" by artists who were seeking new visual strategies to align the capacities of art with the cultural dynamics of the modern world.

We are familiar with a history of modern Western art since the mid-nineteenth century recounted largely as a series of artistic movements identified by their innovations in aesthetic practice. Spurred by their sense of living within a dramatically new and constantly changing era, modern artists asserted that their times demanded an art that reflected and advanced new ways of perceiving and experiencing the world. Through the succession of movements—such as Impressionism, Fauvism (fig. 3), Cubism, Futurism, Constructivism, Surrealism, and beyond into the time of Pop, conceptual, minimal art and the neo-avant-garde forms of postmodernism—artists appear to have been echoing the proclamation of the French poet Rimbaud: “Il faut être absolument moderne” (one must be absolutely modern).[1] This mission required continuous aesthetic innovation, in effect an incessant art world dialectic driven by, on the one hand, the need to break free from the conventions of the past academy—or even the preceding movement—and on the other, the search for, or invention of, new forms of visual articulation.

In the quest for innovative practices, modernist artists apprehended, and often selectively appropriated, elements and strategies of visual expressive behavior found outside the existing art world. They mined not only the visual vocabularies expressive of other social sectors of their culture (as well as in other cultures) but also the seemingly idiosyncratic visual achievements of marginalized individuals within their own society: those who had little, if any, connection to the world of art. Notably, these discoveries helped spur modernist invention. Ultimately, however, they also expanded our ways of understanding art well beyond the formalist concerns that have defined much of modern art history. This led to the appreciation of artworks such as those in the Rosenthal Collection.

Some early modernist artists were drawn to the forms of visual expression in other cultures. Paul Gauguin, for

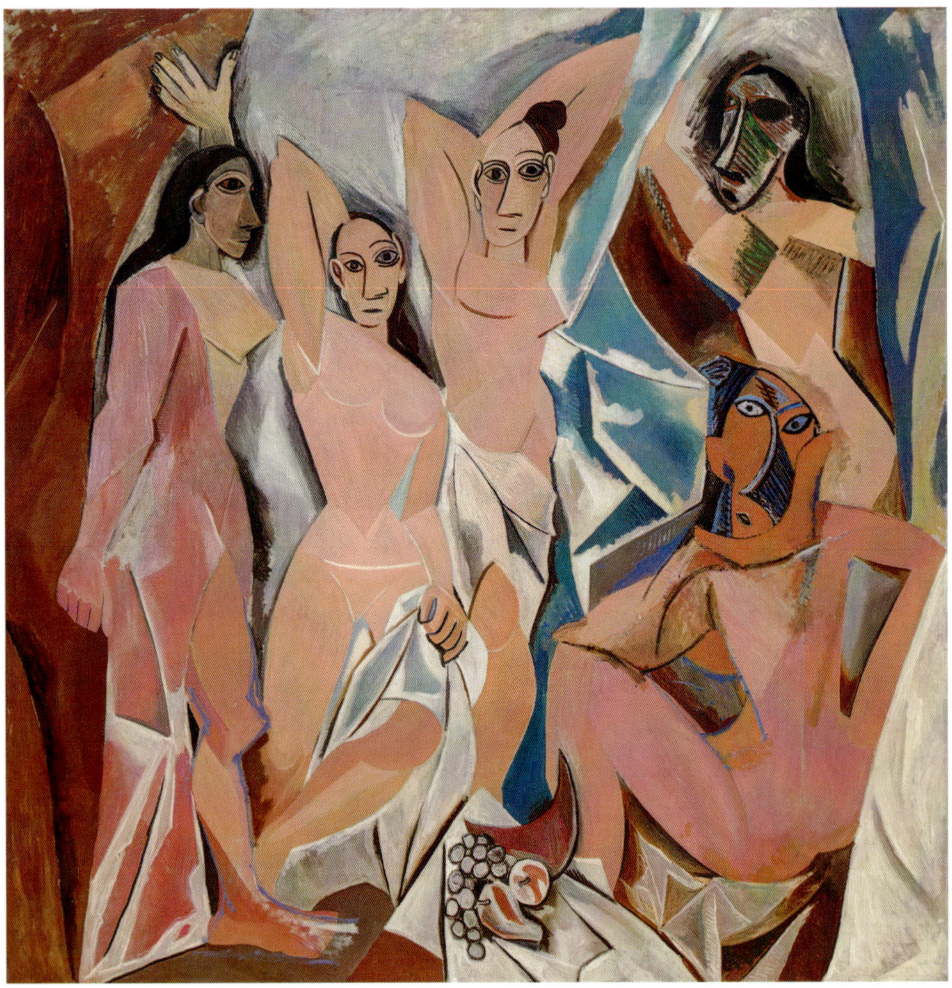

Fig. 5
Pablo Picasso (Spanish, 1881–1973), *Les Demoiselles d'Avignon*, 1907, oil on canvas, 96 × 92 in. (243.9 × 233.7 cm), Museum of Modern Art; Acquired through the Lillie P. Bliss Bequest (by exchange), 333.1939

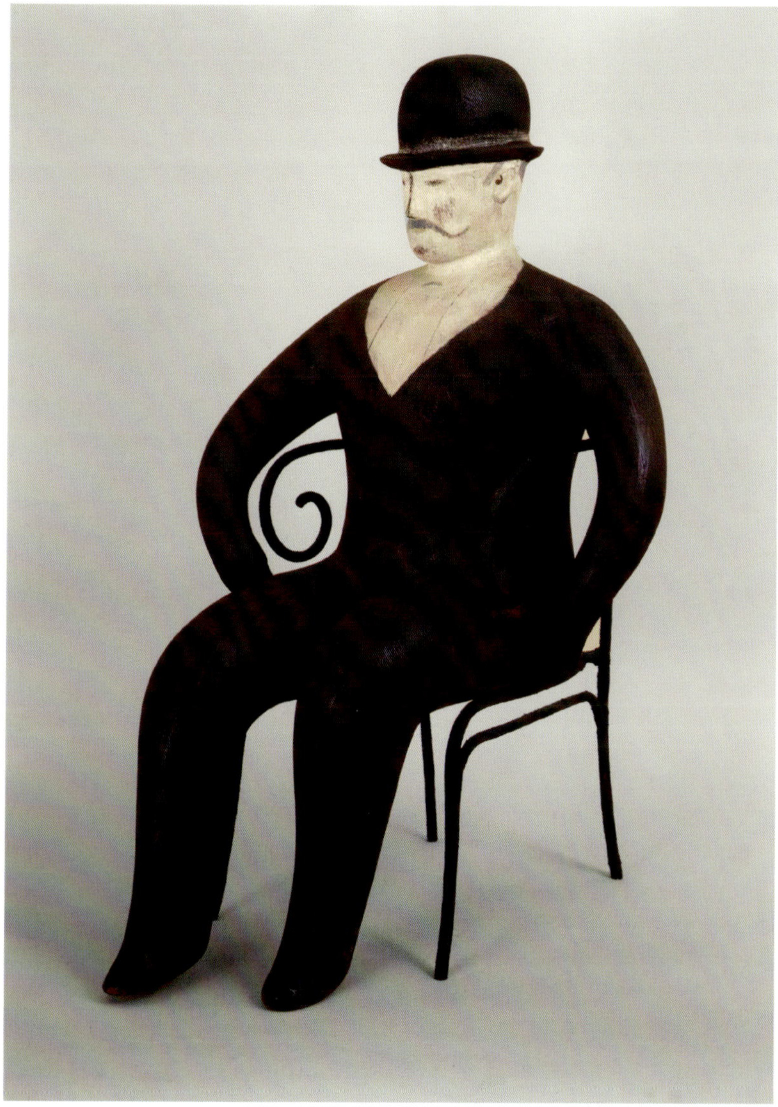

Fig. 6
Elie Nadelman (American, 1882–1946), *Host*, circa 1920–23, cherrywood, gesso, paint, and wrought iron, 28½ × 15 × 18½ in. (72.4 × 38.1 × 47 cm), Columbus Museum of Art; Museum Purchase, Derby Fund and funds from the Sessions and Schumacher Collections, 2001.001

one, responded first to the rustic culture of Brittany and then to that of South Pacific Polynesia (fig. 4). Similarly, many French artists were attracted to Japanese aesthetics, resulting in the popular style of Japonisme, which freely adapted visual elements for modernist purposes with little regard for what they meant to the original culture. More dramatically, the encounter of the Fauves and Matisse, then Picasso (fig. 5), with the expressive and plastic qualities of African cult objects inspired radical inventions in figuration and composition. Yet, even though Picasso and other artists sensed the intended magical force and social agency of a work of African sculpture, neither the identity of the object's creator nor the artwork's particular message was relevant to the aesthetic pursuits of the European appropriators.

A similar appreciation of cultural aesthetic creativity outside the art world inspired American modernists such as Elie Nadelman (fig. 6), Charles Demuth, and Charles Sheeler who found the plain-style visual grammar of early American folk art useful for their own formalist invention. Subsequently, the interest of American curators, critics, and artists shifted from the creations of a past, romanticized folk culture to the visual practices of previously overlooked regional and ethnic populations, such as African Americans and Indigenous Americans. Consequently, in addition to influencing modernist practices, this development both awakened an appreciation of the social dimensions of artistic creation and broadened the recognition of self-taught artists of note.

Such an informed regard for the force and variety of vernacular visual expression is especially observable in the Rosenthal Collection in works by a number of American artists, among them Bill Traylor, Thornton Dial, David Butler,

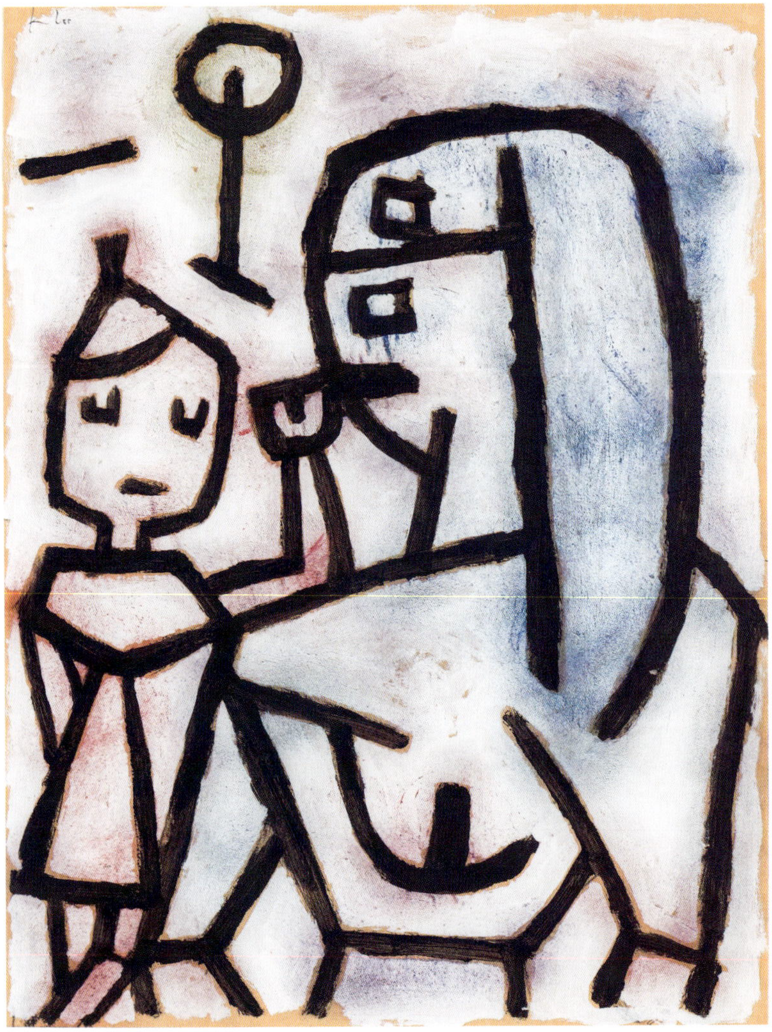

Fig. 7
Paul Klee (Swiss, 1879–1940), *Alte Frau Darf Versuchen*, 1939, oil, colored pastel, and tempera on paper, 23 11/16 × 17 9/16 in. (60.2 × 44.6 cm), Cincinnati Art Museum; Bequest of George Rieveschl, Jr., 2007.222

Sister Gertrude Morgan, Minnie Evans, Bessie Harvey, Nellie Mae Rowe, Ned Cartledge, Earl Cunningham, Victor Joseph Gatto, Louis Monza, Ralph Fasanella, and Mary K. Borkowski, as well as several unidentified creators. These artworks make it particularly clear to the perceptive viewer that while they exemplify types of shared expressive behavior within their immediate culture, they each demonstrate how singular artists find within those communal practices opportunities for unique expressions of personal agency.

A similar recognition of the power and mystery of unexpected, intuitive artistic expression inspired other modernist artists seeking new aesthetic strategies. Individual artists, such as Emil Nolde, Oskar Kokoschka, and Paul Klee (fig. 7), as well as members of the Dada group and Surrealist movement, were intrigued by isolate or marginal figures within their own culture whose work they saw as unfettered expressions of instinctive drives and primal states of being. Presumably unaffected by what the modernist artists considered to be a dominant and ultimately repressive culture, such artists appeared to demonstrate a distinctive state of selfhood on their own visual terms.

Works of such singular European and American artists whose intensely unique creativity seemed to flourish independently of the premises and practices of the art world are found in the Rosenthal Collection. These include examples by Adolf Wölfli, Carlo Zinelli, Henry Darger, and Martín Ramírez, as well as Dwight Mackintosh, Malcolm McKesson, Edmund Monsiel, Damian Le Bas, Paul Duhem, Eddie Arning, and Friedrich Schröder-Sonnenstern.

To the artist Jean Dubuffet (fig. 8), who coined the term *Art Brut*, the works of these untutored or mentally distressed artists indicated a disruptive and essentially "anti-cultural" vision damningly absent from the established art world.[2]

Cat. 37 (detail)
Earl Cunningham, *Mill*

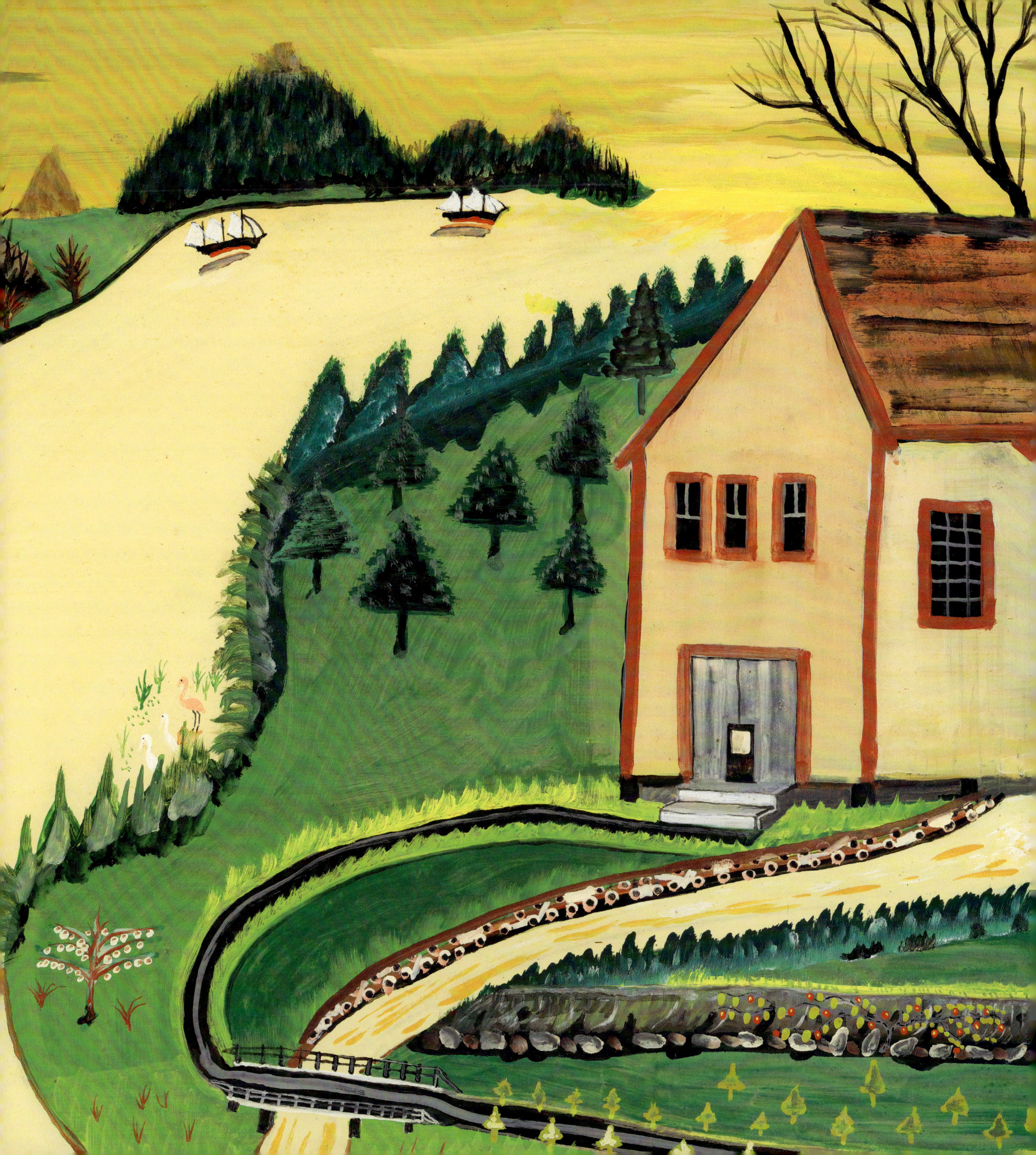

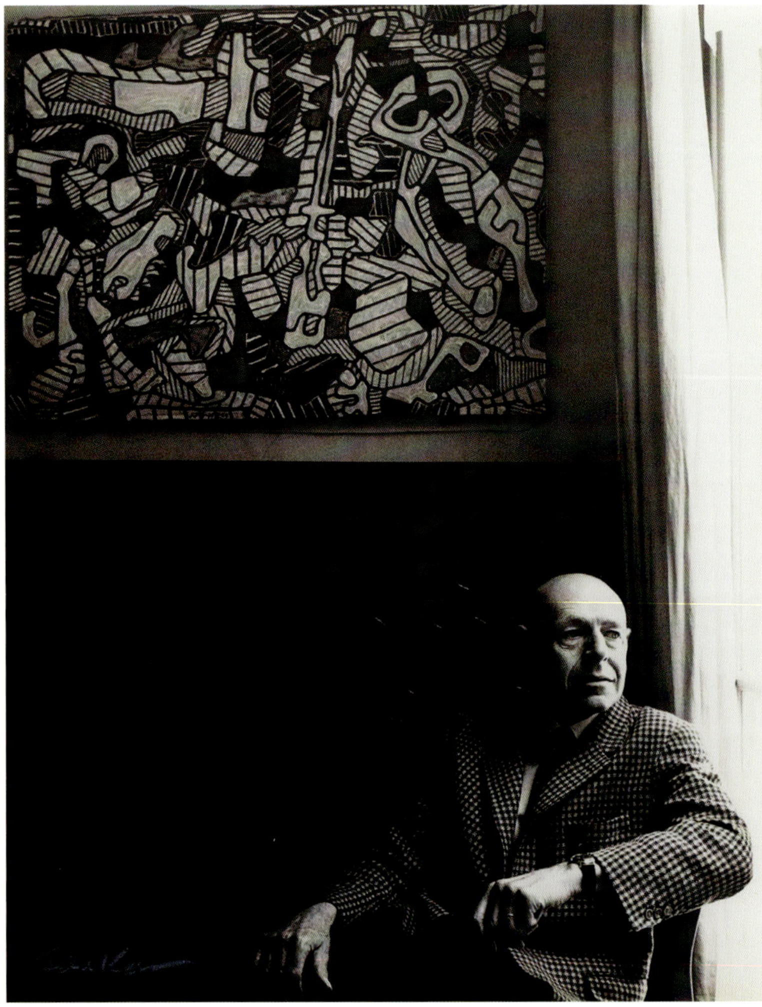

Fig. 8
Ida Kar (1908–1974), *Jean Philippe Arthur Dubuffet*, 1964, bromide print, 7⅛ × 9¼ in. (18.1 × 23.5 cm), National Portrait Gallery, London, NPGx132498

Nonetheless, even while their creations appeared to justify the vanguard vision of challenging existing cultural conventions (and had a clear influence on Dubuffet's own art, seen in cats. 43, 44, 59), they were not perceived as sharing that mission, and their works were preserved—by Dubuffet—outside the frame of the art world. And indeed, until relatively recently, the works of such artists have not been considered relevant to the dominant concerns of the mainstream art world.

With their eyes fixated on how new aesthetic effects might be found in either the art forms of folk or distant cultures or in the work of untutored, marginal figures in their own society, the modernists tended to see only portions of what the art they encountered truly offered. One result has been the plethora of reductive labels applied to the works in the Rosenthal Collection and the many types of self-taught and "Outsider" art, each focused upon elements of formal achievements and personal expression that have been abstracted from, or rather separated from, the integral nature of artistic creation.

For us now to appreciate more fully the artistic achievement and the cultural significance of these non-mainstream artists, we should view artistic creativity from a more integrative approach to personal expression and social engagement. While there are numerous ways of addressing these issues, it is fitting that one especially insightful and still resonant model appeared within an early psychological study of "Outsider Art," the groundbreaking work *Artistry of the Mentally Ill* (1922) by Hans Prinzhorn, a doctor at the psychiatric clinic of the University of Heidelberg, who in addition to his medical and psychiatric training held a doctorate in art history (fig. 9).[3]

Having analyzed thousands of visual creations by hundreds of institutionalized patients, Prinzhorn discerned six recurring patterns within the works' structural configurations, which he identified as manifestations of instinctive drives toward "self-actualization." By this he meant how an individual brings into visible form a conception of self that is projected into the world. By the creative act, the artist presents an expression of self not only *in* the world, but *to* the world. In essence, self-actualization is inherently an effort to bridge an individual's sense of separation from others. Furthermore, Prinzhorn recognized that because the viewers of artworks are themselves subject to similar instinctive drives and desires to overcome the inherent separation between themselves and others, they are predisposed to respond personally to the creator's psychic self-expression.

Although Prinzhorn's insights derived from the study of creative behavior of the mentally ill, he insisted that none of these expressive drives is, in itself, symptomatic of mental illness. Rather, they are to be found in all forms of normal human expressive behavior, and certainly in art, whether mainstream or non-mainstream. The six instinctive configurative drives toward self-actualization that Prinzhorn described are those of self-expression, ordering and/or arranging, imitation, ornamentation, play, and creating symbolic meaning. Prinzhorn also observed that while any one of these may appear dominant in an artwork, they all can contribute to other inflections of self-expression in the work as well. Nor do the individual drives identify distinct types of art. In fact, it is worth briefly considering these drives separately to recognize how commonly they are expressed by different creators of both mainstream and non-mainstream art.

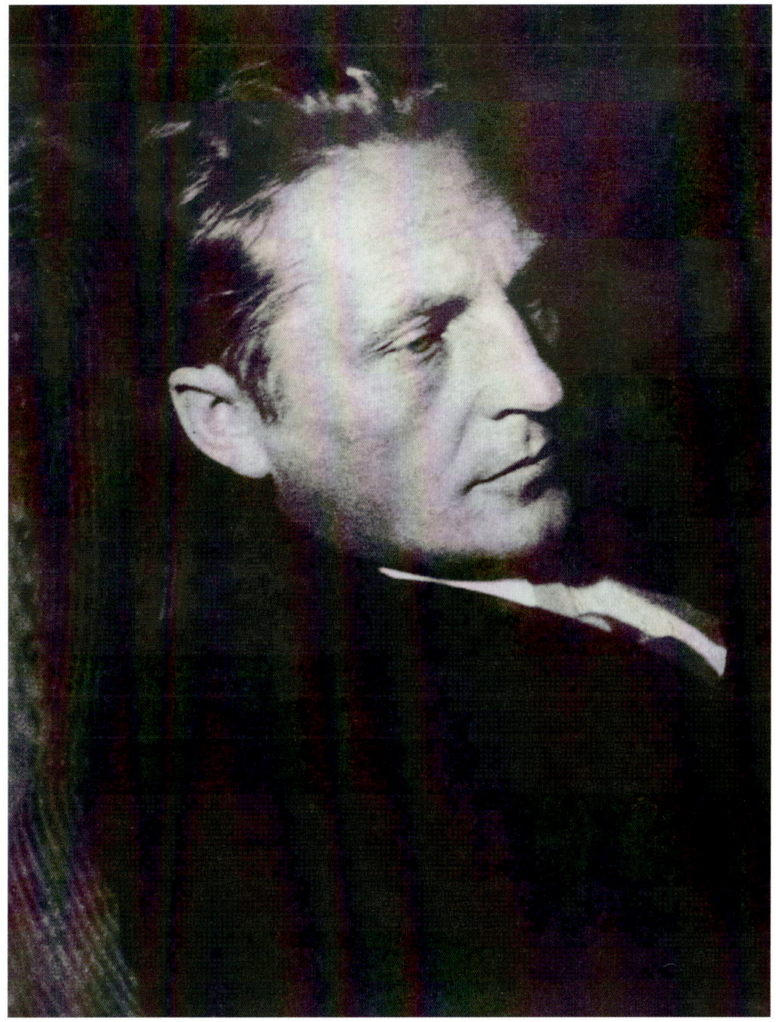

Fig. 9
Hans Prinzhorn (1886–1913), photograph from *Beyond Reason: Art and Psychosis, Works from the Prinzhorn Collection* (London: Hayward Gallery, 1997), 6

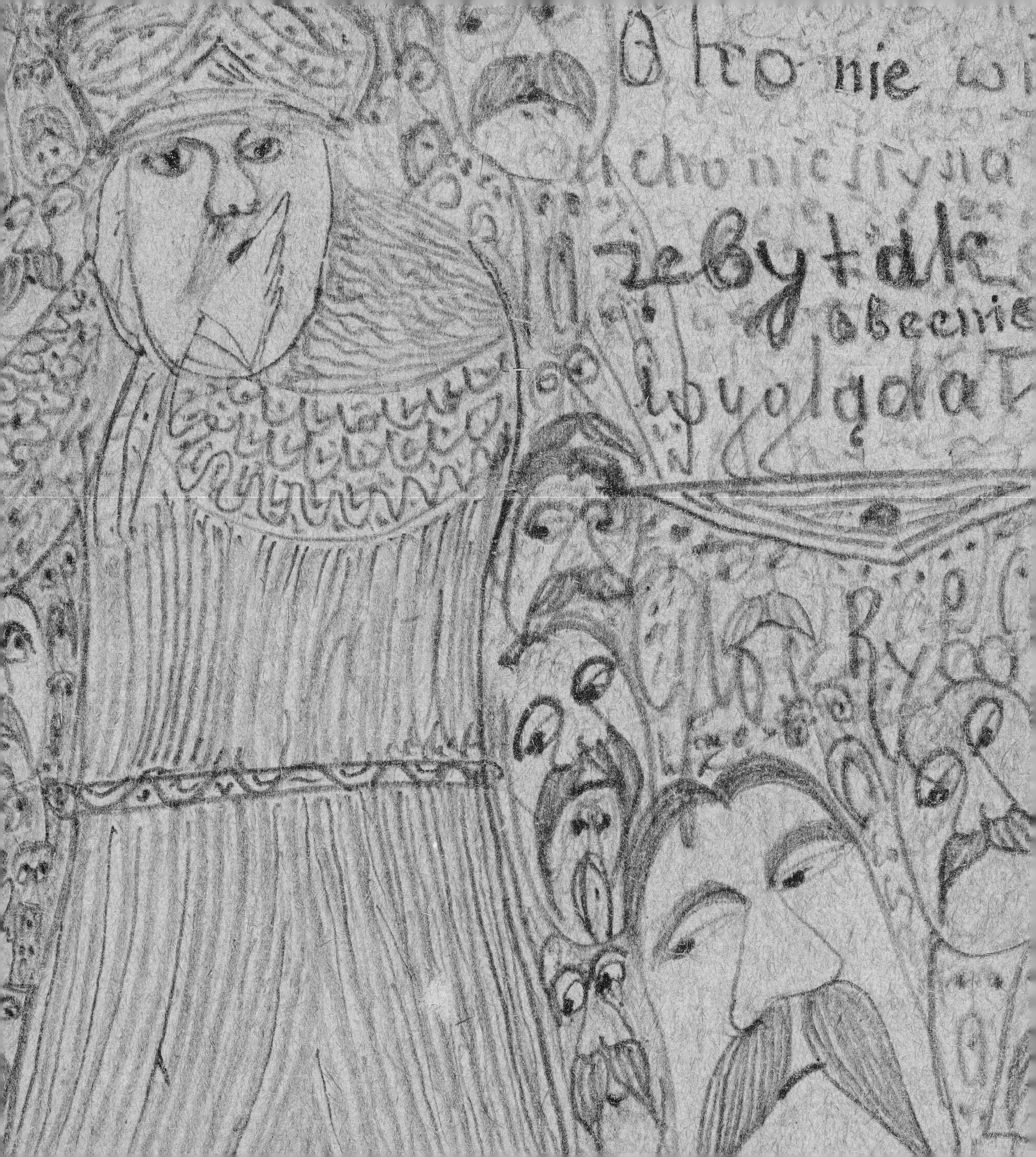
kto nie
żeby tak
obecnie
wyglądał

Self-expression In effect, all six instinctive configurative drives toward self-actualization result in statements of self-expression, but some works bring the articulation of selfhood primarily to view. Probably the most literal form of such expression is the self-portrait, the visual projection of one's inner awareness that reveals a vision of self that is meant to be seen by others. Yet we might even perceive a self-reflective action in the depiction of those others (including ourselves?) looking back at the artist. Thus, a dramatic image of a solitary face on an empty ground, as in Paul Duhem's stark figure (cat. 62) or the image of a face looming toward the viewer in Albert Louden's painting (cat. 61) might be a self-portrait or the imposing mien of an Other. And a sense of the artist may be expressed, if perhaps challenged, when what is depicted is not a single observer but a crowd of staring, interwoven faces, as those in the works of Edmund Monsiel, Nick Blinko, Janet Sobel, and Damian Le Bas (cats. 53, 54, 60, 71, 72).

Ordering/Arranging The fundamental challenge for all artists is to compose the visual image in order to focus the viewer's attention most effectively on both the meanings and feelings expressed within it. The individual artist's act of shaping the composition is an existential expression of both a desired internal order and the need to discern or command patterns of coherence and meaning external to oneself. For some artists, the composition as a rigorously defined visual artifice carries its primary meaning and expresses the satisfactions of singularly personal achievement. For instance, Adolf Wölfli's densely structured yet lyrical compositions (cat. 45) suggest a rich, if mysterious, cosmic order from within which peer dozens of tiny faces, all representing Wölfli. Similarly, Martín Ramírez's ornately patterned drawings (cat. 51) feature profoundly ordered landscapes in which personally meaningful events or figures dramatically occur. In contrast, Ken Grimes shapes minimalist compositions with a mantra-like repetition of words and symbols expressing his profound belief in the existence of traces of alien contact (cat. 69).

Imitation Mimetic depiction of the world is a common means of expression of creative agency evident in many forms of art. By capturing visual aspects of the physical world, the artist positions the self within a known or imagined realm of special import. The depiction may take such diverse forms as the sculptural figures of Thornton Dial and Nek Chand (cats. 11, 12, 31); active scenes of presumably "significant events," as in the art of Bill Traylor (cat. 7); and romanticized projections of observed or imagined landscapes, such as those portrayed by Earl Cunningham, Mary K. Borkowski, and Victor Joseph Gatto (cats. 37, 38, 40). Yet what is "imitated" may also be pictures created by others, such as the magazine or mass culture images that spurred the imaginative works of William Hawkins and Eddie Arning (cats. 24, 49).

Ornamentation The drive for ornamentation expresses both taking pleasure in the world and the desire to improve it—to celebrate and enhance one's experience. It adds to what exists and transforms the ordinary into the extraordinary. The colorful markings on both sides of David Butler's sculpture (cat. 29), the interplay of bright hue and fluid design in Nellie Mae Rowe's work (cat. 32), and the exuberance of the packed visual fields of Erich Grams (cat. 34) demonstrate the drive to see more and to say more. By these means, artists also may demonstrate

Cat. 53 (detail)
Edmund Monsiel, *Untitled*

their mastery of the given, offering to the viewer a vision of delight or beauty, and certainly a sense of stable, if vibrant, order.

Play As in the process of ornamentation, the instinctive drive to play evokes a state of exploration and self-creation not constrained by the limits of given reality. It's a manifestation of imaginative freedom to configure and enjoy realms of fulfilled desire. As an expressive configuration arising from imaginative play, art envisions a willed but unbounded range of thought and emotional possibility. Clearly, there is a playful sensibility at work in the vernacular, or "folk," creations of Clarence and Grace Woolsey (cat. 26) and the carvings and constructions by unidentified artists in the Rosenthal Collection (cats. 1, 3–5, 25, 27). Yet we might well imagine a more intimate state of meditative play in the precisely, if perhaps obsessively, ordered and yet decorative creations of Hiroyuki Doi (cat. 58) and Charles Benefiel (cats. 55–57).

Symbolic meaning The configuration of forms of symbolic meaning manifests perhaps the most complex and outgoing instinctive drive for self-expression: to create a visual image that carries deeply personal yet socially resonant emotional and conceptual insights. By its very nature, a symbol refers to a realm of meaning beyond its particular image, usually evoking a dimension of values or belief shared by others within the culture. Symbolic works make evident that however strong the instinctive drive for self-expression, the artist seeks not only to affirm a singular awareness of self in the world, but to bridge an existential sense of separateness from others. Expressing selfhood through symbolic forms is to insert an individual voice within the collective visual discourse, to reach beyond self to connect to the thoughts and feelings of others.

Symbols, especially those found in a culture's religious beliefs or political contexts, link artists and the viewers within shared frames of resonant social meaning and value. Such symbolic artworks may present intensely individualistic interpretations of widely recognized mythic images, as in Friedrich Schröder-Sonnenstern's death's head within a cut apple offered on a plate (cat. 46), or the Judgment Day scenes of Donald Pass (cat. 63). But often we are offered quieter, more intimate testimonies of spiritual expression, as in the works by Bessie Harvey, Minnie Evans, and Sister Gertrude Morgan (cats. 8–10). In addition, what is communicated through the symbolic image may be the willed declaration of the artist's sense of personal agency, the intention to act in and on the world, to address and affect the thoughts of others. This can be evident especially when the imagery challenges, rather than affirms, the symbols of social order, as do the political critiques of artists, such as Ralph Fasanella's depiction of a massive workers' rally in response to distressing social conditions (cat. 17), Louis Monza's ironic scene of a wounded veteran and smug businessman (cat. 18), and Ned Cartledge's sardonic images of hypocritical distortions of supposedly sacred religious and political symbols (cats. 20–23).

However personal, even idiosyncratic, the individual artist's interpretation of shared symbolic imagery, we may find ourselves responding to the works as meaningful visual statements and find personal connection to the thoughts and emotions of others. We may not only be moved by depictions of previously unknown or familiar images and symbols, and by the manner of their visual configuration,

Cat. 69 (detail)
Ken Grimes, *WOW*

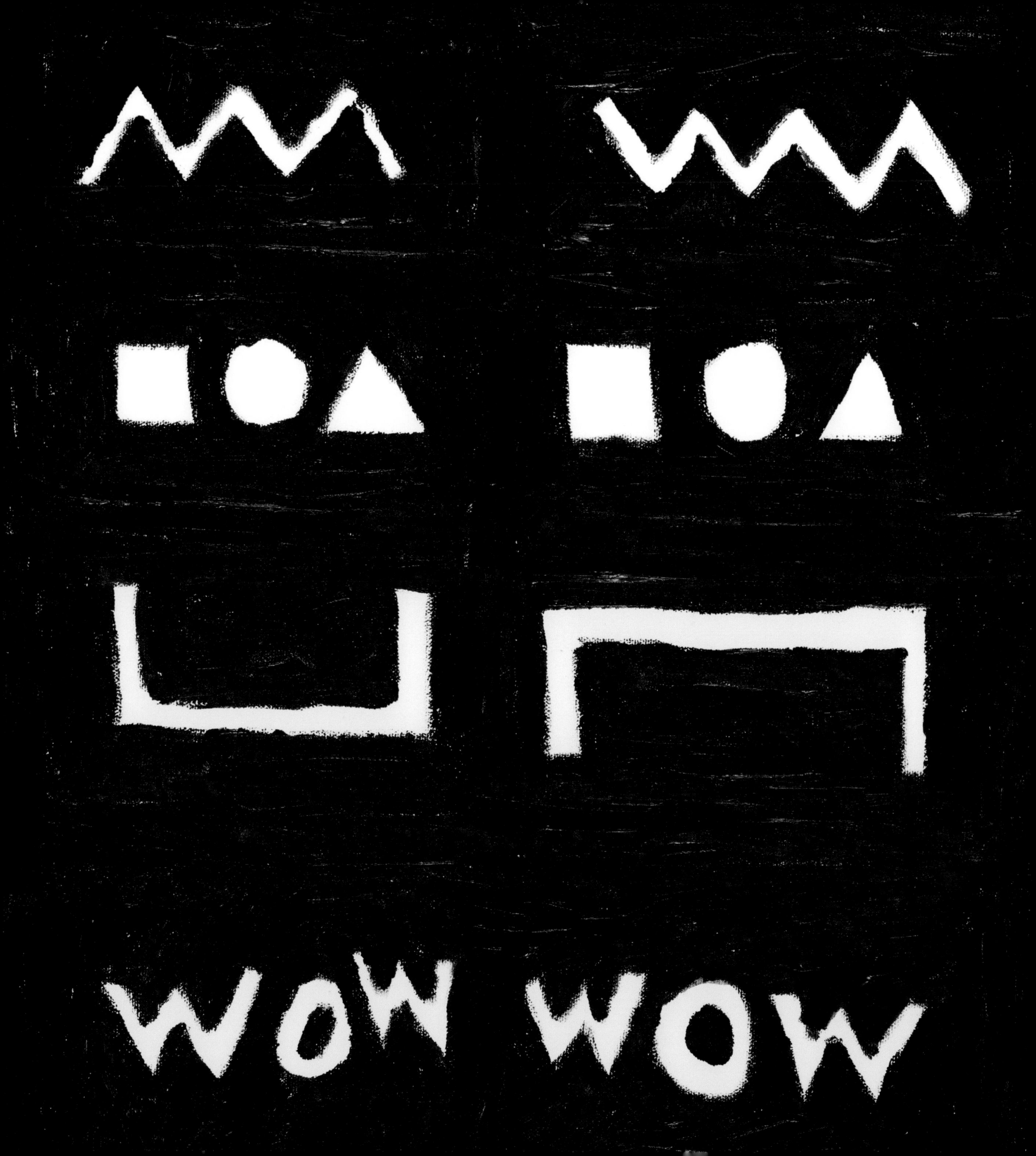
WOW WOW

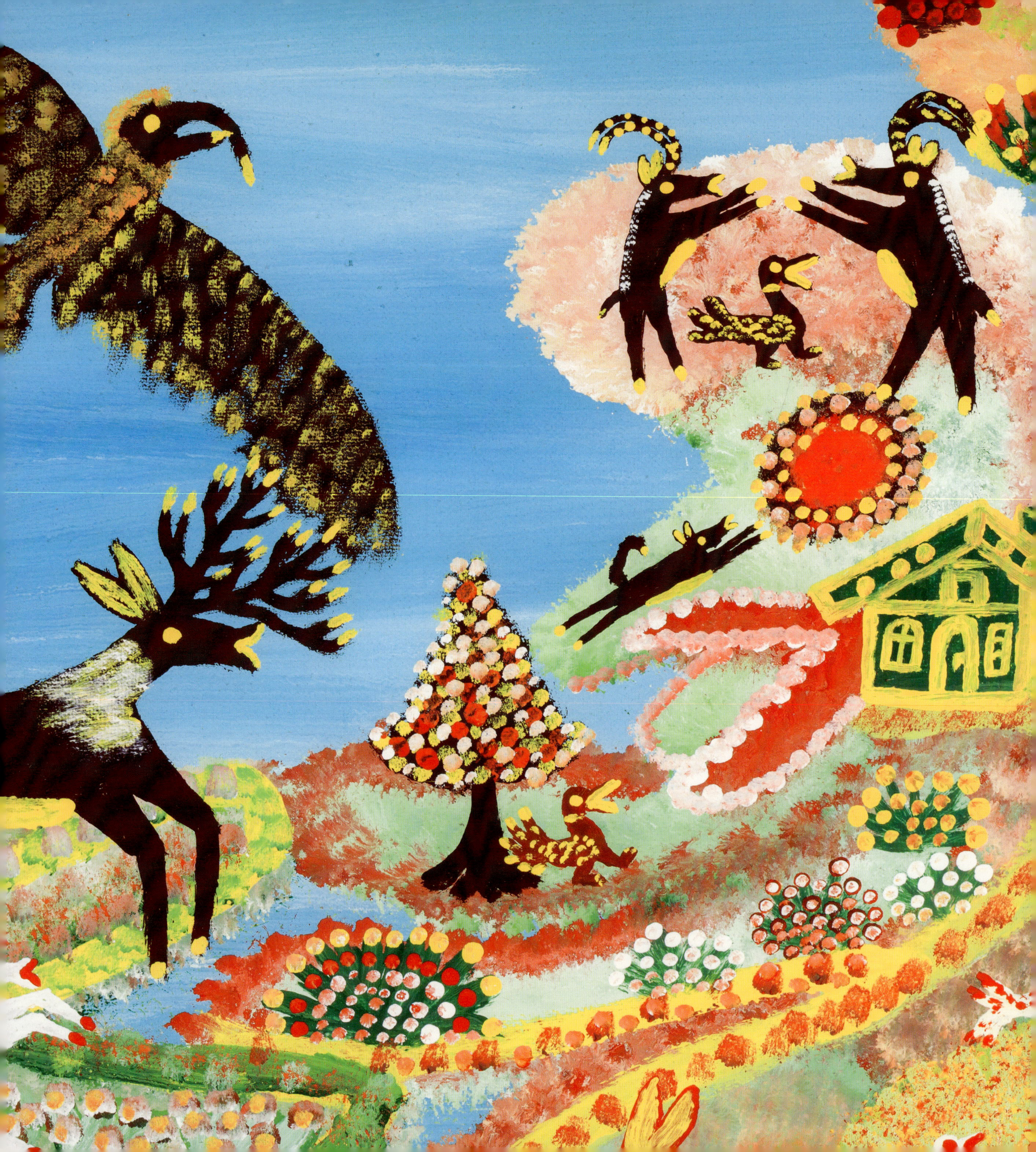

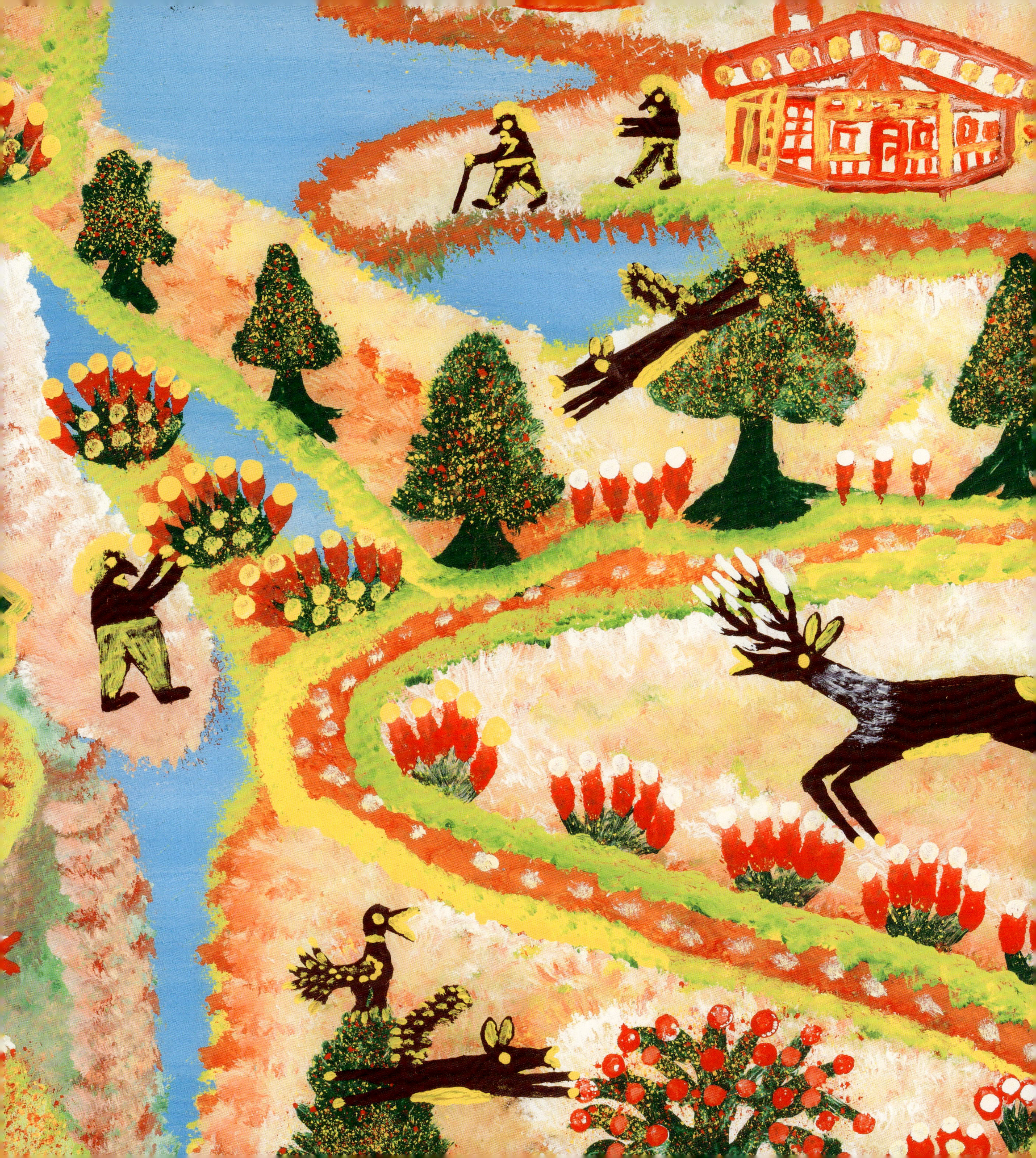

but may feel as well within them stirrings of our own inherent drives for self-expression and connection to others. What is instinctive is universal. We recognize in the works, as we experience in ourselves, the desire to order, arrange, and ornament our lives and visual surroundings. We all know the pleasures of imagining or playing with images of a life led differently or more intensely, perhaps finding a sense of personal agency and connection by imitating or even transgressing culturally prevalent, valued behaviors or symbolic icons.

In effect, the artwork is understood as an existential act of meaning-making in which the artist adapts, whether consciously or unconsciously, shared visual languages to create modes of visual experience that may articulate a profound statement about self and the world in which that artist lives. But, however personal this originating act might be, once others perceive the work and the visual language through which it is expressed, it becomes a cultural statement, participating within collective visual behavior and discourse that connects artist and viewer. It provides a challenge and an opportunity for our own sense of selfhood and our awareness of a degree of commonality with the artist and with the culture we both share.

Through art, any expression of personally charged meaning invariably takes place within and references a collective realm of desired or presumed meaning. The personal statement is always inflected by common cultural values. The connection is experienced through the perspective of individuals struggling to know and articulate themselves through the available images and visual languages. The artwork makes evident this tenuous but necessary dynamic. All experiences of art (especially artworks contemporary with the viewer) are opportunities for self-conscious explorations of what the viewer shares with the artist; both the artwork and the act of viewing illuminate the cultural realm within which they both live. These connections can be found not only in what has been deemed high art, but throughout the popular arts of mass culture as well. They appear in particularly striking manifestations in the creations of self-taught artists and those formerly marginalized, as found in the Rosenthal Collection.

If responding to the work of these unique artists is an unexpected occasion, for the museum world it is also a provocation. Museums are dedicated to presenting significant examples of artistic quality that demonstrate and contribute to the celebration of cultural values. They have traditionally collected and displayed historical creations of high aesthetic achievement by trained artists and respected artisans working in the interests of the primary institutions and beliefs of the cultural order. Integrating the visually distinctive creative work of untrained artists—those living within what have been considered the margins of the social order—has been a constant challenge for art museums, especially in the United States. Generally, these institutions have presented American art history as both an extension of and independent from European aesthetic traditions. They sustain a conception of a national culture grounded in a European heritage and of national identity arising from multiple, widely diverse forms of native "folk," ethnic, and vernacular visual expression.

Russell Bowman, former director of the Milwaukee Art Museum, identified especially well the crux of this challenge of incorporating notable artistic behavior created outside the traditional context of art history when the museum acquired a large collection of "folk" art in the early 1990s (fig. 10). Contrasting—and equating—the creations of the self-taught with those of

Cat. 46 (detail)
Friedrich Schröder-Sonnenstern, *Death Winking in the Moral Apple of Life* (*Der schielende Tod im moralischen Lebensapfel*)

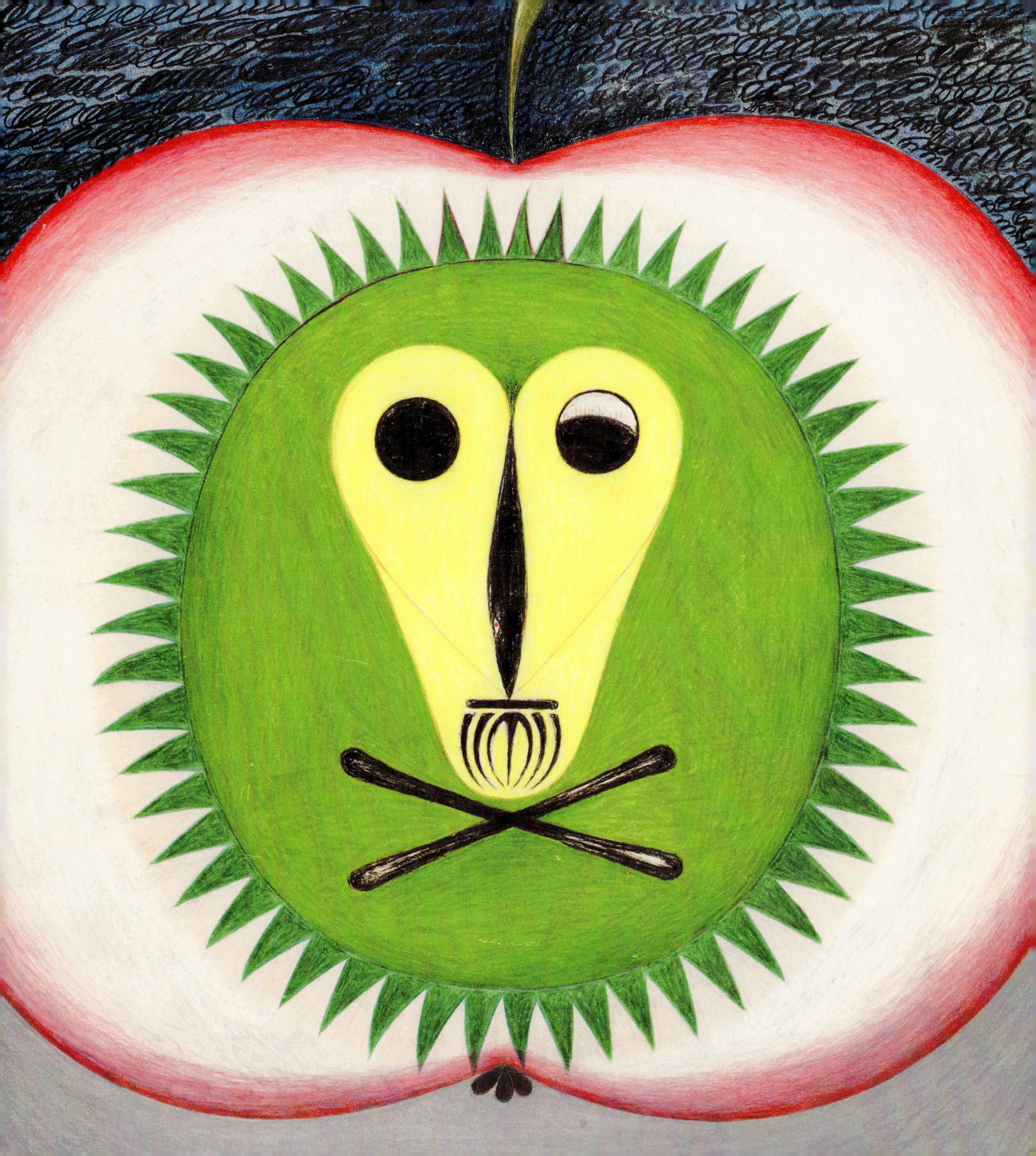

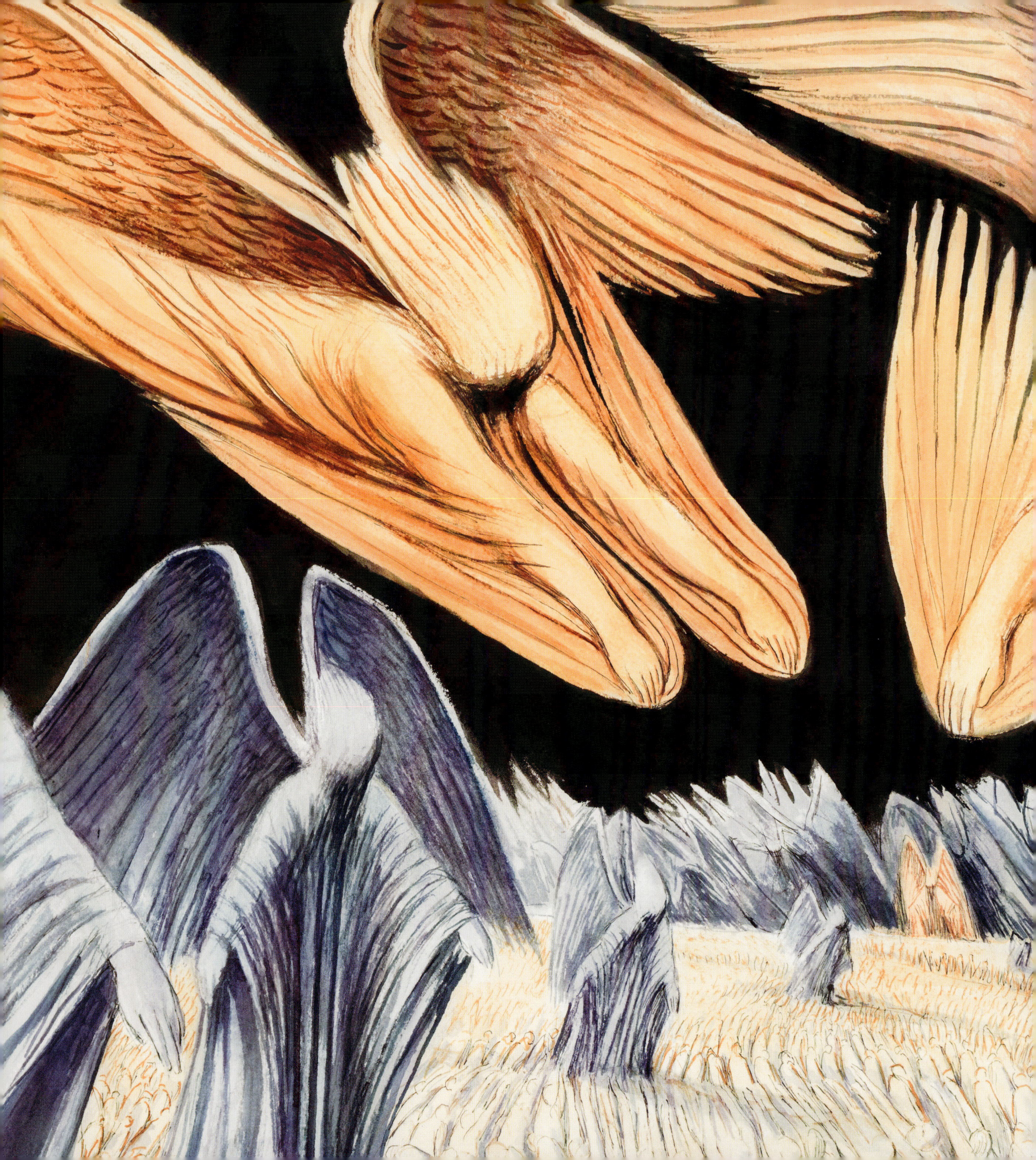

acclaimed modern artists, Bowman stated, “Because they incorporate a powerful and original formal vocabulary to express the artist’s cultural or personal ideals, they are art. Despite being nonparticipants in the dialectical history of what defines art, they do participate in the dialectics of the broader culture and deserve to be seen on a par with any meaningful artistic expression.”[4] Here, Bowman homed in on what strikes us most about these artworks: the distinctiveness of their aesthetic achievement—the visual qualities that make present to us, as do all strong artworks, an individual’s articulation of what is meaningful and valued. And once we look beyond the confines of the “mainstream” art world, we can discover such significant works of art arising throughout our culture that do, indeed, participate in and illuminate life within it.

This is especially true now, when our general social discourse itself calls us to be increasingly attuned to expressions of the “dialectics” of commonality and diversity, when we confront multiple forms of personal and collective expression giving voice and visibility to aspects of a shared local, regional, transcultural, national, or even “universal” vision that we variously may recognize, identify with, and respond to. In them, we may encounter works of especially striking visual and personal expression that at once capture our attention and allow us to envision perspectives on life quite different from what we have known.

The works of those artists who find their inspiration and means of aesthetic expression less in the practices of the art world than in their immediate physical and social environments may initially appear unfamiliar, particularly idiosyncratic, and hence challenging to their viewers. Or alternatively, they may prove surprisingly familiar. The lived or symbolic world the artist presents may be hard to identify

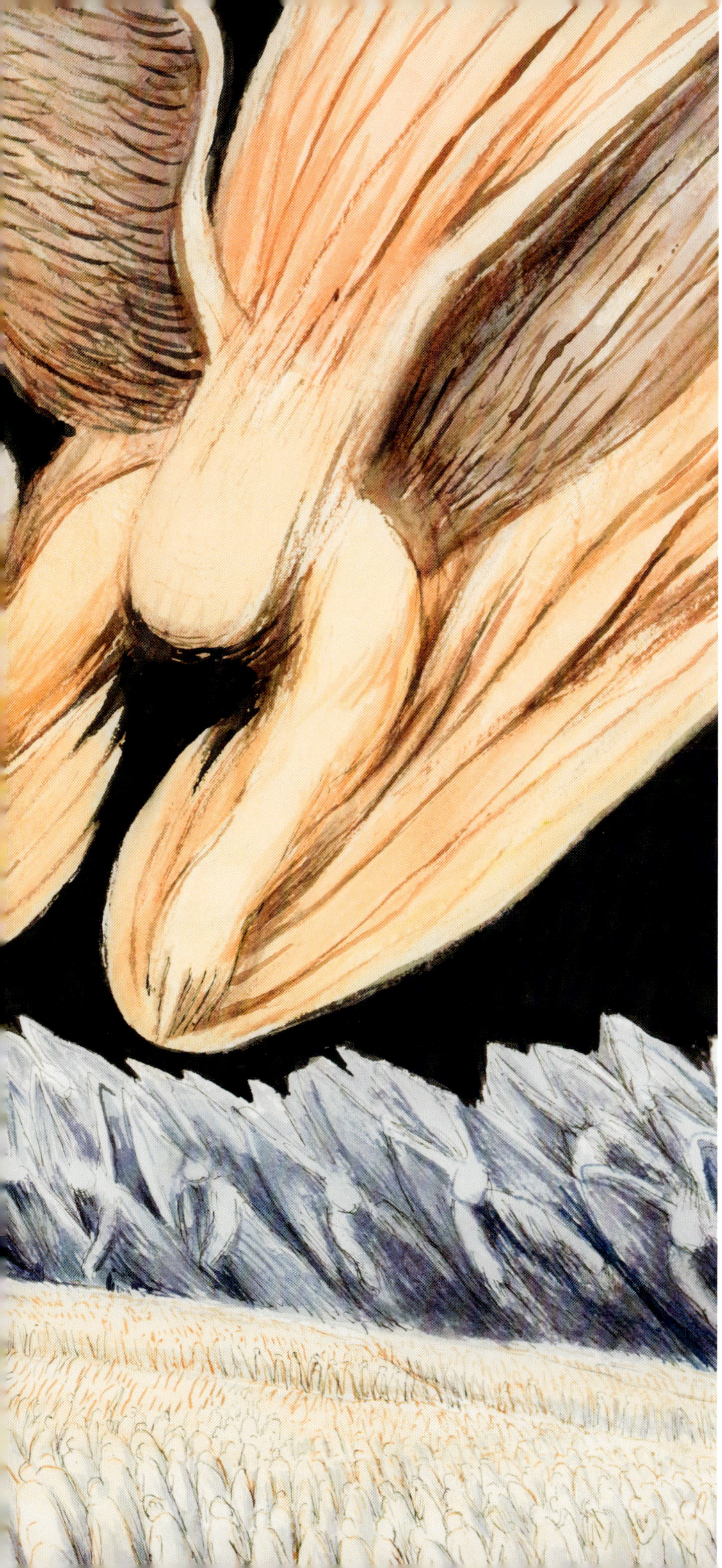

Cat. 63 (detail)
Donald Pass, *Landscape beyond the Veil*

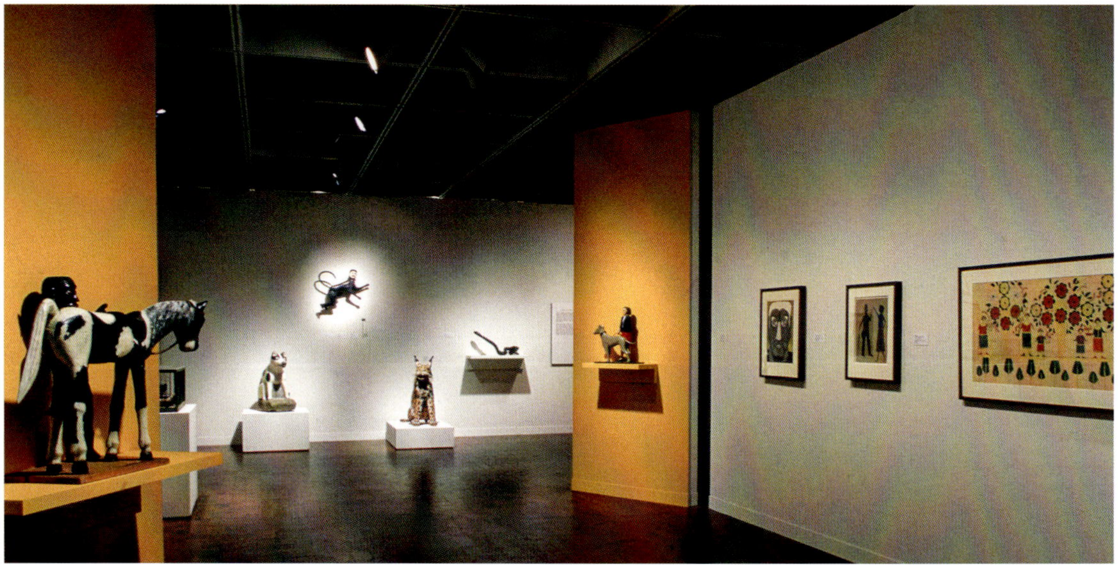

Fig. 10
Common Ground/Uncommon Vision: The Michael and Julie Hall Collection of American Folk Art exhibition installation, Milwaukee Art Museum, April 16–June 20, 1993

and understand, or it might be one we readily perceive in our own personal experience or recognize from the shared pool of imagery encountered across the ubiquitous popular media. Similarly, whether the artist might be an isolated, perhaps deeply disturbed person or one ingrained in their social realm, the visual distinctiveness and power of the particular artistic creation might stir us to feel and discern the nature and the degree of connection or difference between us and that artist's expressed self. Yet is not the experience of such distinctive individual vision one of the primary reasons we seek out and respond to art—why we go to art, and to museums? To see what we have never seen, as well as to see what we have known, once again, only perhaps more intensely and from another person's perspective, in order to feel life more fully?

Through the artwork, through another's imaginative vision—through another's eyes—we may find that a world of thought and emotion is shared, and essentially recognize that we are not alone and that we can experience personal affirmation through aesthetic connection to another and within our common life. Alternatively, the creation of someone distinctly dissimilar may enable us to apprehend in that otherness a sense of greater possibility, perhaps even freedom. The world might be lived differently, and that which engages us more consciously in the "dialectics of the broader culture" situates us more fully in life. By responding to these artists, we find we respond to ourselves; it's a receptivity and breadth of vision to be celebrated.

Endnotes

1. Arthur Rimbaud, *Une saison en enfer* [A season in hell] (Brussels: Alliance Typographique, 1873), 52, https://gallica.bnf.fr/ark:/12148/btv1b86108277/f64.item.
2. Jean Dubuffet, "Art Brut in Preference to the Cultural Arts," in *Art Brut: Madness and Marginalia*, ed. Allen S. Weiss, trans. Paul Fuss and Allen S. Weiss (Sydney: Art and Text, 1988), 33.
3. Hans Prinzhorn, *Artistry of the Mentally Ill*, trans. Eric von Brockdorff, 2nd ed. (New York: Springer-Verlag, 1955).
4. Russell Bowman, "Introduction: A Synthetic Approach to Folk Art," in *Common Ground/Uncommon Vision: The Michael and Julie Hall Collection of American Folk Art*, by Jeffrey Russell Hayes, Lucy R. Lippard, and Kenneth L. Ames, exh. cat. (Milwaukee: Milwaukee Art Museum, 1993), 18.

Cat. 40 (detail)
Victor Joseph Gatto, *The Train through the Mountains*

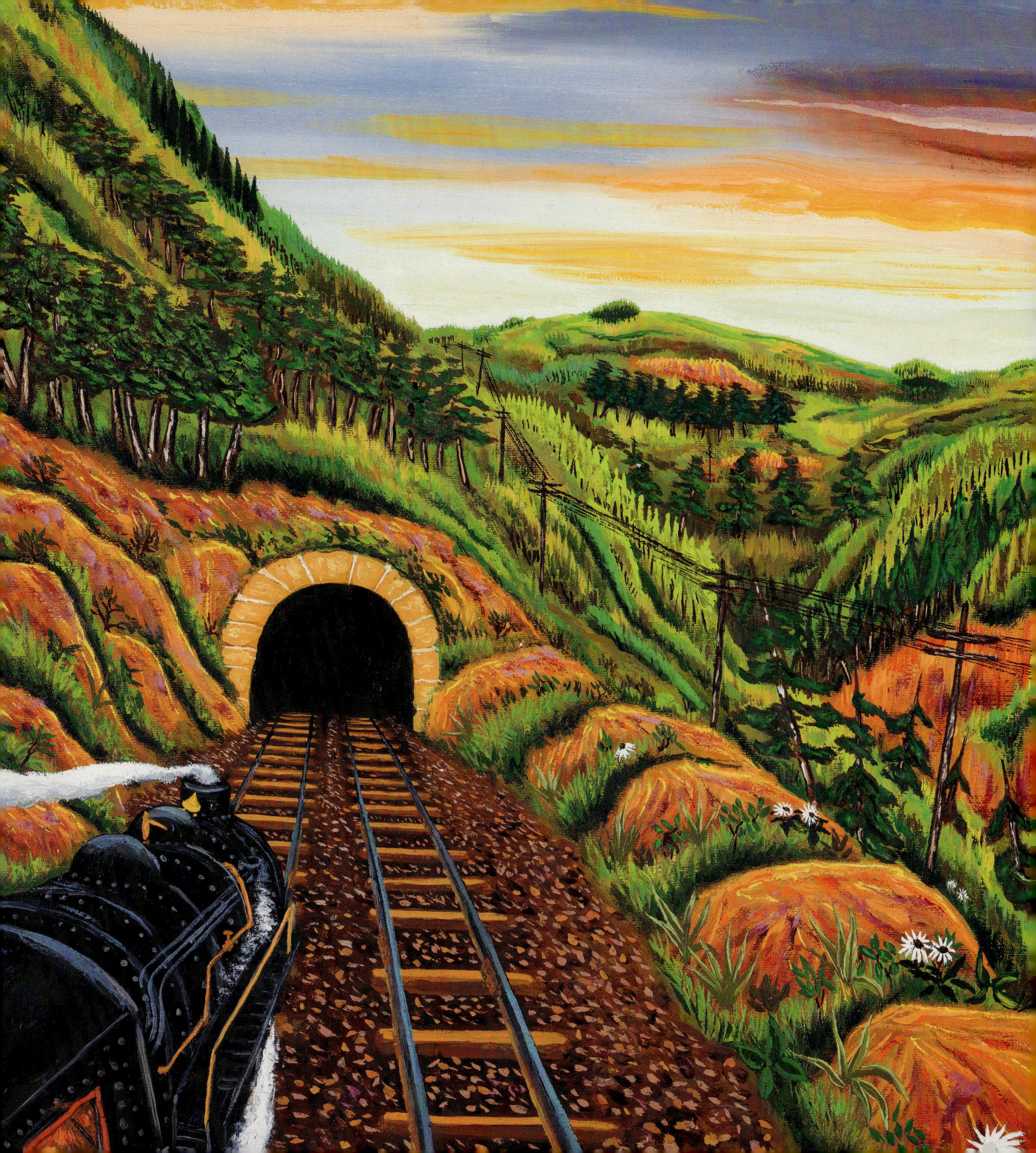

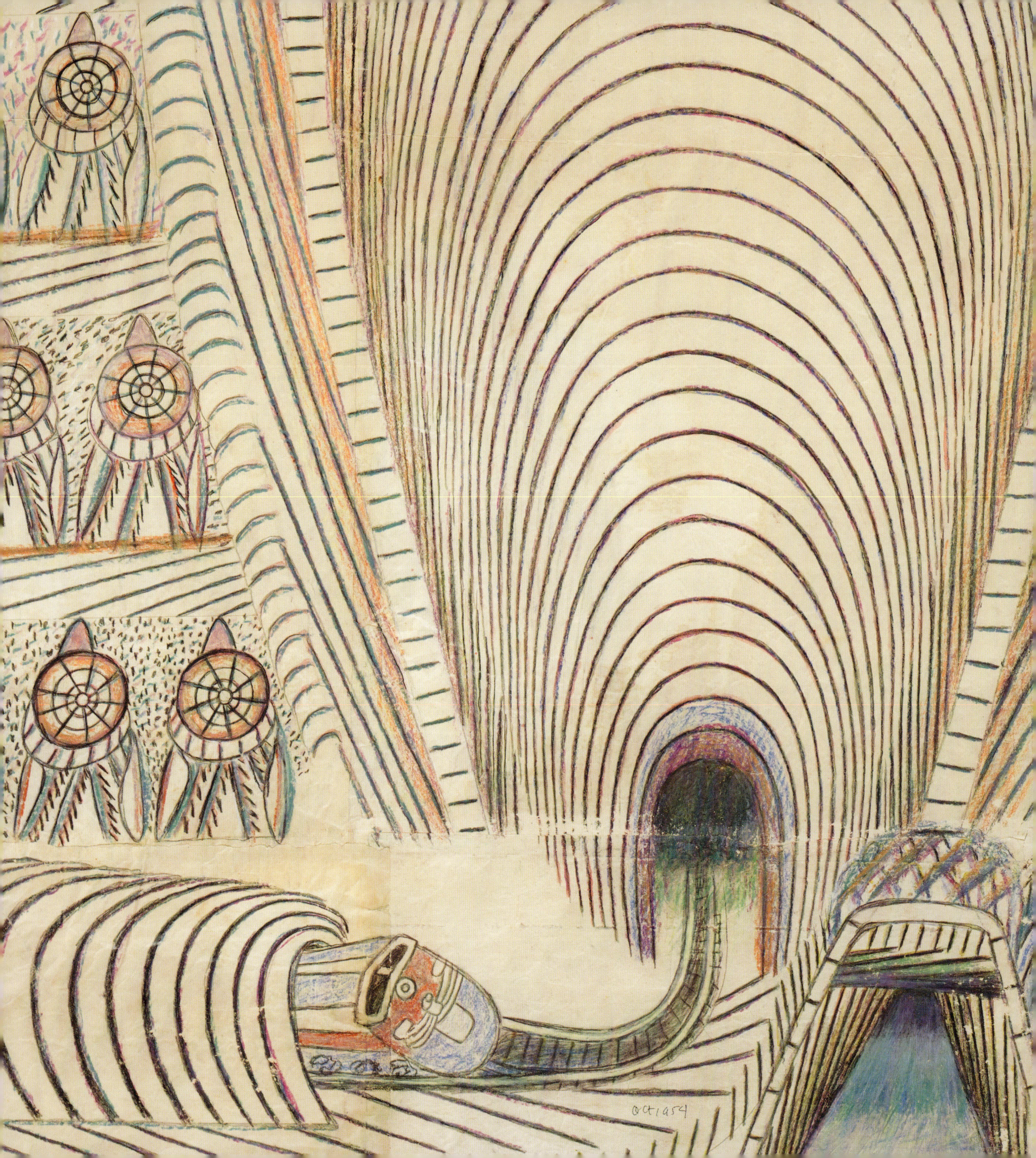
Oct 1954

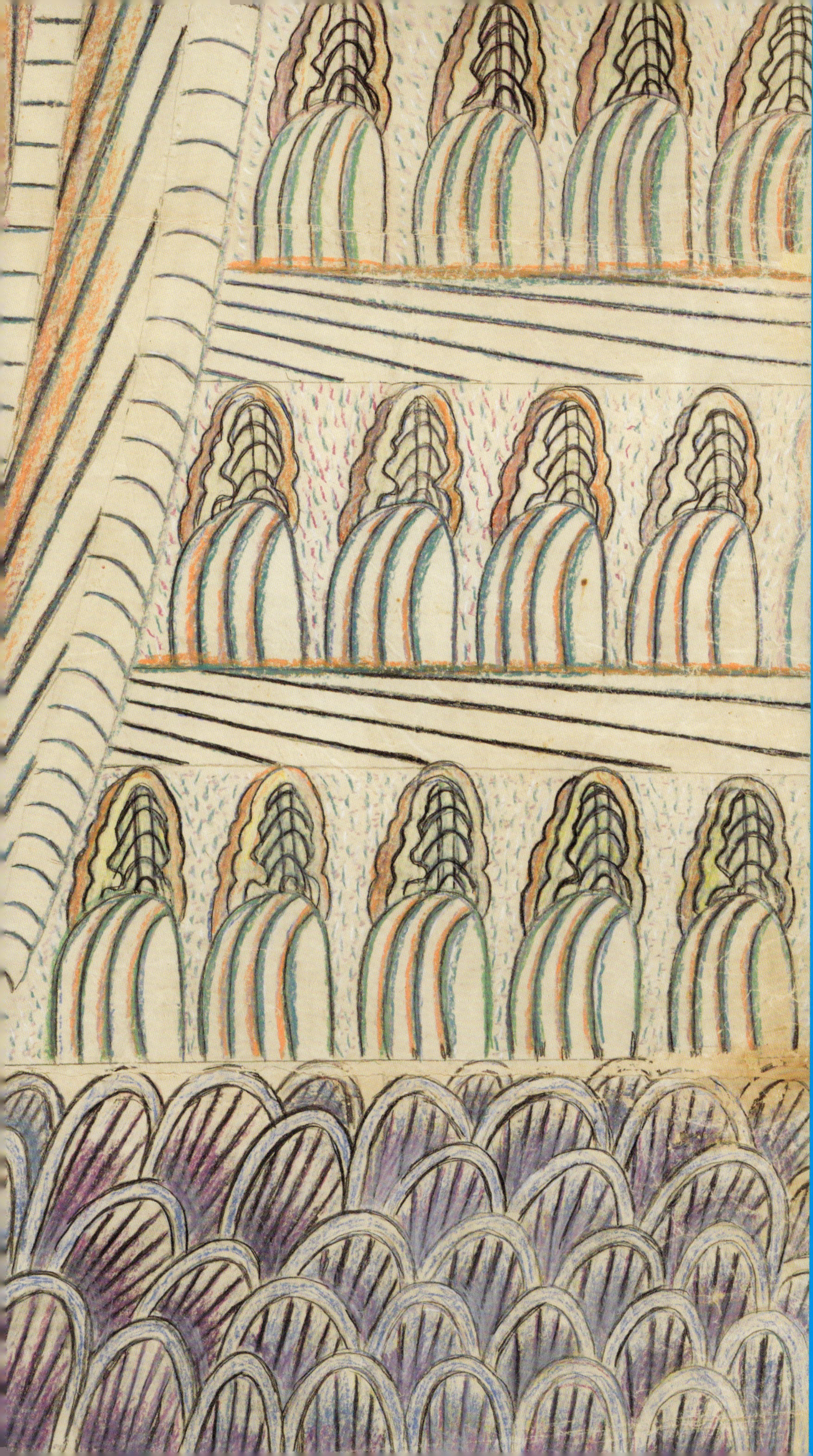

Part 2

Cat. 43
Jean Dubuffet
Born 1901 Le Havre, France
Died 1985 Paris, France

Annal XII (Annale XII)
1978
pen and black ink with collage elements on paper
13 13/16 × 20 3/16 in. (35.1 × 51.3 cm)

Jean Dubuffet studied art in Paris, yet, seeking more honest and humanistic work than the art world endorsed, he rejected conventional beauty and embraced the art of those on the periphery of established cultural spheres. He found "more art and poetry in the words of the barber—in his life—in his head—than in those of the so-called specialists." Dubuffet initiated a collection of work he admired in 1945, then in 1948 formed the Compagnie de l'Art Brut with Surrealist artists, writers, and art dealers.

Jean Dubuffet quoted in *Prospectus et tous écrits suivants*, comp. and ed. Hubert Damisch, 2 vols. (Paris: Éditions Gallimard, 1967), 2:62.

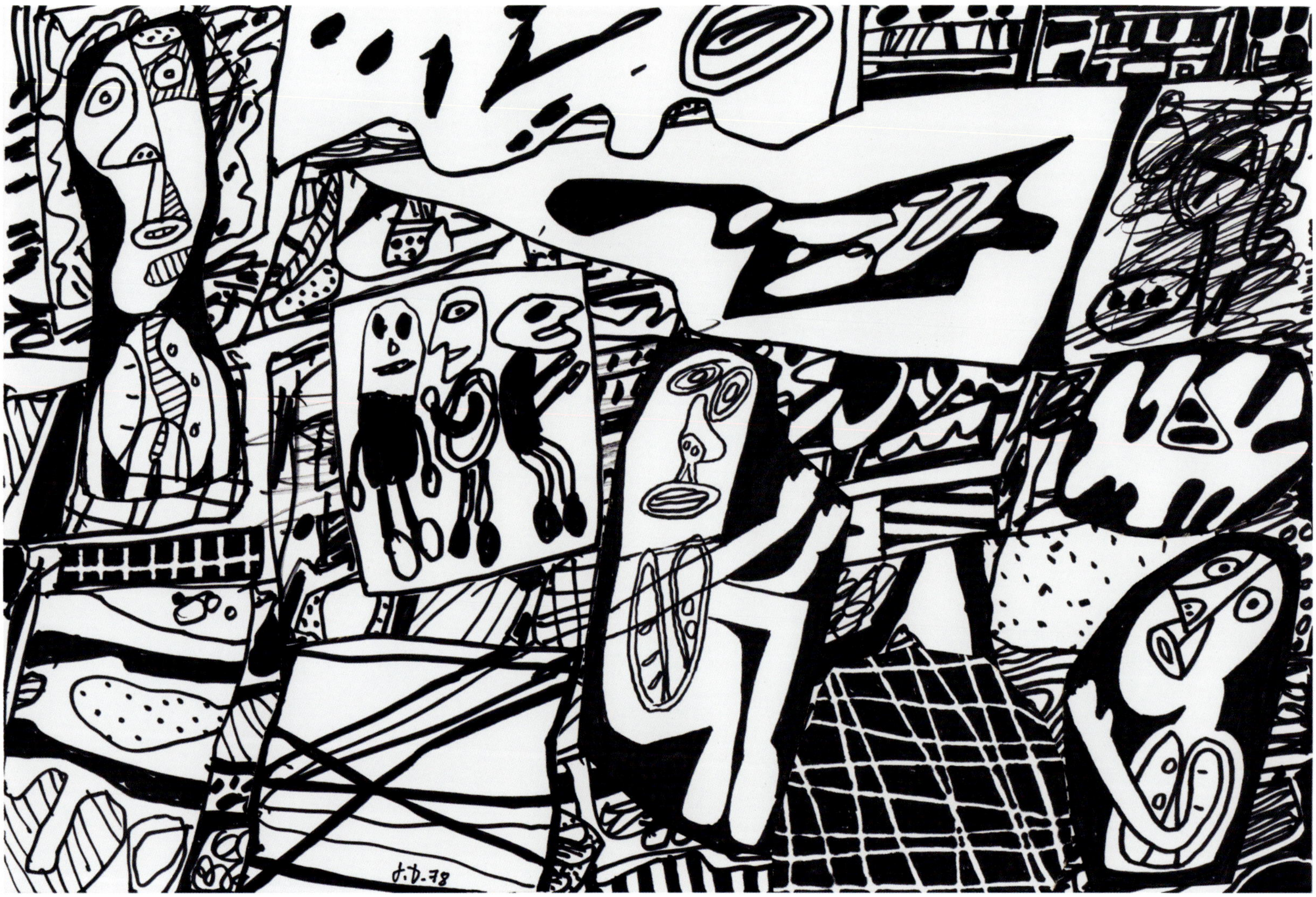

Cat. 44
Jean Dubuffet

Le Circulus I
1984
acrylic on paper
mounted on canvas
39 3⁄16 × 52 13⁄16 in. (99.6 × 134.1 cm)

"I feel that every work of art should in the highest degree lift one out of context, provoking a surprise and a shock."

Jean Dubuffet quoted in *Jean Dubuffet: Retrospective* (Dallas: Dallas Museum of Fine Arts, 1996), 47.

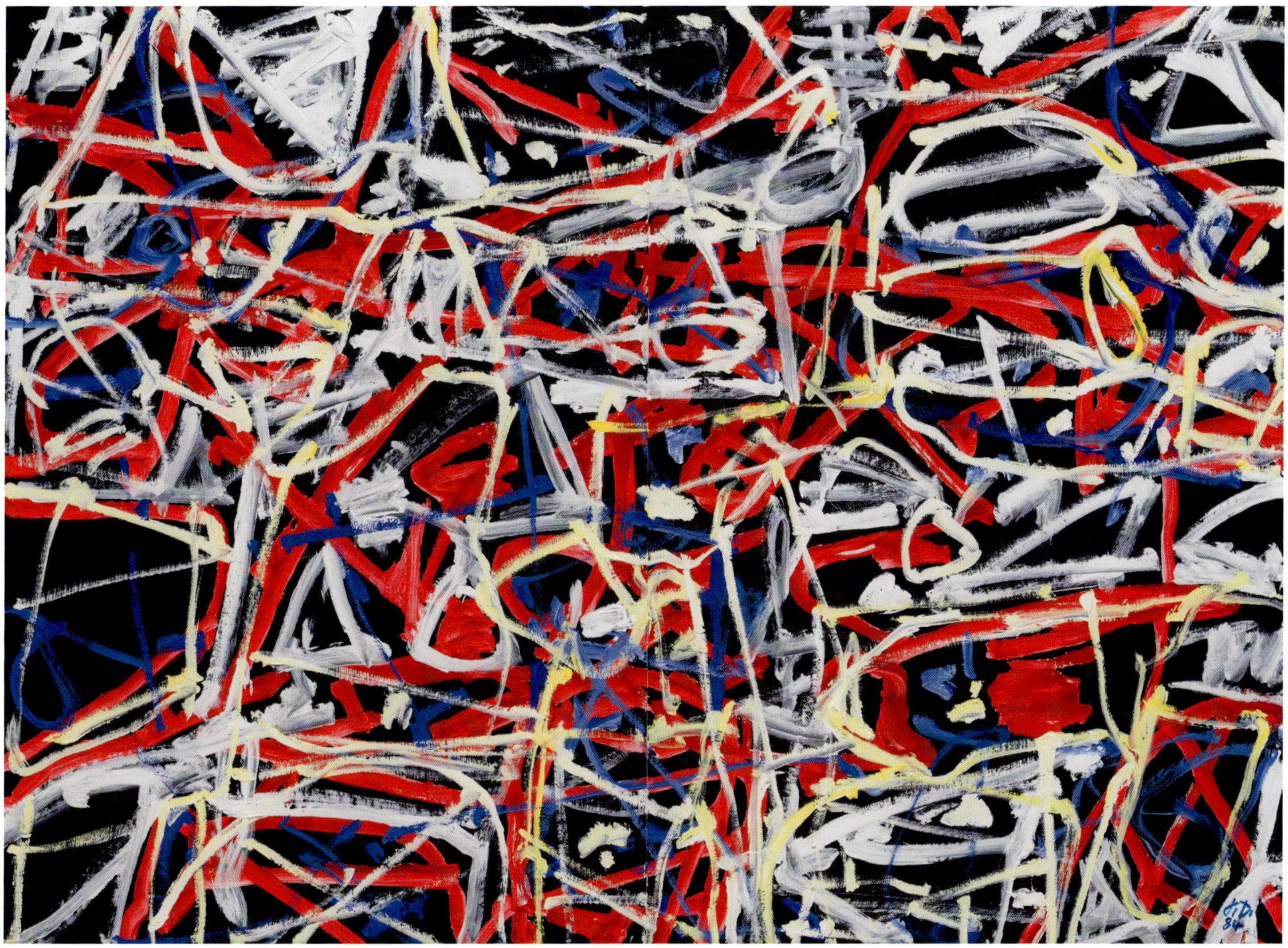

Cat. 45

Adolf Wölfli

Born 1864 Bern, Switzerland
Died 1930 Bern, Switzerland

Elisabeth Bieri

1907
graphite pencil and
crayon on paper
35½ × 47¼ in. (90.1 × 120 cm)

This elaborate drawing on conjoined sheets of paper may be among the first made in color by Adolf Wölfli, who spent most of his adult life in the Waldau Clinic in Bern as a psychiatric patient. Amid vivid and dense scrolling patterns that make the work resemble a textile, he included his name in large letters and a plethora of heads, birds, musical notations, and (near the bottom) the name Elisabeth Bieri from his troubled boyhood.

Cat. 46

Friedrich Schröder-Sonnenstern

Born 1892 Kaukehmen, East Prussia (now in Russia)
Died 1982 Berlin, Germany

Death Winking in the Moral Apple of Life (Der schielende Tod im moralischen Lebensapfel)

1956
crayon on cardboard
28¾ × 20$\frac{1}{16}$ in. (73 × 51 cm)

Inscribed in an apple is an insect-like death's head atop crossbones. This motif appears more than once in the fantastical colored drawings and unique symbolism of Friedrich Schröder-Sonnenstern. The Surrealists and Jean Dubuffet embraced his highly inventive artwork, some of which features sexual imagery and conflations of human and animal forms.

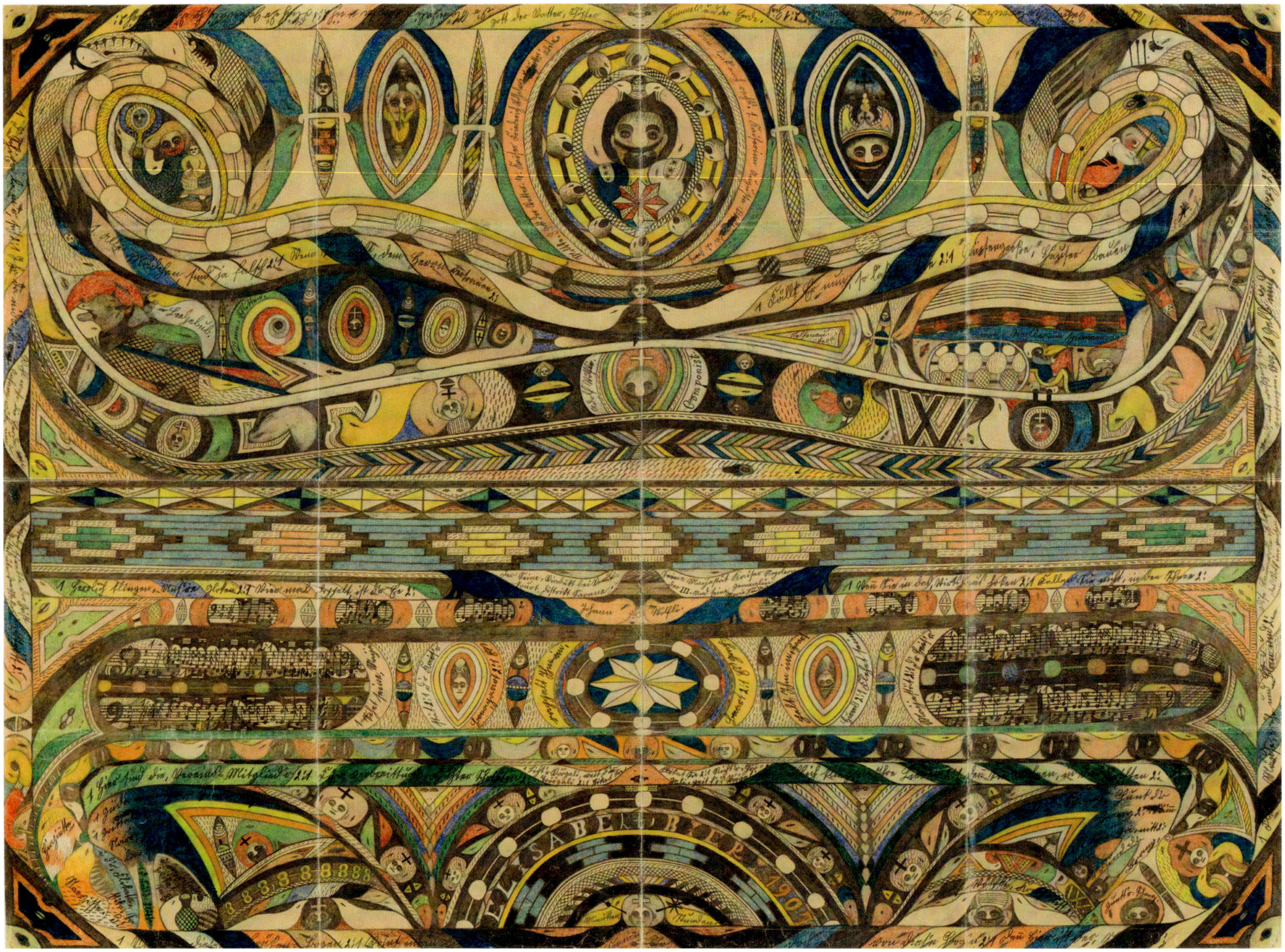

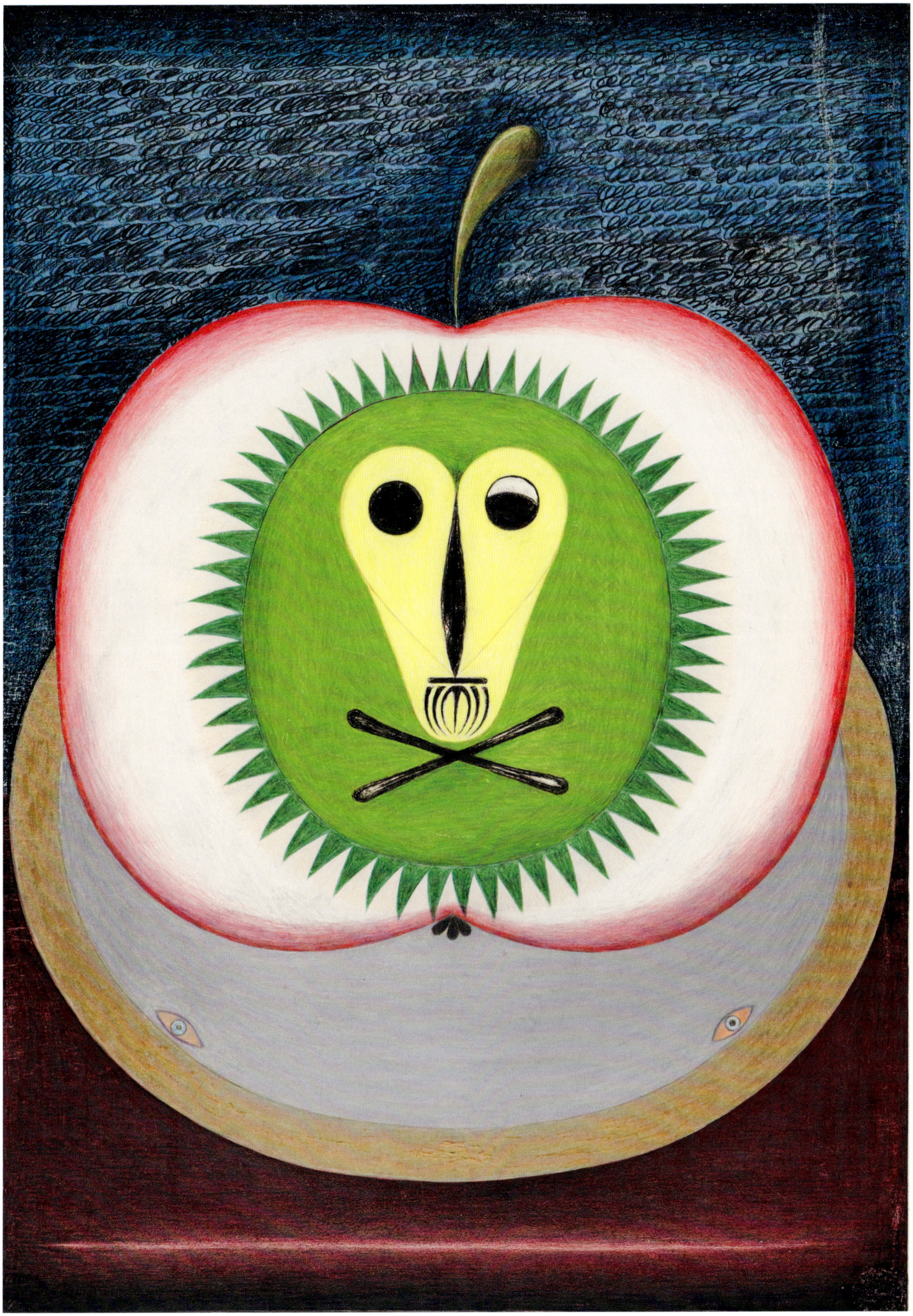

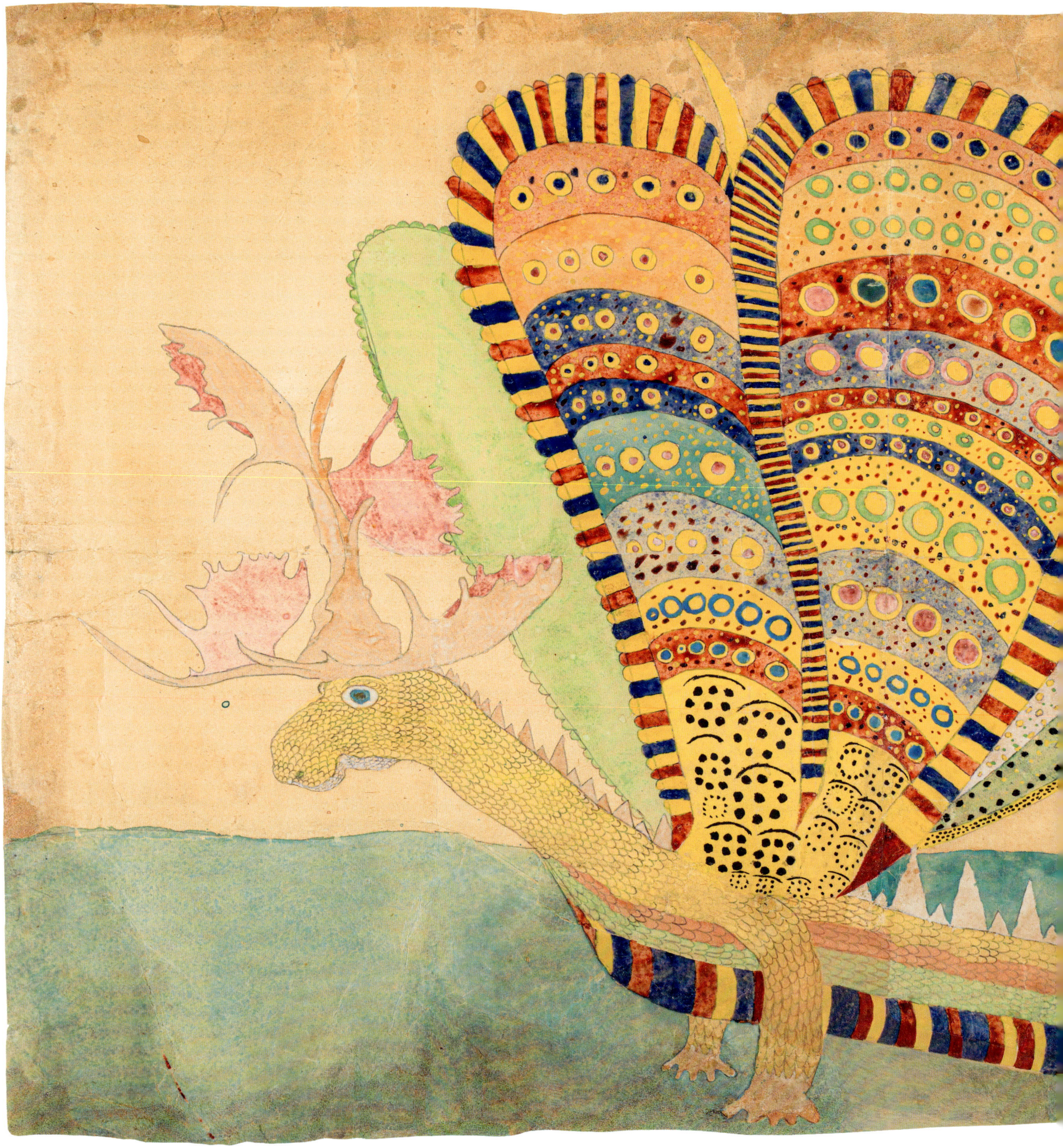

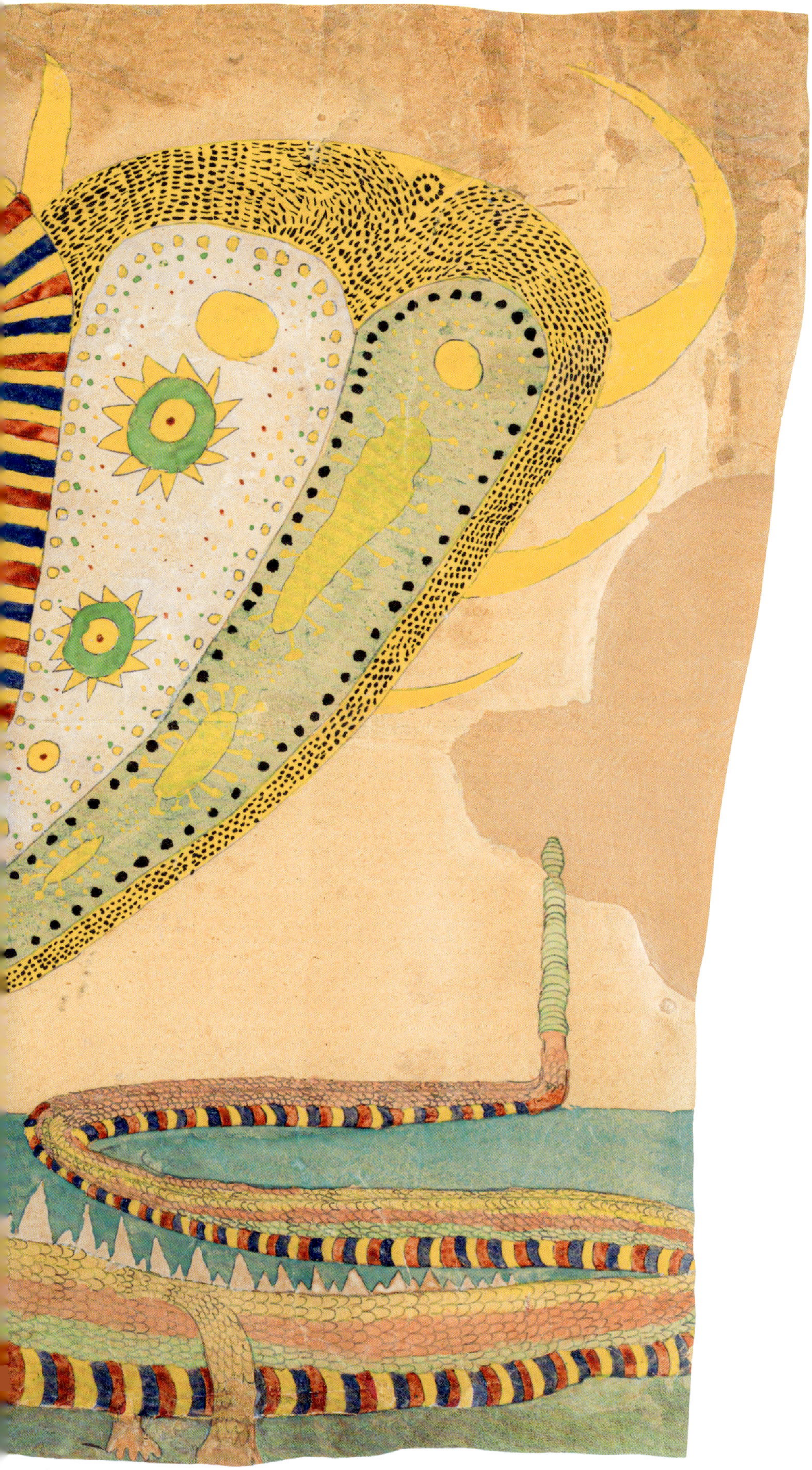

Cat. 47

Henry Darger

Born 1892 Chicago, Illinois

Died 1973 Chicago, Illinois

Blengin

circa 1920–30

watercolor, graphite pencil, and blue carbon transfer on paper

23½ × 34 15⁄16 in. (59.7 × 88.7 cm)

In the rich fantasy world of Henry Darger, a solitary hospital janitor and dishwasher, *Blengin* is short for *Blengiglomenean*, a serpent with human and animal characteristics. Unlike the artist's later works in which he extensively appropriated details from printed matter, this early depiction is of a fanciful creature he largely drew by hand, adding decorative patterns and vibrant, candy-like colors.

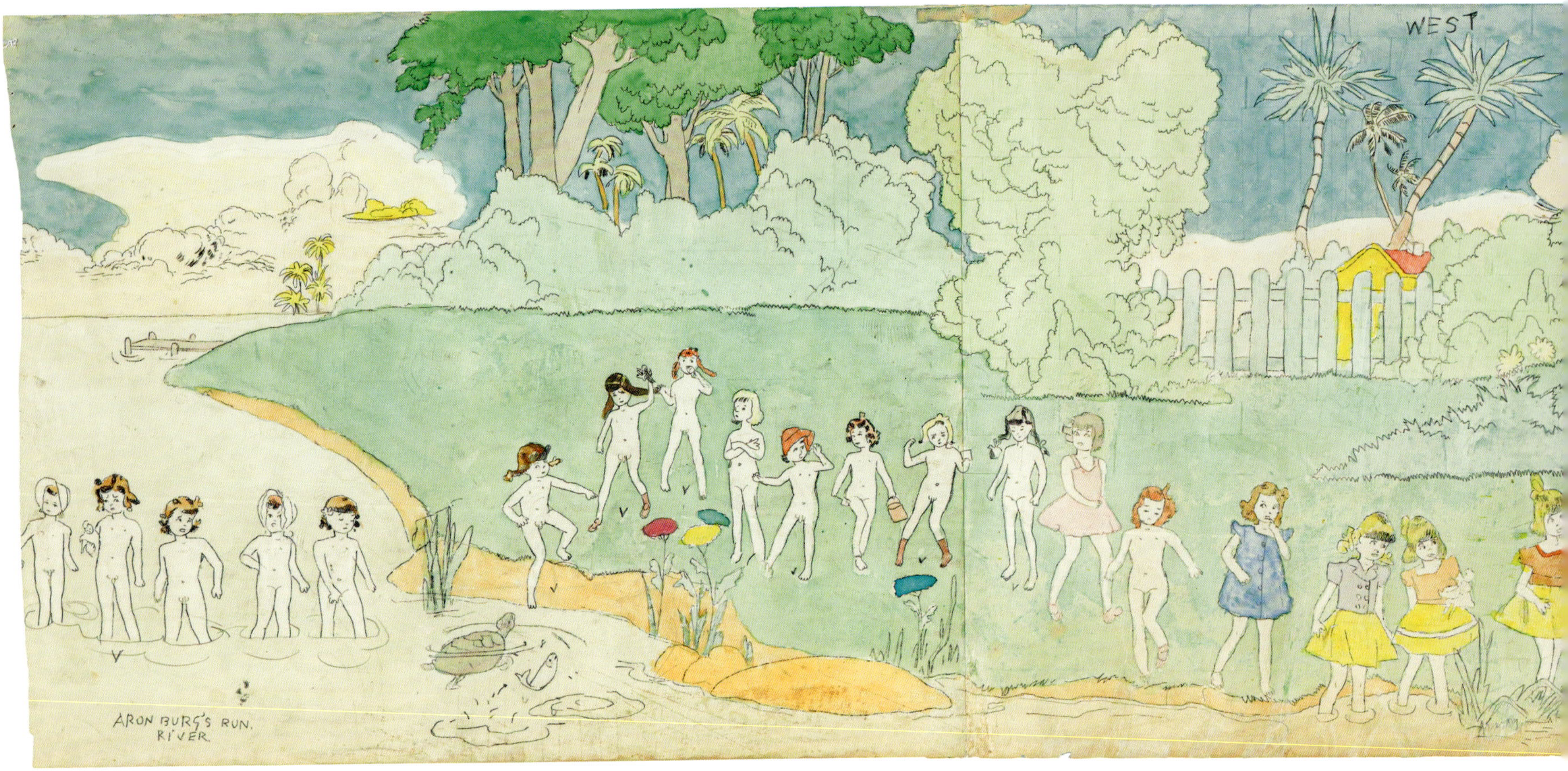
WEST
ARON BURG'S RUN.
RIVER

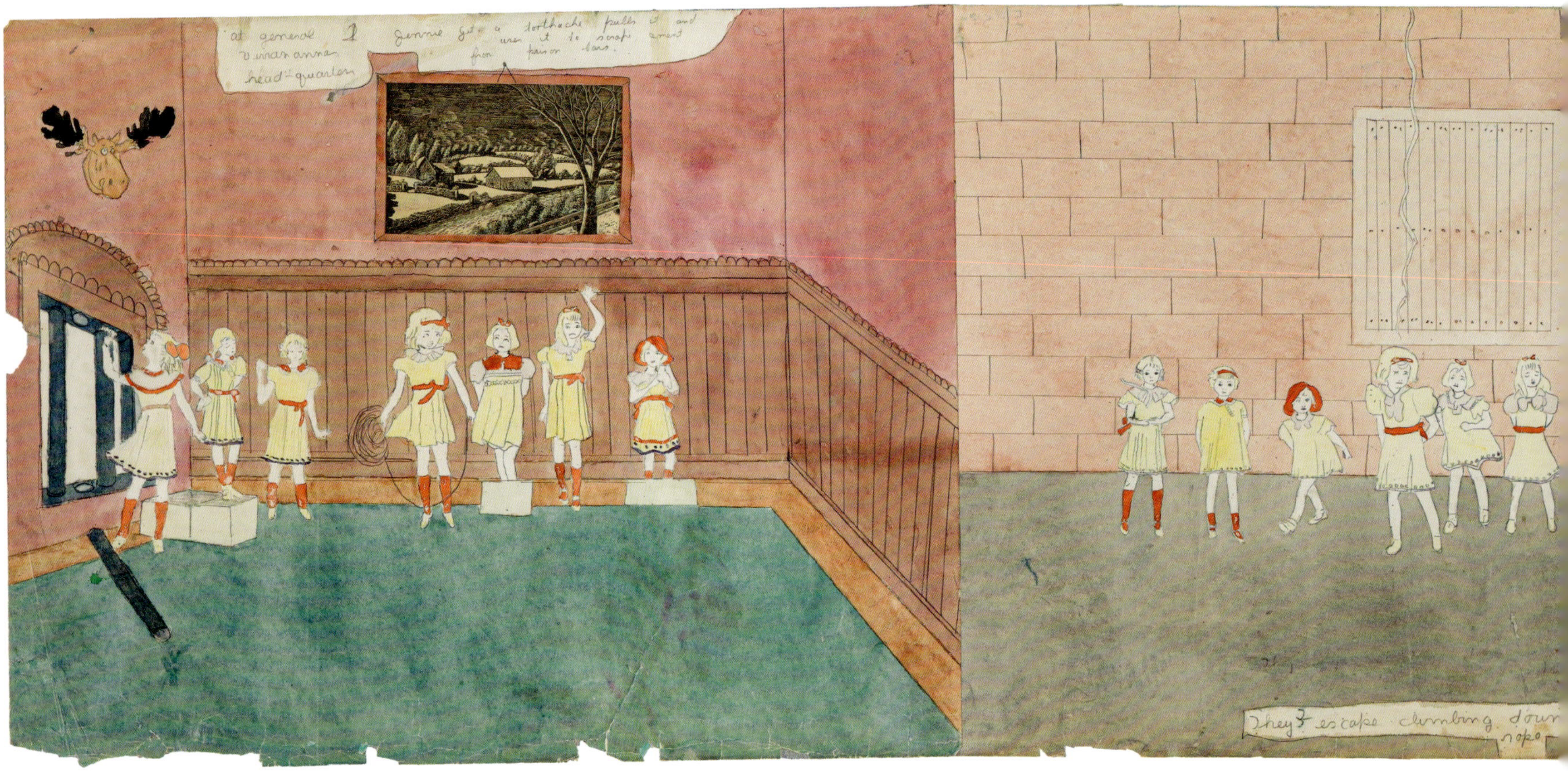
at general 1
head-quarters
from prison bars.
They escape climbing down
rope

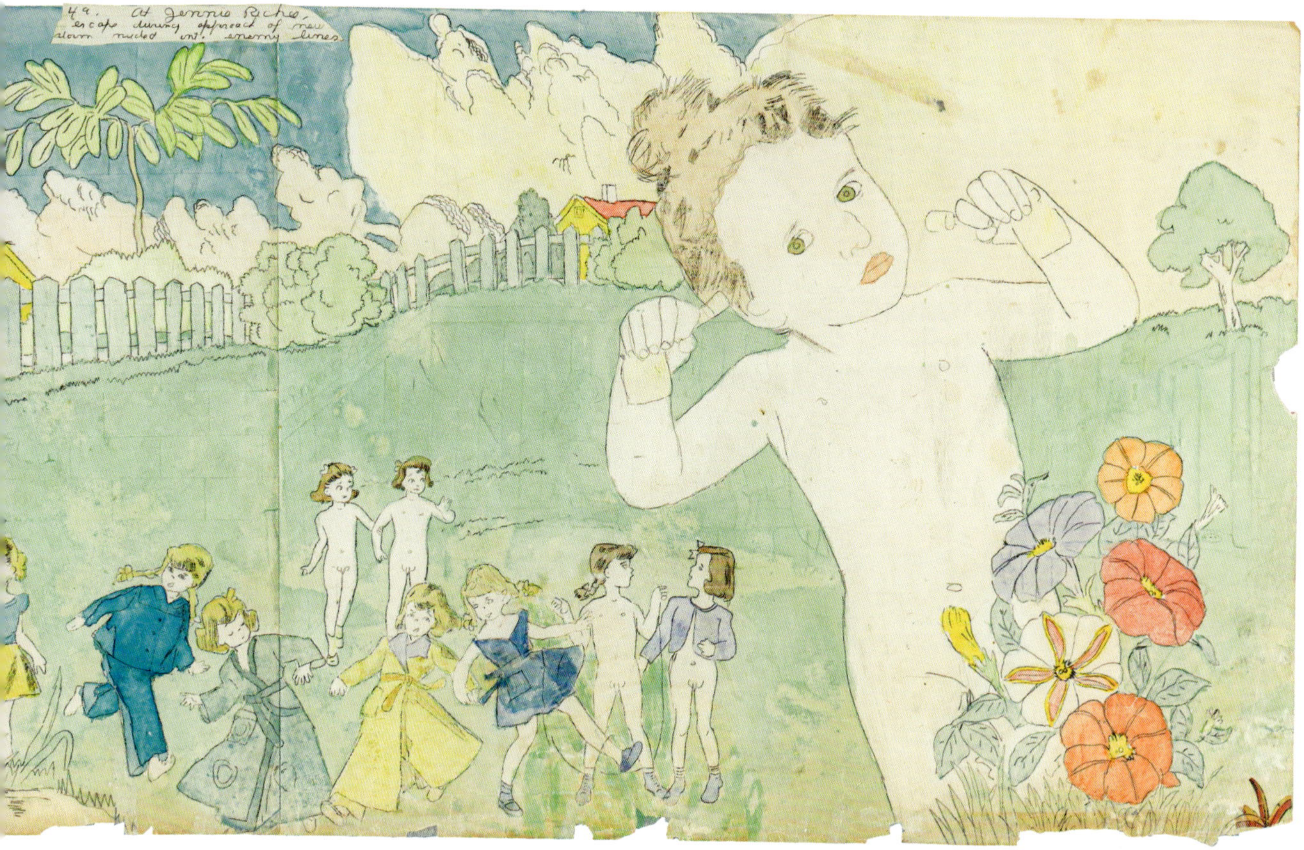

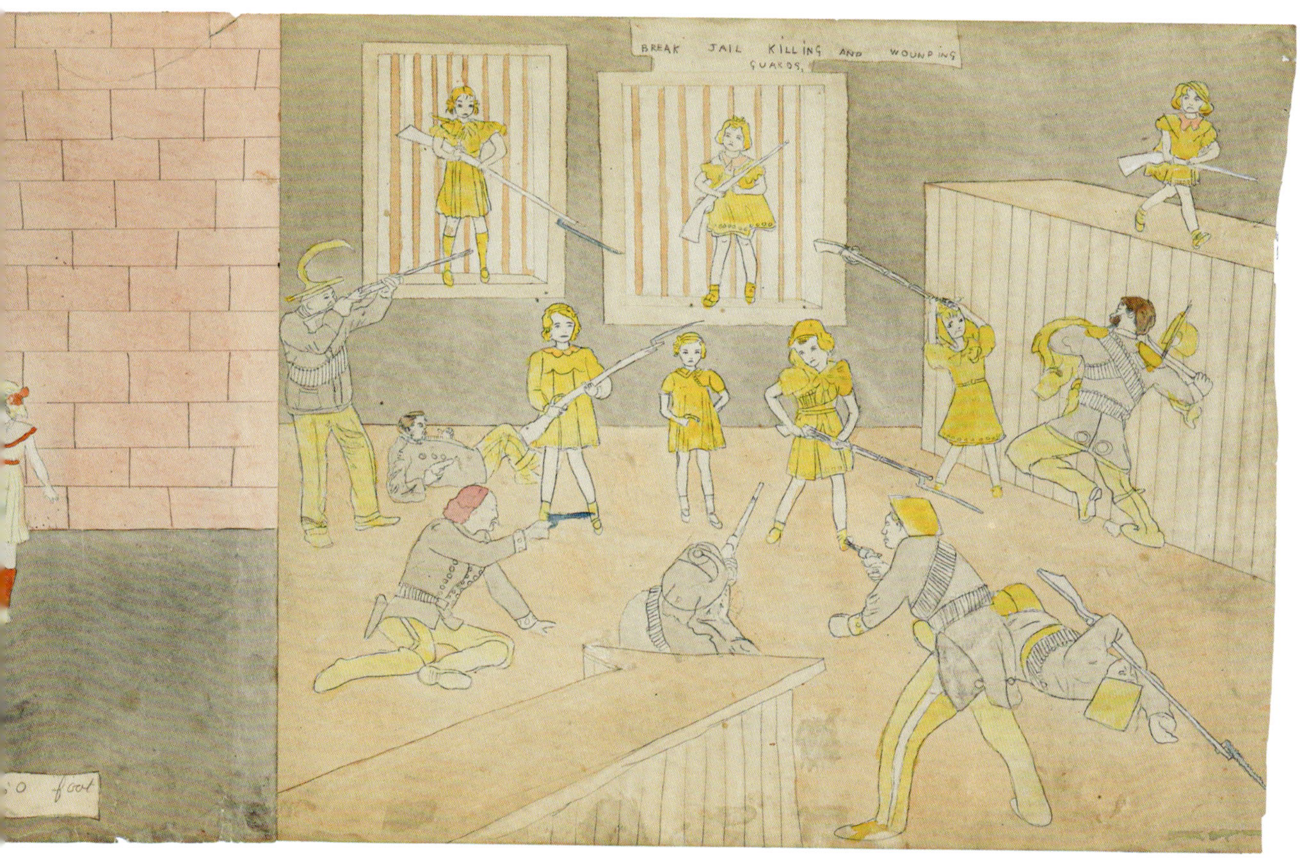

Cat. 48
Henry Darger

49. At Jennie Richee, escape during approach of new storm nuded [sic] into enemy lines (recto)
circa 1950–60

At general Viviananna head-quarters 1 Jennie gets a toothache pulls it and uses it to scrap [sic] cement from prison bars (verso)
circa 1930–40
watercolor, graphite pencil, and carbon transfer on paper
19 ⅛ × 70 ½ in. (48.6 × 179 cm)

Henry Darger's exquisitely colored watercolors illuminate a 15,000-page epic describing a war between forces of good (represented by the Vivian Girls) and evil (the Glandelinia empire that enslaves children). The Chicago artist imaginatively selected, combined, then traced imagery he collected from catalogues, comic books, magazines, and newspapers, and embellished the pages with freehand drawing.

Cat. 49
Eddie Arning
Born 1898 Germania, Texas
Died 1993 McGregor, Texas

Untitled
circa 1964–74
oil pastel and graphite pencil on dark blue paper
19¾ × 25 11/16 in. (50.1 × 65.3 cm)

Popular magazines provided source material for Texan Eddie Arning, who made distinctive, stylized, heavily worked drawings as a psychiatric hospital and nursing home resident. For this couple in a landscape, he perhaps referenced an advertisement for wine; the woman raises a glass in her hand.

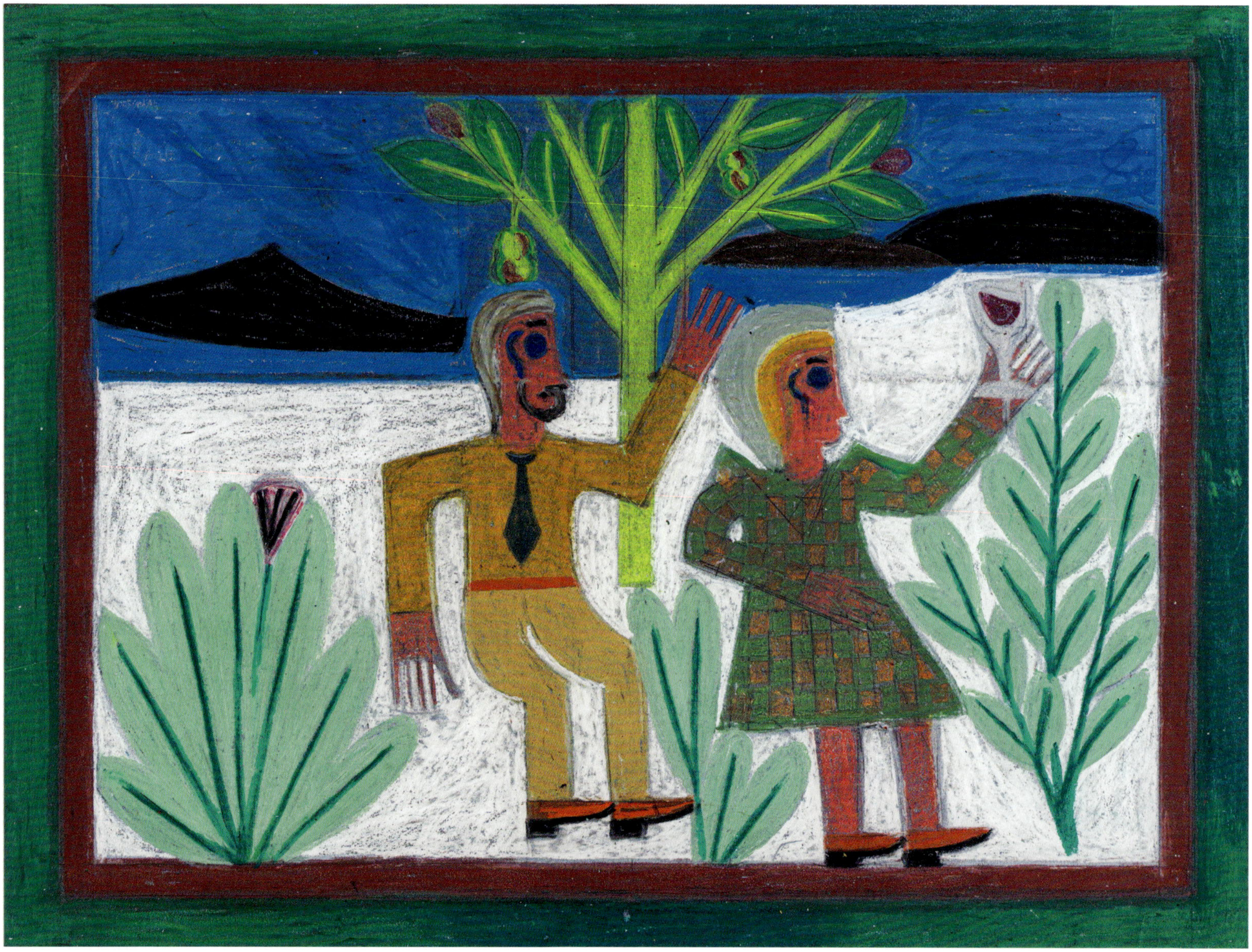

Cat. 50
Carlo Zinelli
Born 1916 Verona, Italy
Died 1974 Verona, Italy

Untitled
1962–64
watercolor and gouache on paper
13¾ × 19⅞ in. (35 × 50.5 cm)

Carlo Zinelli left over 3,000 compelling drawings with mysterious symbolism known only to him. Profile silhouettes of women and handbags are the principal motifs in this allover composition with an urban sensibility. Confined to a Veronese psychiatric facility after seeing combat during Italy's engagement in the Spanish Civil War (where he worked as a stretcher bearer), Zinelli took encouragement from a visiting artist and found a refuge in the art studio.

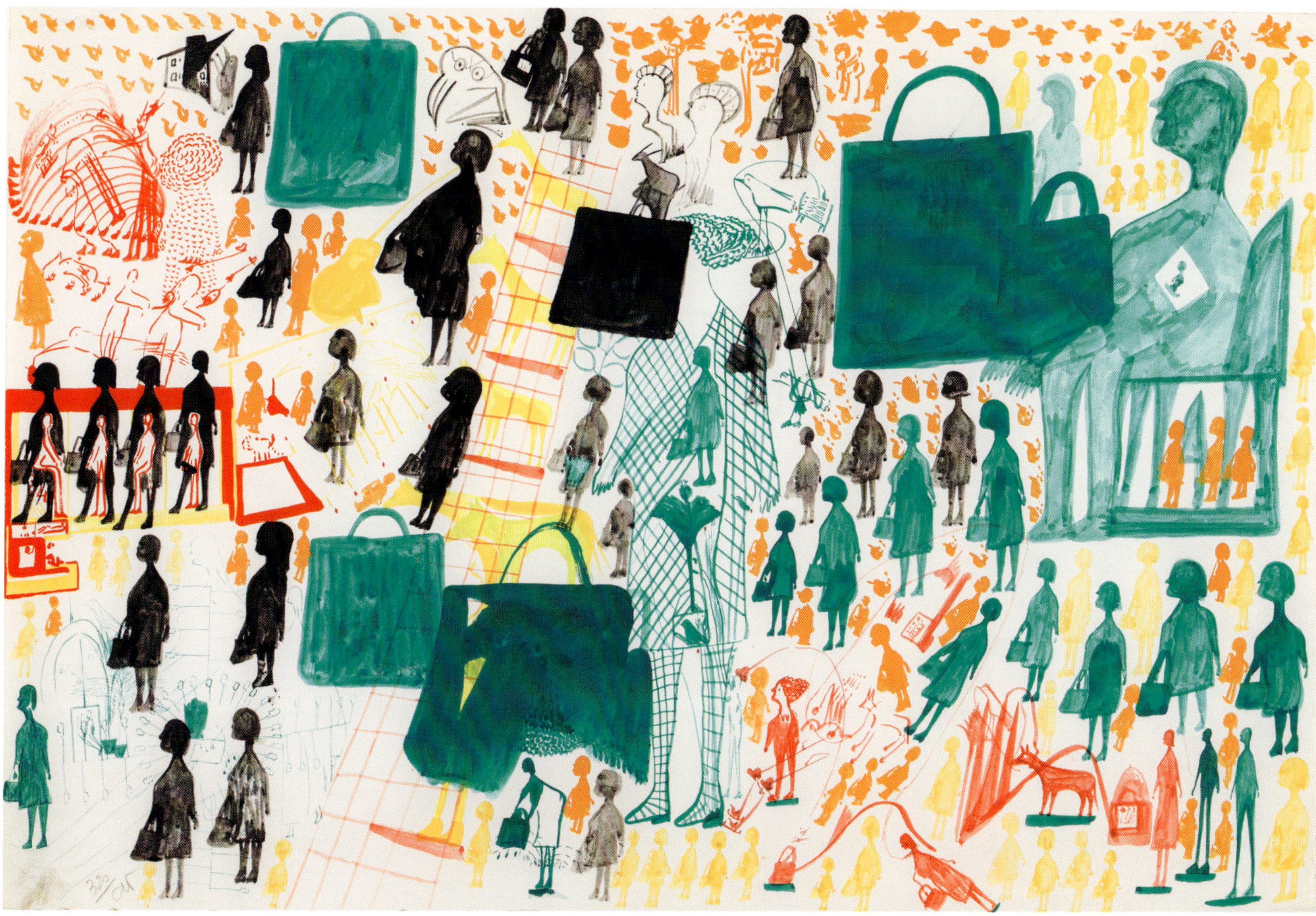

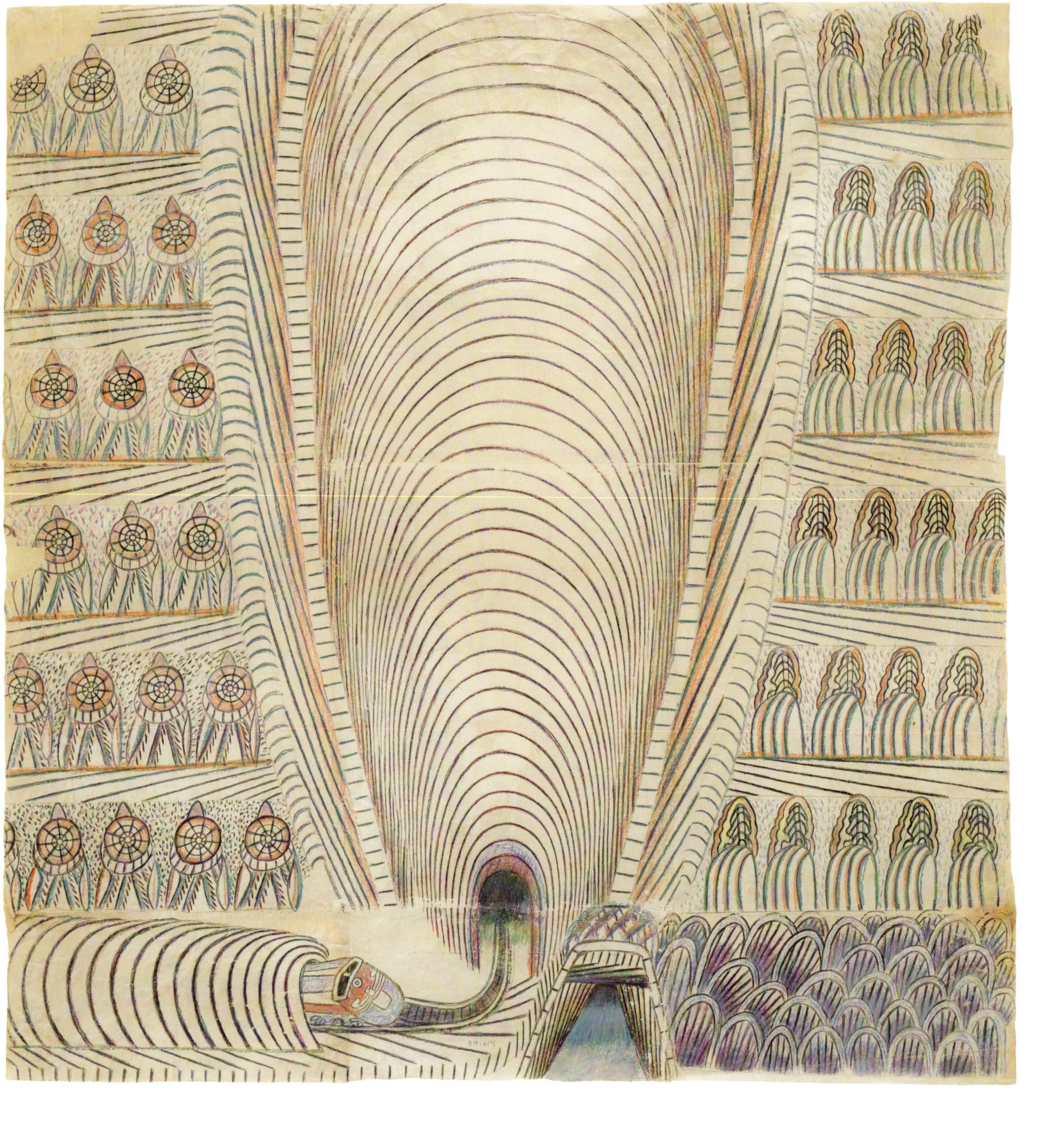

Cat. 51
Martín Ramírez
Born 1895 Tepatitlán, Mexico
Died 1963 Auburn, California

Untitled, Super Chief
1954
graphite pencil and pastel (est.) on paper
55 9/16 × 51½ in. (141.2 × 130.8 cm)

The tunnel at the center of this large, dramatic work creates the illusion of deeply receding perspective that pulls you in. The tilting train, requiring an abrupt turn to enter the tunnel, seems to barrel ahead at lightning speed. Trains were a favorite motif of Martín Ramírez, a former railroad worker who made exquisite and distinctive choices in line, patterns, and materials. To this immigrant artist confined in an institution, trains may have represented freedom.

Cat. 52
Dwight Mackintosh
Born 1906 Hayward, California
Died 1999 Berkeley, California

Untitled (Large Horse)
1992
pen and black ink on paper
22 1/16 × 30 1/16 in. (56 × 76.3 cm)

"The one animal that Mackintosh seems to have had an early experience with is the horse. . . . The continuous line enveloping the body, the multiple hooves, the wildly scribbled mane, and the lopsided and slightly sick expression, bring this horse convincingly, and amusingly, to life. One is reminded that Dwight possesses a fleeting sense of humor—and an oddly furtive smile."

John M. MacGregor, *Dwight Mackintosh: The Boy Who Time Forgot* (Oakland, CA: Creative Growth Art Center, 1992), 26.

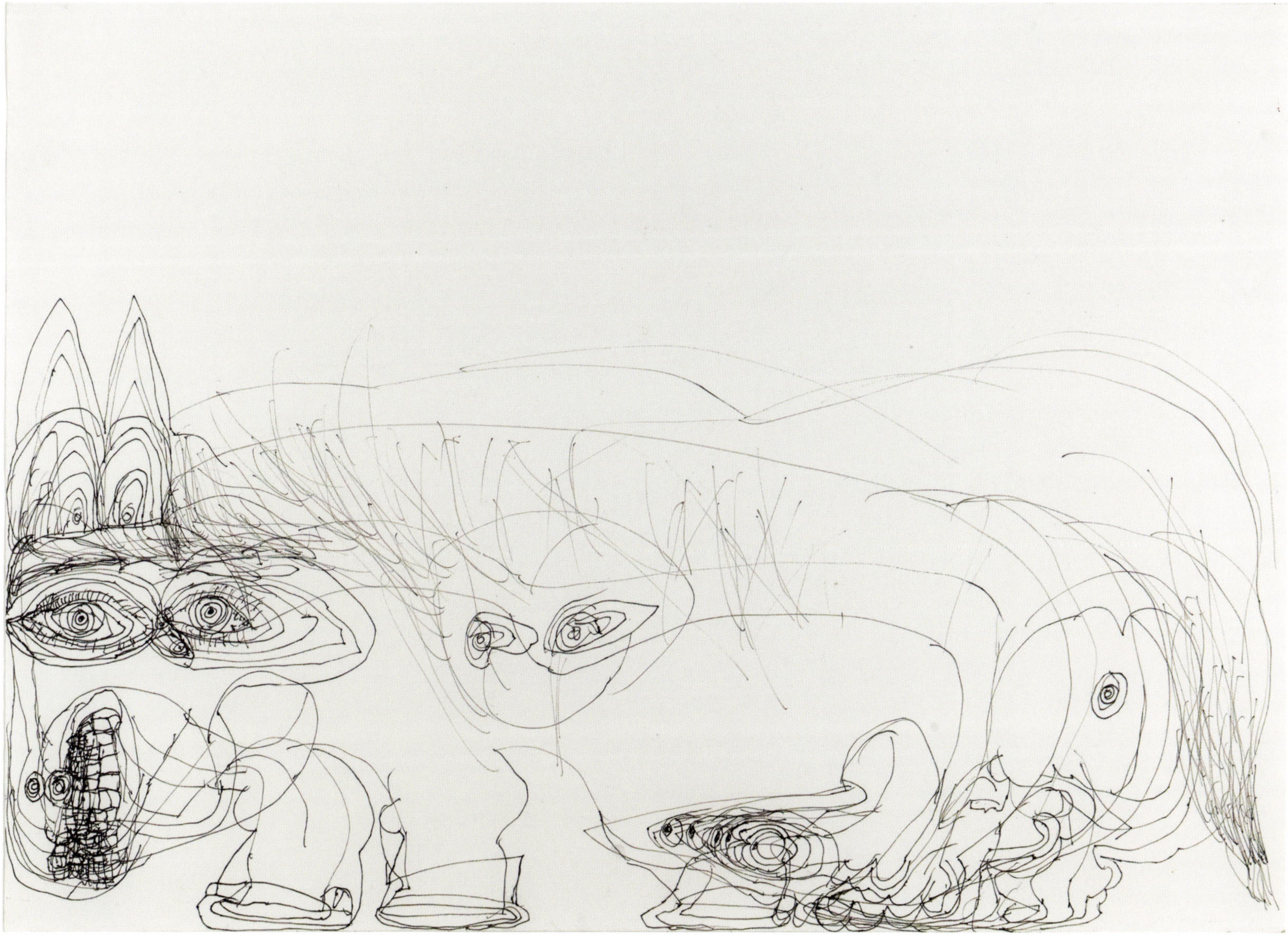

Cat. 53

Edmund Monsiel

Born 1897 Wożuczyn, Poland
Died 1962 Tomaszów Lubelski, Poland

Untitled

1958
graphite pencil on paper
8 1/8 × 5 11/16 in. (20.6 × 14.5 cm)

Edmund Monsiel created a body of intricately detailed drawings in the last twenty years of his life. These drawings portray figures surrounded by faces with staring eyes and usually include a messianic or religious inscription. Monsiel used art to help cope with his untreated schizophrenia. Each drawing was a manifestation of his struggles with the evils he saw in everyday life.

Cat. 54

Nick Blinko

Born 1961 Watford, Hertfordshire, England

Untitled

1985
pen and black ink on paper
16 9/16 × 16 9/16 in. (42.1 × 42.1 cm)

Nick Blinko "doesn't have a single methodology, although very often a central figure somewhere in the middle of the sheet is where things start. . . . Larger forms are usually drawn first, often in outline, and then space is incrementally occupied, sometimes almost obliterating the original image, and at others forming a kind of holding web or visual soup."

Colin Rhodes, interview by Michael Bonesteel, April 17, 2020, quoted in Bonesteel, unpublished notes on Rosenthal Collection, Richard Rosenthal files.

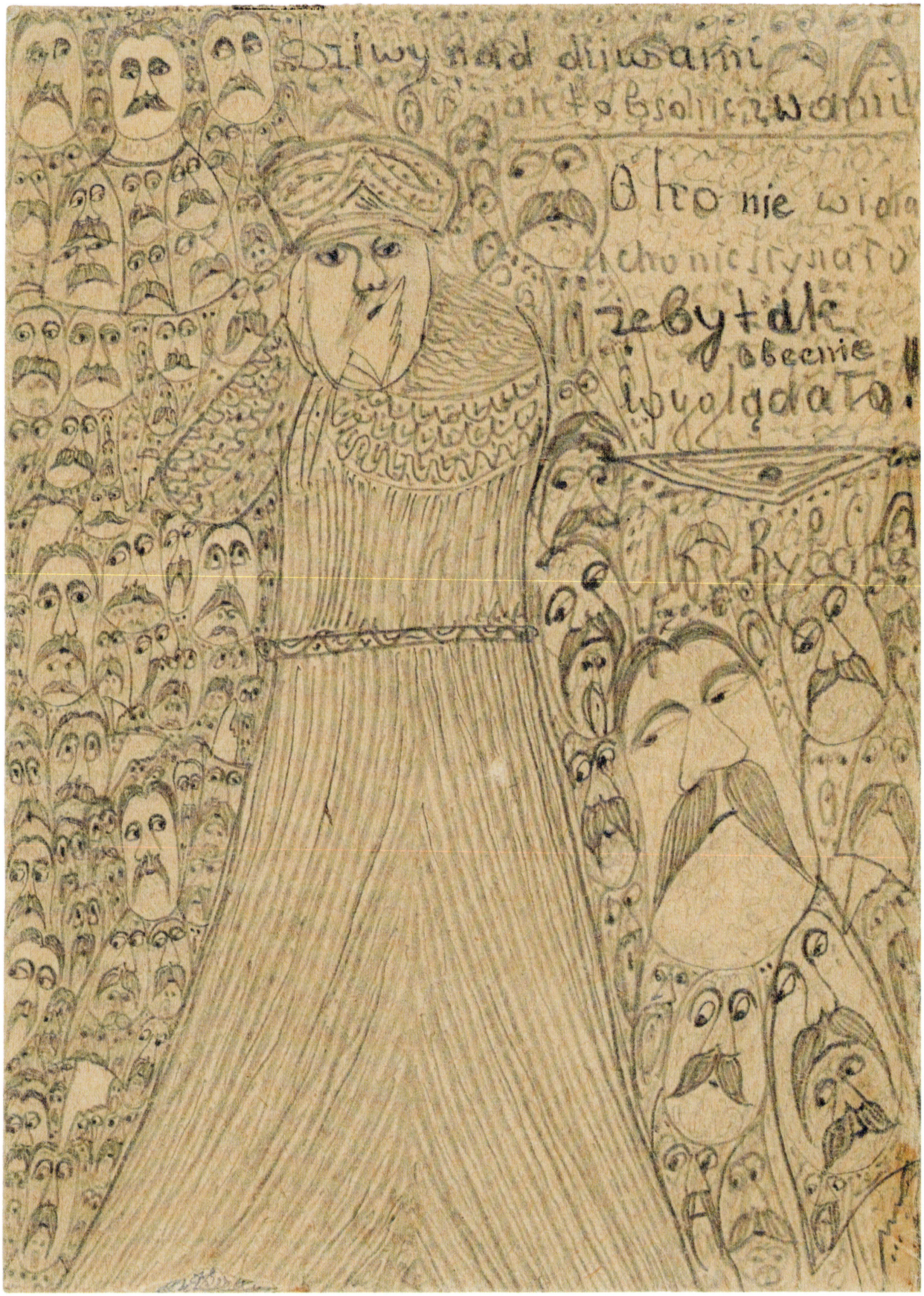

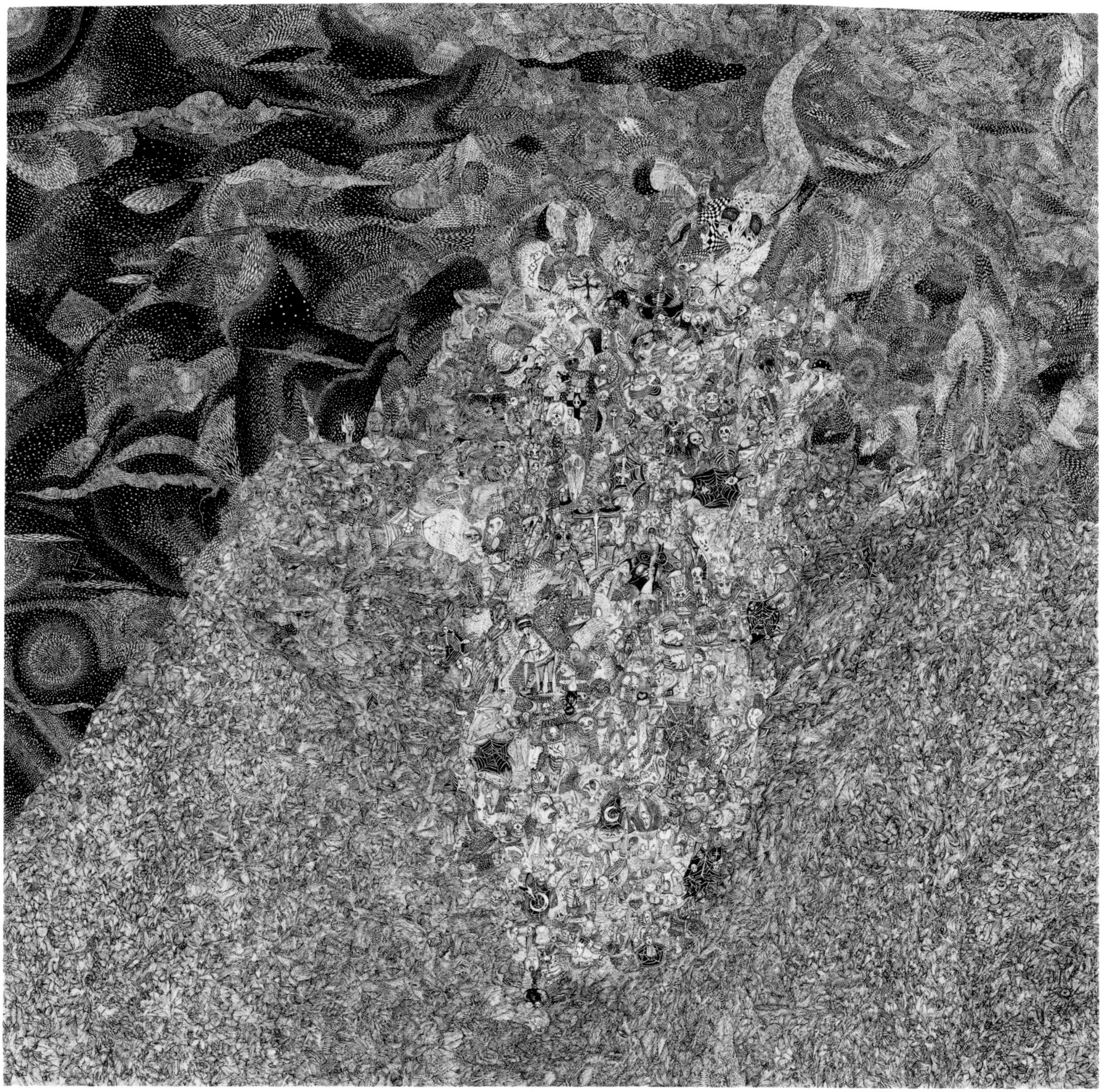

Cat. 55

Charles Benefiel

Born 1967 Venice Beach, California

Untitled #9

circa 1995–96

pen and black ink, tea, and furniture varnish on paper

22 15⁄16 × 15 3⁄16 in. (58.3 × 38.6 cm)

Charles Benefiel's drawings are a complex layering of stippling created by working from the center of the composition out. Diagnosed with obsessive compulsive disorder, Benefiel uses art making to exert control over his life. The focus on broken dolls is personal: "I needed to draw them and see how I felt. They were meant to embody very, very negative things. [They are] depersonalized, isolated, contained, torn up, used—violated, but they are still there."

Charles Benefiel quoted in Bernard L. Herman, "Charles Benefiel," *Raw Vision* 30 (Spring 2000): 34.

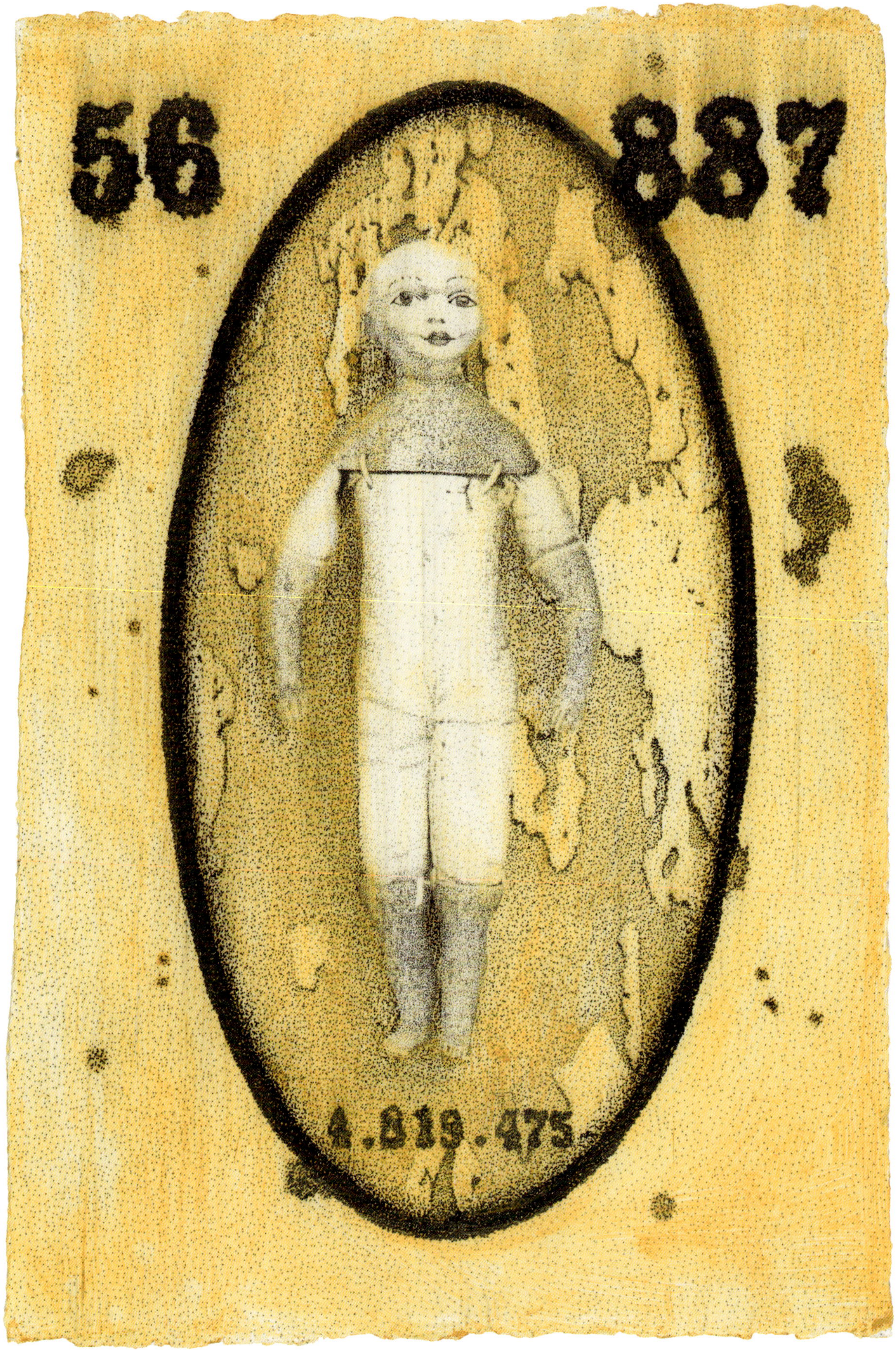

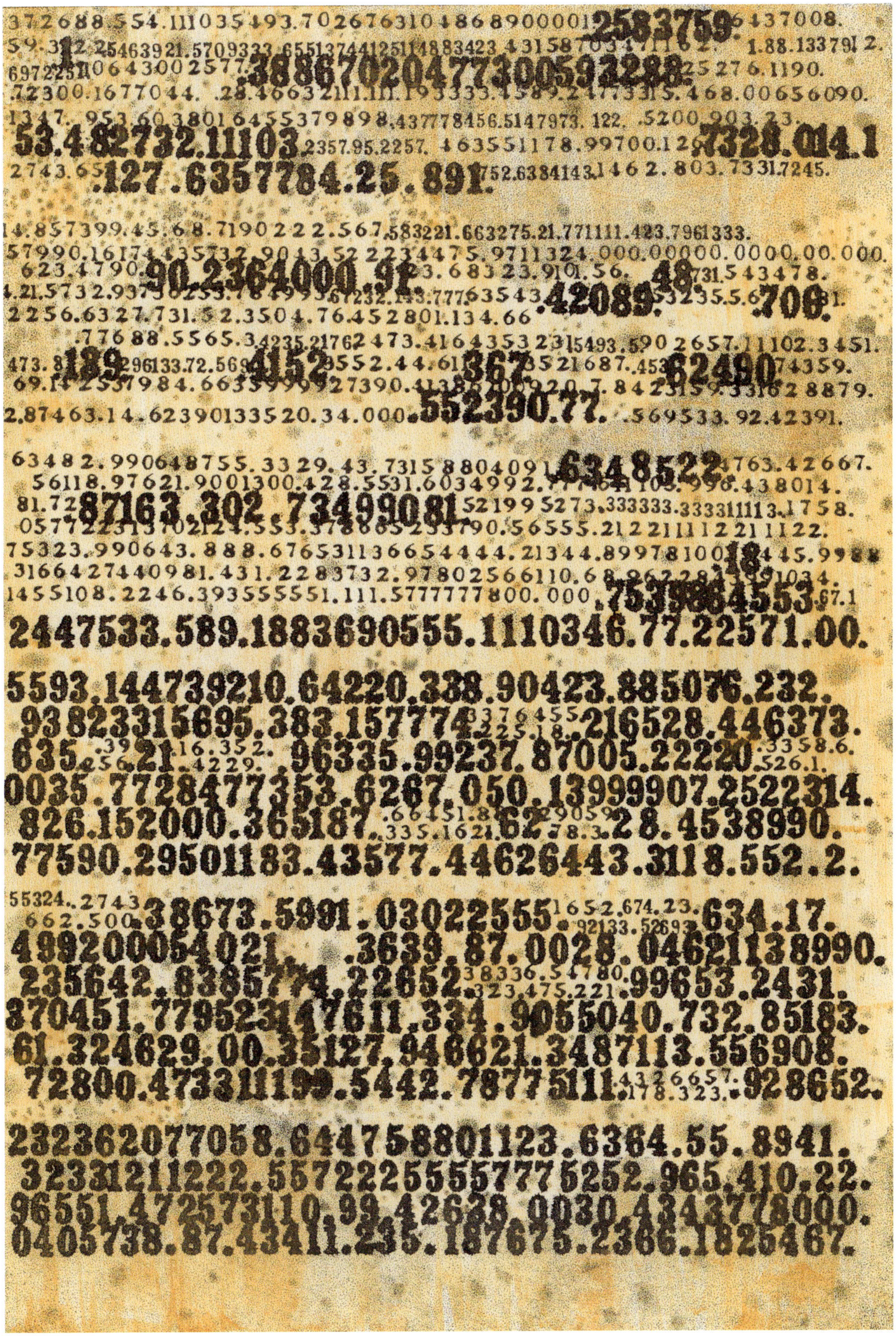

Cat. 56

Charles Benefiel

Hygienic Toys 4

1996

pen and black ink, tea, and varnish on paper

59⅛ × 39³⁄₁₆ in. (150.1 × 99.6 cm)

"In his drawings of rows of numbers he stipples the characters from left to right as they would appear on a typed or printed page. As he draws, he counts the dots, an act that apparently takes place in sequences rather than as a continuous inventory. The sequences (counting to a certain number, then beginning anew) help him to focus his thoughts and 'chain' his mind to the drawing process."

Bernard L. Herman, "Charles Benefiel," *Raw Vision* 30 (Spring 2000): 32.

Cat. 57

Charles Benefiel

Random Numeric Repeater #5

2001

pen and ink on paper

49 5/16 × 35 1/4 in. (125.3 × 89.5 cm)

"Each [Random Numeric Repeater] drawing was made up of more than 20,000 characters written in stream of consciousness and represented a pheonetic [sic] numeric language that I had created as a zen drawing exercise."

Charles Benefiel, Facebook post, May 12, 2013.

Cat. 58

Hiroyuki Doi

Born 1946 Nagoya, Japan

Untitled

2002

pen and black ink on paper

38 3/8 × 74 5/16 in. (97.5 × 188.7 cm)

Composed of tiny circles, often on washi (Japanese handmade paper), the contemplative works of Hiroyuki Doi may bring to mind drifting cloud formations or pulsing galaxies. Therapeutic for both artist and viewer, their creative process, as Doi explains, has a calming effect that helped him grieve the death of his brother.

Hiroyuki Doi quoted in Edward M. Gómez, "A Universe in Tiny Form," *Raw Vision* 79 (Summer 2012): 51.

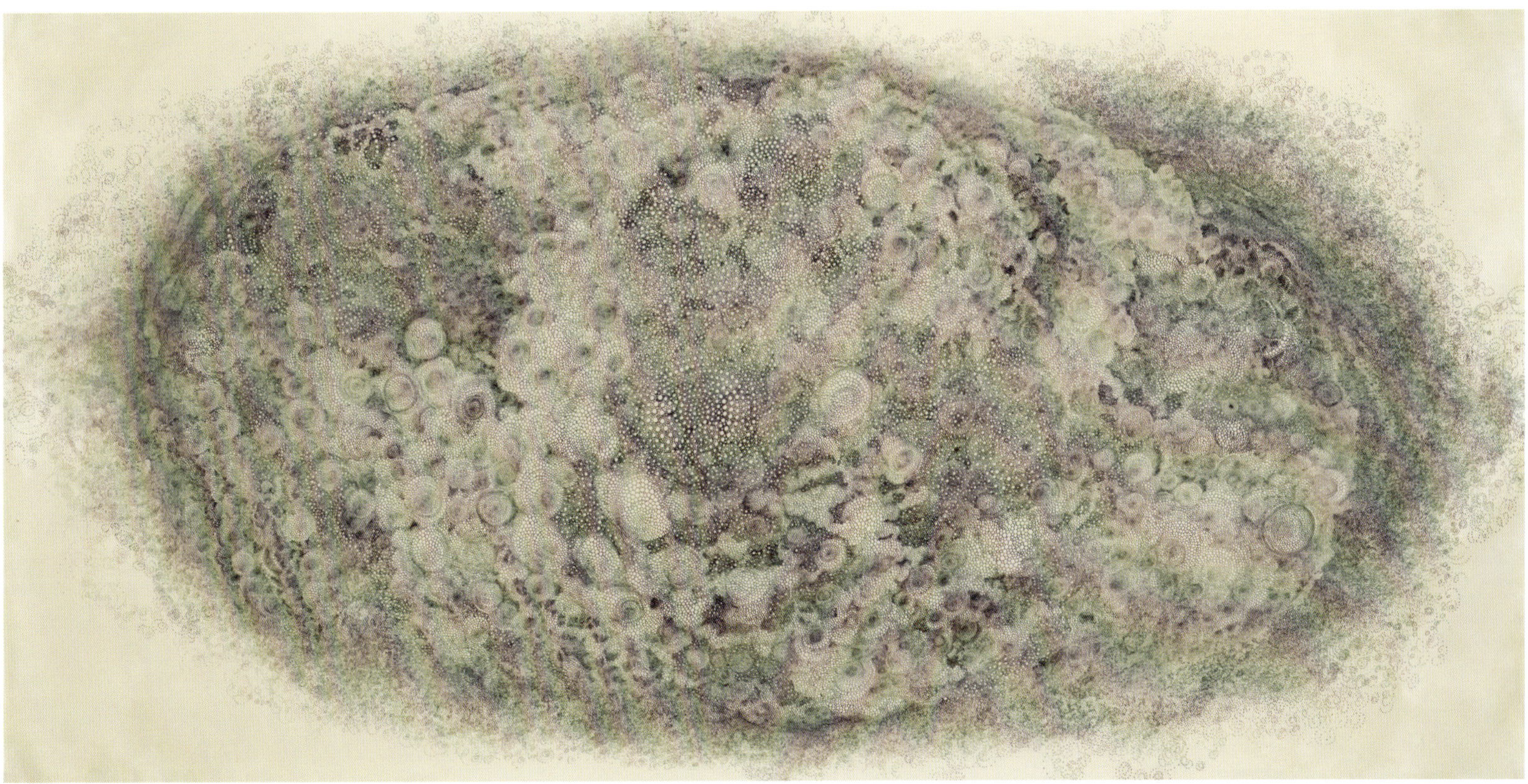

Cat. 59
Jean Dubuffet
Born 1901 Le Havre, France
Died 1985 Paris, France

Landscape (Paysage)
1980
fiber-tipped pen and black ink on paper
13¾ × 10 1⁄16 in. (35 × 25.6 cm)

Jean Dubuffet, the trailblazing advocate of the work of the self-taught, stated of art, “It is a duet between the artist and his medium. Each must speak freely and directly and visibly his own language. One must allow all the fortunes proper to the material to emerge. . . . To try to prevent these vagaries of fortune would be to deprive the work of vitality.”

Jean Dubuffet quoted in *Prospectus et tous écrits suivants*, comp. and ed. Hubert Damisch, 2 vols. (Paris: Éditions Gallimard, 1967), 2:233.

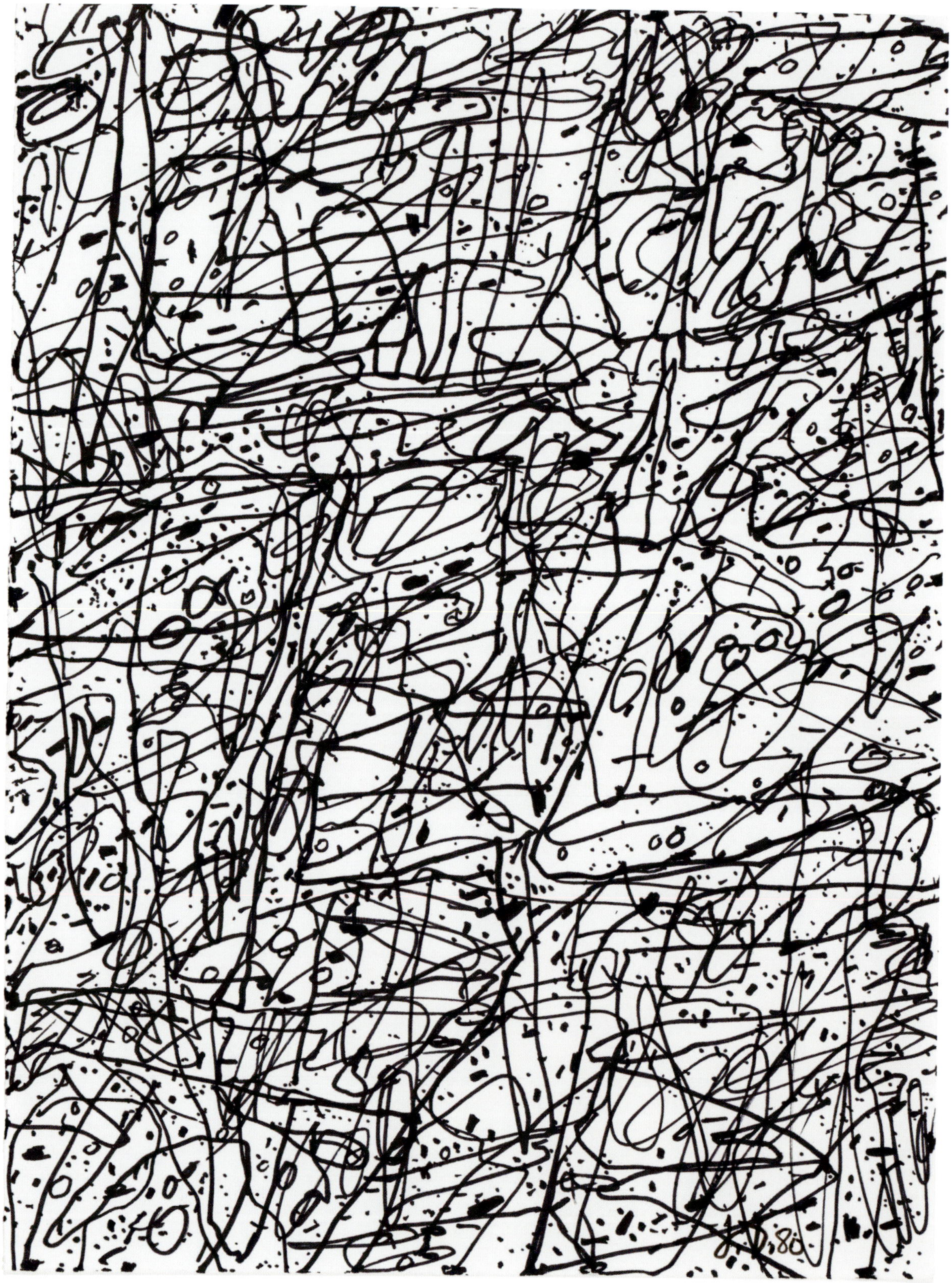

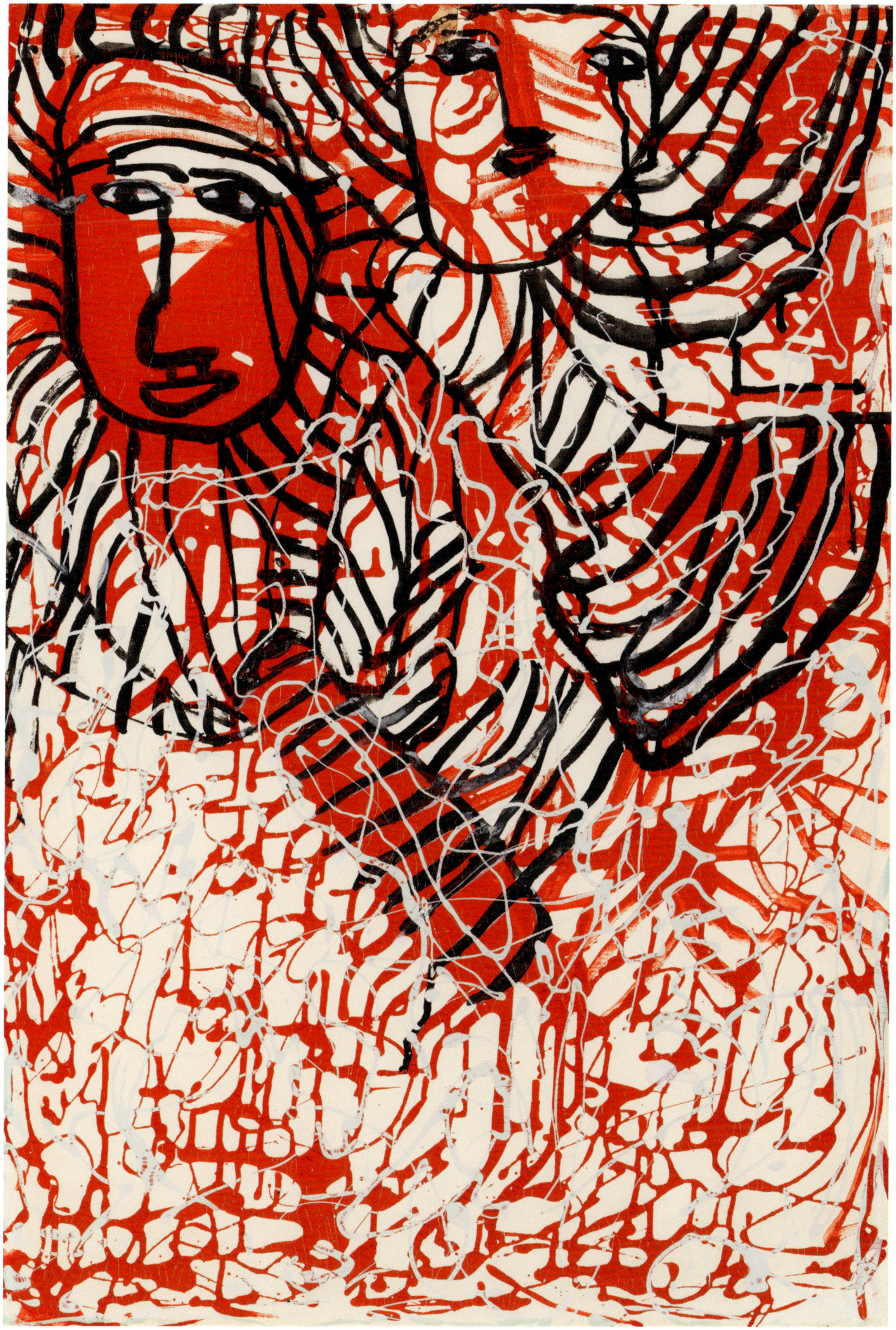

Cat. 60

Janet Sobel

Born 1893 as Jennie Olechovsky, Ekaterinoslav, Ukraine

Died 1968 Plainfield, New Jersey

Untitled (JS-070)

1946–48

enamel paint on canvas board

30 × 20 in. (76.2 × 50.8 cm)

Renewed attention has come recently to Janet Sobel (who tried painting one day with her son's materials) for inventing the celebrated Abstract Expressionist drip. Of the faces that often hover in her work, Sobel's granddaughter recalled, "Although Gramma left many of her siblings behind in the Ukraine, she remembered them in her art. Faces from her past—people who spoke her language—were there on canvas or paper, or envelopes or whatever surface was under her hand. The eyes and bodies spoke, and they created the familiar in a country that was never quite her own."

Ashley Shapiro, interview by James Barron, January 2018, in *Janet Sobel and Ashley Shapiro: Spiritual Connection* (South Kent, CT: James Barron Art, 2022), 26–27.

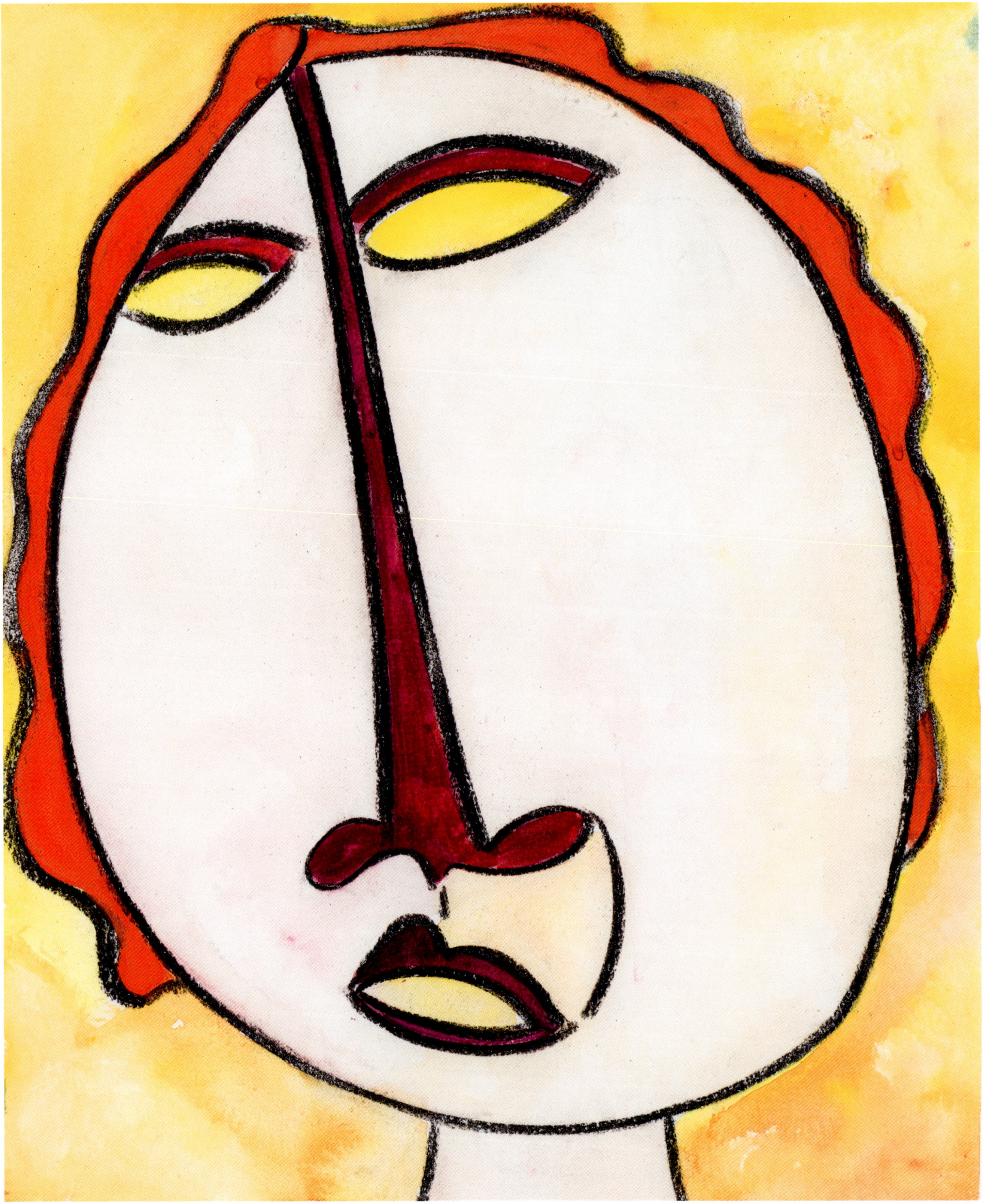

Cat. 61
Albert Louden
Born 1943 Blackpool, England

Untitled
late 20th–early 21st century
watercolor, gouache, and black pastel on paper
19⅝ × 15⅞ in. (49.9 × 40.4 cm)

When Albert Louden creates art, he does not know what the outcome will be. Says the artist, "When I try to hold onto images and experiment, even something as straightforward as a tree, when I try to paint it—can't do it, and anger comes over me and the tree is forgotten; it becomes something else—hair!"

Albert Louden quoted in Nina Milburn, "Outsider Art: Can Art be Taught?," https://prezi.com/zfycqh3zkj0s/outsiders-art/, accessed July 20, 2022.

Cat. 62
Paul Duhem
Born 1919 Blandain, Belgium
Died 1999 Ellignies-Sainte-Anne, Belgium

Untitled
circa 1989
acrylic and graphite pencil on paper
21¾ × 14⅜ in. (55.2 × 36.5 cm)

At age seventy, Paul Duhem began making art in a workshop at the Centre La Pommeraie, a Belgian organization for people with disabilities. An observer noted of his process: "Before choosing a color he would place the entire contents of the tube in the tin. He worked in series. As he emptied the tin, the next color would be mixed with the previous one, the dirty brushes helping in the process. . . . He had a marvelous rapport with oils and paper."

Quoted in "Paul Duhem," Fondation Paul Duhem, https://fondationpaulduhem.eu/the-artists/paul-duhem/?lang=en, accessed June 28, 2022.

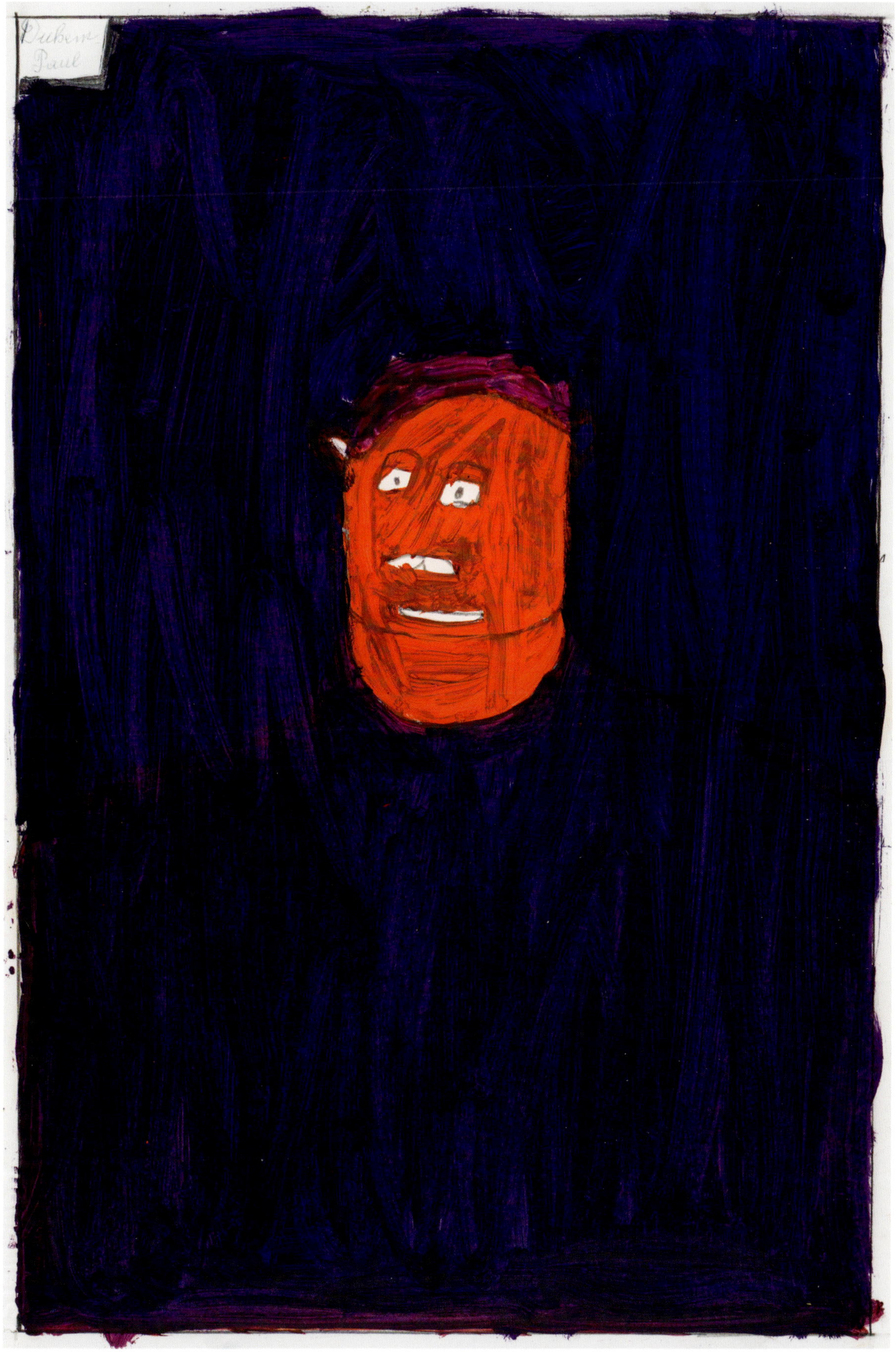

Cat. 63

Donald Pass

Born 1930 Cheshire, England
Died 2010 Oxford, England

Landscape beyond the Veil

2000
watercolor and pen and ink on paper
29 13⁄16 × 40 11⁄16 in.
(75.7 × 103.3 cm)

In a Cuckfield, Norfolk, graveyard, Donald Pass became unsettled when he encountered a tomb in the winged shape of the Royal Air Force insignia. "Everything began to change and a tremendous darkness surrounded me. . . . The whole landscape, churchyard, near and distant fields, seemed filled with thousands of figures Stretching to the horizon. In the blackness was a tremendous light; large winged figures with faces like lions. . . . A veil had been lifted and I would never again see anything in the same way."

Donald Pass quoted in "Donald Pass," Henry Boxer Gallery, https://www.outsiderart.co.uk/artists/donald-pass, accessed June 23, 2022.

Cat. 64

Malcolm McKesson

Born 1909 Monmouth Beach, New Jersey
Died 1999 New York City

We are led into service

1979
pen and blue, brown, and black ink, and graphite pencil on paper
13 11⁄16 × 11 in. (34.7 × 28 cm)

"When I draw, I attempt to see the form in the undrawn . . . this is therapeutic for me." Malcolm McKesson wrote, "I want to rediscover a buried tradition, to rediscover the female in the man; I've looked for a long time for a social dimension to all this, maybe now the world is ready for this sort of thing."

Malcolm McKesson quoted in Tony Thorne, "The Reclusive World of Malcolm McKesson," in *Malcolm McKesson: An Exquisite Obsession* (Richmond, England: Henry Boxer Gallery, n.d.), unnumbered pages.

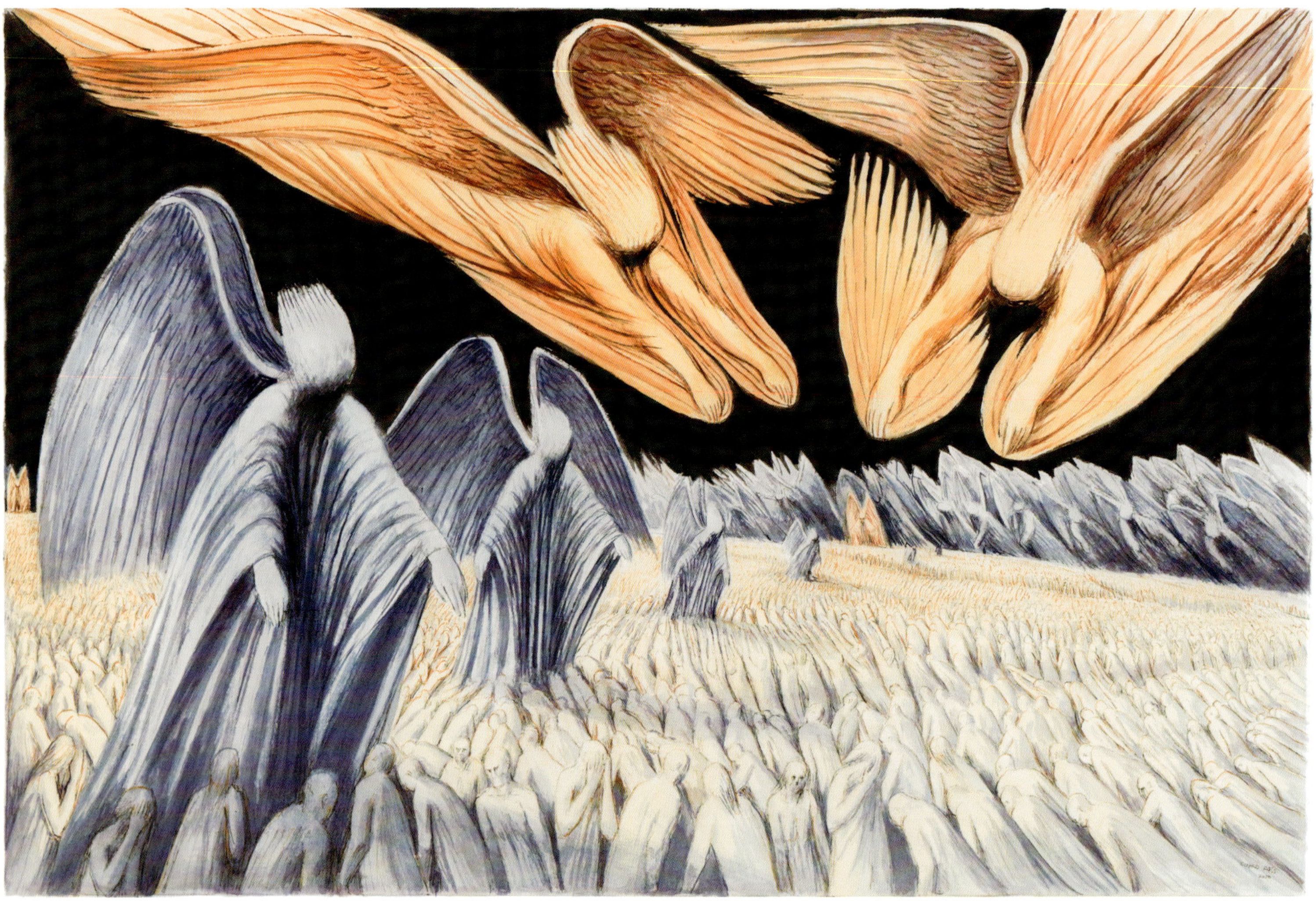

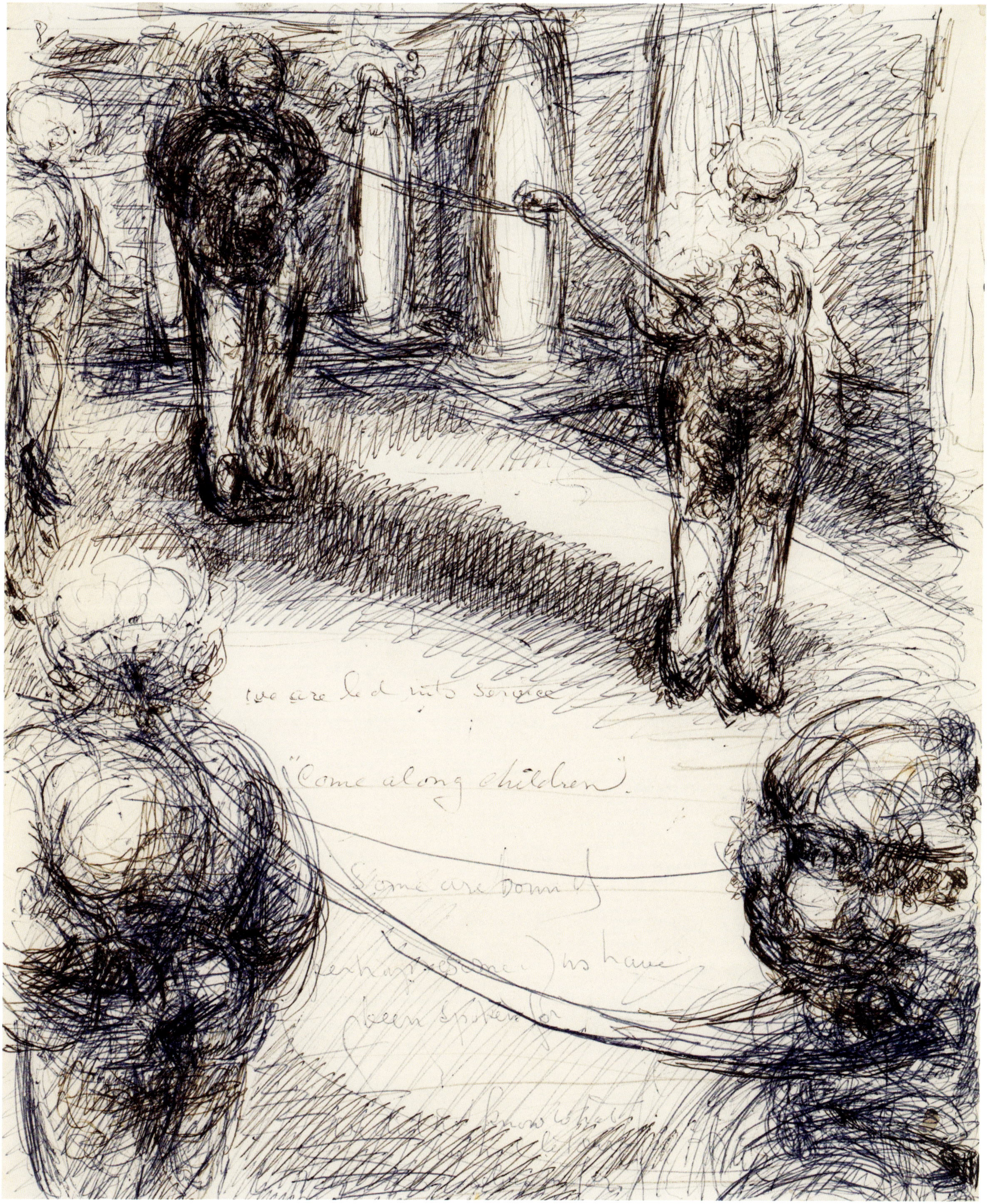
we are led into service
"Come along children"
Some are born
been spoken for

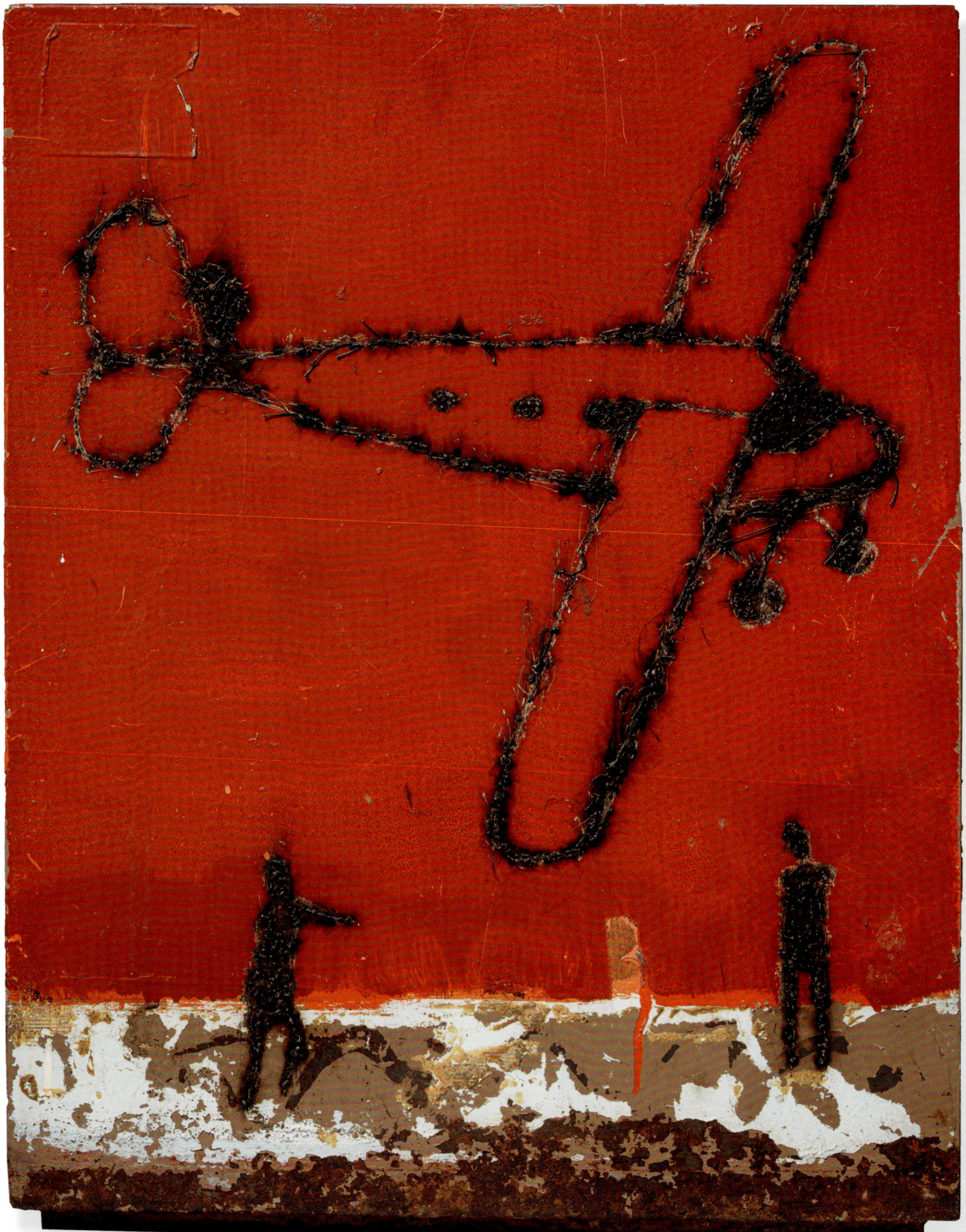

Cat. 65
Scott Griffin
Born 1970 Oshawa, Canada

Runway Walk
circa 2000
arc welding on metal
29 ½ × 22 ½ × ¾ in.
(74.9 × 57.2 × 1.9 cm)

"I am a scrapper and collector of interesting things that people abandon. I use a MIG welder to draw onto the metal objects. It is a controlled burn of old paint and rust. With this drawing tool, my vision is limited but [I] work intuitively. My welding contribution is only to complement the found surface."

Scott Griffin to Michael Bonesteel, August 17, 2020, quoted in Bonesteel, unpublished notes on Rosenthal Collection, Richard Rosenthal files.

Cat. 66
Scott Griffin

Scapegoats
2001
arc welding on metal
12 × 25 ½ × 1½ in.
(30.5 × 64.8 × 3.8 cm)

"In the piece *Scapegoats,* there is a lonely space and distance."

Scott Griffin to Michael Bonesteel, August 17, 2020, quoted in Bonesteel, unpublished notes on Rosenthal Collection, Richard Rosenthal files.

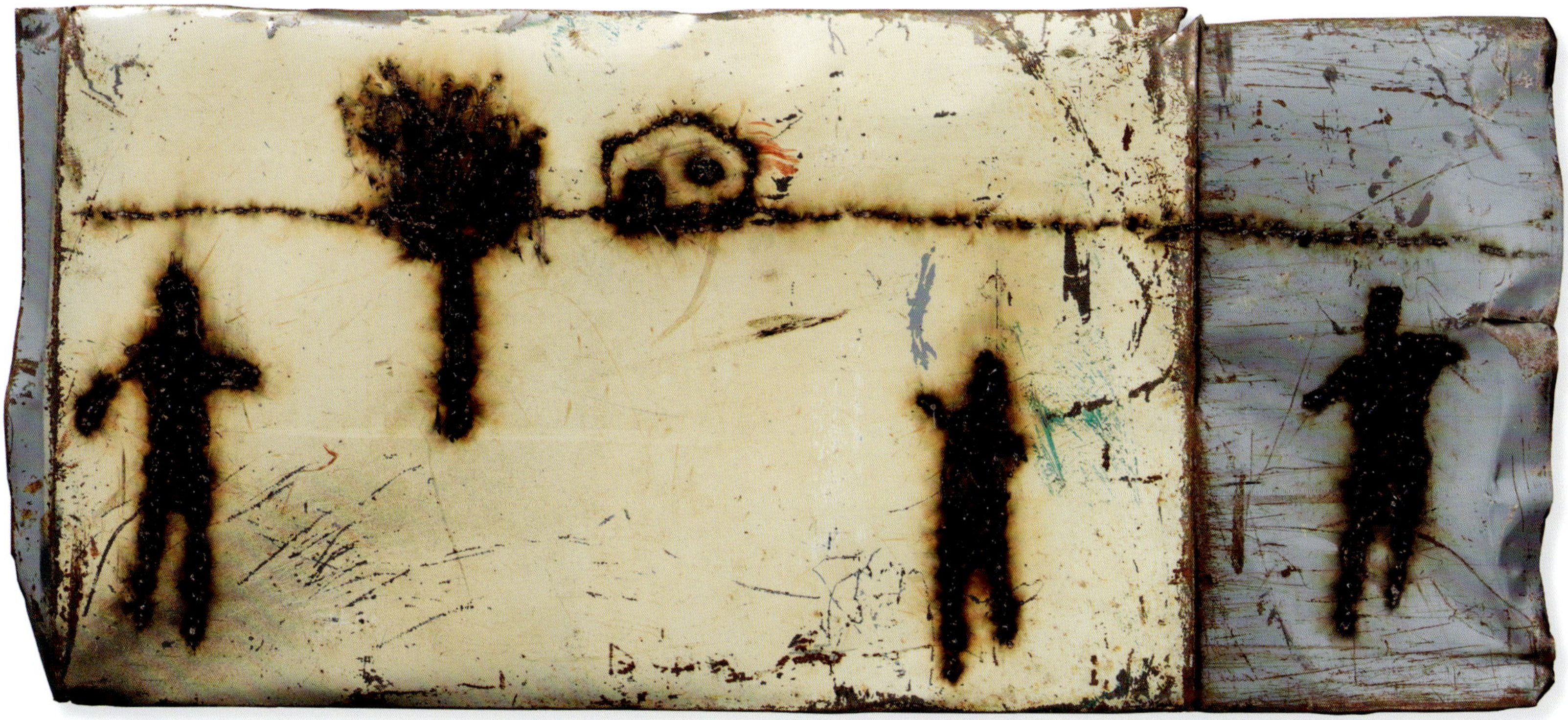

Cat. 67

Hipkiss

Born 1964 (both artists) England, working in France

Slit in Molko Oi

2000

graphite pencil, silver ink, and brown paint or resin on paper

34 × 25$\frac{7}{16}$ in. (86.3 × 64.6 cm)

Hipkiss is the pseudonym of British artists Alpha and Christoper Mason, who collaborate on precise, detailed drawings in which silver ink applied under graphite pencil subtly enhances the pencil's reflective qualities. Binaries, such as industrial versus natural landscapes, intrigue the creative duo, now based in France.

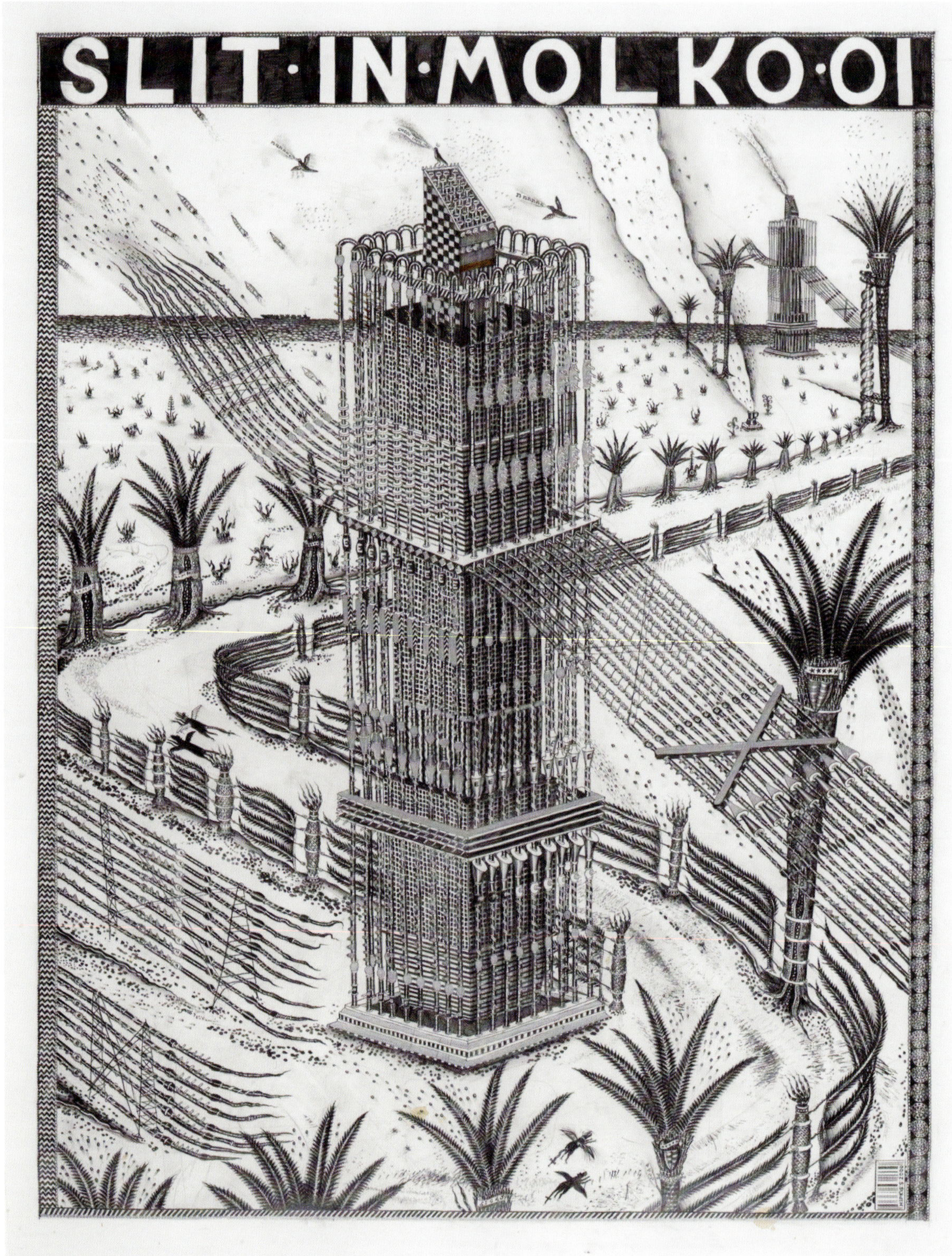

Cat. 68
Hipkiss

My Hole with an East
2001
graphite pencil and silver
ink on paper
25 ½ × 45 ½ in. (64.8 × 115.6 cm)

"Eschewing a formal art education, the couple [known as Hipkiss] chose to pursue university studies in subjects such as mathematics, political geography, sociology and media production, all of which inform their artistic universe to this day."

"Biography," Hipkiss, https://www.hipkissart.com/biography.html, accessed June 20, 2022.

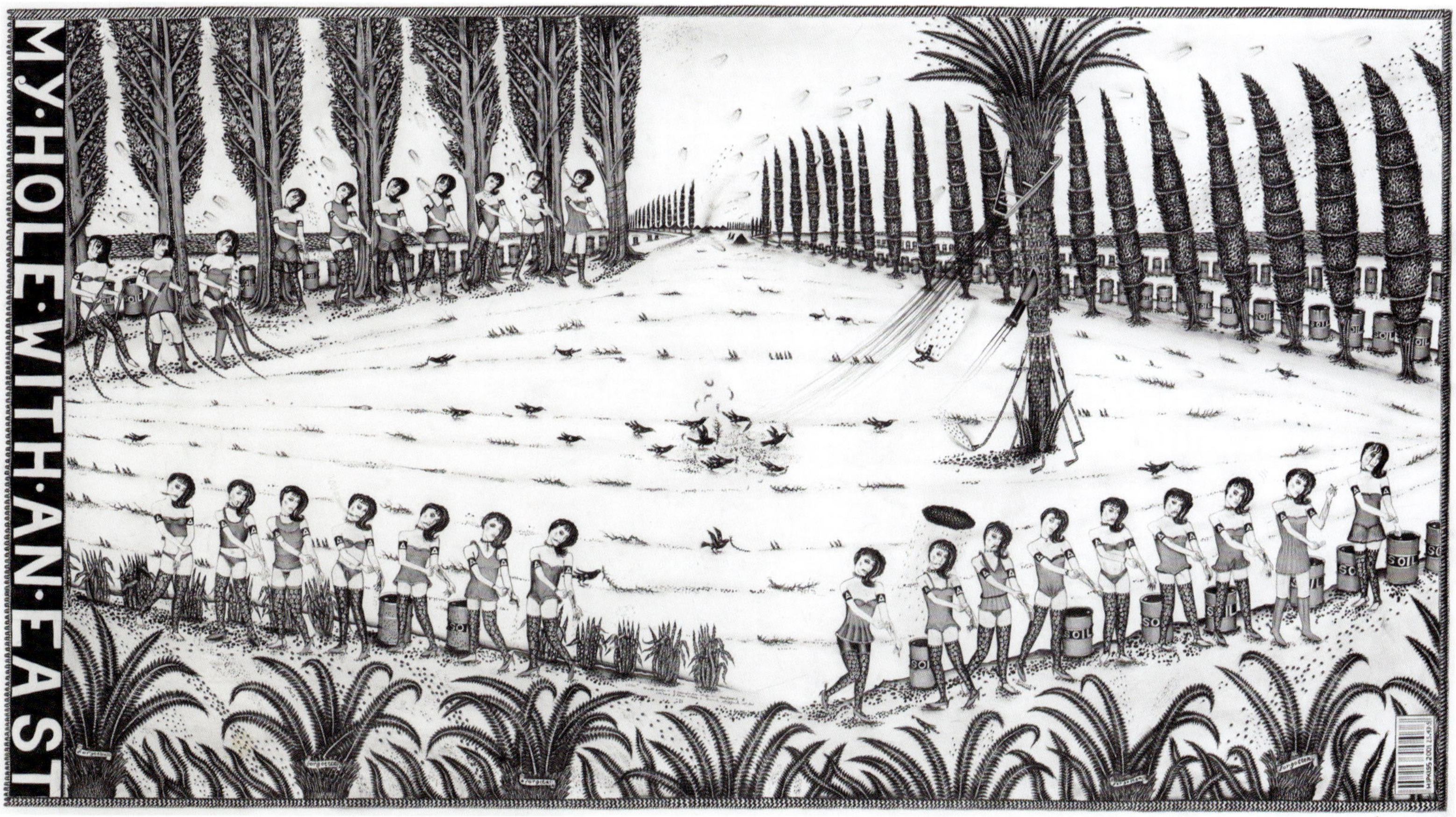

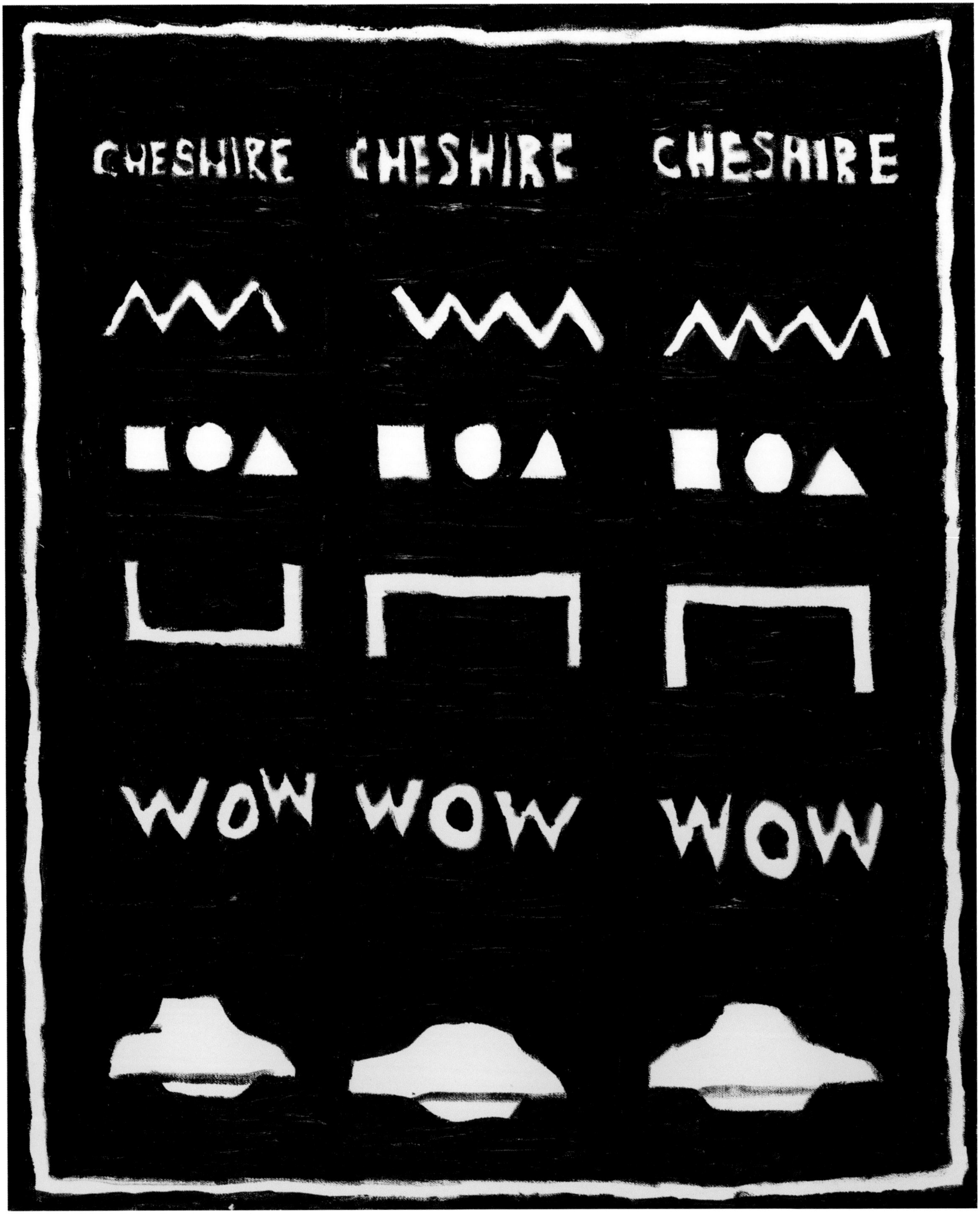
CHESHIRE CHESHIRE CHESHIRE
WOW WOW WOW

Cat. 69
Ken Grimes
Born 1947 New York City

WOW
1992
acrylic on canvas
30 × 24 in. (76.2 × 61 cm)

"Synchronicities," for Ken Grimes, are signs of extraterrestrial intelligence and alien intervention. Thus Cheshire, repeated at the top of this painting, is both the Connecticut town where the artist grew up and the home in England of another Ken Grimes who won a huge soccer pool by calling seven straight ties at odds of 1.5 million to one.

"Ken Grimes," Ricco/Maresca Gallery, https://www.riccomaresca.com/artists/46-ken-grimes/biography/, accessed June 23, 2022.

Cat. 70
Ionel Talpazan
Born 1955 Petrachioaia, Romania
Died 2015 New York City

UFO: ART & SCIENCE #7
1997
black fiber-tipped pen, crayon, colored pencil, and graphite pencil on paper
30 1/16 × 71 5/8 in. (76.4 × 182 cm)

"My art is about the big mystery in life. How did we get here on planet Earth? Why are we here? Is there life on other planets?"

Ionel Talpazan, interview by *Western Folklore*, 2008, quoted in William Grimes, "Ionel Talpazan, Whose U.F.O. Art Had Sightings All Over, Dies at 60," *New York Times*, September 29, 2015.

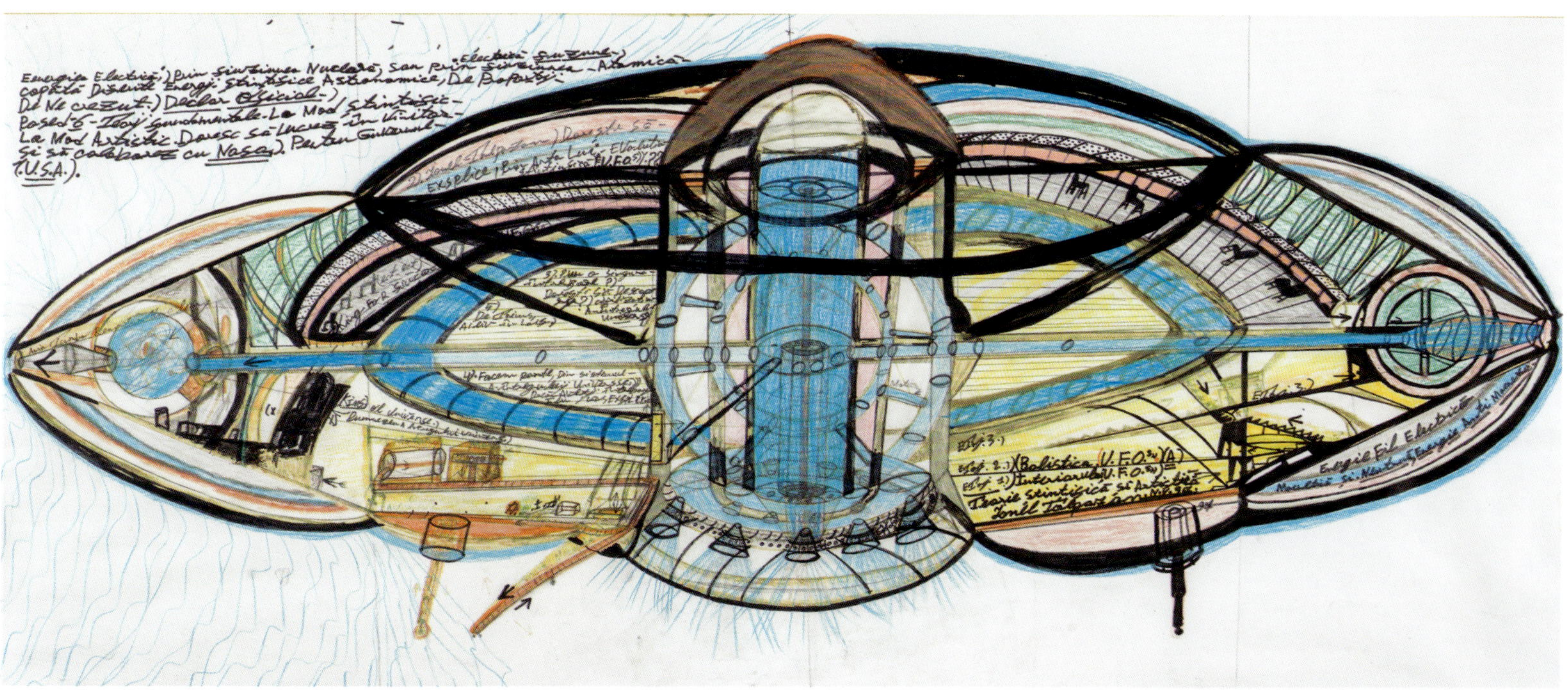

Cat. 71
Damian Le Bas
Born 1963 Sheffield, England
Died 2017 Worthing, England

Untitled
1999
graphite pencil on paper
11$\frac{11}{16}$ × 8$\frac{5}{16}$ in. (29.7 × 21.1 cm)

Each picture began as a blank page ready to be filled: "I never have any plan. No theory. I probably start off with a little face, an eye. The rest follows."

Damian Le Bas quoted in Philip Vann, "Romany Visions," *Raw Vision* 13 (Winter 1995/96): 41–42.

Cat. 72
Damian Le Bas

Untitled
1999
graphite pencil on paper
16½ × 12$\frac{1}{16}$ in. (41.9 × 30.7 cm)

"One of these faces is my soul. I am lucky enough to have recorded my soul in the pictures. I've also recorded my love for [my wife] Delaine and little Damian [our son] in the bargain."

Damian Le Bas quoted in Philip Vann, "Romany Visions," *Raw Vision* 13 (Winter 1995/96): 41–42.

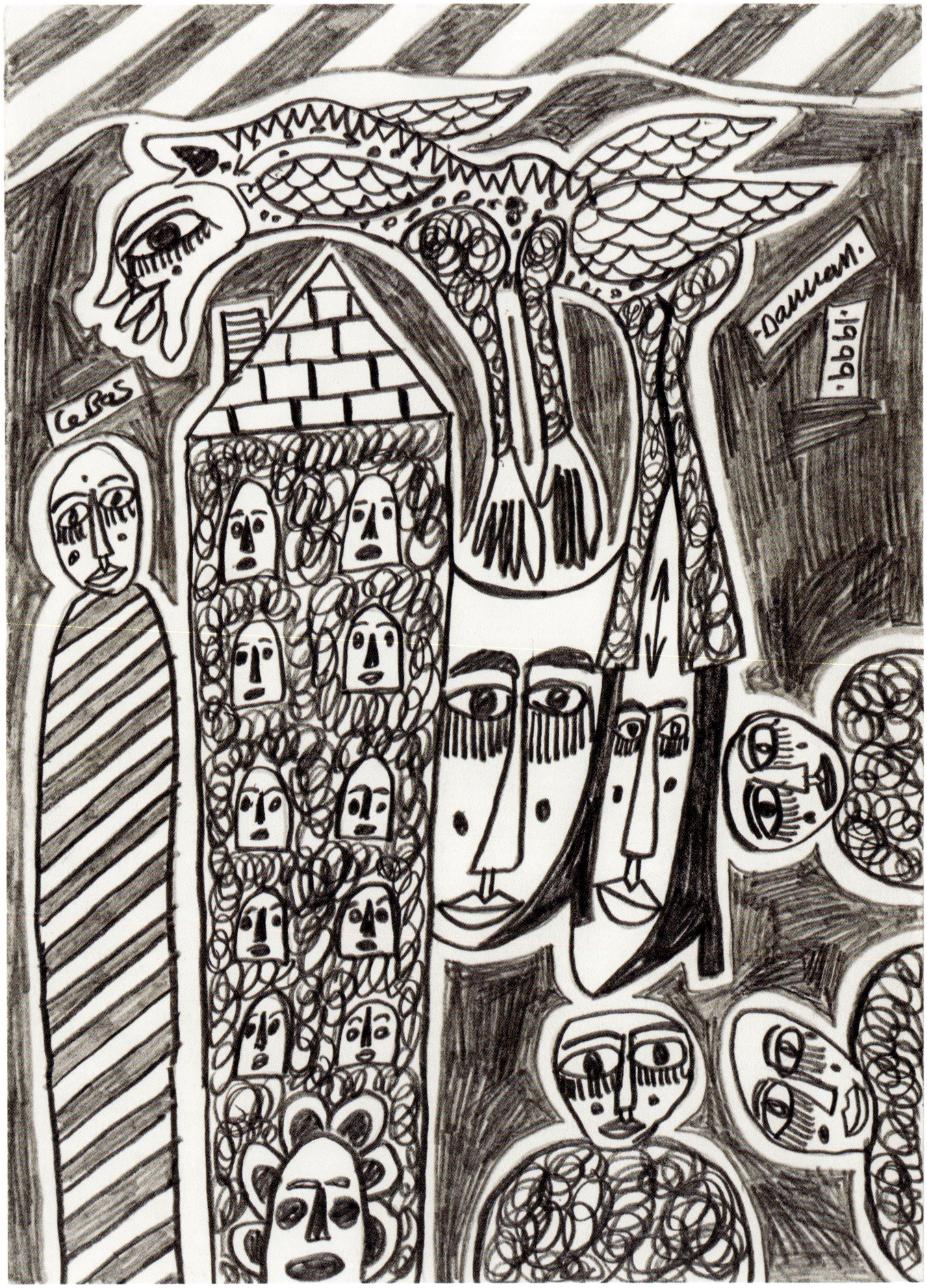

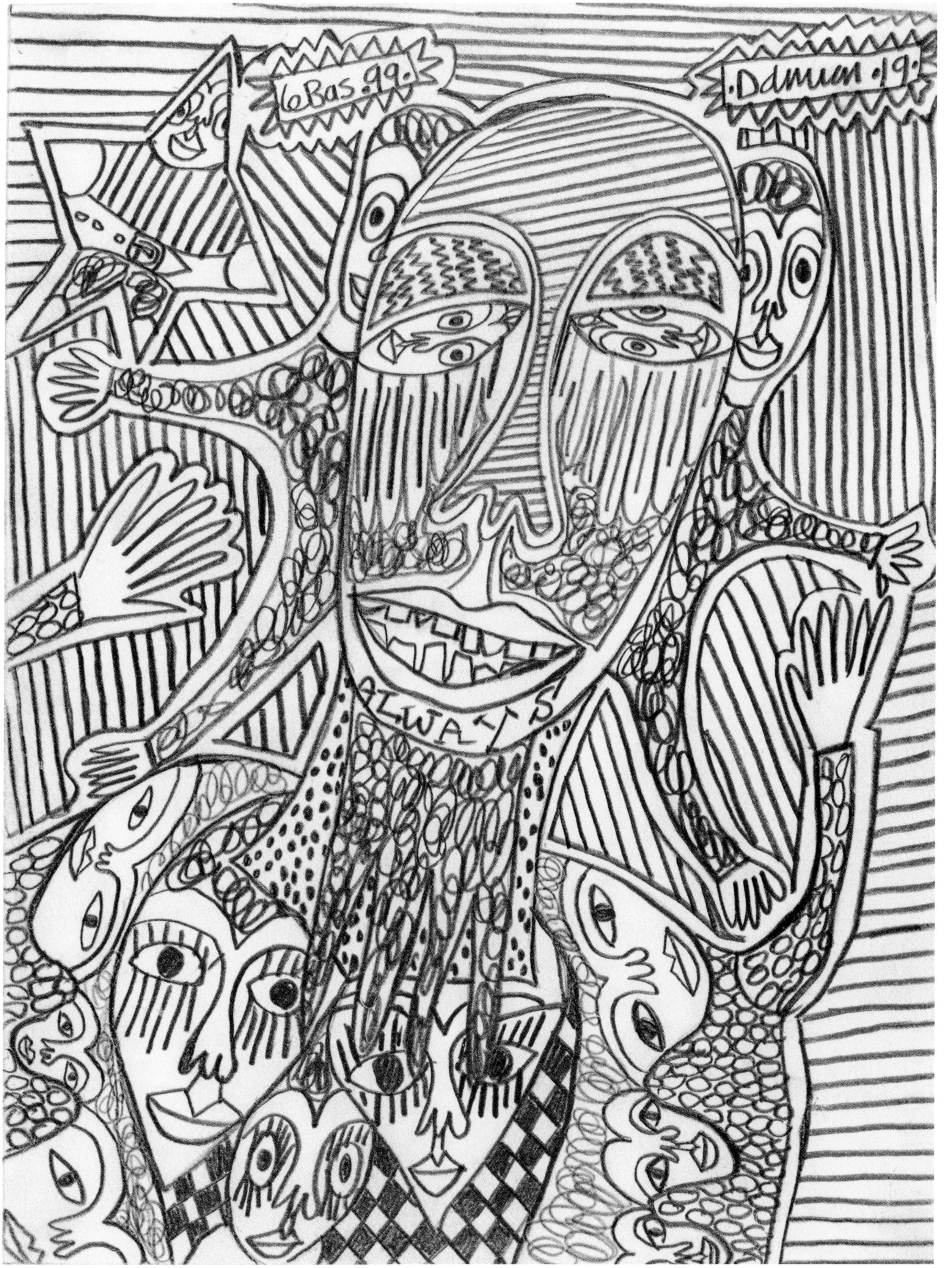
leBas.99.
.Damien.19.
ALWAYS

Cat. 73
Lidia Syroka
Born 1956 Poland, works in Paris, France

Map Book
late 20th century
mixed media on handmade paper
closed: 8⅞ × 5⅞ in. (22.5 × 14.9 cm);
open: 8⅞ × 54⅛ in. (22.5 × 137.5 cm)

Lidia Syroka's richly textured maps of imagined cities include this accordion-folding work of art. Born in Poland, Syroka moved to Paris as a young woman. Her extensive journeys—to Mongolia, Siberia, India, Pakistan, Nepal, and China—have been transformational, deeply impressing themselves upon her work.

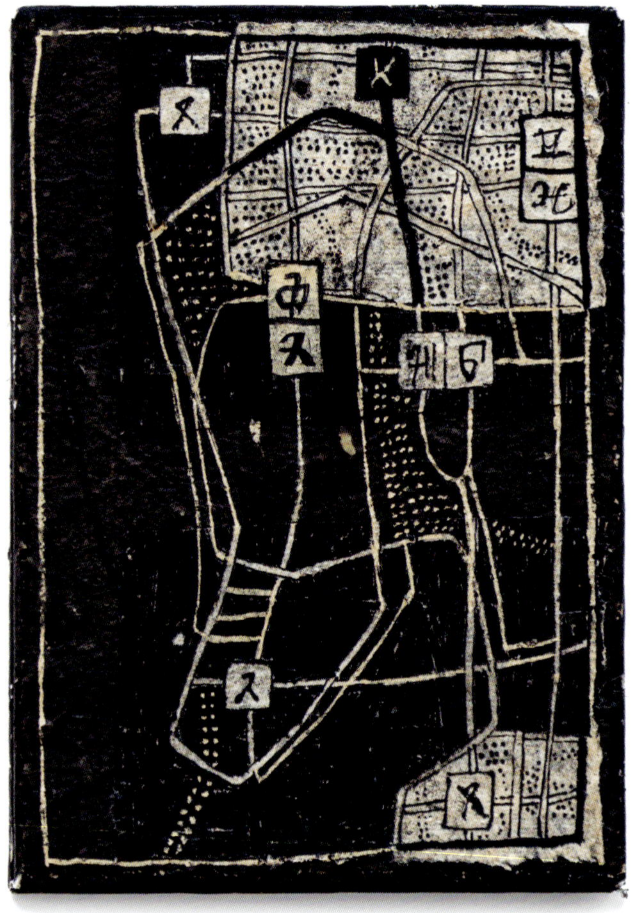

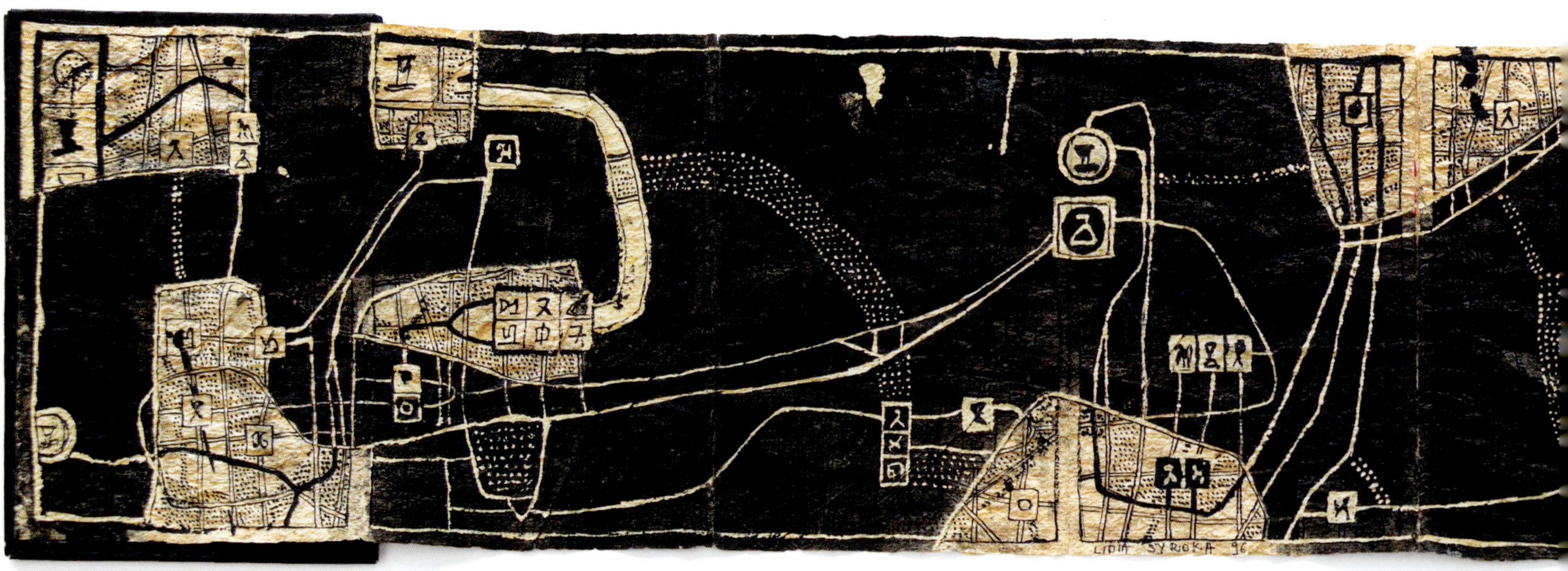

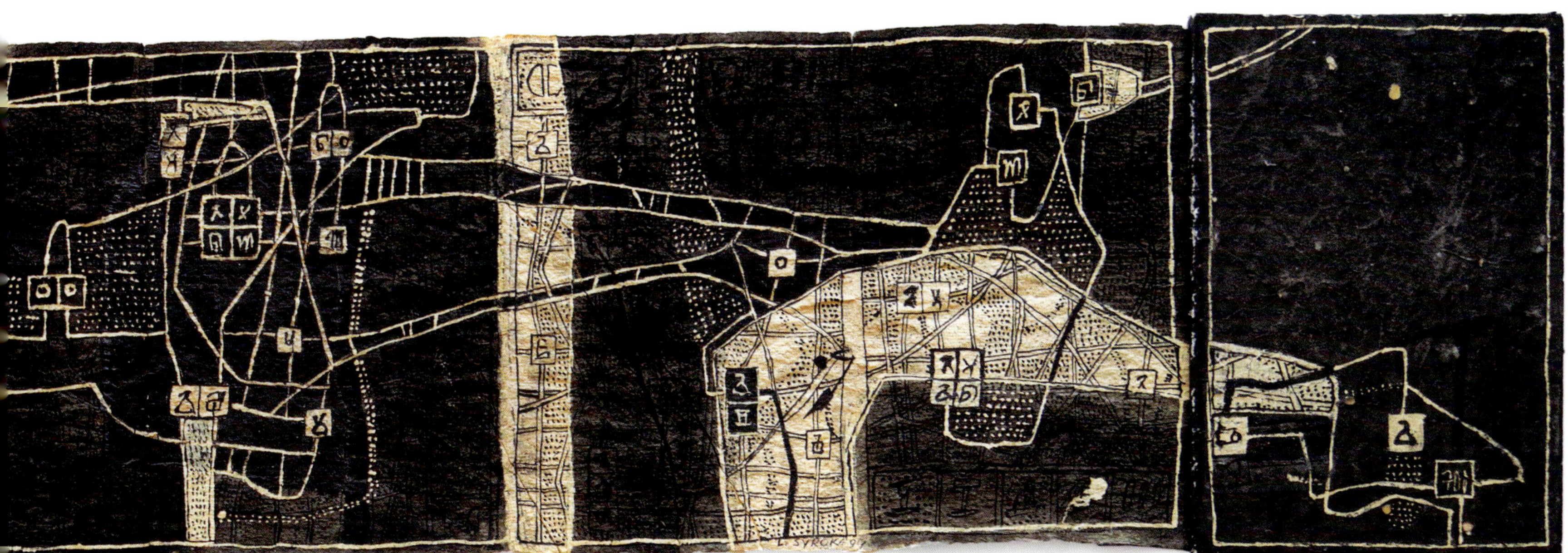

Cat. 74
Lidia Syroka

Map of Fictional City
1996
pen and black ink, and watercolor on sewn collage of handmade paper
19 5/16 × 54 15/16 in. (49 × 139.5 cm)

"In my sewn paper work, I concentrate on the intimate reality of paper matter. I've always worked with paper; inspected its 'inner' dimension to extract its beauty. To touch its secret, I stuck it, sewed it, tore it, and stuck it again. Yet after many years in this line of work, it felt necessary for me to return to drawing."

Lidia Syroka quoted in "Lidia Syroka," Ricco/Maresca Gallery, https://www.riccomaresca.com/artists/59-lidia-syroka/biography/, accessed June 22, 2022.

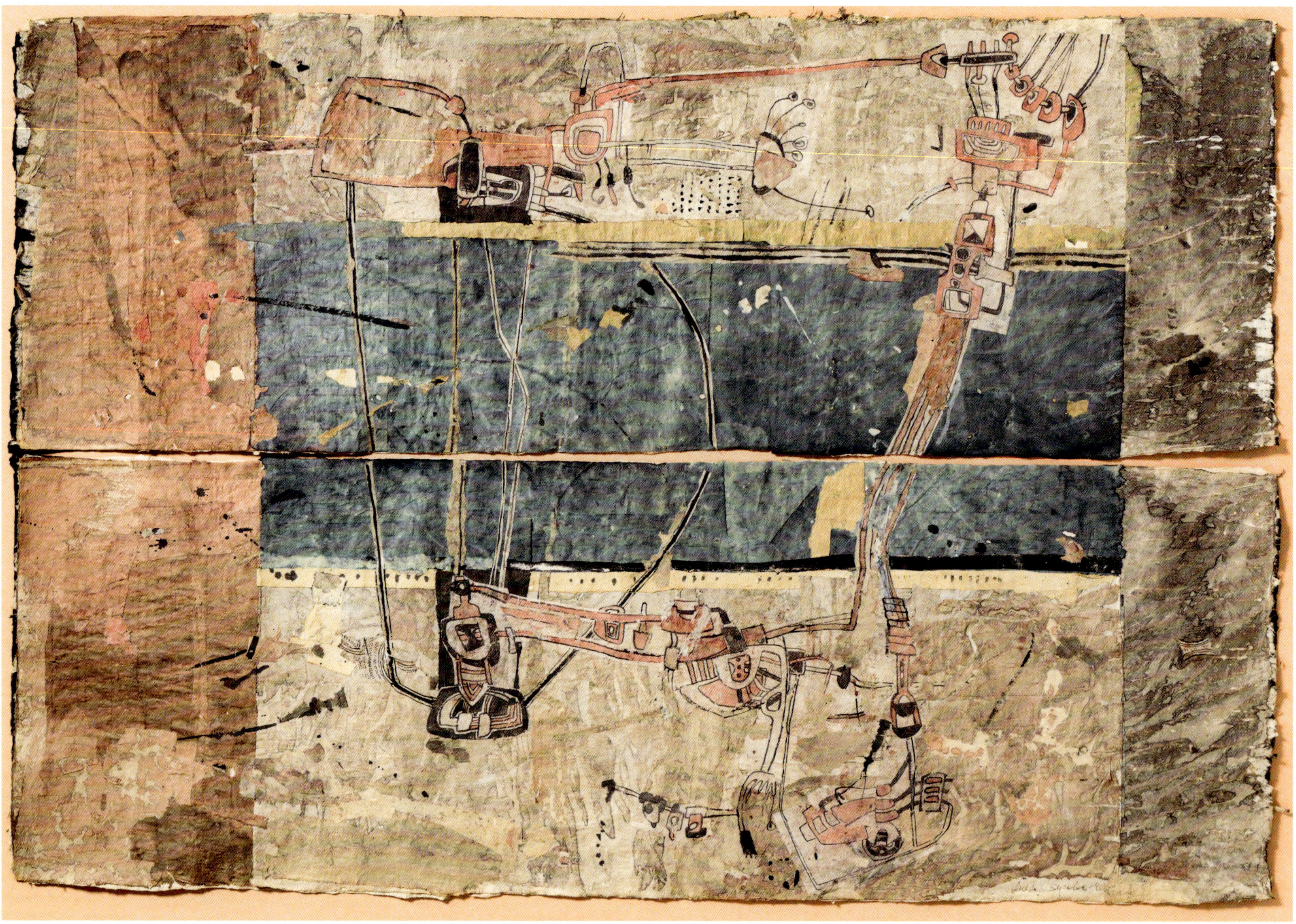

Cat. 75
Lidia Syroka

Genese
late 20th century
collage with string on
handmade paper
11 panels, each 6 × 24 in.
(15.2 × 61 cm)

The body is a preoccupation of artist Lidia Syroka, who is deeply concerned with the emotional resonance of textures. The word *GENESE*, which appears in the topmost bar of this multipanel wall piece, may allude to the creation and origins of life.

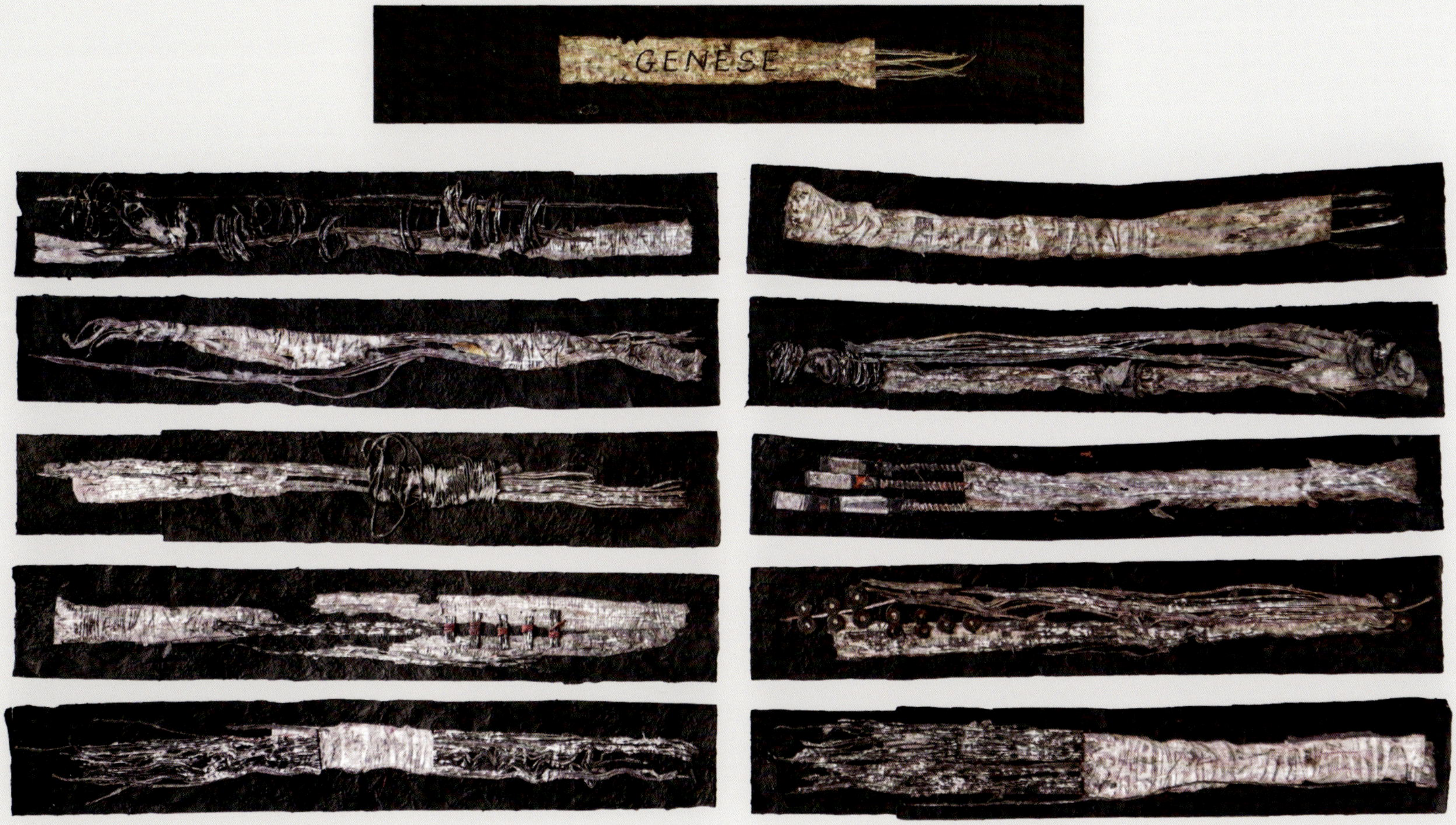

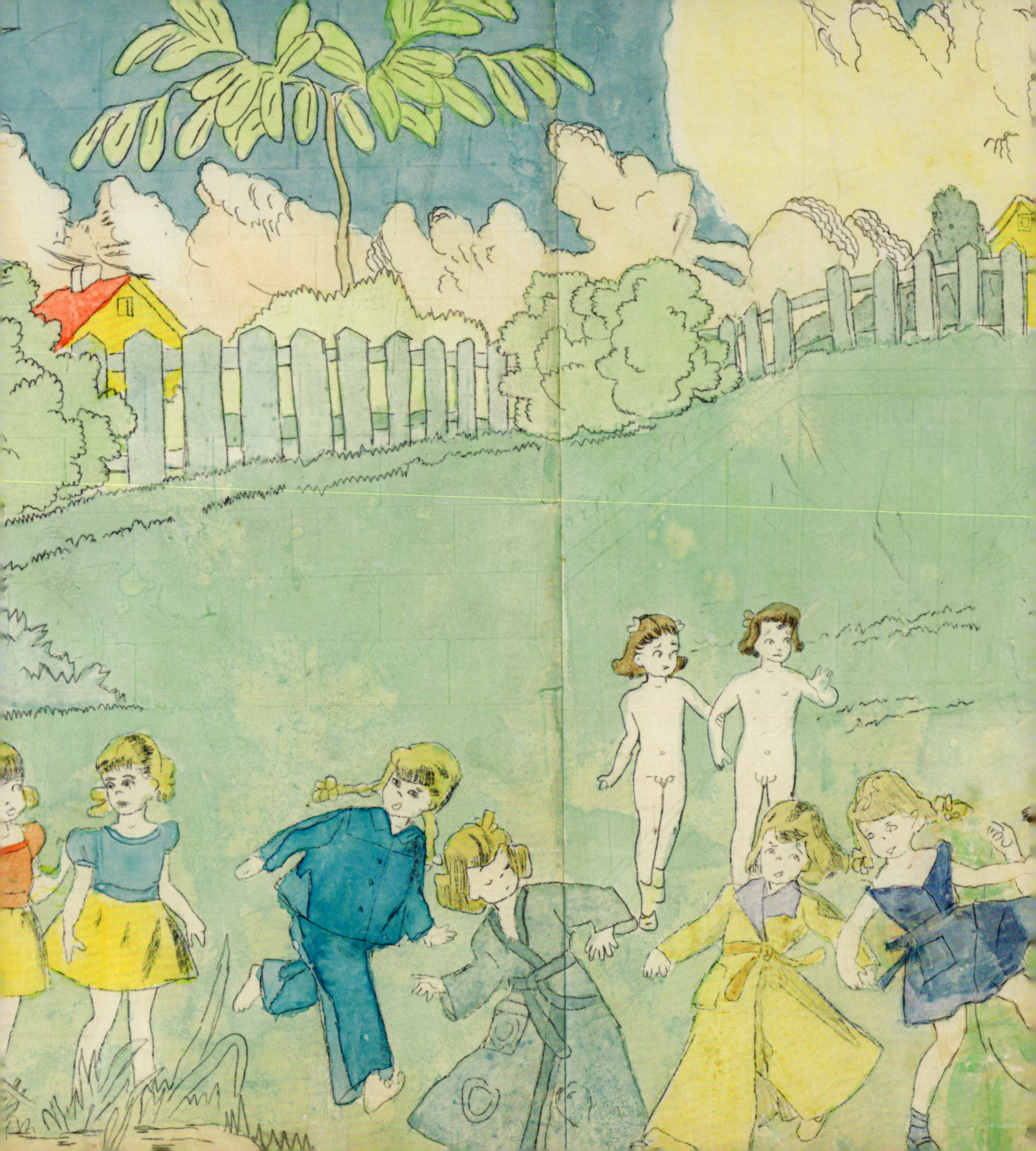

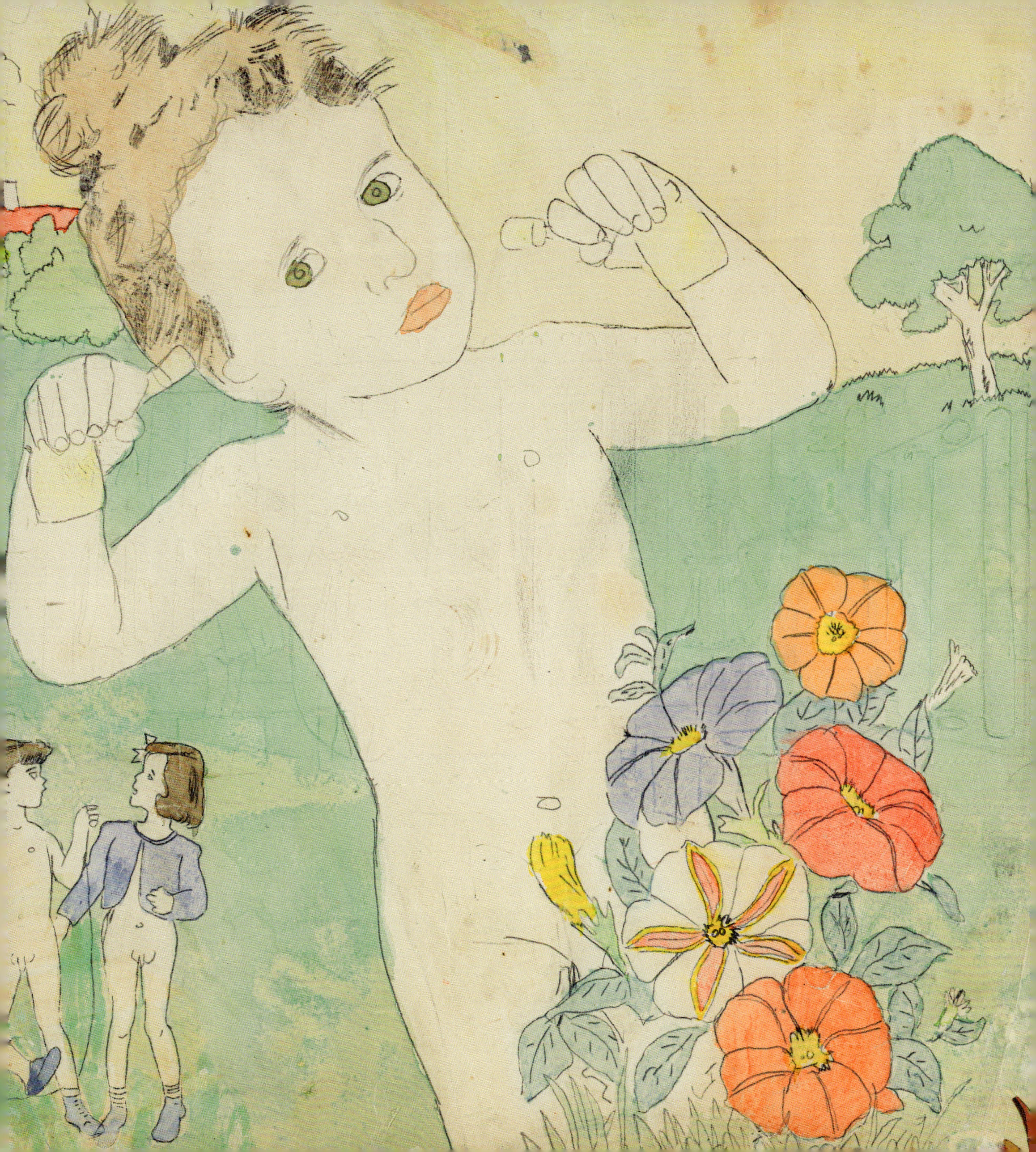

Exhibition Checklist

*Promised Bequest to the Cincinnati Art Museum

*Eddie Arning (American, 1898–1993)
Untitled
circa 1964–74
oil pastel and graphite pencil on dark blue paper
19¾ × $25\frac{11}{16}$ in. (50.1 × 65.3 cm)
Cat. 49

Charles Benefiel (American, born 1967)
Random Numeric Repeater #5
2001
pen and ink on paper
$49\frac{5}{16}$ × 35¼ in. (125.3 × 89.5 cm)
Cat. 57

*Nick Blinko (British, born 1961)
Untitled
1985
pen and black ink on paper
$16\frac{9}{16}$ × $16\frac{9}{16}$ in. (42.1 × 42.1 cm)
Cat. 54

*Mary K. Borkowski (American, 1916–2008)
House Huntin'
1967
hand stitching, quilting, and appliqué on fabric
15¾ × 18¾ in. (40 × 47.6 cm)
Cat. 35

*Mary K. Borkowski (American, 1916–2008)
Toil, Strength, and Devotion
1973
hand stitching with silk thread on velvet
20⅛ × 29¼ in. (51.1 × 74.3 cm)
Cat. 38

*Mary K. Borkowski (American, 1916–2008)
Her Last Goodnight
1985
hand stitching and appliqué on fabric
26⅛ × 19⅛ in. (66.4 × 48.6 cm)
Cat. 36

David Butler (American, 1898–1997)
Nativity Scene
circa 1980
painted cut sheet metal, plastic beads, and wire
28 × 42½ × 3 in. (71.1 × 108 × 7.6 cm)
Cat. 28

Ned Cartledge (American, 1916–2001)
Hell Ain't Half Full
1986
carved and painted wood
17¼ × 33½ in. (43.8 × 85.1 cm)
Cat. 23

*Nek Chand (Indian, 1924–2015)
Standing Man
circa 1951–80
painted fired clay, broken china, rocks,
and concrete
34½ × 12 × 12 in. (87.6 × 30.5 × 30.5 cm)
Cat. 31

*Earl Cunningham (American, 1893–1977)
Mill
1949–77
oil on fiberboard
18 × 24 in. (45.7 × 61 cm)
Cat. 37

*Henry Darger (American, 1892–1973)
Blengin
circa 1920–30
watercolor, graphite pencil, and blue carbon
transfer on paper
23½ × $34\frac{15}{16}$ in. (59.7 × 88.7 cm)
Cat. 47

*Henry Darger (American, 1892–1973)
49. At Jennie Richee, escape during approach of new storm nuded [sic] *into enemy lines* (recto)
circa 1950–60

At general Viviananna head-quarters 1 Jennie gets a toothache pulls it and uses it to scrap [sic] *cement from prison bars* (verso)
circa 1930–40
watercolor, graphite pencil, and carbon
transfer on paper
19⅛ × 70½ in. (48.6 × 179 cm)
Cat. 48

*Thornton Dial (American, 1928–2016)
Street People
1988
painted cut sheet metal and concrete
a: 15 × 4½ × 3¼ in. (38.1 × 11.4 × 8.3 cm)
b: 15 × 3¼ × 2½ in. (38.1 × 8.3 × 6.4 cm)
c: 9⅛ × 3 × 2½ in. (23.2 × 7.6 × 6.4 cm)
d: 10¾ × 11½ × 3 in. (27.3 × 29.2 × 7.6 cm)
e: 14⅜ × 3¼ × 3 in. (36.5 × 8.3 × 7.6 cm)
f: 14¼ × 4¼ × 2¾ in. (36.2 × 10.8 × 7 cm)
Cat. 11

Cat. 33 (detail)
Malcah Zeldis, *Peaceable Kingdom*

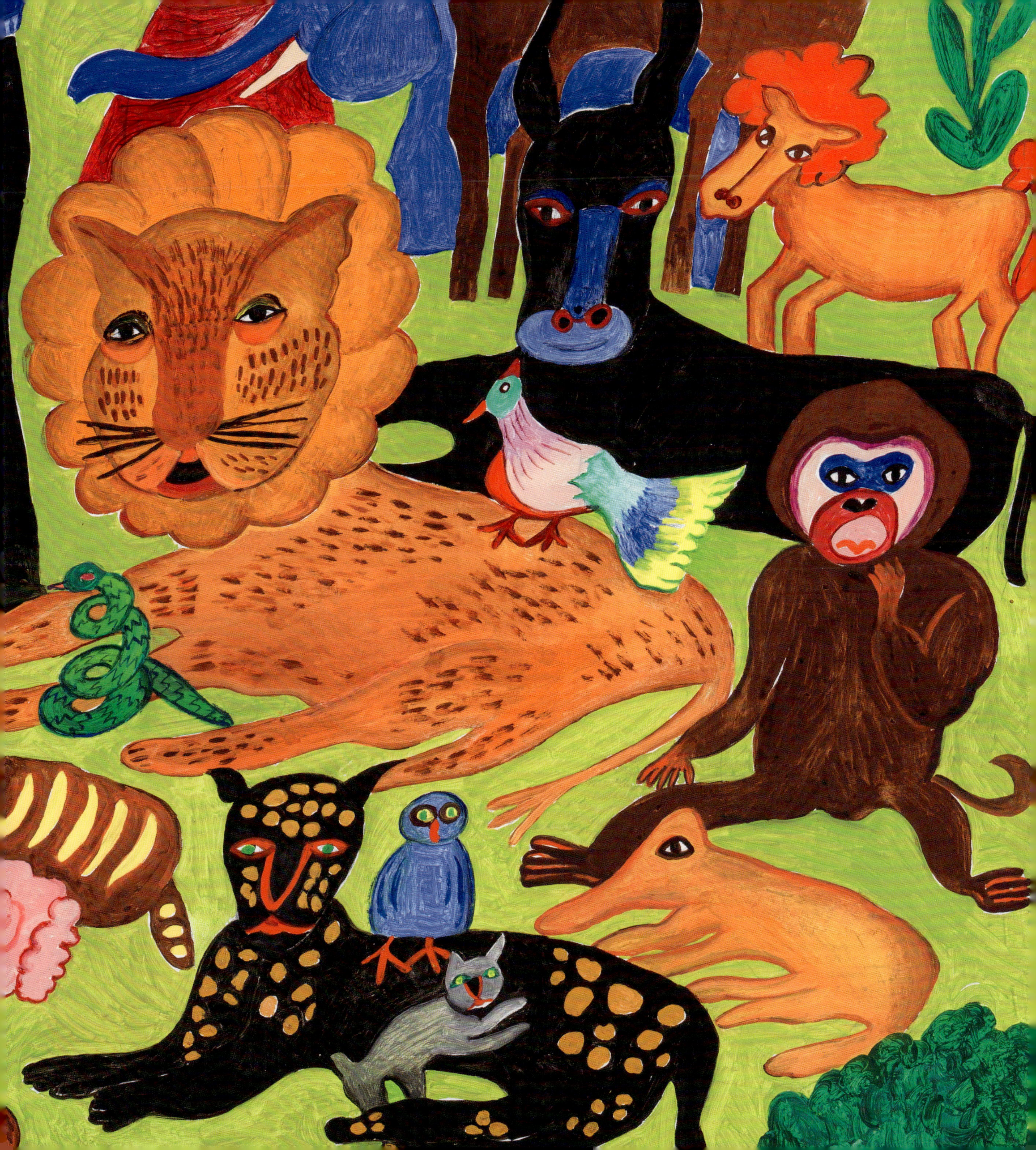

*Thornton Dial (American, 1928–2016)
A Moose That Has a Back Can Do Anything in the Woods
1989
paint and cut and painted high-pile carpet on canvas mounted on board
in frame 36½ × 48¼ in. (92.7 × 122.6 cm)
Cat. 13

Hiroyuki Doi (Japanese, born 1946)
Untitled
2002
pen and black ink on paper
38⅜ × 74$\frac{5}{16}$ in. (97.5 × 188.7 cm)
Cat. 58

*Jean Dubuffet (French, 1901–1985)
Annal XII (Annale XII)
1978
pen and black ink with collage elements on paper
13$\frac{13}{16}$ × 20$\frac{3}{16}$ in. (35.1 × 51.3 cm)
Cat. 43

*Jean Dubuffet (French, 1901–1985)
Le Circulus I
1984
acrylic on paper mounted on canvas
39$\frac{3}{16}$ × 52$\frac{13}{16}$ in. (99.6 × 134.1 cm)
Cat. 44

Minnie Evans (American, 1892–1987)
No. 79
1946
crayon, pen and ink (several colors), and graphite pencil on paper mounted on a second sheet of paper
8¾ × 11⅝ in. (22.2 × 29.6 cm)
Cat. 9

*Ralph Fasanella (American, 1914–1997)
Meeting at the Commons—Lawrence 1912
1977
oil on canvas
50 × 120 in. (127 × 304.8 cm)
Cat. 17

Ken Grimes (American, born 1947)
WOW
1992
acrylic on canvas
30 × 24 in. (76.2 × 61 cm)
Cat. 69

*Bessie Harvey (American, 1929–1994)
Peace
1987
found wood, beads, and paint
41 × 32 × 30 in. (104.1 × 81.3 × 76.2 cm)
Cat. 8

*William Hawkins (American, 1895–1990)
Did Comets Kill the Dinosaurs? #1
circa 1986
enamel house paint, cornmeal, and collage on Masonite
48 × 56½ in. (121.9 × 143.5 cm)
Cat. 24

Hipkiss (British, working in France, both artists born 1964)
Slit in Molko Oi
2000
graphite pencil, silver ink, and brown paint or resin on paper
34 × 25$\frac{7}{16}$ in. (86.3 × 64.6 cm)
Cat. 67

*Ronald Lockett (American, 1965–1998)
Traps
circa 1989
wire, painted wood, chainlink fencing, found sticks, cut sheet metal, and nails
49 × 54 × 4 in. (124.5 × 137.2 × 10.2 cm)
Cat. 14

*Edmund Monsiel (Polish, 1897–1962)
Untitled
1958
graphite pencil on paper
8⅛ × 5$\frac{11}{16}$ in. (20.6 × 14.5 cm)
Cat. 53

Sister Gertrude Morgan (American, 1900–1980)
Mothers Day
circa 1960–74
crayon, tempera or gouache, and pen and ink (blue, black, and silver) on cardboard
7$\frac{13}{16}$ × 12$\frac{3}{16}$ in. (19.9 × 30.9 cm)
Cat. 10

Donald Pass (British, 1930–2010)
Landscape beyond the Veil
2000
watercolor and pen and ink on paper
29$\frac{13}{16}$ × 40$\frac{11}{16}$ in. (75.7 × 103.3 cm)
Cat. 63

*Martín Ramírez (American, born Mexico, 1895–1963)
Untitled, Super Chief
1954
graphite pencil and pastel (est.) on paper
55$\frac{9}{16}$ × 51½ in. (141.2 × 130.8 cm)
Cat. 51

*Nellie Mae Rowe (American, 1900–1982)
Pink Pig
mid-20th century
crayon on paper
$16\frac{1}{16} \times 20\frac{1}{16}$ in. (40.8 × 50.9 cm)
Cat. 32

Friedrich Schröder-Sonnenstern (German, 1892–1982)
Death Winking in the Moral Apple of Life (Der schielende Tod im moralischen Lebensapfel)
1956
crayon on cardboard
$28\frac{3}{4} \times 20\frac{1}{16}$ in. (73 × 51 cm)
Cat. 46

*Janet Sobel (American, born Ukraine, 1893–1968)
Untitled (JS-070)
1946–48
enamel paint on canvas board
30 × 20 in. (76.2 × 50.8 cm)
Cat. 60

*Bill Traylor (American, circa 1853–1949)
Exciting Event in Blue: Four Wild Men, Barking Dog, Perched Bird, and Construction
circa 1939–42
tempera, graphite pencil, and ink (or watercolor) on thin cardboard
$14\frac{7}{8} \times 13\frac{7}{8}$ in. (37.8 × 35.2 cm)
Cat. 7

*Adolf Wölfli (Swiss, 1864–1930)
Elisabeth Bieri
1907
graphite pencil and crayon on paper
$35\frac{1}{2} \times 47\frac{1}{4}$ in. (90.1 × 120 cm)
Cat. 45

*Clarence Woolsey (American, 1909–1987) and Grace Woolsey (American, 1921–1992)
Caparena Figure
1961–71
bottle caps, wire, wood, and nails
$40 \times 18\frac{1}{2} \times 13$ in. (101.6 × 47 × 33 cm)
Cat. 26

Malcah Zeldis (American, born 1931)
Peaceable Kingdom
1977
enamel paint on Masonite
35 × 35 in. (88.9 × 88.9 cm)
Cat. 33

Carlo Zinelli (Italian, 1916–1974)
Untitled
1962–64
watercolor and gouache on paper
$13\frac{3}{4} \times 19\frac{7}{8}$ in. (35 × 50.5 cm)
Cat. 50

Unidentified American Artists

Spotted Hen
circa 1890
painted pine, sheet copper, and metal with mount $13\frac{7}{8} \times 8\frac{1}{2} \times 14\frac{1}{2}$ in. (35.2 × 21.6 × 36.8 cm)
Cat. 4

**All We Ask Is a Fair Trial*
late 19th–early 20th century
oil on canvas mounted on wood panel
36 × 46 in. (91.4 × 116.8 cm)
Cat. 6

**Bird House*
circa 1920–30
carved and painted wood and wire
$18\frac{1}{2} \times 10 \times 11\frac{1}{2}$ in. (47 × 25.4 × 29.2 cm)
Cat. 1

**Cat Post*
20th century
painted wood and found objects
$63\frac{1}{2} \times 14 \times 14$ in. (161.3 × 35.6 × 35.6 cm)
Cat. 3

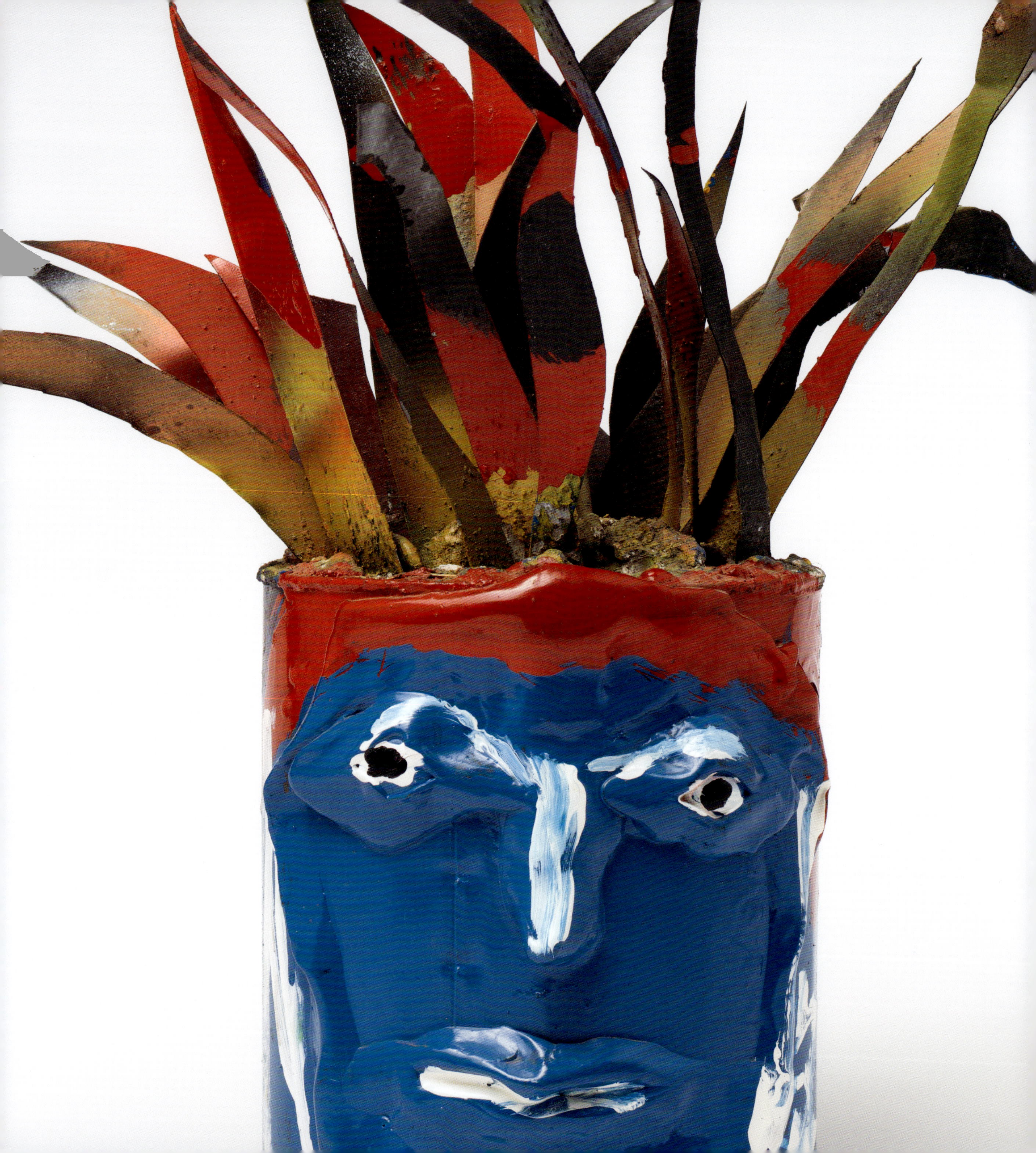

Bibliography

Akerman, Sean, and Suzanne C. Ouellette. "What Ricoeur's Hermeneutics Reveal about Self and Identity and Aesthetic Experience." *Theory & Psychology* 22, no. 4 (August 2012): 383–401.

Arnett, Paul, and William Arnett, eds. *Souls Grown Deep: African American Vernacular Art*. 2 vols. Atlanta: Tinwood Books, 2000–2001.

Bakhtin, Mikhail. *The Dialogic Imagination*. Edited by Michael Holquist. Translated by Caryl Emerson and Michael Holquist. Austin: University of Texas Press, 1981.

Bion, Wilfred Ruprecht. *Attention and Interpretation*. London: Karnac Books, 1970.

Bourdieu, Pierre. *The Logic of Practice*. Translated by Richard Nice. Cambridge: Polity Press, 1990.

Bowman, Russell. "Introduction: A Synthetic Approach to Folk Art." In *Common Ground/ Uncommon Vision: The Michael and Julie Hall Collection of American Folk Art*, by Jeffrey Russell Hayes, Lucy R. Lippard, and Kenneth L. Ames, 13–21. Milwaukee: Milwaukee Art Museum, 1993.

Buber, Martin. *I and Thou*. New York: Howard Books, 2008.

Cardinal, Roger. *Outsider Art*. New York: Praeger Publishers, 1972.

Carlano, Annie, ed. *Vernacular Visionaries: International Outsider Art*. New Haven: Museum of International Folk Art, Santa Fe, in association with Yale University Press, 2003.

Charmaz, Kathy. "Stories and Silences: Disclosures and Self in Chronic Illness." *Qualitative Inquiry* 8, no. 3 (June 2002): 302–28.

Cooke, Lynne, et al. *Outliers and American Vanguard Art*. Chicago: University of Chicago Press, 2018.

Cropley, Arthur J. "The Dark Side of Creativity: What is it?" In *The Dark Side of Creativity*, edited by David H. Cropley et al., 1–14. Cambridge: Cambridge University Press, 2010.

Csikszentmihalyi, Mihaly. *Creativity: Flow and the Psychology of Discovery and Invention*. New York: Harper Collins, 1996.

Cubbs, Joanne. "Rebels, Mystics, and Outcasts: The Romantic Artist Outsider." In *The Artist Outsider: Creativity and the Boundaries of Culture*, edited by Michael D. Hall and Eugene W. Metcalf Jr., 76–95. Washington, DC: Smithsonian Institution Press, 1994.

Davies, James. *Sedated: How Modern Capitalism Created Our Mental Health Crisis*. London: Atlantic Books, 2021.

Deleuze, Gilles, and Félix Guattari. *A Thousand Plateaus*. London: Bloomsbury Academic, 2013.

Dissanayake, Ellen. "Ethology, Interpersonal Neurobiology, and Play: Insights into the Evolutionary Origin of the Arts." *American Journal of Play* 9, no. 2 (Winter 2017): 143–68.

Dissanayake, Ellen. *Homo Aestheticus: Where Art Comes From and Why*. Seattle: University of Washington Press, 1995.

Dubuffet, Jean. "Art Brut in Preference to the Cultural Arts." In *Art Brut: Madness and Marginalia*, edited by Allen S. Weiss, translated by Paul Fuss and Allen S. Weiss, 30–33. Sydney: Art and Text, 1988.

Ehrenzweig, Anton. *The Hidden Order of Art*. Los Angeles: University of California Press, 1971.

Eigen, Michael. *Emotional Storm*. Middletown, CT: Wesleyan University Press, 2005.

Fine, Gary Alan. *Everyday Genius: Self-Taught Art and the Culture of Authenticity*. Chicago: University of Chicago Press, 2004.

Foucault, Michel. *Discipline & Punish: The Birth of the Prison*. 2nd ed. Translated by Alan Sheridan. London: Vintage Books, 1995.

Fricker, Miranda. *Epistemic Injustice: Power and the Ethics of Knowing*. Oxford: Oxford University Press, 2009.

Glover, Nicky. *Psychoanalytic Aesthetics: An Introduction to the British School*. London: Harris Meltzer Trust, 2009.

Gosso, Sandra, ed. *Psychoanalysis and Art: Kleinian Perspectives*. London: Karnac Books, 2004.

Hahl, Oliver, Ezra W. Zuckerman, and Minjae Kim. "Why Elites Love Authentic Lowbrow Culture: Overcoming High-Status Denigration with Outsider Art." *American Sociological Review* 82, no. 4 (August 2017): 828–56.

Jentleson, Katherine. *Gatecrashers: The Rise of the Self-Taught Artist in America*. Oakland: High Museum of Art, Atlanta, in association with University of California Press, 2020.

Cat. 12b (detail)
Thornton Dial, *Can Man (Blue)*

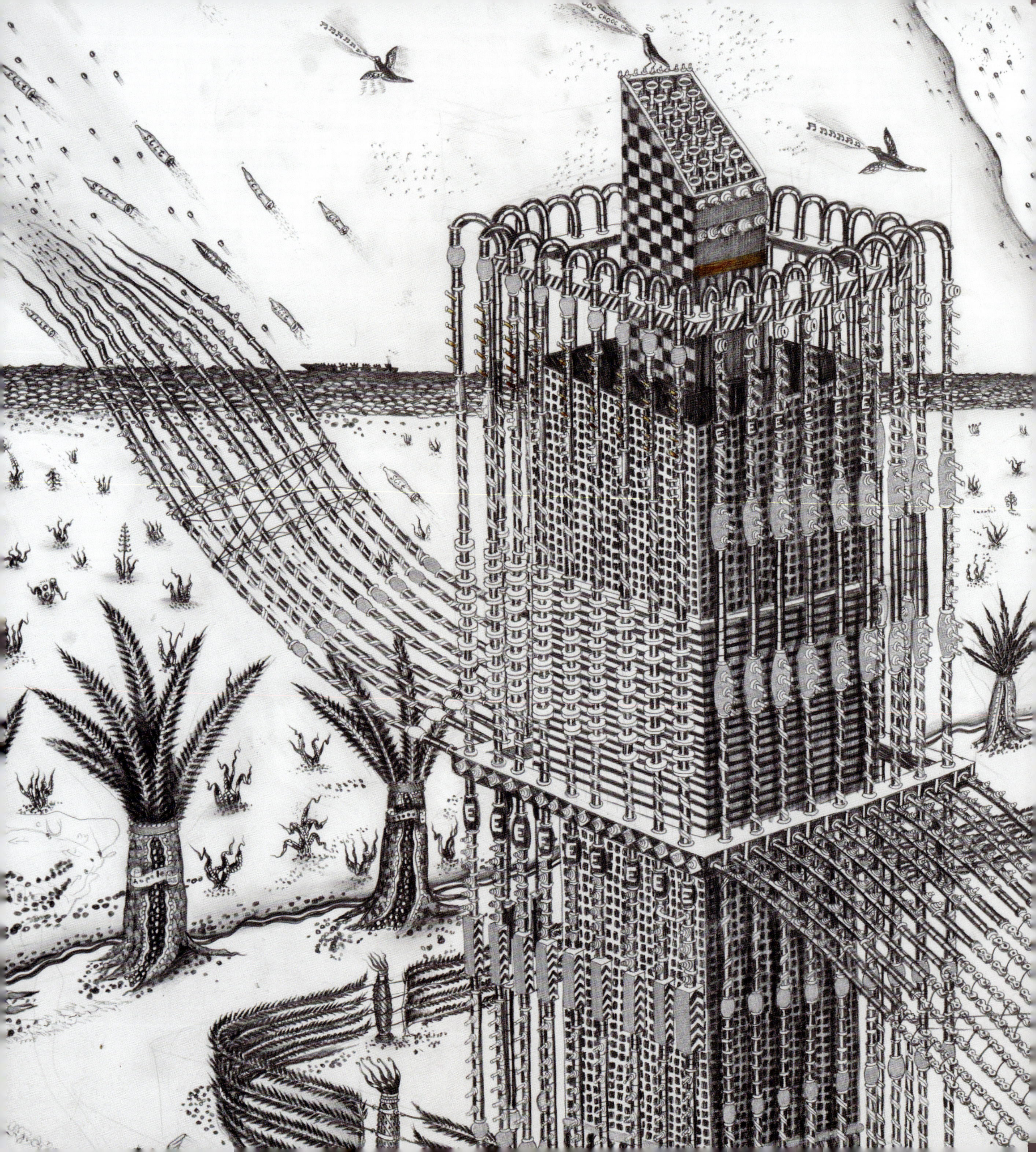

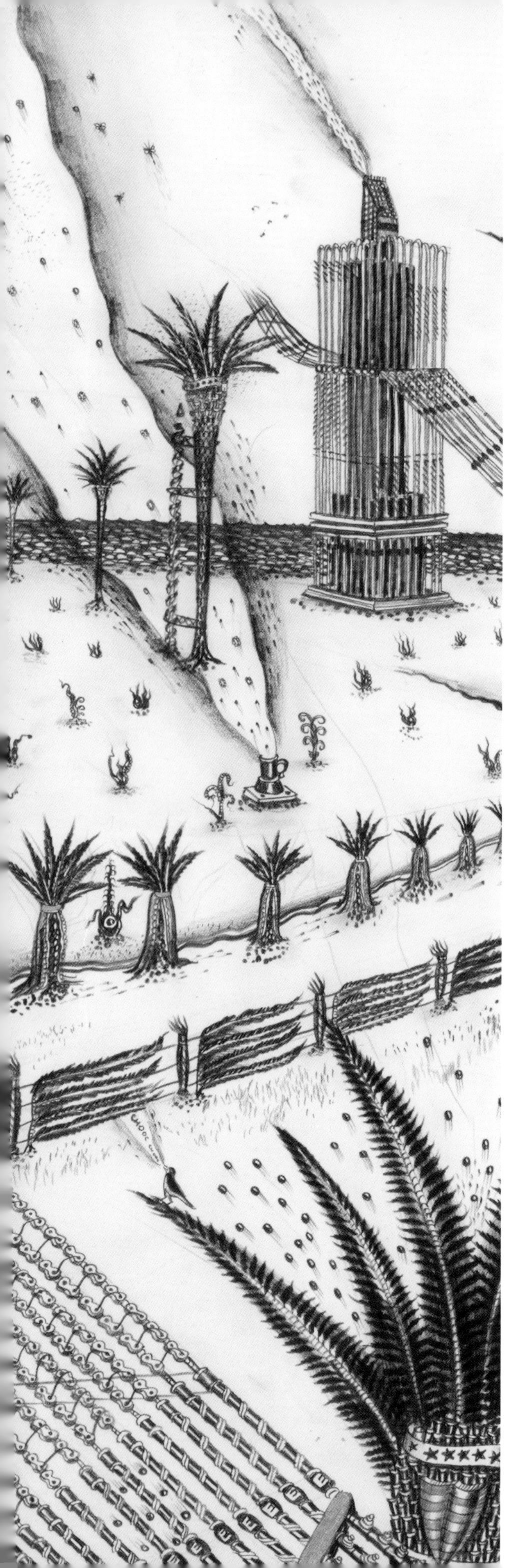

Kjellman-Chapin, Mónica. "Fake Identity, Real Work: Authenticity, Autofiction, and Outsider Art." *SPECS Journal of Art and Culture* 2, no. 1 (2009): 148–59.

Kohler, Catherine Riessman. "Analysis of Personal Narratives." In *Handbook of Interview Research: Context and Method*, edited by Jaber F. Gubrium and James A. Holstein, 695–710. London: Sage Publications, 2000.

Kuri, Erin. "Toward an Ethical Application of Intersectionality in Art Therapy." *Art Therapy* 34, no. 3 (September 2017): 118–22.

Kwon, Miwon. *One Place after Another: Site Specific Art and Locational Identity*. Cambridge, MA: MIT Press, 2002.

Maclagan, David. *Outsider Art: From the Margins to the Marketplace*. London: Reaktion Books, 2010.

Molino, Anthony, ed. *Freely Associated: Encounters in Psychoanalysis with Christopher Bollas, Joyce McDougall, Michael Eigen, Adam Phillips, Nina Coltart*. New York: Free Association Books, 1997.

Nakamura, Jeanne, and Mihaly Csikszentmihalyi. "The Concept of Flow." In *The Handbook of Positive Psychology*, edited by Shane J. Lopez and Charles R. Snyder, 89–105. New York: Oxford University Press, 2002.

Odell, Jenny. *How to Do Nothing: Resisting the Attention Economy*. New York: Melville House, 2019.

Ogden, Thomas. *The Matrix of the Mind: Object Relations and the Psychoanalytic Dialogue*. London: Karnac Books, 1992.

Pitt, Alice, and Deborah Britzman. "Speculations on Qualities of Difficult Knowledge in Teaching and Learning: An Experiment in Psychoanalytic Research." *Qualitative Studies in Education* 16, no. 6 (November 2003): 755–76.

Prinz, Jesse. "Against Outsider Art." *Journal of Social Philosophy* 48, no. 3 (September 2017): 250–72.

Prinzhorn, Hans. *Artistry of the Mentally Ill*. 2nd ed. Translated by Eric von Brockdorff. New York: Springer-Verlag, 1955.

Rexer, Lyle. *How to Look at Outsider Art*. New York: Harry N. Abrams, 2005.

Rhodes, Colin. *Outsider Art: Spontaneous Alternatives*. New York and London: Thames and Hudson, 2000.

Rimke, Heidi. "Introduction—Mental and Emotional Distress as a Social Justice Issue: Beyond Psychocentrism." *Studies in Social Justice* 10, no. 1 (August 2016): 4–17.

Rosenak, Chuck, and Jan Rosenak. *Contemporary American Folk Art: A Collector's Guide*. New York: Abbeville Press, 1996.

Rosenak, Chuck, and Jan Rosenak. *Museum of American Folk Art Encyclopedia of Twentieth-Century American Folk Art and Artists*. New York: Abbeville Press, 1990.

Rousseau, Valérie, et al. *The Hidden Art: 20th- and 21st-Century Self-Taught Artists from the Audrey B. Heckler Collection*. New York: American Folk Art Museum in association with Skira Rizzoli, 2017.

Cat. 67 (detail)
Hipkiss, *Slit in Molko Oi*

Russell, Charles. *Groundwaters: A Century of Art by Self-Taught and Outsider Artists*. New York: Prestel, 2011.

Sagan, Olivia. "Art-Making and Its Interface with Dissociative Identity Disorder: No Words That Didn't Fit." *Journal of Creativity in Mental Health* 14, no. 1 (August 2018): 23–36.

Sagan, Olivia. *Narratives of Art Practice and Mental Wellbeing: Reparation and Connection*. London: Routledge, 2014.

Shriver, Lionel. *So Much for That*. London: HarperCollins, 2010.

Slominski, Lisa. *Nonconformers: A New History of Self-Taught Artists*. New Haven: Yale University Press, 2022.

Stanley, Liz. *The Auto/Biographical I: Theory and Practice of Feminist Auto/Biography*. Manchester: Manchester University Press, 1992.

Stern, Daniel. *The Interpersonal World of the Infant*. New York: Basic Books, 1985.

Strout, Elizabeth. *Olive, Again*. London: Penguin Books, 2020.

Tamboukou, Maria. "Machinic Assemblages: Women, Art Education and Space." *Discourse: Studies in the Cultural Politics of Education* 29, no. 3 (September 2008): 359–75.

Teo, Thomas. "Critical Psychology: A Geography of Intellectual Engagement and Resistance." *American Psychologist* 70, no. 3 (January 2015): 243–54.

Trechsel, Gail, ed. *Pictured in My Mind: Contemporary Self-Taught Art from the Collection of Dr. Kurt Gitter and Alice Rae Yellen*. Jackson: University Press of Mississippi, 1995.

White, Michelle. *As Essential as Dreams: Self-Taught Art from the Collection of Stephanie and John Smither*. New Haven: Menil Collection, Houston, in association with Yale University Press, 2016.

Winnicott, Donald Woods. *Playing and Reality*. New York: Pelican Books, 1985.

Wojcik, Daniel. *Outsider Art: Visionary Worlds and Trauma*. Jackson: University Press of Mississippi, 2016.

Woolf, Virginia. *A Room of One's Own*. London: Hogarth Press, 1929.

Wright, Kenneth. *Mirroring and Attunement: Self-Realization in Psychoanalysis and Art*. London: Routledge, 2009.

Further Reading about Individual Artists

Anderson, Brooke Davis. *Martín Ramírez*. Seattle: Museum of American Folk Art, New York, in association with Marquand Books, 2007.

Arnett, Paul, Joanne Cubbs, and Eugene W. Metcalf Jr., eds. *Thornton Dial in the 21st Century*. Atlanta: Tinwood Books, 2006.

Baumann, Daniel, Edward M. Gomez, Elka Spoerri, and Gerard C. Wertkin, with texts by Adolf Wölfli. *The Art of Adolf Wölfli: St. Adolf-Giant-Creation*. Translated by Andrew Shields. Princeton, NJ: American Folk Art Museum, New York, in association with Princeton University Press, 2003.

Biesenbach, Klaus, ed. *Henry Darger*. 3rd ed. Munich, London, and New York: Museum of American Folk Art, New York, in association with Prestel, 2019.

Bonesteel, Michael. *Henry Darger: Art and Selected Writings*. New York: Rizzoli, 2000.

Cubbs, Joanne, and Eugene W. Metcalf, eds. *Hard Truths: The Art of Thornton Dial*. New York: Indianapolis Museum of Art in association with Delmonico Books/Prestel, 2011.

Espinosa, Victor M. *Martín Ramírez: Framing His Life and Art*. Austin: University of Texas Press, 2015.

Fagley, William A. *David Butler*. New Orleans: New Orleans Museum of Art, 1976.

Fasanella, Marc, Leslie Umberger, and Paul S. D'Ambrosio. *Ralph Fasanella: Images of Optimism*. Portland: Pomegranate, 2017.

Garret, Wendell, Virginia M. Mecklenburg, and Carolyn Weekley. *Earl Cunningham's America*. Washington, DC: Smithsonian American Art Museum, 2007.

Gómez, Edward M. "A Universe in Tiny Form." *Raw Vision* 79 (Summer 2013): 50–55. (About Hiroyuki Doi.)

Gorsen, Peter. "The Fabulous Co-Equality of Man and Animal: Friedrich Schröder-Sonnenstern and His Heretical Bestiary." *Raw Vision* 80 (Winter 2013): 26–33.

Herman, Bernard L. "Charles Benefiel." *Raw Vision* 30 (Spring 2000): 30–34.

Jean Dubuffet: Retrospective. Dallas: Dallas Museum of Art, 1966.

Kogan, Lee. *The Art of Nellie Mae Rowe: Ninety-Nine and a Half Won't Do*. Jackson: Museum of American Folk Art, New York, in association with University Press of Mississippi, 1998.

Levin, Gail. "Janet Sobel: Primitivist, Surrealist, and Abstract Expressionist." *Woman's Art Journal* 26, no. 1 (2005): 8–14.

Lyons, Mary E. *Painting Dreams: Minnie Evans, Visionary Artist*. Boston: Houghton Mifflin, 1996.

MacGregor, John M. *Dwight Mackintosh: The Boy Who Time Forgot*. Oakland, CA: Creative Growth Art Center, 1992.

Maizels, John. "Nek Chand: 25 Years of the Rock Garden." *Raw Vision* 35 (Summer 2002): 22–31.

The Museum of Everything Presents Carlo Zinelli. London: Museum of Everything, 2013.

Nek Chand Foundation. "About Nek Chand." Accessed June 30, 2022. https://nekchand.com/about-nek-chand.

Rowell, Margit. *Jean Dubuffet: A Retrospective*. New York: Solomon R. Guggenheim Museum in association with New York Graphic Society, 1973.

Sarchant, Pamela Jane. "Pamela Jane Sarchant Follows Eddie Arning's American Dream." *Raw Vision* 28 (Fall 1999): 28–33.

Spoerri, Elka. *Adolf Wölfli: Draftsman, Writer, Composer*. Ithaca, NY: Cornell University Press, 1997.

Swislow, William. "Big Some Day: The Woolsey Bottle-cap 'Caparena.'" *Raw Vision* 92 (Winter 2016/17): 16–21.

Thorne, Tony. "The Reclusive World of Malcolm McKesson." In *Malcolm McKesson: An Exquisite Obsession*, unnumbered pages. Richmond, England: Henry Boxer Gallery, n.d.

Umberger, Leslie. *Between Worlds: The Art of Bill Traylor*. Princeton, NJ: Smithsonian American Art Museum in association with Princeton University Press, 2018.

Vann, Philip. "Romany Visions." *Raw Vision* 13 (Winter 1995/96): 41–42. (About Damian Le Bas.)

William L. Hawkins: An Imaginative Geography. Milan: Figge Art Museum, Davenport, Iowa, in association with Skira, 2018.

Yau, Elaine Y. "Acts of Conversion: Sanctification and the Sense of Race in the Art of Sister Gertrude Morgan." In *Sensation Religion: Sensory Cultures in Material Practice*, edited by Sally Promey, 403–11. New Haven: Yale University Press, 2014.

Zalman, Sandra. "Janet Sobel: Primitive Modern and Origins of Abstract Expressionism." *Woman's Art Journal* 36, no. 2 (2015): 20–29.

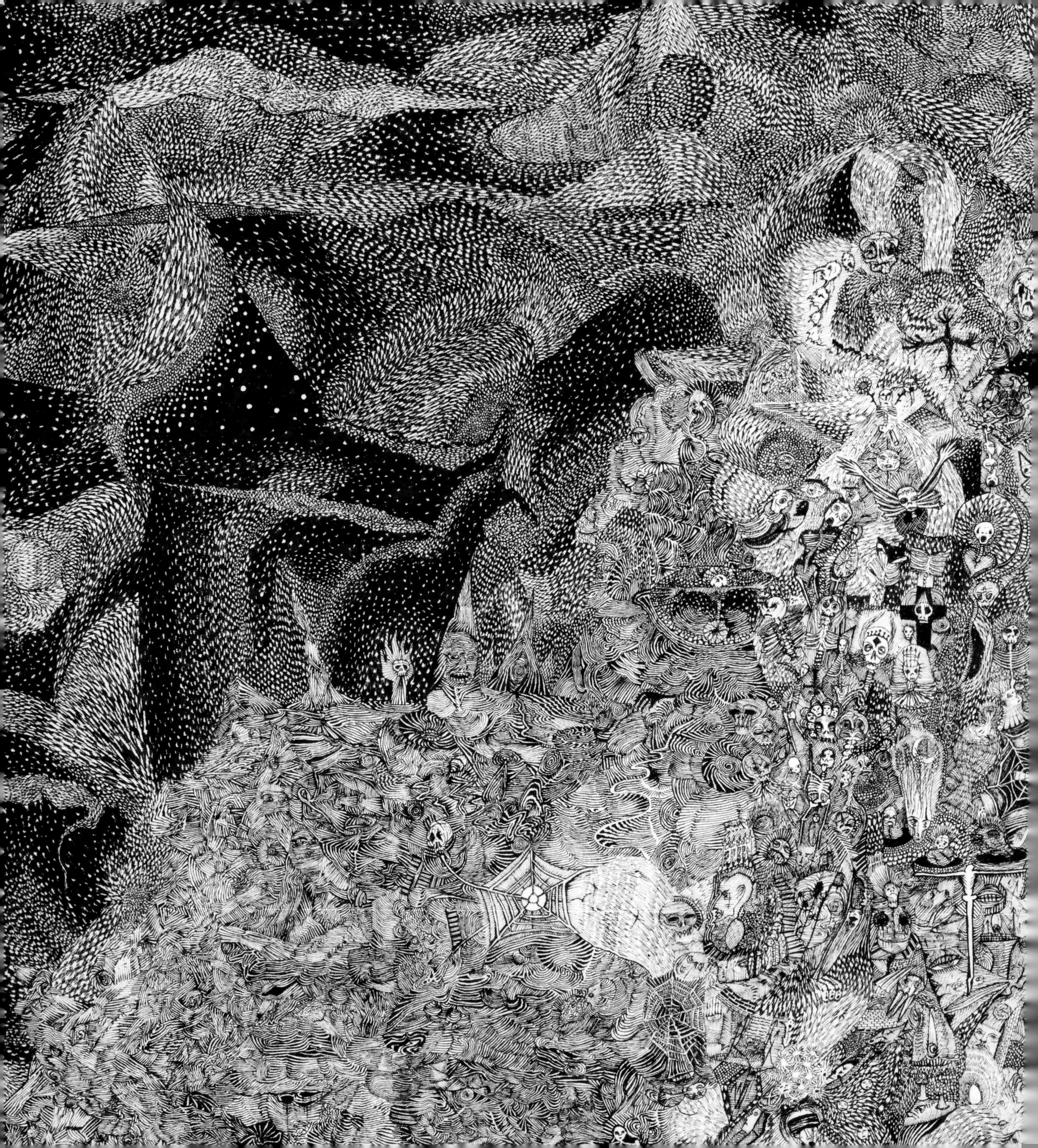

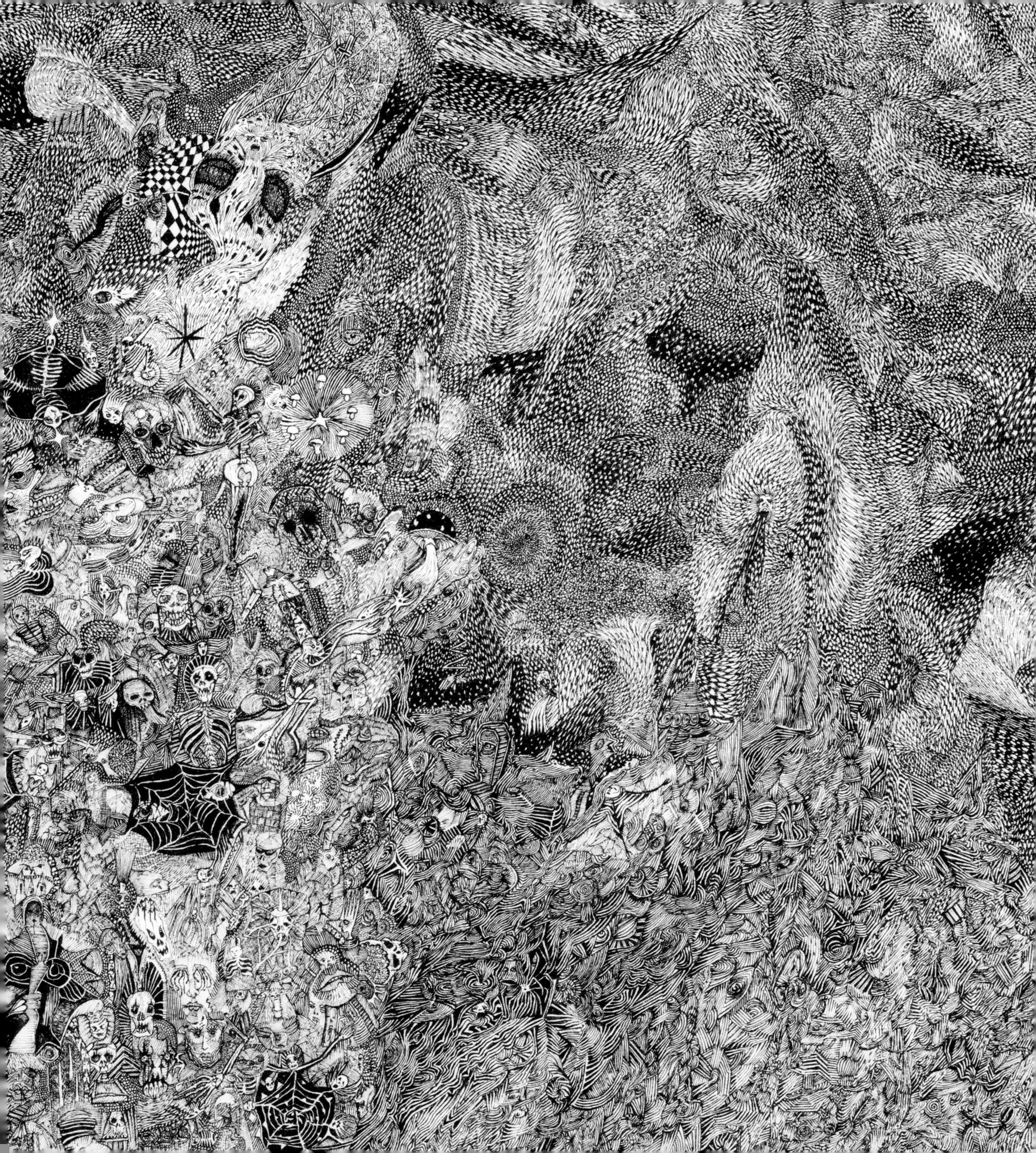

Index

Page numbers in *italics* refer to the illustrations and their captions.

Cat. 62 (detail)
Paul Duhem, *Untitled*

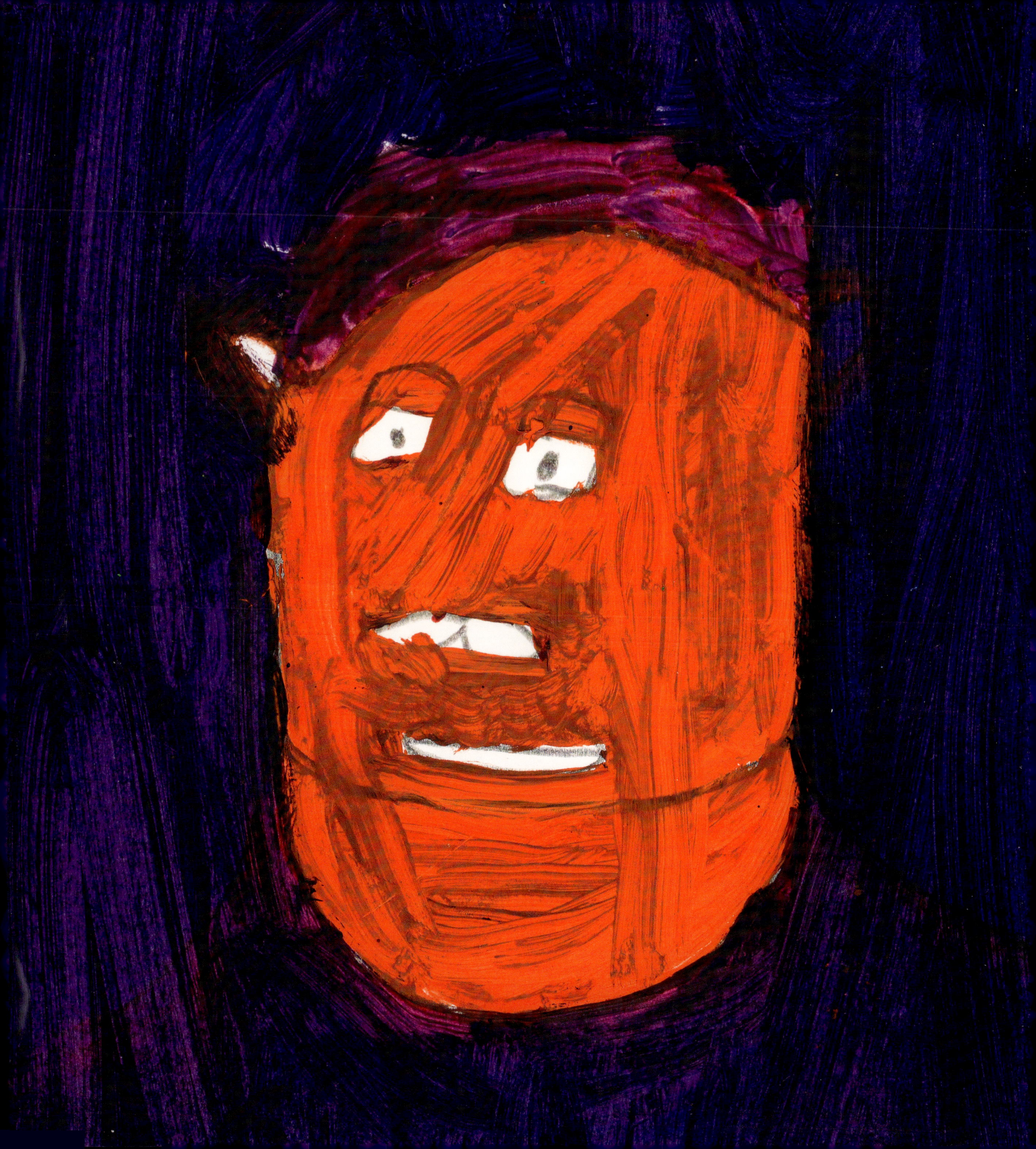

Photography Credits

All photography of the works in the Rosenthal Collection is by Rob Deslongchamps unless otherwise noted. Other photography credits appear below.

Page 31 Tony Walsh

Pages 32–33 Tony Walsh

Pages 38–39 Tony Walsh

Pages 42–43 Tony Walsh

Fig. 3 © 2022 Artists Rights Society (ARS), New York / ADAGP, Paris

Fig. 5 © 2022 Estate of Pablo Picasso / Artists Rights Society (ARS), New York

Fig. 7 © 2022 Artists Rights Society (ARS), New York

Fig. 8 © National Portrait Gallery, London

Fig. 10 Image courtesy of the Milwaukee Art Museum

Cat. 7 © Bill Traylor Family Trust

Cat. 8 Tony Walsh

Cat. 11 © 2022 Estate of Thornton Dial / Artists Rights Society (ARS), New York

Cat. 12 © 2022 Estate of Thornton Dial / Artists Rights Society (ARS), New York

Cat. 13 © 2022 Estate of Thornton Dial / Artists Rights Society (ARS), New York

Cat. 14 © 2022 Estate of Ronald Lockett / Artists Rights Society (ARS), New York

Cat. 17 © Estate of Ralph Fasanella

Cat. 24 © Ricco/Maresca Gallery, Courtesy Ricco/Maresca Gallery

Cat. 30 Tony Walsh

Cat. 31 Nek Chand Foundation

Cat. 32 © 2022 Estate of Nellie Mae Rowe / Artists Rights Society (ARS), New York

Cat. 33 © 2022 Malcah Zeldis / Artists Rights Society (ARS), New York

Cat. 39 © Courtesy artofandykane.com

Cat. 41 © 2022 David Zeldis / Artists Rights Society (ARS), New York

Cat. 43 © 2022 Artists Rights Society (ARS), New York / ADAGP, Paris

Cat. 44 © 2022 Artists Rights Society (ARS), New York / ADAGP, Paris

Cat. 46 © 2022 Artists Rights Society (ARS), New York / VG Bild-Kunst, Bonn

Cat. 47 © 2022 Kiyoko Lerner / Artists Rights Society (ARS), New York

Cat. 48 © 2022 Kiyoko Lerner / Artists Rights Society (ARS), New York

Cat. 51 © Estate of Martín Ramírez, Courtesy of the Ricco/Maresca Gallery

Cat. 54 Image courtesy of the Henry Boxer Gallery

Cat. 55 © Charles Benefiel

Cat. 56 © Charles Benefiel

Cat. 57 © Charles Benefiel

Cat. 59 © 2022 Artists Rights Society (ARS), New York / ADAGP, Paris

Cat. 61 Image courtesy of the Henry Boxer Gallery

Cat. 62 © Fondation Paul Duhem

Cat. 63 Image courtesy of the Henry Boxer Gallery

Cat. 64 Image courtesy of the Henry Boxer Gallery

Cat. 67 © 2022 Artists Rights Society (ARS), New York / ADAGP, Paris

Cat. 68 © 2022 Artists Rights Society (ARS), New York / ADAGP, Paris

Cat. 69 © Ken Grimes, Courtesy Ricco/ Maresca Gallery

Cat. 71 Courtesy Delaine and Damian Le Bas

Cat. 72 Courtesy Delaine and Damian Le Bas

Cat. 73 © Lidia Syroka, Courtesy Ricco/Maresca Gallery, Photograph Tony Walsh

Cat. 74 © Lidia Syroka, Courtesy Ricco/ Maresca Gallery

Cat. 75 © Lidia Syroka, Courtesy Ricco/Maresca Gallery, Photograph Tony Walsh

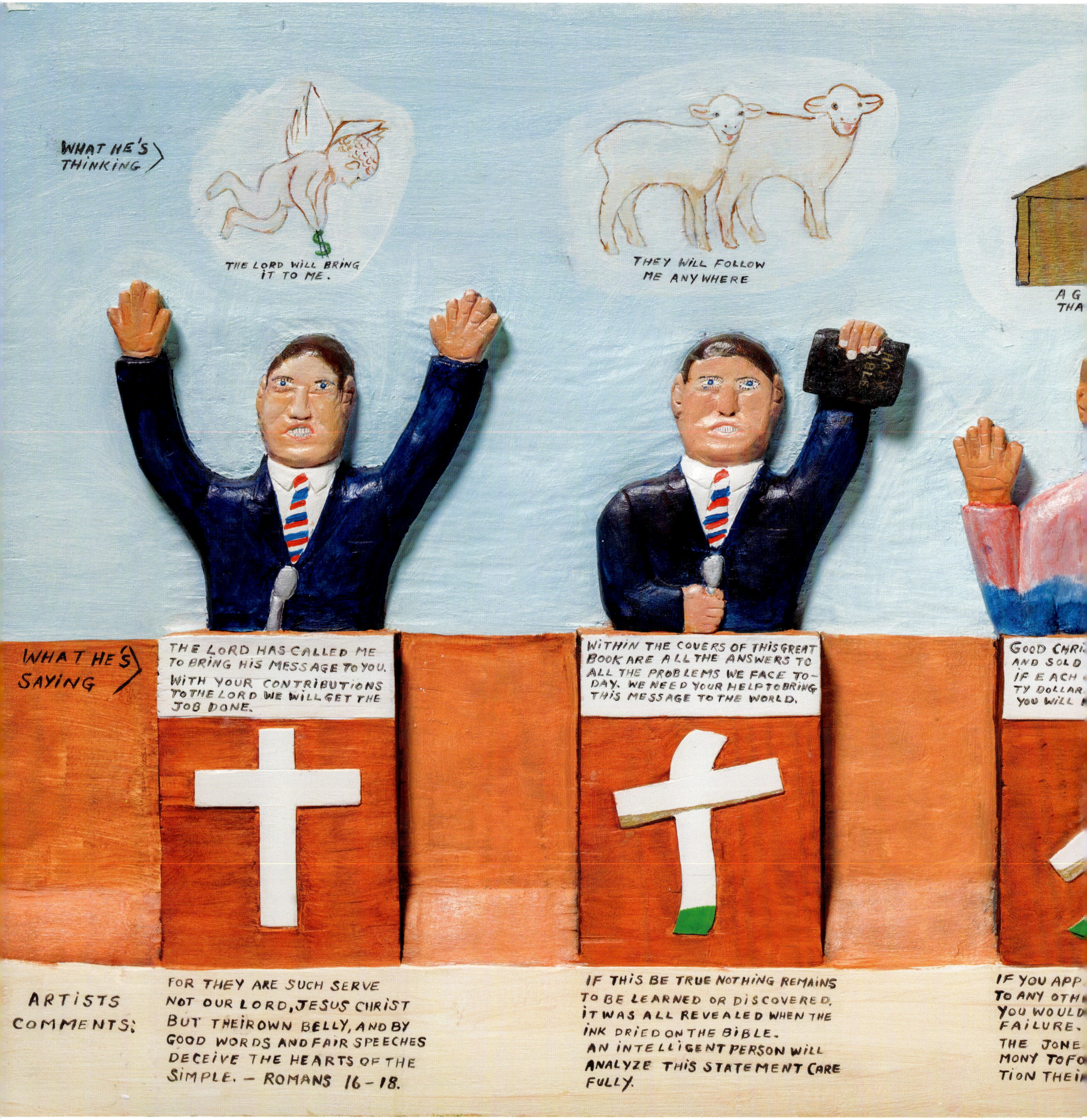
WHAT HE'S THINKING
THE LORD WILL BRING IT TO ME.
THEY WILL FOLLOW ME ANYWHERE
WHAT HE'S SAYING
THE LORD HAS CALLED ME TO BRING HIS MESSAGE TO YOU. WITH YOUR CONTRIBUTIONS TO THE LORD WE WILL GET THE JOB DONE.
WITHIN THE COVERS OF THIS GREAT BOOK ARE ALL THE ANSWERS TO ALL THE PROBLEMS WE FACE TODAY. WE NEED YOUR HELP TO BRING THIS MESSAGE TO THE WORLD.
ARTISTS COMMENTS:
FOR THEY ARE SUCH SERVE NOT OUR LORD, JESUS CHRIST BUT THEIR OWN BELLY, AND BY GOOD WORDS AND FAIR SPEECHES DECEIVE THE HEARTS OF THE SIMPLE. – ROMANS 16-18.
IF THIS BE TRUE NOTHING REMAINS TO BE LEARNED OR DISCOVERED. IT WAS ALL REVEALED WHEN THE INK DRIED ON THE BIBLE. AN INTELLIGENT PERSON WILL ANALYZE THIS STATEMENT CAREFULLY.

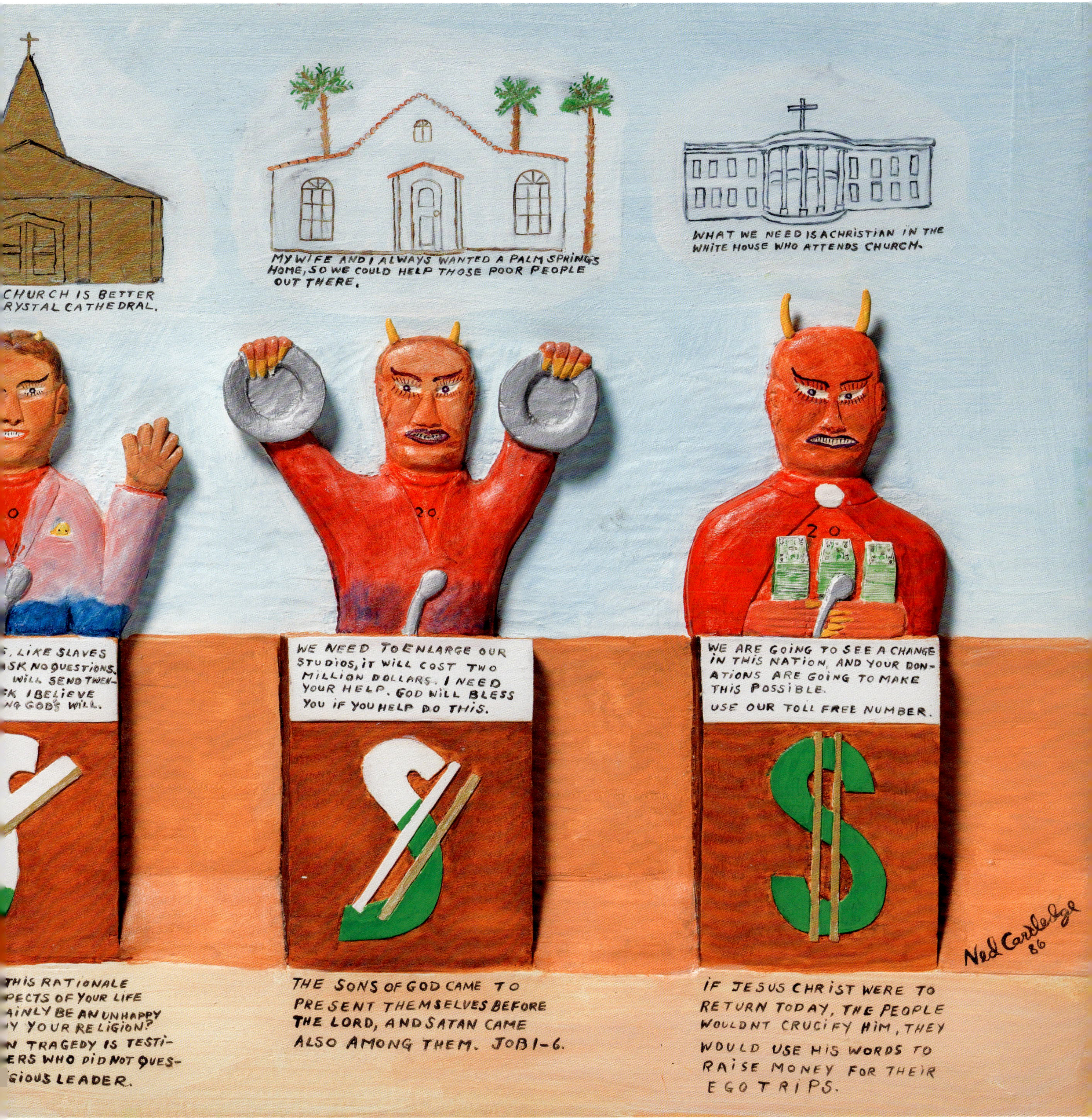

CHURCH IS BETTER
RYSTAL CATHEDRAL.
MY WIFE AND I ALWAYS WANTED A PALM SPRINGS HOME, SO WE COULD HELP THOSE POOR PEOPLE OUT THERE.
WHAT WE NEED IS A CHRISTIAN IN THE WHITE HOUSE WHO ATTENDS CHURCH.
20
20
20
, LIKE SLAVES
SK NO QUESTIONS.
WILL SEND TWEN-
K I BELIEVE
NG GOD'S WILL.
WE NEED TO ENLARGE OUR STUDIOS, IT WILL COST TWO MILLION DOLLARS. I NEED YOUR HELP. GOD WILL BLESS YOU IF YOU HELP DO THIS.
WE ARE GOING TO SEE A CHANGE IN THIS NATION, AND YOUR DON-ATIONS ARE GOING TO MAKE THIS POSSIBLE.
USE OUR TOLL FREE NUMBER.
Ned Cartledge 86
THIS RATIONALE
PECTS OF YOUR LIFE
AINLY BE AN UNHAPPY
Y YOUR RELIGION?
N TRAGEDY IS TESTI-
ERS WHO DID NOT QUES-
GIOUS LEADER.
THE SONS OF GOD CAME TO PRESENT THEMSELVES BEFORE THE LORD, AND SATAN CAME ALSO AMONG THEM. JOB 1-6.
IF JESUS CHRIST WERE TO RETURN TODAY, THE PEOPLE WOULDNT CRUCIFY HIM, THEY WOULD USE HIS WORDS TO RAISE MONEY FOR THEIR EGO TRIPS.

The Cincinnati Art Museum gratefully acknowledges the operating support provided by ArtsWave, The Ohio Arts Council, the City of Cincinnati, and our members.

This catalogue accompanies the exhibition *Creating Connections: Self-Taught Artists in the Rosenthal Collection* on display at Cincinnati Art Museum from June 9–October 8, 2023

First published in 2023 by GILES
An imprint of D Giles Limited
66 High Street,
Lewes, BN7 1XG, UK
gilesltd.com

ISBN: 978-1-913875-41-1

The exhibition was curated by Julie Aronson, Curator of American Paintings, Sculpture, and Drawings, Cincinnati Art Museum

For the Cincinnati Art Museum:
Julie Aronson, Curator of American Paintings, Sculpture, and Drawings
Anne Buening, Curatorial Assistant, American Paintings, Sculpture, and Drawings
Rob Deslongchamps, Head of Photographic Services

For D Giles Limited:
Copyedited and proofread by Jodi Simpson
Designed by Alfonso Iacurci
Produced by GILES, an imprint of D Giles Limited
Printed and bound in China

All measurements are in inches and centimeters; height precedes width precedes depth.

Front and back cover: Cat. 17 (detail)
Frontispiece: Cat. 32 (detail)
Pages 4–5: Cat. 61 (detail)
Pages 8–9: Cat. 24 (detail)
Pages 48–49: Cat. 11 (detail)
Pages 108–9: Cat. 34 (detail)
Pages 116–17: Cat. 51 (detail)
Pages 154–55: Cat. 48 (detail)
Pages 166–67: Cat. 54 (detail)
Pages 174–75: Cat. 23 (detail)

Library of Congress Cataloging-in-Publication Data

Names: Aronson, Julie, editor. | Russell, Charles, 1944- | Sagan, Olivia. | Cincinnati Art Museum organizer, host institution.
Title: Creating connections : self-taught artists in the Rosenthal collection / edited by Julie Aronson ; interview with Richard Rosenthal by Julie Aronson ; contributions by Olivia Sagan and Charles Russell.
Other titles: Creating connections (Cincinnati Art Museum)
Description: [Cincinnati] : Cincinnati Art Museum ; Lewes : in association with D Giles Limited, [2023] | Includes bibliographical references and index. | Summary: "Creating Connections features over 70 paintings, sculptures, drawings, and watercolors from the Rosenthal Collection of work by self-taught artists. This richly illustrated publication explores the mysterious connections we have with works of art and examines the journey into the meaning of art for its creators. It looks at the historic approaches to the creations of self-taught artists and the problems inherent in their interpretation. It also considers where we should go to achieve a more equitable and inclusive art history. The Rosenthal Collection comprises a significant and notably varied grouping. Not only does it cover a broad mix of US names including Earl Cunningham, Henry Darger, Thornton Dial, Bill Traylor, Sister Gertrude Morgan, Ralph Fasanella, Martín Ramírez, and Janet Sobel, it also includes non-US artists Carlo Zinelli, Hiroyuki Doi, Adolf Wölfli, Donald Pass, and Nek Chand, among others. Jean Dubuffet, the French painter who famously promoted the study of self-taught artists, is also featured. An illustrated interview by Julie Aronson with Richard Rosenthal provides special insight into the collector who has brought together this exceptionally diverse array of work. Essays by Olivia Sagan and Charles Russell look at the need for a more nuanced approach to these artists and their work, at the history of its appreciation (including terminology such as "Outsider Art"), and examine the work in the context of autobiography, trauma, connection, and remembering"-- Provided by publisher.
Identifiers: LCCN 2022047831 | ISBN 9781913875411 (hardcover)
Subjects: LCSH: Outsider art--United States--Exhibitions. | Rosenthal, Richard (Richard H.)--Art collections--Exhibitions. | Rosenthal, Lois--Art collections--Exhibitions. | Outsider art--Private collections--United States--Exhibitions.
Classification: LCC N7432.5.A78 C74 2023 | DDC 709.04/09--dc23/eng/20221026
LC record available at https://lccn.loc.gov/2022047831